Studying Society: Sociology at Work

Second Edition

Rebekah Ellis & Ethan Embry-Saunders

ISBN-13: 978-1975928537

Studying Society: Sociology at Work
Second Edition

Chapter 1: What is Sociology?

In my Introductory Sociology course I like to ask students what their college major is. Hands go up and I hear "psychology," "computer science," "nursing," "education", and "criminal justice." Rarely do I hear a student say "sociology." Very few students declare sociology as their major when they first matriculate. Why? They don't know what it is. So, next I ask, "Who knows what sociology is?" Silence. Sometimes a hand or two will go up and I hear things like "it's the study of society" or "it's the study of groups." Very few high schools teach sociology as a separate and distinct discipline, so that few students know what sociology is shouldn't be surprising. Some students will have had social sciences while in high school, but social science is such a broad arena students don't come to have an understanding of sociology as a discipline.

In the 1800's, most Americans lived in rural areas. Children learned to read, write and do math problems at home or in a one-room school house if they lived in a town. Children of all different ages would attend the same school and attend class in the same room. If the family lived in a more urban area, most likely their children of 6 or 7 years old might work in a mill or a factory. Work started before sunup and generally everyone was in bed as the sun went down. Ninety percent of Americans lived in rural areas in the 1850's, and while they made occasional trips to towns for supplies, most of those rural Americans led relatively isolated lives in comparison to today. Except for the occasional visit to town, farmers and their families were dependent on themselves. Further, again with those few occasional visits to town, they interacted with themselves (Morse Society, 2016).

Sociology as scientific discipline is relatively young - maybe at best 200 years old. To speak about why sociology has only been around such a relatively short time, we have to understand what sociology studies. Sociology studies human social life, societies, and groups. So, let's begin by discussing what life was like for those Americans living in the 1800's in comparison to today. Imagine this scenario, your alarm clock goes off at 7:30 a.m., you jump out of bed, brush your teeth, throw on some clothes, and then move to the kitchen where you make yourself a cup of coffee. You have class at 8 a.m., so you gulp down your coffee, run out the door and jump into your car, back out onto the street, and drive to school. You arrive right on time - at 8 a.m. We're talking about a span of time of 30 minutes or less. Now I want you to think about how many people you depend on during the course of those 30 minutes. Did you make your alarm clock? No. By the time that you bought that clock, dozens if not hundreds of people who have been involved in the process of manufacturing and distributing that clock. What about the toothpaste you squeeze out of the tube. Did you make it yourself? In thinking about that cup of coffee you gulped down, did you pick the coffee beans? Grind the beans? Did you make the cup for the coffee in a pottery class? No? How many people were responsible for getting that coffee from the field to the coffee cup that was made by someone else? Hundreds if not thousands. You run out the door and jump into that thing parked in the driveway. Did you make that car? Thousands of people took part in the manufacture and distribution of that car. And what about the road you use to drive to school? Or maybe the bridge you have to cross on the way? Did you build the road? Build the bridge? Nope. Again, hundreds of people have helped to put those roads and bridges into place.

Let's return to 1800's America. In thinking about what life was like for Americans living in rural areas in the 1800's, how many people do you suppose they were dependent on for their survival? Can you guess? The answer is pretty well themselves—the family. While the family may have made occasional trips to town for a few supplies, they were fairly well independent. They raised their own crops, slaughtered their own livestock, made their own clothes, candles, and the homes they lived in. So, during those past 160 years or so, people have become more and more dependent on others for their survival. Dependence also means connections—interactions. Today's world is built on interdependence—connections with others that help provide us with those things it would be difficult for us to provide ourselves.

So, now let's look at interactions between people. Again, I want to think about your own life. From the time you get up in the morning until you go to bed at night, how many people do you suppose in an average day do you interact with? Make a list. Did you stop and get gas or cup of coffee on the way to school? If so, did you interact with others? Once at school, as you sit in your classroom, how many people share that class with you? Do you talk to them? Do you listen to them as they express their thoughts or answer questions when posed by the instructor? You are likely enrolled in more than one class. If you're a full-time student, taking maybe four classes per term, take the number of interactions you may have had in that one class and now multiply it by four. On the way home, maybe you have to stop at the store to pick up some things, or stop at the bank, or God forbid, have to deal with the financial aid office at school. Can you see that the number of people you are potentially interacting with is increasing dramatically as the day goes by? What if instead of going home after school, you had to go to your job—there are even more interactions to add to your list. By the end of just that one day, you may have interacted with dozens or more people—and that's just in one day. Now, let's revisit life in the 1800's rural America. In a typical day, how many people did these Americans interact with? Can you guess? For the most part, themselves—their family. Today, it is estimated that we interact with more than 80,000 people during our lifetime (Edmund, 2015).

New Science

W hy is sociology a relatively new science? Largely because of population changes and shifts that led to huge changes in the number of people on whom we depend and interact. So, while in the 1800's as many as 90% of Americans lived in rural areas, today that number is pretty well reversed—more than 80% of Americans live in urban areas today. That change in population and where people live today when compared to the past, provides the research ground for sociology—studying groups, which can be small to large. But sociology, because it is a science and uses scientific steps to discover facts, can empower people by providing research facts that often dispel myths and stereotypes. It also broadens personal viewpoints. For instance, sociology helps to appreciate the value of diversity by helping people discover the facts about those of a different race, ethnicity, religion, or sexual orientation. Sociology provides some of the tools necessary to understand and fight prejudice and discrimination.

Common Sense Versus Sociology

I f you ask Americans why they choose to marry someone, they will respond by saying that they love that person. But in many parts of the world, this kind of "love marriage" is not the norm. Instead, marriages are arranged by parents for political or economic reasons. When you attempt to measure marital satisfaction, while holding constant cultural reasons for marriage, the research indicates that marital satisfaction is higher in cultures that practice arranged marriage (Schoenberg, 2012). Why? In the U.S., if the reason the vast majority of people get married is because they fall in love, it seems only reasonable that the main reason they divorce is because they fall out of love. Love is such an intangible affect, and because so many factors affect it, not the least is sexual attraction and fulfillment, it is easy to see that it makes for a poor basis for marriage. However, in cultures that practice arranged marriage, love is something a couple might hope for someday, but it is not the basis for the marriage. The basis for marriage in these cultures that practice arranged marriage is having children, stability, physical (and possibly emotional) support, and communal cohesiveness.

Another issue that finds common sense in conflict with reality is "welfare." During virtually every presidential election campaign, candidates will attack the idea of something they call welfare, and they will justify their attack as saying that recipients are lazy, receiving something for nothing, turn down paid jobs, and have children just to receive more benefits from the state. When we dig deeper, we find that the term "welfare," as used by politicians, really refers to one program, Aid to Families with Dependent Children (AFDC). It is easy to say that recipients are lazy and lack a strong work ethic, largely because most Americans don't personally know people on AFDC and get their information, which is often distorted, from their politicians or the media. However, the research finds that more than 80% of AFDC recipients are working full-time jobs, therefore do not lack a strong work ethic, and are not lazy. Additionally, most states limit the amount of benefits to two children—if an AFDC recipient has more than children they do not receive additional benefits. So, while politicians have historically liked to use the term welfare to incite voters, they did this knowing that their facts were distorted.

As a sociologist, one my jobs in this book and in my in-class lectures is to "push buttons." It is my job to challenge your thinking. I'm not asking students to accept what I write or tell them, but I am asking them to think about the issues and form their own opinion rather than simply accepting someone else's opinion. With that in mind, let me challenge you with this.

Money for Nothing

If the term "welfare" is meant to connote people who get something for nothing, are there other more acceptable things in American culture that could be defined in the same way, but are not seen in that same negative way? Unemployment insurance is a great example.

Most Americans think that they have unemployment insurance premiums deducted from their paychecks, but that's not true. When someone files for unemployment, the funds used to provide support to unemployed workers comes from two places—employer contributions and matching funds from the state. Workers themselves do not pay a dime into unemployment insurance. Could we not say that those receiving unemployment compensation are receiving something for nothing?

Social Security is another example. The average monthly Social Security benefit in 2016 was $1,341 per worker according to the Department of Social Security (Social Security Fact Sheet, 2016). While workers do pay Social Security taxes, that tax that is paid from their paycheck does not go into a fund with their name on it. Instead, the Social Security taxes being deducted from a worker's paycheck is actually going to pay the benefits being paid out to those currently receiving social security benefits. Further, because people are living longer today than ever, the amount of Social Security benefits paid out to retirees far exceeds the amount that was paid by the Social Security taxes deducted from their paychecks—even if it were to have drawn interest during those many work years, retirees will still be paid substantially more than they paid into the fund. Again, at least in part, is that not receiving something for nothing? If it is true that we do not look at unemployment insurance and Social Security retirement benefits in the same way we do welfare recipients, why do we look at the latter so differently? Could it be because the stereotype we have of welfare recipients is that of African-American women?

Another example has to do with crime and poverty. The non-sociologist says, "The poor commit more crime than the rich," but the sociologist says the poor are prosecuted more because of:

1. stereotyping,

2. they live in areas where there are more police on patrol, which makes crime more easily discovered than in areas where there are fewer police on patrol,

3. the poor have less money for legal defense,

4. the rich have a network of ties that can be used to help keep their crimes hidden from prosecution, and

5. the rich are more likely to commit white-collar crime which is less likely to be prosecuted.

6. the rich are the ones who make the laws—laws which favor their actions over that of others.

For instance, why is prostitution illegal but charging 30 – 45% interest on credit cards legal? Don't claim that is it a Biblical or moral issue. The Bible identifies usury (making money by lending money) as wrong. With the Bible in mind, both are sinful.

- You must not lend them money at interest or sell them food at a profit. Leviticus 25:37

- The rich rule over the poor, and the borrower is slave to the lender. Proverbs 22:7

The interest rate a consumer pays depends on where the credit card issuing company is incorporated—ever wonder why so many credit card companies are based in South Dakota? The title pawn industry has an even worse record. Consumers can pay as much as 300% interest on a title loan—and it's perfectly legal. The average title loan in the U.S. was $951, which equates roughly to 26% of the car's value, and cost the borrower $2,142 in interest. While some states have enacted legislation to greatly reduce the maximum allowable interest rate for title loans, many have not. Who gets hurt by this kind of interest rate? Those who need the credit the most—the poor. What do you think is the primary reason for credit card debt in the U.S.? Hospital bills. Who benefits from the high interest rates of credit cards? The banks and their shareholders. Also, credit card companies often target college students and young people in general. In fact, many colleges and universities sell student information to credit card companies so that they can be targeted.

As for prostitution, there is only one state that currently allows it, which is Nevada, but even so, it is only legal in eight counties. In those eight counties, brothels are licensed as are their "employees." These "employees" must undergo regular medical evaluations so they can have their licenses renewed every six months; without a license they cannot legally work. As of June–July 2008 there were 28 legal brothels in Nevada. While many people believe that prostitution is legal in major Nevada cities like Las Vegas and Reno, that is a myth—it is illegal.

Major Contributors to Sociology

Auguste Comte (1798 – 1857) a French philosopher, is credited for coining the term "Sociology". Originally, Comte referred to sociology as social physics because he believed that the fledging discipline of sociology should be modeled after the science of physics, which was also in its infancy. By studying human behavior, and using the knowledge gained to predict, control, and modify human behavior, Comte believed that sociology could be used to benefit humanity. Further, the development of positivism, a view that science could discover social facts, is credited to Comte.

Emile Durkheim (1858 – 1917) discouraged that Auguste Comte failed to successfully establish sociology as a new science, Emile Durkheim advocated the development of a method to discover facts scientifically. Therefore, in order to establish social facts (i.e, facts about humans acting in their social world), Durkheim advocated for the use of the scientific method—procedures necessary to study sociology systematically and empirically. In other words, just as a biologist studies different forms of life as "things," a sociologist can study social facts as "things," too.

      In studying people, Durkheim believed that a society's institutions must function as an integrated whole—in other parts, those institutions, or parts, must function as an interdependent unit for the society to survive. This "social cohesion" was identified by Durkheim as organic solidarity. He also believed that social cohesion could be based on social connections based on shared experiences (e.g., education, work, religion). He called the latter mechanical solidarity.

Emile Durkheim

      Durkheim later went on to study the division of labor within the industrializing society. While he had at one time argued that religion served to foster organic solidarity, he believed that industrialization would continue to increase the dependence of humans on one another and lead to an even greater division of labor. This enhanced division of labor would then replace religion as the primary mechanism for social cohesion or organic solidarity.

One of Durkheim's greatest achievements was to apply the scientific method to the study of humans. Specifically, he wanted to investigate organic solidarity between peoples of different religions—specifically, between Protestants and Catholics, and the term he chose to label as the measure of any differences in organic solidarity was **anomie**. Anomie is social estrangement, isolation, feeling lost, alienated, and unclear of social norms. Emile Durkheim was the first to use scientific principles in the relatively new science of sociology. He was also the first to advocate that the social world affected people's behaviors.

In the 1800's, Durkheim studied European religions and believed that Catholics experienced less anomie than did Protestants. His reasoning was that Catholicism advocated that they approached God as a community and therefore were accountable to God as a community. Protestantism on the other hand, with the Protestant work ethic widely accepted in the Protestant community, believed that they approached God as individuals and were therefore individually accountable to God.

Durkheim believed that the bonds between Protestants were weaker than they were for Catholics. Based on this premise, Durkheim believed that Protestants would have higher rates of anomie than Catholics. Using the scientific principles he wanted to employ within sociology, he proposed that Protestant countries would have higher rates of anomie than would Catholic countries.

To test this, Durkheim reasoned that people who suffered from the effects of anomie would be more likely to commit suicide than others. After finding that Catholic (European) countries reported almost non-existent suicide rates and Protestant (European) countries reporting significantly higher rates, he concluded that his hypothesis had been proven correct: Protestants were more likely to suffer from the effects of anomie. While there were methodological problems with Durkheim's study, he is still credited for being the first to make sociology a science.

Max Weber (1864 – 1920) was lrgely influenced by the works of Marx , though he is usually associated with **structural functionalism**, Weber was interested in the development of capitalism and expressly in the influence of religion, specifically Christianity, in the formation of capitalism. Unlike Marx, Weber believed that social forces (i.e., cultural ideas and values) were more important in explaining the development of capitalism than was economic forces. Weber believed that man was rational is his behaviors. Weber's work on rationality can be divided into four general themes:

- behavior aimed at higher-level values,

- behavior that supported the development and adoption of habits,

- behavior aimed at affect (i.e., a person's feelings), and

- behavior which worked in favor of self-interest (sometimes referred to as rational actions).

Weber's work on rationality led to what is called rational choice theory. While this theoretical perspective is sometimes challenged because of the notion of altruism, and other seemingly irrational actions, it is not widely used as theoretical perspective when trying to explain human social life. Another area of sociology in which Weber heavily contributed was his work on bureaucracies. We will look at bureaucracies in greater depth in the module on groups and organizations.

Harriet Martineau (1802 – 1876) was an English writer, philosopher, a perhaps the first female sociologist. Martineau believed that the social conditions of women's lives should be included in the study of sociology and in particular issues of marriage, children, and family. Martineau published a number of books including *Society in America* (1837), in which she describes the social and political place of women in America. On her visit to America in 1834, she supported Northern abolitionists in their efforts to abolish slavery in the U.S. and often visited with then president James Madison.

W.E.B. Du Bois (1868 – 1963) was an American sociologist who fought institutionalized racism by urging African-Americans to political action. He was instrumental in leading African-Americans away from the Republican Party, which they had supported since the time of Abraham Lincoln, because of their lack of support of African-American rights and causes. He was the first African-American to earn a doctorate from Harvard. W.E.B. Du Bois also founded the N.A.A.C.P. (National Association for the Advancement of Colored People) in 1909.

George Herbert Mead (1863 – 1931) created the Symbolic Interactionist approach. Mead was a philosopher who advocated the importance of language because it was symbolic in nature and it is therefore interpreted. Our interpretations, he believed, are the result of societal consensus. His work led to his formulation of the development of the self—a major theoretical treatise that reveals how the self is developed as a result of interaction with others in our social world. Mead suggested that we learn to see ourselves through the eyes of others in that social world—in other words, as children we began to see ourselves as different from others, and that is when we learn to distinguish between our individual identity (i.e., to see ourselves as an "I") and the identities of others. This is when, Mead argued, we began to develop self-consciousness. Generally, this is what sociologists refer to as a **micro theory** because it has very limited applicability. We will learn more about George Herbert Mead in the module on social theory.

Robert Merton (1910 – 2003) developed another major theoretical perspective within sociology called the structural functionalist perspective. Merton believed that society could be examined and studied just like the human body. A system, like society, was made up of parts and that those parts worked together, the parts were interdependent. Interdependence means that they depend on each other; if one part fails, the system cannot function and may die. He proposed, like the human body, a system is surrounded by an environment that provides raw resources to the system. The system utilizes those resources to meet its goal(s) much like the body uses food and food water from the environment to meet its goal of survival. Further, he believed that as environments change, systems need to change in order to meet their goal(s). When looking at humans, we can say that man has adapted to changes in his environment with the addition of heavier (or lighter) clothing, air-conditioning or more effective ways of staying warm, and changes in the diet resulting from changes in agricultural production. For instance, during the sixteenth through the nineteenth centuries, a dramatic change in climate resulted in what is referred to as the "little ice age." Significant colder temperatures and harsher winters led to considerable changes in agricultural production. While the English, Irish, and Germans adapted by switching their agricultural production to more potatoes and less grains, the French did not. Some historians believe that the "little ice age" had a causal impact on the French revolution because it led to massive starvation and a general discontent with the French monarchy.

System Boundaries, Dysfunction, and Moral Consensus

Merton suggested that all systems had identifiable boundaries. Just like the body, Merton maintained you can see where a system stops and the environment begins. Evidence of boundaries can be found in borders between states, badges, ID cards, parking stickers, and clothing. Merton believed that systems have functions. He argued there are intended functions, also known as manifest functions, and unintended functions, latent functions. For example, the Native American rain dance has the manifest function of making it rain, but it also has a latent function, which is to increase the cohesiveness of the tribe by bringing everyone together in the religious ritual. Merton also discussed the idea of dysfunctions, which have the potential to increase instability within a system. Some might consider crime a dysfunction, and while there are certainly negative consequences to crime, there are also positive consequences. Crime may increase the solidarity and cohesiveness of a people if they share a feeling of victimization. Likewise, law enforcement and the criminal justice system in general provide millions of jobs which is good for the economy.

Structural functionalists suggest that people develop shared values which then lead to what Merton referred to as "moral consensus." Moral consensus is necessary for the system as leads to the normal or desired state of the system—balance and equilibrium=homeostasis.

Conflict Perspective

We have explored two of the major theoretical frameworks in sociology, symbolic interaction and structural functionalism. The third more influential theoretical perspective is referred to as the conflict perspective.

Karl Marx (1818 – 1883) was a philosopher and political economist. He believed social change resulted from economic influences. Capitalism as an ideology caused divisions between people, but that society, uninfluenced by capitalism, was naturally cohesive. Unlike Weber, who saw social inequality as resulting from differences in status and power, Marx believed that inequality exists between the workers and the owners of the means of productions—industry, financial holdings including companies and corporations. The conflict perspective is a macro theory and therefore has broad applicability.

Karl Marx

Charles Cooley (1864 – 1929) was a prominent sociologist who developed the concept called the looking glass self (i.e., essentially a mirror). Cooley's concept of the looking glass self suggests that people develop their self-image (i.e., the self) from social interactions and feedback from others. Cooley identified three steps involved in the process he conceptualized as the looking glass self in his book Human Nature and the Social Order (1902). Those steps are:

- the imagination of our appearance to others,

- the imagination of his judgment of that appearance, and

- some sort of self-feeling, such as pride or mortification.

The Sociological Imagination & the Power Elite

C. Wright Mills (1916 – 1962) was an American sociologist known for his Sociological Imagination. In his work on the sociological imagination, Mills investigated how the average person tries to understand his or her place in everyday social life. Mills believed that we try to make sense of that social world by examining and reacting to the social situations in which we are involved in our daily lives.

Unfortunately, this leads humans to develop a very myopic view in our understandings of our social world because our interactions with that social world are so very limited in scope. Most humans are incapable of understanding the broader factors in our social world that affect their personal lives and their problems. Mills advocates that people should think beyond their immediate social world and try to understand the social forces from a larger and more objective manner. In other words, Mills suggests that humans need to step aside from their daily lives and their immediate social world and look at themselves and their behaviors from a more expansive and objective manner. He called this ability the sociological imagination—the ability to step back and look at one's life and culture objectively, dispassionately, and from the perspective of functionality. For example, is unemployment the result of an individual's inabilities or deficiencies or is the result of social and economic forces? In most cases, both are likely true. The non-sociologist says, "Unemployment is a personal problem," but the sociologist says that unemployment is usually the result of both personal and public factors and that unemployment has both personal and public consequences—many of them long-term.

Mills was a conflict theorist and approached class divisions and inequality in the U.S. from that point of view. In the *Power Elite* (1956), Mills wrote how power in the U.S. was centralized in the hands of a small group of powerful and rich people. The members:

- Came from one or several influential groups (i.e., politicians, military, and upper classes),

- Tended to be male, white, Protestant, share the same general social upbringing, and tended to socialize with each other. Because of these similarities and interactions, they tended to

- Shared the same general agenda for the U.S., and that shared view or agenda was what came them power collectively.

While Americans believe that they 'run' America by the act of voting in a democracy, Mills adamantly disagreed stating that power was in fact in the hands of the aforementioned power elite.

Social Construction of Reality

Building on Mead's work with symbolic interactionism, humans construct social reality by consensus. If a group or a larger society interprets and defines situations in the same way, they have socially constructed reality. While bricks, flooring, toilets, and automobiles may all be real in their physical form, social reality only exists when humans create it by their shared agreement as to what that social reality is. We'll come back to this issue when we discuss social interaction.

Why is Sociology a Valuable Science?

Every science, be it a "hard" science like biology, chemistry, or physics, benefits mankind in a number of ways. Likewise, the social and behavioral sciences like sociology, psychology and economics do the same. So how does knowing sociology benefit people as individuals and the cultures and societies in which they live?

First, having what C. Wright Mills called a sociological imagination allows us to see the influences of personal and public problems and how they are often intertwined. As sociology students you should now be aware that divorce is both a personal and public issue. Yes, people divorce because they fall out of love, but what social factors might increase the likelihood of them having significant enough marital problems that divorce is the result? The second most commonly named reason for divorce is financial problems (Doherty. 2016). Couples having a hard time making ends meet and paying their bills will almost certainly be stressed. That stress, left unmanaged, can lead to fights. Likewise, if one of the marital partners loses his/her job because the employer had to cut costs, the loss of their job, through no fault of their own will almost certainly lead to financial problems. As I previously stated, this can introduce a tremendous amount of stress into a marriage—sufficient enough to lead to a divorce.

Another personal issue related to divorce is the immediate and long-term consequences on the divorced couple's children. Did you know that most children at one point blame themselves for their parent's divorce (Moses, 2013)? The vast majority of research has found that divorce can traumatize children for years and even decades. In addition to divorce as a personal issue, it is a public issue as well. First, changes in the economy may lead to a downturn that results in employers laying off employees. The financial consequences are not only felt by the divorcing couple, but also by society as it struggles to help women and children financially deal with divorce. Regardless the reasons for divorce, there are financial and social consequences for society as well. Using the economy as an example, there is a chicken and egg relationship here. Not only could the economy contribute to a divorce, but it could reap a financial cost because of increasing divorce and thereby dependency of women and children.

Further, the sociological imagination encourages us to view our lives and the cultures in which we live and interact objectively—like an outsider might look at those things. By so doing we may learn a great deal about ourselves and our social world—things that might lead to research which results in information that has the potential to positively affect our lives and aspects of our culture. It may seem like common sense, sociological research is what contributed to the notion of bringing people of different backgrounds together on a level playing field to decrease levels of prejudice. This scientific knowledge has had a dramatic effect on the relations between diverse groups in America.

Second, by studying people and their interactions with one another, sociology helps us develop a sense of empathy. Empathy refers to a person's ability to understand things from another person's point of view. Seeing things from another person's perspective provides us with immensely valuable information. For instance, research has consistently found that single female-headed households are far more likely to produce juvenile delinquents. This could be for several reasons including a sudden change Socio Economic Status (SES) (Rekker et al., 2015). From a naïve point of view, that seems to demonstrate that there are a lot of divorced women with children in America who are bad mothers. But by using qualitative research, which allows us to see issues from other people's perspectives, has shown us that social and economic forces are the real culprit when explaining why single female-headed households are far more likely to produce juvenile delinquents. Though some research shows that women may not be as badly effected by divorce as previously thought (Bedard & Deschenes, 2005), women are more likely to come out of divorce financially worse off when compared to their former husbands, but emotionally better off than their ex-husbands (Laurence, 2016).

Divorced women raising children have a difficult time making financial ends meet—even if they are receiving child support. The amount of the child support may not be enough to sufficiently make ends meet and that's assuming that the ex-husband is even paying child support. Just because the court mandates it doesn't mean it's being paid. According to the U.S. Census Bureau (2011), child support is only paid in full 41% of the time. So, using empathy as our basis for doing qualitative research on single female-headed households we find:

- The majority of single divorced women heading households with children, work full-time.

- These women tend to have minimum wage jobs, which more often than not, even with child support being paid in some amount, is not enough for them to make ends meet.

Imagine this situation - Carla is a divorced woman raising two children. Because her ex-husband has a minimum wage job, she only receives $200 per month for child support. Carla has a full-time job, and like her husband, also makes minimum wage.

Between her job and child support, Carla brings home $1,200 per month. Because her AFDC benefits have expired, Carla is forced to seek additional income, which means if her employer offers over-time opportunities, she takes them.

One day, she comes home from work around 5:30 p.m. only to find her 10-year-old son has not taken out the trash as she asked him to do before leaving for work that morning. Carla depends on her children to help out with household chores because she works full-time and often works over-time. Carla punishes her son for not taking out the trash by sending him to his room and takes away his Playstation for the evening.

The next day, she is offered over-time at work and stays at work an additional two hours. On the way home from work, she stops at the grocery store. Carla finally gets home at 8:30 p.m., exhausted, only to find that her son didn't take out the trash for the second day in a row. Whereas she punished him the day before for not taking out the trash, Carla is exhausted and says to herself, "I just can't deal with this tonight," and doesn't discipline her son for not taking out the trash.

Research has shown that inconsistent discipline is actually just as likely to reinforce a behavior when compared to no discipline (Halgunseth, 2013). Though not intentional, Carla has just taught her son that he can get away with not taking out the trash. Research reveals that Carla's inaction could result in a greater likelihood that her son begins to test her on other things he has been asked to do, and that this behavior eventually gets taken out of the home.

Though unintentional, Carla has laid the groundwork for her son to potentially become a juvenile delinquent. Is Carla solely to blame if her son does become a juvenile delinquent or are there other forces at work that have played a part in the aforementioned outcome? One of the problems here is role overload (i.e., when two or more social statuses exist, the expected roles that go along with those statuses, compete with another for someone's time). Research has found that single-parents who are overloaded with responsibilities and duties have children who are at a higher chance of adolescent risky behavior (Han, 2010).

Carla is just too overwhelmed because she is solely responsible for providing a home, food, clothing, and other necessities for her children while also monitoring their behavior and administering discipline when necessary, whereas in a two-parent household, those duties are shared. So, while society might naively blame Carla for producing a juvenile delinquent because of poor or inattentive parenting, economic and social forces in most cases are far more to blame. Further, in 82% of divorces the primary child custodian is the mother (U.S. Census Bureau, December 2011).

Creating Informed Citizens

T hird, because sociology helps us to understand society, we have the potential to be active citizens in a democracy. By using research to discover social facts, which was what Durkheim believed could serve as the main contribution of sociology, informed people can participate in government from a position of facts and not from one of fear of the unknown.

George Simmel, a German sociologist, believed that the easiest way groups can increase cohesiveness among its members was to impose an outside threat. Simmel was right. Throughout history people have easily been led to deny rights or even life to groups different than themselves simply because they were induced by influential people to believe they were a threat and needed to be dealt with. The classic example would be the Nazi Holocaust. Adolf Hitler used anti-Semitism to arouse the German people and incite them to acts previously thought of as unconscionable by a civilized society.

One of the most well-known former Supreme Court justices, Oliver Wendell Holmes, a well-known proponent of eugenics, advocated that "imbeciles" (i.e., people with low I.Q.) be forcibly sterilized so that they would no longer damage the gene pool (Buck v. Bell, 1927). While many succumbed to the fear he generated, educated and informed people actively opposed the eugenics movement and no such policy of forced sterilization was ever implemented in the U.S.—unlike Germany which not only forced sterilization on those judged as mentally inferior, but went further by euthanizing (i.e., killing) them. In fact, Thomas Jefferson's idea for free mass public education was based on the idea that democracies must have educated citizens in order to exist. Sociology through research provides facts so that reasonable and rational people use facts when investigating an argument rather than giving into emotional arguments designed to generate fear from a perceived threat to society.

Sociology is Empowering

F ourth, sociology empowers people. After the American Civil War ended in 1865, the institution of slavery was officially ended, but the Southern policy of segregation began. For one hundred years, if you were an African-American living in the South, you were at best a second-class citizen. If while walking down a sidewalk whites walked toward you, by law you had to step out onto the street and let them pass. If you were hungry and had money to eat at a restaurant, and it was a white restaurant, you ate out back on picnic tables. If you were African-American living in the South during segregation, you drank out of a "colored-only" fountain, you used a "colored-only" restroom, and you sat at the back of the bus. While Rosa Parks was not the first African-American to refuse to give up her seat on a bus to a white man, and go to jail for it, she represented the beginning of what later became known as the civil rights movement.

This movement was organized and led by educated and informed people, both black and white, who used that knowledge to change the status quo. Many of those civil rights leaders, people who helped lead this country out of its longest national disgrace, earned their degrees in sociology. Men and women like Martin King, Jr., Jesse Jackson, Ralph Abernathy, Roy Wilkins, and Shirley Chisholm, empowered by the knowledge and facts that sociology had provided them, used their strength and personal religious beliefs to dare and stand up to demand equality. For those heroes, they understood that knowledge is power, and when coupled with strength of conviction, cannot be conquered by fear and hatred.

To What End?

While it is clear that there are important reasons and benefits for individuals to study sociology, can it or should it be used at a broader societal level? How do sociologists themselves view the purpose of their research? Many sociologists believe that the use of sociological research findings is not their concern; this is not a case of not caring about social problems that could be addressed by society, but rather the result of a sense of helplessness and frustration that U.S. policy-makers rarely use social research findings to effect public policy. Instead, in the U.S. sociologists are more concerned about developing a knowledge base through the collection of sociological research findings. This, they believe, builds a body of knowledge for the discipline as it is with other sciences, too. When the goal of sociology is to use research to build a body of knowledge is called pure sociology.

Some sociologists believe that sociological research should be used to better our social world and human conditions within that social world. This is one of the major differences between American and European sociologists. European governments often directly elicit help from sociologists to improve social and living conditions for their citizens. This use of sociology to benefit and reform society in some way is referred to as applied sociology or clinical sociology. Public sociology attempts to analyze and critique society and social policy, and then based on those criticisms, offer suggestions for improvement.

Now that you have an understanding of what sociology is, let's move forward and examine the development of sociological theory and how those theories are used to study our social world.

Terms, Concepts and Names to Know:

- Karl Marx

- Haves versus the have-nots

- Organic versus mechanical solidarity

- Applied sociology versus pure sociology

- Civil disobedience

- Max Weber

- Clinical sociology

- Social Security

- AFDC

- The Looking-Glass Self

- Anomie

- Harriet Martineau

- W.E.B. Du Bois

- NAACP

- George Mead

- C. Wright Mills

- Charles Cooley

- Georg Simmel

- Martin Luther King

Be Able to Discuss:

- What is meant by the social construction of reality?

- Auguste Comte and his role in the development of sociology

- Emile Durkheim and his role in the development of sociology

- The importance of the Sociological Imagination

- Functionalism

- Systems theory

- The conflict perspective

- Symbolic interactionism

- Durkheim's study on anomie

- Micro versus macro theory

- The little ice age and its effect on history

References

Bedard, K. (2005). "Sex Preferences, Marital Dissolution, and the Economic Status of Women." Journal of Human Resources, 40(2), 411-434.

Buck versus Bell, 274 United States Supreme Court (1927).

Doherty, W. (2016). "How common is divorce and what are the reasons?" Retrieved January 13, 2016, from http://www.divorce.usu.edu

Edmund, M. (2015, February 15). How many people does the average person physically meet in a lifetime? Retrieved July 13, 2016, from https://www.quora.com/How-many-people-does-the-average-person-physically-meet-in-a-lifetime

Halgunseth, L. C. (2013). "Delinquent-oriented attitudes mediate the relation between parental inconsistent discipline and early adolescent behavior." Journal of Family Psychology, 27(2), 293-302.

Han, W. (2010). "Parental work schedules and adolescent risky behaviors." Developmental Psychology, 46(5), 1245-1267.

Laurence, R. (2016). "Ted's (Painful, Expensive, but Otherwise Perfect) Divorce." Men's Health, 31(3), 104-134.

Moses, M. (n.d.). "Helping Children Endure Divorce." Tennessee Bar Journal, 49(1), 34-38.

Morse Society. (2016). Life in the 1800s. Retrieved July 13, 2016, from http://www.mors-esociety.org/cpage.php?pt=11

Rekker, R. (2015). "Moving in and out of Poverty: The Within- Individual Association between Socioeconomic Status and Juvenile Delinquency." PLoS One, 10(11), 1-17.

Schoenberg, N. (2012, August 22). A surprising new look at arranged marriages. Chicago Tribune. Retrieved from http://articles.chicagotribune.com/2012-08-22/features/sc-fam-0821-arranged-marriage-20120821_1_marriages-free-choice-satisfaction

United States Census Bureau. (2011). "Custodial Mothers and Fathers and Their Child Support: 2009." Retrieved from http://www.census.gov/prod/2011pubs/p60-240.pdf

United States Social Security Department. (2016). Social Security Fact Sheet: 2016 SOCIAL SECURITY CHANGES. Retrieved July 13, 2016 from https://www.ssa.gov/news/press/factsheets/colafacts2016.html

Chapter 2: Social Theory

What is theory? Theory helps us to understand and explain how and why facts are related. Sociology not only explores how things happen but also why they happen; theories help us understand these phenomena. One of the greatest outcomes of a successful theory is that it helps us make predictions. Humans like to be able to predict things. The ability to predict means that we understand something well enough to allow us to make those predictions.

For instance, let's say you were going to meet a friend for lunch. Whether you realize it or not, you have made predictions about that lunch. Yes, you're probably predicting your friend will show up and that you will both pay for your own lunch, but you're predicting more than that. One of the most basic predictions you've made is that you will have a good time. I doubt you would want to have lunch with that friend if you thought you were going to have a miserable time. Well, in some sense, that's what science and theory allows us to do—predict. So, why do we need theory when investigating social facts?

- First, sociology not only explores how things happen by also why they happen.

- Second, we need theories to help us make sense of facts.

- Third, facts obtained from research allow us to gather strength for the support of a theory.

- Fourth, when facts support a theory, we are then able to make predictions.

Theories have several components. All theories contain **concepts** and **propositions**, and are preceded by axioms. A concept is simply the thing a theory is attempting to explain (e.g., prejudice). Propositions simply offer an explanation of why two or more variables are related in some way (e.g., rates of prejudice decrease as the amount of post-high school education increases).

To help you understand that theory is nothing to run away from, I will use an example of a sociological theory. There is an economical model of exchange that attempts to explain exchange outcomes and their likelihood of being repeated. The economical model posits that as a result of an economic exchange, each actor of that exchange will have their rewards and costs and a feeling of whether they were profited by the exchange. The theory is generally written as Rewards – Costs = Profit.

As an example, let's say I go to a car dealership to buy a car. A deal is struck and I leave the car dealership unconsciously calculating whether I profited or not. So, I do the calculation. What was my reward? A brand new turbo-charged shiny red car. My costs? The cost I paid for the vehicle. Do I think it was a fair price? Maybe I even think that I got a good deal and paid below sticker. So, I decide my costs were fair and maybe even minimal. I conclude that my reward exceeded my costs and therefore I feel profited. On the other hand, let's say that I owed $25,000 on my current car and wanted to trade it for a newer model. The newer model is priced at $30,000 and the dealership offers me $18,000 in trade on my current car—what is called in the business "negative equity." Therefore, I would need to finance to $37,000 if I decided to accept the deal and trade-in my vehicle for the newer model. There is nothing wrong with my car, it runs and looks just like the day I purchased it three years earlier, I just want the newer model. Thinking about the deal I am being offered, I begin to get angry. Why? Even though I have not ac-cepted the deal, I project that if I accepted the deal my costs would far exceed my reward and thereby I anticipate feeling un-profited by the exchange. So, while I would probably be angry that I more or less gave the dealership $7,000 and my perfectly good car, I imag-ine the dealership being happy that they made such a large profit from the exchange. I feel that our costs and rewards are not equally distributed. I therefore would reject the deal, and because I would believe the dealership tried to unfairly profit by the trade, not return to that dealership in the future. That's the economic model of exchange. A man by the name of George Homans decided that people enter into social exchanges, much like economic exchanges, and therefore those exchanges can be described and calculated in the same way: **Rewards – Costs = Profit**.

Homans put forth a number of propositions explaining and predicting subse-quent actions (Homans, 1958).

Homans' First Proposition - Success Proposition

For all actions taken by persons, the more often a
particular action of a person is rewarded,
the more likely a person is perform that action.

Imagine this situation. You're just getting ready to walk out the door to leave for class. You're running a little late, but you think you can make it in time. The phone rings as you walk out the door. It's your friend Dave. Dave says, "Hey, man, sorry to bother you, but my car won't start. Can you give me a ride to school?" Dave's a good friend, so you agree. When you get to Dave's house, he's outside standing on the curb waiting for you. As he climbs into the car, he says, "Thanks, man, I really appreciate it. Let me buy you a beer this weekend to pay you back." As you drive to school the two of you talk and share a few laughs. When you get to school and park the car, Dave says, "Thanks again. I appre-ciate it. This weekend. The beers on me."

As Dave walks away your brain begins to subconsciously work through the exchange. Were you rewarded? Yes. You had a good time, Dave thanked you, and promised to repay you with a beer over the weekend. What were your costs? You had to go a little out of your way to pick him up, but he was waiting outside for you so that your cost in time was minimal. Your brain does the calculation and reaches the conclusion you profited.

So, Homan's first proposition thoroughly explains the phenomenon and makes a prediction: you will be more likely to repeat the exchange because you profited from this exchange. So, the next morning when you're getting ready to walk out the door, your phone rings, you look at the caller ID and see that's it Dave. Do you answer the phone? Homans would say yes. If you profited yesterday you predict that you will profit again today.

On the other hand, let's say instead of Dave calling its Steve on the phone. He asks if you could pick him up because his car won't start. You get to Steve's house, but he's nowhere to be seen. You have to honk your horn. After a couple of minutes he walks out the door in no hurry. After he climbs into your car, he says, "Hey." You drive to school in silence—not one word is said between you. When you get to school and park the car, he says, "See, ya," and gets out of the car and walks away. What were your rewards? Ah, none. What were your costs? Well, you had to go out of your way to pick him up, you were late to class, there was no offer to pay for gas or buy you a beer, and your feelings are a little hurt because of this. Your brain does the calculation and concludes you weren't profited. Therefore, you are less likely to repeat the exchange.

Stimulus Proposition

> If, in the past, the occurrence of a particular stimulus has resulted in a reward, then the more similar the present situation to the past the more likely the person is to perform that same action.

Homans' second proposition is called the stimulus proposition, Let's revisit your old friend Dave. You gave Dave a ride to school yesterday, and when all was said and done, you felt that you profited from the exchange. Today as you walk out the door your phone rings and it's another friend of yours, Cindy. Cindy asks if you could give her a ride to school. The stimulus proposition suggests that because you profited in the same type of exchange with Dave, you are more likely to enter into a similar exchange with Cindy. Feeling profited or un-profited from exchanges will carry over from one actor to another in similar situations. So, what if Cindy calls the day after you gave ol' deadbeat Steve a ride to school? What do you think Homans' stimulus proposition would predict you would do? If you guessed not answer your phone, you're right—because you didn't profit with Steve you predict you won't profit from Cindy in a similar situation.

Distributive Justice Proposition

A person in an exchange relationship with another will expect

> that the rewards of each person be proportional to their cost – the greater the rewards, the greater the cost – and that the net rewards (profits) of each man be proportional to their investment.

Homan's third proposition is called the distributive justice proposition. Let's come back to our economic model for a minute. We will say you went to a used car dealership and bought a car. You handed the dealer $5,000 in cash and he/she handed you the keys, the title, and the sticker that had been on the window of the car and that states, "No Warranty." You leave the lot in your new ride, but about two blocks from the dealer, the car makes a loud noise before coming to a grinding halt in the middle of the road. "WTF!?!?" you mutter as you get out of the car. Once you're out of the car you're frozen by what you see. It's good that your mother isn't around this time when you yell, "WTF!?!?" as you notice the car engine laying in the road. As you stand there waiting for the tow truck to get there, and after re-reading the "No Warranty" statement, you're pissed because all you can think of is the car dealer back on his lot counting your money with a big smile on his face. From an economic point of view, did you profit? I don't think we need even go there, right? No, you didn't profit. But the distributive justice proposition goes further than just suggesting you won't repeat an exchange with that same dealer, the proposition suggests that when people enter into exchanges they expect each others' rewards, costs, and profits to be equitable.

As you stare at your worthless car with the engine sitting on the pavement, do you feel that your rewards/costs/profits were equal to that for the dealer? That's the distributive justice proposition in action. But like the other economic exchanges that Homans believed could be applied to social interactions, he felt the same was true of the distributive justice proposition.

Let's say you're a red-blooded American male college student. All semester you've had your eye on girl named Susan you see occasionally with a mutual friend. At some point you managed to ask her out on a date, but she turned you down because she had something to do. Several months go by. It's the night before your big chemistry exam. You've procrastinated and decided you'd just do an all-niter to study for the exam. About 7 p.m. you sit down at the table to study when the phone rings. It's Susan. "OMG!" as your brain synapses begin to fire. "Hey," she says, "I don't have anything to do tonight. Do you want to go out?" "There is a God!" you shout silently to yourself. "Sure!" you say. As you hang up the phone you remember the major chemistry exam you haven't started studying for yet. You tell yourself you'll just study when you get home later that night. So, you get to Susan's house and pick her up. The second she gets in the car she starts whining in this high-pitched irritating voice. You get to the restaurant. She hasn't stopped talking the whole time. You're hoping she'll stop talking over dinner, but somehow between bites of steak that she chews with her mouth open, dinner isn't any better. You consider dumping her there. No, you can't do that.

You take her to the movie you'd planned on seeing. This nightmare just isn't go-

How would you define "true" love?

1. John and Mary have been married for five years. Every morning before leaving for work they give each other a kiss, say good-bye, and tell each other "I love you."

2. Every St. Valentine's Day John buys Mary a big box of chocolates, some roses, and takes her out for a romantic dinner for two.

3. Without being asked, John has Mary's car washed and waxed and then fills up the gas tank. That's how John shows Mary he loves her.

4. John comes home from work dead tired. All afternoon he has imagined walking in the door, kicking off his shoes, and just collapsing into a living room chair and turning on the TV. But when John walks in the house, he sees Mary laying on the couch-she's been sicker than a dog all day. He decides it's more important to take care of her than to kick his shoes off and crash in the chair.

ing away. Finally, the movie ends and it's time to take her home. She is absolutely nothing like you thought she was. You had a miserable evening. You drive home, but when you get there you realize you're just too tired to study for the chemistry exam.

The next morning you go to class, take the chemistry exam, bomb it, and then head home. This was a major part of your course grade and you absolutely bombed it. Once you walk in the door, you flop down on the sofa—tired and just wanting to forget everything that happened the last 24 hours. What were your rewards and costs? Rewards: not a damn thing. Costs: you could have used the time to study, you paid for dinner and the movie, and you had to put up with the date from hell.

Did you profit? No way. As you lay on the couch the phone rings. You pick it up without looking at the caller ID: it's Susan. In that high-pitched irritating squeaky voice she says, "Hey, I just wanted to call and tell you that I had an absolutely wonderful time last night! I really, really enjoyed spending time with you and wanted to see if you'd like to go out again." The next thing Susan hears is dead air. "Are you there? Is there anybody there?"

You not only hang up on her, but throw the phone across the room in rage. She didn't have any costs. Because she had a good time, and you paid for dinner and the movie, she profited. Again, the distributive justice proposition suggests that the outcomes for both parties should be equitable, but in this case, they were not. What does Homans say is a typical human emotion when exchanges like these are inequitable? Anger.

Homans social exchange theory is what is called a micro-theory. It is a theory that has relatively narrow applicability. In this case it can really only be used to explain one-on-one interactions. It can't be used to describe some larger sociological themes like gender inequality, crime, socialization, and others. To explain those larger themes, we need theories that have broad applicability— called macro theories. Within sociology there are a number of dominant theories and we will be using these dominant theories to explain concepts and processes as we progress through this book.

Now that you have some idea what theory is and does, let's look at the some of the dominant theories in sociology. We will be using these dominant theories as we explore the many topics of this book.

Symbolic Interaction

Sociologist **George Herbert Mead** (1863 – 1931) is credited as the founder of symbolic interactionism. The perspective argues that people interact with each other and social institutions on the basis of the consensual interpretation of shared symbols. These shared meanings allow for the social construction of reality. Only when people are in agreement as to the interpretations of these symbols is there meaning (Blumer, 1973).

Harold Blumer (1900 – 1987) is credited for providing the name "symbolic interaction" to the theory devised by George Herbert Mead. Blumer believed that humans create their own social reality by shared interactions and these shared interactions are continuous and ongoing (Blumer, 1969). Blumer coined the term in 1937.

Our world is full of symbols, with only a few exceptions, you could argue that are world is primarily built on symbols. Words are a great example of symbols. This book is written on paper. You can see the paper. You can feel the paper. In that sense paper is real. But for you to read or hear the word "paper" is symbolic. Symbols always elude to something because in themselves, symbols have no meaning. If I were to speak about a car, a wall, a hospital, or an exam, those words are symbolic representations of the real thing. In order for those words to have meaning, they must be understood as a representation of that thing.

Having Meaning

In order for symbols to have meaning, there must be shared agreement as to what they're supposed to represent, but shared understanding doesn't change the fact they are still just symbols. If I use the word "deviant," which is a symbol, is there shared agreement as to what deviance is? Generally, there must be widespread agreement about symbols before we can say it reality exists. Would we all agree on what deviance is? Probably not, but there are some forms of deviance that I think most of us Americans would agree on—e.g., incest, murder, and child molestation to name a few. But what about a 'whistle-blower?' Is that deviant? Edward Snowden rocked the world by releasing information about how the U.S. spies on its own citizens and other countries. Is that deviant? In this example, is Edward Snowden a traitor or a patriot? So, while we may have shared understandings of incest and murder as acts of defiance, we don't necessarily have shared understandings of all acts that are deviant or not.

For a symbol to have meaning there needs to be shared understanding as to what the symbol means or represents. There are certain symbols within our culture that are overwhelmingly shared, such as murder, but there are also symbols within our culture that are not shared when understanding or defining deviance, such as marijuana use. Is marijuana use deviant? Well, according to a recent Pew poll, approximately 55% of Americans say it should be decriminalized. Therefore, is there shared agreement that marijuana use is deviant? No.

Another word that is so often used that its meaning may be hopelessly ambiguous is the word "love." It is often used to refer to places, things, and people. A Google search for "love you" came back with 547 million hits, while a Google search of "love it" came back with 490 million hits. People will say they love a particular TV show or a movie, they love a particular restaurant or type of food, they love a particular time of day, they love watching the sunrise or the sunset, they love this or that. Because the word love is used so often, symbolic interactionists would question its meaning since there may be little consensus on its meaning. To make this hit you a little closer to home, either now or at some point in your life you have no doubt been in a relationship in which that other person has said to you, "I love you." Symbolic interaction would ask you this question: how do you know they love you? In other words, what does that word mean to you? And, for the word to have any real meaning, your definition has to be similar to the definition offered by other people. There must be consensus on meaning for something to be real.

Other cultures will have their own interpretations of symbols and that may differ from ours. So, if we come back to the word "deviant," we would almost certainly see that being representative of a child-molester. Most U.S. states allow sex between 16 and older, while sex between a 35-year-old and a 13-year-old would be deviant and illegal. But recently there was a case in Saudi Arabia where a man, who was deeply in debt, sold his eight-year-old daughter to a 35-year-old Saudi man and he married her. According to Saudi law, it was perfectly legal. From our perspective as Americans, it was an act of child-molestation and would you get you major time in prison. The story caught the attention of the world press, and the Saudi man under pressure, issued a statement saying that he would not have sex with his new wife until she became a women—something that would happen when she turned 12 years old. That didn't seem to reduce the world outcry, so the Saudi man divorced her. Symbols are interpreted differently by time, context, and culture. But for them to have any meaning, there must be shared agreement as to their meaning.

Symbols have no meaning in themselves, and always represent something else, the study of language is important to understanding societies, cultures, and groups. Social structures don't physically exist—they exist through a process of social interactions where people share the same meaning of that social structure. So, for instance, if I talked about the "educational system," most of us would understand that to mean private and public educational systems from kindergarten up through high school including students, schools, administrators, teachers, state and federal laws that govern how students are educated, and so forth. If I spoke about "government," most of us would understand that to mean city, county, state, and federal entities that passed laws, taxed us, and essentially told us what we could and couldn't do. These are shared meanings attached to words or phrases that are symbolic representations of something.

While we use shared symbolic understandings to define and explain cultures, societies, and groups, we also use symbols to communicate with one another through a process called social interaction. When we interact with others, we act and react to those symbols—those words. Meaning results from defining and interpreting those symbols and words, in shared ways. Imagine having a conversation with someone who used words that you didn't understand. By not having a mutual understanding of the symbols used, what would you get out of the interaction? Not much.

What if words as symbols are interpreted in different ways by people engaged in an interaction? The following are two examples of how words can be interpreted differently because they are symbolic and there must consensus to have any real meaning.

Example 1. There is an urban legend that goes like this. A white woman and her husband have just won a lot of money at a casino in Las Vegas. The husband looks towards the restaurant and sees a line starting to form for dinner. He turns to his wife and says, "Honey, why don't you take our winnings upstairs to our hotel room while I get us a table for dinner and then you come back down and join me?" She agrees, and carrying their winnings in her arms, she gets on the elevator and then presses the button for the appropriate floor. Before the elevator doors can close, Eddie Murphy and Michael Jordan get on the elevator with her, but she doesn't know who they are. Eddie Murphy is standing to her left and slightly behind her and Michael Jordan is standing to her right and slightly behind her. The elevator doors close and Eddie Murphy says to Michael Jordan, "Hit the floor." The next thing that Eddie Murphy and Michael Jordan know is that the woman has fallen to the floor of the elevator with her winnings scattered all over the floor. They both stand staring down at her. As the urban legend goes, the next morning there is a knock at the woman's door. She opens the door to find a bellboy with a dozen roses. Attached to the roses is a note that reads, "Thanks for the best laugh we've had in years," signed Eddie Murphy and Michael Jordan. Keeping in mind that this is only an urban legend, and both Eddie Murphy and Michael Jordan deny this ever happened, had it been real, can you explain what happened? Both the woman and Michael Jordan had heard Eddie Murphy say the same thing, "hit the floor." But while the woman was falling to the floor, Michael Jordan was reaching out to press the elevator button for the floor they wanted. The woman and Michael Jordan had interpreted "hit the floor" in completely different ways. Because of this, we can say they did not share the same meaning for "hit the floor." There was no consensus between them on the meaning of "hit the floor." Instead, because the woman was white, was carrying a great deal of money, and was trapped in an elevator with two African-American males, because she stereotyped African-American males she felt threatened and therefore interpreted "hit the floor" in that mindset.

Example 2. Last week, Susan received an e-mail from an old college friend named Jeremy. During their college days, Susan had a huge crush on Jeremy, but Jeremy had a girlfriend at the time. After graduating college, Jeremy had moved to another city, and though they didn't see each other much, they kept in touch via e-mail. While e-mail has some significant advantages, it has disadvantages, too. The biggest disadvantage to e-mail is that you can't see a person's facial expression or listen to the tone of their voice. One day, Susan opens her e-mail to find one from Jeremy. In his e-mail to Susan, Jeremy let's her know that he will be coming home for the weekend and wants to know if she wants to go out. Susan writes back immediately agreeing to go out and they work out a time for him to come by her apartment Saturday night around 7 p.m. Saturday afternoon Susan goes out and has her hair and nails done, and buys a new dress for her date with Jeremy. Susan assumes they'll probably go out for dinner, maybe catch a movie, and with luck, Jeremy will come back to her place at the end of the evening. Around 7 p.m. the doorbell rings. "It's him!" Susan screams excitedly to herself. Taking one last look in the mirror, she heads to the door and opens it. There stands Jeremy ... and two of his friends. Jeremy smiles and gives her a kiss on the cheek, and then asks, "Are you ready?" Needless to say, Susan is devastated. What happened? Susan had read Jeremy's e-mail, and after talking with her friends, had interpreted Jeremy's request to "go out" to mean "go out on a date." In other words, using symbolic interaction, Susan had interpreted the meaning of "go out" differently than had Jeremy.

Because symbolic interaction is a macro theory, it can be used to study most sociological areas of interest. For instance, marriage and divorce. First, we have to ask what is the meaning of marriage? What is the meaning of divorce? Up until perhaps fifty years ago, marriage was defined as "for life"—hence the phrase, "till death do us part." In those days, people waited to have sex until they were married, they didn't cohabitate before marriage, couples married at earlier ages than today (i.e., the average age of first marriage for a man is 31.8 years and 29.7 years for a woman), and it was considered as sacred. Today, sex prior to marriage is common, maybe even expected, cohabitation prior to marriage is becoming more common, marriage is seen more as "just a piece of paper" and less as an important institution, and divorce so common it is almost the norm. In the past, marriage was seen as one demanding commitment, understanding, and support. Consequently, divorce was seen as a failure and very few couples divorced. Divorce was the deviant thing to do. In fact, it bordered on being immoral and was almost always viewed by society as being caused by immoral wives or wives who didn't take care of their husbands, as they should. Just as the shared meaning of marriage has changed in the past fifty years, so has the meaning of divorce. Today, divorce is seen as liberating and offers the chance for a new, independent and more fulfilling life.

Structural Functionalism

The next dominant theory used in sociology is called structural functionalism and it is a macro theory. It has broad applicability and be used to study a great number of phenomenon. Probably the single most important figure in the development of structural functionalism was a man named Emile Durkheim. He believed that society could be studied much like the human body. As the human body is made up of interdependent parts that work together for the survival of the body, Durkheim maintains that society operates in a similar way. Often called systems theory, structural functionalism and systems theory are virtually synonymous. Systems are made up of parts that are interdependent and they must work together for the system to survive. Survival is the ultimate goal of any system. Systems have goals, and while the primary goal of any system is survival, there are often secondary goals as well as unstated goals. Surrounding the system is an environment. The environment provides raw resources to the system, and after the system has worked those raw resources into a finished "product," the system outputs that product back to the environment. Systems theory also argues that since the primary goal of any system is survival, just like the human body, the system must adapt to changes in the environment; failure to adapt to these changes could lead to the death of the system. A system also has identifiable boundaries so that members can be distinguished from non-members.

Let's use a college or university as a system we can discuss using systems theory. First, colleges and universities are made of interdependent parts that include faculty, staff, and students. These parts are interdependent and must work together for the system to survive. The college or university exists within an environment and is separated from that environment by a boundary. Boundaries are always visible. Because colleges and universities often have facilities throughout cities and counties, boundaries are seldom geographical—there's no nice neat line you can draw separating the college or university from its environment. So where does evidence of a boundary come from? All colleges and universities in the U.S. issue ID cards for faculty, staff, and students. The ID serves as an indication of the boundary: if you have an ID card, you are a member of the system, if you don't you're not a member. If we were investigating the post office as a system, can you think what might indicate who is a member of the system and who is not? A uniform or ID might serve as an indication of a boundary for the post office as it probably does in many U.S. agencies, organizations, and companies.

Environments Provide Raw Resources for the System

What kind of raw resource might the environment provide for a college or university? We would probably agree that the environment provides the system with non-degreed high school graduates who want a college/university education. If that's the case, these non-degreed students enter the system, the system works its magic on them, and hopefully four years later they are spit back out into the environment as graduates. All systems have goals, and as I've already mentioned, the primary goal for any system is survival. Using our example, the primary goal of colleges and universities is survival, but they have secondary and additional goals. While most college or university presidents would not tell a group of parents of prospective student that their goal is to make money, it is nevertheless an unspoken goal. Generally, goals are very specific, but sometimes can be too specific. A case in point is the March of Dimes.

The March of Dimes is an organization set up in 1938 with the explicit goal of raising funds to provide for research to eradicate infantile paralysis (polio). The 32nd president of the U.S., Franklin Delano Roosevelt, was thought to be afflicted with polio in his late 20's and it left him paralyzed from the waist down. It was a horrible and catastrophic disease. The March of Dimes was designed to help eradicate that disease. Unfortunately for the March of Dimes, a man by the name of Jonas Saulk invented a vaccine in the mid-1950's that virtually eradicated polio within a decade. The March of Dimes had met its goal, but the problem was, they had no reason to exist anymore. So, the March of Dimes reformulated its goal(s) and is still in existence today. The reformulated goal of the March of Dimes? To help provide funds for research to eradicate all childhood diseases. They got smart—that's a goal that can never be realized.

Structural Functionalism helps us to understand the value of individual functions as they contribute to society. Again, social structure is unseen and is the result of repetitive interactions between people, but these interactions must be relatively stable which in turn promotes a stable society. Robert Merton believed that all systems have functions. Sometimes these functions are positive and sometimes they are negative. Likewise, sometimes functions are intended and sometimes they are unintended. Intended functions are called manifest functions—intended to produce some good for the society. Latent functions are unintended functions, but that doesn't necessarily mean they are negative, just unintended.

Let's look at the Native American rain dance. The manifest function of the rain dance is to make it rain. Simple enough. But researchers have discovered that there are latent functions attached to the rain dance. The rain dance is a spiritual part of a tribe's culture and involves every member of the tribe. The rain dance tends to increase the bonds or cohesiveness of group members.

If we were revisit the former example of a college or university, the manifest function would be educate those who have not yet been educated, but there are many latent functions. For instance, colleges and universities often have a dramatic effect on the region's culture (e.g., music and the arts), provide jobs for faculty and staff, which in turn brings money into the local economy, as do the students themselves, and this increases local tax revenues. A recent study released from Facebook revealed that 28% of Facebook users met their spouses at their college/university (Macskassy 2013). Now you have an additional reason to stay in school!

Merton also believed that some functions could hurt a social system. He argued that manifest functions were never designed to hurt a system, but that latent functions could. He labeled these hurtful functions as latent dysfunctions. For instance, if we return to our example of marriage and divorce, if there is a breakdown between the husband and wife (e.g., social forces like financial issues, loss of a job, death of a loved one), the marital unit loses function. Fifty years ago, husbands and wives led interlocking lives—they depended on each other financially, emotionally, and physically, and worked together to restore function to the marital unit. However, today spouses often lack the depth of dependency (e.g., they have separate bank account) and either have no interest in working hard to restore function to the marital unit or the emotional tools to do so.

The Conflict Perspective - Karl Marx and the Evolution of Stratification

Karl Marx is most famous for his analysis of history, summed up in the opening line of the introduction to the *Communist Manifesto*: "The history of all hitherto existing society is the history of class struggles. Free man and slave, patrician and plebeian, lord and serf, guild-master and journeyman, in a word, oppressor and oppressed, stood in constant opposition to one another, carried on an uninterrupted, now hidden, now open fight, a fight that each time ended either in a revolutionary reconstitution of society at large, or in the common ruin of the contending classes" (Harmon, 2010).

Within sociology Marx is known for his ideas on the evolution of social stratification (i.e., dividing people into classes or categories), which often referred to as the **conflict perspective**. The conflict perspective is a macro-level theoretical approach because it has broad applicability. Marx believed that there would be a class struggle between those who owned the means of production (i.e., the haves or the ruling class) and those who worked for a wage (i.e., the have-nots or the working class). In fact, Marx believed that society was primarily based on inequality and conflict—conflict that arose when the "haves" struggled with the "have-nots" for limited resources. Further, he argued that the ruling or upper classes try to exploit the workers by turning their labor into profit.

"Religion is the opiate of the masses," Karl Marx wrote. Have you ever heard that expression? Marx believed that religion was being used by those with power and resources to keep those without power and resources in place. What most people don't know is that Marx was referring to the American institution of slavery. Marx felt that slaveholders forced Christianity on their slaves so that they could maintain control over them and they would do as they were told. If slaves were to be indoctrinated into Christianity, Christian beliefs would keep them in their place. For a slave to runaway from his master, was theft—something identified as wrong in the 10 Commandments. Slaves wouldn't dare rise up in the middle of the night and kill their masters because as the Bible says, "thou shalt not kill." And there are many passages in the Bible justifying slavery:

- Slaves, obey your earthly masters with respect and fear, and with sincerity of heart, just as you would obey Christ (Ephesians 6:5).

- And masters, treat your slaves in the same way. Do not threaten them, since you know that he who is both their Master and yours is in heaven, and there is no favoritism with him (Ephesians 6:9).

- Slaves, obey your earthly masters in everything; and do it, not only when their eye is on you and to win their favor, but with sincerity of heart and reverence for the Lord (Colossians 3:22).

- Slaves, submit yourselves to your masters with all respect, not only to those who are good and considerate, but also to those who are harsh (1 Peter 2:18).

- Masters, provide your slaves with what is right and fair, because you know that you also have a Master in heaven (Colossians 4:1).

- Teach slaves to be subject to their masters in everything, to try to please them, not to talk back to them (Titus 2:9).

The conflict perspective can be used to study phenomenon of inequalities. For instance, the rich versus the poor, males versus females, industrialized versus non-industrialized countries. For each of the aforementioned we can more simply classify them as "the haves" versus "the have-nots."

For instance, if the proportion of males to females in the U.S. population is 48/52, and if all things were equal, we should expect to see that 52% of physicians in the U.S. are female, 52% of the top 500 C.E.O. positions in the U.S. are held by women, that 52% of all U.S. presidencies were held by women, and that 52% of all automobile mechanics in the U.S. are women.

Conversely, all things being equal, we would expect to find that 48% of all clerical positions (i.e., secretaries) in the U.S. were held by men, 48% of all retail workers in the U.S. were male, 48% of all homemakers in the U.S. were male, and 48% of all daycare workers were male. But in fact, none of the above are found, which indicates that all things are not equal.

In reality, only 14% of the top 500 C.E.O. positions in the U.S. are held by women, 33.4% of physicians are female, 13% of all automobile mechanics in the U.S. are female, and of course, to date there have been no female U.S. presidents. When investigating the ratio of males working in predominantly female occupations, we find that only 4% of all secretaries are male, 5.2% of daycare workers are male, only 3% of all pre-school teachers are male, and only 3.4% of all stay-at-home homemakers are male. Something is amiss. All things are not equal. Using the conflict perspective, which suggests that those with more wealth, higher status and power, use those things to keep the status quo. We can suggest that males use their political and financial power and status to value those skills typically assigned to males and devalue those skills typically assigned to females. So, how do men exercise the economic and political power necessary to keep the status quo? In an article published in The Nation (March 7, 2014), the author Steven Hill writes: "... compared to other nations, the United States is losing ground. America now ranks ninety-eighth in the world for percentage of women in its national legislature, down from 59th in 1998. That's embarrassing: just behind Kenya and Indonesia, and barely ahead of the United Arab Emirates. Only five governors are women, including just one Democrat, and twenty-four states have never had a female governor. The percentage of women holding statewide and state legislative offices is less than 25 percent, barely higher than in 1993. Locally, only twelve of our 100 largest cities have female mayors."

Now that you understand the role of theory and the dominant theories used in sociology, let's move on to the next chapter on social research. Social research is the bedrock of sociology as a science. That research allows us to offer facts rather than opinions when explaining social phenomena. Only by understanding how sociology discovers facts or truths can you understand what those facts and truths say to us.

Terms, Concepts and Names to Know:

- Theoretical proposition
- Axioms
- George Homans
- George Herbert Mead
- Harold Blumer
- Symbols
- Emile Durkheim
- Robert Merton
- Anomie
- Karl Marx

Be Able to Discuss:

- Economic model of exchange
- Homan's social exchange theory
- Success proposition
- Stimulus proposition
- Distribute justice proposition
- Macro theory
- Micro theory
- Symbolic Interaction
- Structural functionalism
- Social construction of reality

- System

- Manifest functions

- Latent functions

- Latent dysfunctions

- Social stratification

- Religion is the opiate of the masses

- Conflict perspective

References

Blumer, H. (1973). A note on symbolic Interactionism. American Sociological Review. 38,(6).

Blumer, H. (1969). Symbolic Interactionism; Perspective and Method. Englewood Cliffs, NJ: Prentice-Hall.

Bureau of Labor Statistics, Household Data Annual Averages, Employed persons by detailed industry, sex, race, and Hispanic or Latino ethnicity. Retrieved 05/01/2016 from http://www.bls.gov/cps/cpsaat18.htm

Harmon, C. (2010). The Manifesto and the World of 1848. The Communist Manifesto (Marx, Karl and Engels, Friedrich). Bloomsbury, London.

Hill S. (2014). Why Does the US Still Have So Few Women in Office? The Nation, March 14, 2014. Retrieved 05/01/2016 from: http://www.thenation.com/article/why-does-us-still-have-so-few-women-office/

Homans, G. (1958, May). Social Behavior as Exchange. American Journal of Sociology, 63(6), 597-606.

Macskassy, S. (October 7, 2013). From Classmates to Soulmates. Retrieved May 11, 2016 from: https://www.facebook.com/notes/facebook-data-science/from-classmates-to-soulmates/10151779448773859/

Merton, R. (December 1936). The Unanticipated Consequences of Purposive Social Action;. American Sociological Review 1 (6): 894–904.

Merton, R. (1949). This Week's Citation Classic: Merton R K. Social Theory and Social Structure. New York: Free Press.

Chapter 3: Foundations of Knowledge: Research — Facts not Opinion

When we think of sciences, we think of biology, chemistry, and physics. But social sciences are just as valid and follow the same path to discovering facts as do those "hard" sciences. Science in general is a body of knowledge that has been collected as a result of the scientific method—a methodology that uses systematic steps to discover facts. To say something is systematic means there are precise steps and procedures that must be followed in order to establish scientific validity. The social sciences study humans in interaction with their environment—which consists of people and things. As previously discussed, sociology studies groups, and the way people affect the groups to which they belong, but also the groups affect their members. Sociology is not only interested in studying the interactions between people and groups, but also in studying how people's attitudes and beliefs are influenced by those interactions.

All social sciences study people, and people are much more difficult to study, studying humans is significantly different in the approach we use to study them. For instance, if I hold up a pen in the air and let go, it will fall. If I hold that same pen up one hundred times and let go, it will fall one hundred times. Even if I held up that pen in the air one million times and let go, it would still fall one million times. That's simple physics. Though I am over simplifying the hard sciences, if we found that each time we evoke a stimulus of some kind, and we get the same reaction each and every time we could state it as: if a given stimulus produces the same response each time, we have a law.

Therefore, we could write it as: S > R. But because sociology studies humans and human interactions, it's not that simple. No single stimulus will produce the same reaction each and every time.

For instance, let's say I walk into my introductory class one morning, and the students could see that I was irritated or angry about something. I stand behind the podium and begin lecturing. As I lecture I notice several students in the back row are talking to each other while I am lecturing. My anger peaks. I can't control it anymore. Furious and out of control, I reach into the back of the podium and whip out my Super Soaker. As I began to waive it around angrily, students begin to react. If studying humans was as predictable as studying organisms, or rocks, or Newton's Law of Gravitation, I would know how the students would react because they would all react in the same way. Do you think that you and your classmates would all react in the same way? Of course not. Some students would run out of the room not wanting to get squirted by their crazed professor. Some students might shriek and hide under their desk. Some students would laugh, and some not wanting to get wet, would try to stare me down as if saying "don't you dare get me wet!"

Humans don't react in the same way to a singular stimulus and that is why there are no laws in sociology. Instead, we react the way we do because we are all different and have a lifetime's worth of different experiences. It is those experiences, stored in the brain, that mediate between a given stimulus and our response to that stimulus.

For instance, let's say the night before you came to class you had seen a news report about a crazed professor who had thrown water balloons at his or her students. Having seen that news report it is stored in your brain as information that will influence you in some future way. Now, you come to class the next morning and experience me waiving my Super Soaker around. Do you think you would react in the same way after having seen the news report the previous night as you would if you had not seen that news report? Almost certainly you would react differently. Why? Because when we experience our social world, all those experiences are stored in the brain and serve to affect the way we react to things.

Me waiving my Super Soaker around is a stimulus. Your reaction to that stimulus is the response. In this case you will not simply react innately like you would when a nurse sticks a needle into your arm. Instead, even though the processing time might be measured in milliseconds, you will react to my stimulus of waiving the Super Soaker around only after accessing your memory in order to interpret the stimulus and decide your reaction.

When studying humans, the equation would be like this: S › I › R (i.e., stimulus › interpretation of the stimulus › response). With the exception of a few innate reactions to stimuli (e.g., pain, hunger, thirst, or the sex drive), we are social creatures and act according to who we are as a result of all those myriad things we've experienced during our lifetime. Those experiences that make us wonderfully unique make us incredibly difficult to study scientifically.

Should sociologists throw up their hands and state categorically that humans cannot be studied therefore we shouldn't study them? Of course not! Even though there are no laws in the social sciences, we can still study humankind in their social environment and discover facts. These facts benefit humans, their cultures, and their societies in some way. We need to utilize the same tools to study humans in their social environments as we use to study plants, or planets, or organisms. Those tools are called the steps of science or the Scientific Method.

Emile Durkheim was a French sociologist and considered the father of sociology. Durkheim wanted sociology to be completely distinct from other disciplines like philosophy and psychology and have its own methods for discovering social facts. Emile Durkheim was the first to use scientific principles in the relatively new science of sociology. He used those principles to study people and groups. Durkheim was the first to advocate that the social world affected people's behaviors. Anomie is the state of being unclear of social norms; in other words, being alienated from other members of the group. Emile Durkheim was the first to use scientific principles in the relatively new science of sociology. He used those principles to study people and groups.

Having identified a concept he called "anomie" (i.e., social estrangement, isolation, feeling lost, and alienated), he sought to study this phenomenon. In the 1800's, Durkheim studied European religions and believed that Catholics experienced less "anomie" than did Protestants. His reasoning was that Catholicism advocated that they approached God as a community and therefore were accountable to God as a community. Protestantism on the other hand, with the Protestant work ethic widely accepted in the Protestant community, believed that they approached God as individuals and were therefore individually accountable to God.

Therefore, Durkheim believed that the bonds between Protestants were weaker than they were for Catholics. Based on this premise, Durkheim believed that Protestants would have higher rates of anomie than Catholics. Using the scientific principles he wanted to employ within sociology, he proposed that Protestant countries would have higher rates of anomie than would Catholic countries. To test this, Durkheim reasoned that people who suffered from the effects of anomie would be more likely to commit suicide than others. After finding that Catholic (European) countries reported almost non-existent suicide rates and Protestant (European) countries reporting significantly higher rates, he concluded that his hypothesis had been proven correct: Protestants were more likely to suffer from the effects of anomie. While there were methodological problems with Durkheim's study, he is still credited for being the first to make sociology a science.

The Axioms of Science

Before we can use the steps of science to study humans in their social world, there are things we must accept and acknowledge before doing so. All sciences share in that there are axioms, taken for granted assumptions, which must pre-exist the steps of science (the scientific method). The following would be regarded as axioms for all sciences:

- Axiom 1: This is a real(ist's) world. A world of "things in themselves" objectively out there whether we can perceive them or not).

- Axiom 2: The world is ordered. Even a world that was chaotic. If one of the main goals of science is the ability to predict, there could be no such thing as science if the world was not ordered.

- Axiom 3: We can perceive this world. Our five senses allow us to come into contact with 'things in themselves.' Axiom 3: The world is ordered. We can discover order, logic, meaning, explanations, understanding and reason.

The axioms of science are necessary assumptions because without them science could not exist. If we could not perceive our world, there would be nothing to study. If we could not use our senses to perceive this world, there would be nothing to perceive. Finally, if the world was chaotic, and not ordered, science could not exist because the primary goal of science is to understand a phenomenon so well that we can use that knowledge to predict future outcomes of that phenomenon.

The Steps of Science

The steps of science, or the scientific method, are those steps and processes used in science to discover and collect facts about our world. Ultimately, the collection of these facts tell us something about our world and may result in our ability to predict.

- Step 1: We first perceive a phenomenon or phenomena (things we have not yet labeled or named).

- Step 2: We conceptualize (we name the phenomenon or phenomena).

- Step 3: We hypothesize (we construct a hypothetical cause and effect relationship between two or more concepts).

- Step 4: We arrive at a fact. After testing empirically (i.e., scientifically by experiment or study) we attempt to verify our hypothesis.

- Step 5: We now construct a theory. After testing and retesting our hypotheses many times, and collecting facts that support our hypothesis, we now attempt to put them together and construct a theory.

- Step 6: If we empirically verify our theory, we have a scientific law.

Steps in the Social Research Process

- Step 1: Define the Problem. What is the particular problem you wish to investigate? The more specific you are, the more definitive will be your research results.

- Step 2: Review the Literature. The next step is to review the existing literature related to the problem you wish to study. Prior research findings may influence your research methodology.

- Step 3: State your Hypothesis. A hypothesis is a testable statement between two or more variables. Hypotheses are formulated from previous research. In other words, there must be a scientific basis for a hypothesis.

- Step 4: Identify the Research Design. After formalizing the hypothesis, researchers must then decide what research method would be best in order to collect the information necessary to prove the hypothesis. Questions to be dealt with at this point include:
(1) how will the variable or variables be measured?
(2) how will the research sample be selected from the research population?
(3) what type of statistical analysis will be used (if it is a quantitative study)?

- Step 5: Collect the Data. There are a number of research tools that can used to gather information. For instance, surveys, experiments, interviews, participant observation, or content analysis.

- Step 6: Analyze the Data. Using the appropriate data analysis tool, analyzing the data will tell researchers if their hypothesis is supported or not.

- Step 7: Report your Findings. Researchers need to publish their findings as this potentially provides the basis for future research. This is how the body of knowledge in each scientific field is increased.

- Step 8: State your Conclusions and Introduce a Discussion. Drawing conclusions involves trying to answer your specific research questions. For instance, was your research question supported? If not, why not? What limitations in the study should be considered in evaluating the results? Do your research findings suggest directions for future research on the same topic? Were there methodological issues with your research that might be important for future research?

Types of Social Research

Surveys

The most common type of research design used in sociology is surveys. Survey research is the most common type of research utilized in sociology and can be either quantitative or qualitative in nature.
Advantages of survey research include:

- Answers are easily quantifiable as data,

- Large groups can be studied,

- Researchers can employ others to collect response data,

- Survey research is quick, and

- Inexpensive when compared to other designs.

Disadvantages of survey research include:

- Research findings might be superficial or doubtful, and

- Return rates may be low and therefore challenge the validity and reliability of the study.

In order to reduce the potential for research bias, researchers often use a pilot study to verify that their survey instrument is valid. Validity refers to the idea that researchers are measuring what they intend to measure. For instance, if I propose that the more time students spend studying, the higher their GPAs, I might unintentionally be measuring intelligence rather than study time. There is a positive relationship between hours spent studying and GPA. The more time students spend studying, the higher their GPA. However, we all know that some students don't have to study as many hours as others to earn good grades. In some cases, intelligence is the more important factor than is time spent studying.

Scales

A scale is a type of composite measure that is composed of several items that are logically related to one another and is used to extract data on a relatively complex variable or phenomenon. For instance, depression is a relatively complex phenomenon to measure. You can't ask just one question about some issue related to depression and expect to know just how depressed someone really is. You need a scale because there are a number of factors that are needed to adequately assess depression.

The most commonly used scale is the Likert scale, which contains response categories such as "strongly agree," "agree," "disagree," and "strongly disagree." For instance we are interested in measuring self-esteem. The following is the Rosenberg Self-Esteem Scale:

1. On the whole I am satisfied with myself.
   Strongly Agree (3) Agree (2) Disagree (1) Strongly Disagree (0)

2. At times I think that I am no good at all.
   Strongly Agree (0) Agree (1) Disagree (2) Strongly Disagree (3)

3. I feel that I have a number of good qualities.
   Strongly Agree (3) Agree (2) Disagree (1) Strongly Disagree (0)

4. I am able to do things as well as most other people.

Strongly Agree (3) Agree (2) Disagree (1) Strongly Disagree (0)

5. I feel I do not have much to be proud of.
   Strongly Agree (0) Agree (1) Disagree (2) Strongly Disagree (3)

6. I certainly feel useless at times.
   Strongly Agree (0) Agree (1) Disagree (2) Strongly Disagree (3)

7. I feel that I am a person of worth, at least the equal of others.
   Strongly Agree (3) Agree (2) Disagree (1) Strongly Disagree (0)

8. I wish I could have more respect for myself.
   Strongly Agree (0) Agree (1) Disagree (2) Strongly Disagree (3)

9. All in all, I am inclined to feel that I am a failure.
   Strongly Agree (0) Agree (1) Disagree (2) Strongly Disagree (3)

10. I take a positive attitude toward myself.

    Strongly Agree (3) Agree (2) Disagree (1) Strongly Disagree (0)

For this scale, each response is coded with a number. The higher the number for each scale item, the more it is associated with high self-esteem. If we code the items towards high self-esteem, the range of possible scores for this scale is 0 (for those who always chose the response associated with low self-esteem) to 30 (for those who always chose the response associated with high self-esteem). Therefore, the higher the score, the higher the self-esteem.

Sampling

Social research is almost always concerned about specific populations of people—for example, people in the U.S. 65 years of age and older. However, if I were to attempt to survey all Americans 65 years of age and older, I would need to survey almost 50 million people. As you can imagine, that would take a great deal of money and time. Instead I would use a smaller sample instead. Sampling is the process of selecting people from a research population so that by studying the sample we may generalize our results back to the population from which they were chosen.

The logic of random sampling is that if the sample is drawn randomly from the research population (i.e., the population we wish to study), everyone in the population has an equal chance of being selected for the sample. If that's the case, the random sample we drew should mirror the characteristics of the research population being studied. The average annual income of elderly in the U.S. is $25,000 per year. I should expect to see that same average income, or close to it, in my randomly drawn sample. Additionally, maybe I also know that the average age of Americans 65 years and older is 75.1 years and I find that the average age of my sample members is about the same. Therefore we can legitimately say that what is true of the sample, is also true of the population. Once we have drawn our random sample, we perform our research using that sample. When we get done with our research on our sample, and reach some conclusions based on the data we have collected from them, we are ready to generalize our results from the sample to our research population. If that sample was randomly drawn from our research population, the sample should mirror the characteristics of the research population. This allows us to say that if the sample mirrors the characteristics of our research population, sample results should be true for the population as well. See also, Generalization.

Experiments

Experiments usually occur in laboratories or carefully controlled environments where the independent variable can be manipulated. The manipulation of the independent variable ideally will lead to a corresponding change in the dependent variable. If there is a change in the dependent variable, and in the predicted direction, researchers would consider the result supporting the stated hypothesis. Advantages of experiments are that they are easily controlled and repeated. Disadvantages of experiments include that they can only collect information from small groups, subjects might not behave as they would in the real world, they take time to collect sufficient data, and they can be expensive. To help you understand the experimental research process, I have provided two famous examples.

Example 1. The following is an excerpt from Brad Bushman's 1988 article titled, "The Effects of Apparel on Compliance." Past research indicates that apparel influences our behavior and our impressions of others. One type of apparel that is both noticeable and symbolically significant is the uniform. Few studies, however, have examined the influence of uniforms on behavior, especially with female authority figures. In this study a female confederate who was dressed in uniform, professional attire, or sloppy clothing told subjects to give change to a person who was parked at an expired parking meter (Bickman, 1974). The results showed that compliance was higher when the confederate was dressed in a uniform. Verbal reasons given for complying also differed across conditions. The study shows that a uniform is a certificate of legitimacy (Joseph & Alex, 1972) for females as well as males and that both sexes are influenced by a female dressed in a uniform.

In 1988, Brad Bushman decided to take the experiments on compliance to perceived authority one step further. As in previous experimental studies, he had a female research confederate stand on the street next to a parking meter pretending to search her purse for the necessary change. As she frantically searches for coins to feed the meter, another woman, either dressed in a uniform or dress, would walk by and order passers-by to give the first woman a nickel for the meter. In this research, the independent variable is manipulated. That variable was perceived authority, and the dependent variable was obedience. And, like in previous research, Bushman operationalized perceived authority by varying the apparel the second female (i.e., the one who yelled at passers-by to give the other woman a nickel) wore. So, in the fist condition, passers-by would start to walk by a woman frantically searching her purse for change and beside her stood a woman dressed in something like a uniform, in the second condition, passers-by would start to walk by a woman frantically searching her purse for change and beside her stood a woman dressed in a business suit, and in the third condition, passers-by would start to walk by a woman frantically searching her purse for change and beside her stood a woman dressed like a panhandler. Bushman's results showed that more passers-by gave money to the woman needing money for the parking meter when they were ordered to do so by the woman wearing something that looked like a uniform. Bushman's hypothesis was supported: subjects in his study were more likely to comply with an order given by someone they perceived as having authority.

Example 2. In another classic experimental study, Solomon Asch (1951) wanted to investigate the effects of peer-pressure (i.e., social pressure) on conformity. Asch recruited fifty undergraduate male students to participate in an experiment they were told was designed to "test vision." A total of eight undergraduates were selected to participate in the study, though only one was a real subject, the other seven were actually research confederates of Asch, but of course, the real subject was unaware of this latter fact. All eight subjects were brought into a room and were seated around a large square table (so that all research subjects could see each other). Research confederates of Asch, had previously been instructed on how to act and respond during the experiment.

As the experiment began, subjects were seated around the table so the real research subject was the last. Asch handed two placards to the first subject (who was a research confederate). One placard had a single line on it and the other placard had three line lengths labeled A, B, and C. Asch then asked the first subject of lines A, B, and C, which is the single line closest to in length? The first subject responded by stating that clearly the single line was closest to the line labeled A. The researcher would thank the subject who then passed the placards to the subject seated to his right. Again, Asch asked the second subject of lines A, B, and C, which is the single line closest to in length? The second subject gave the same answer. Each of the seven subjects gave the same obviously incorrect answer. The real subject showed visible signs of confusion.

At the end of his research, Asch found that about 1/3 of the "real" subjects conformed to the majority opinion even though the majority opinion was clearly wrong. While some of the subjects said they really did not believe that the majority opinion was correct, but that they had went along with the group because they felt pressured to do so; in other words, they were afraid of being ridiculed or thought of as strange or deviant.

Asch concluded that people conform for two reasons:

- they wanted to fit in with the group and not stand out. Asch called this the normative influence, and

- because they believed the majority were better informed then them. Asch called this the informational influence.

Participant Observation

Participant observation is a research method in which the researcher observes while taking part in the activities of the social group being studied to some level of involvement—that involvement ranges from pure observation and therefore no involvement to the other end of the spectrum where there is pure observation and involvement. There are four roles of participant observation:

- Complete participant. In complete participation the researcher completely engages with the group being studied and their true identity is hidden from the group.

- Participant as observer. The researcher engages with the group, but makes no pretense as their true identity as researchers.

- Observer as participant. In this type of participant observation the researcher observes, but does not participate.

- Complete observer. In this situation the researcher is completely detached from the group being studied and simply records observations for future analysis. For instance, a researcher might decide to sit in a corner of a bar and record their observations of how people act when in a bar while drinking and socializing with others.

Ethnography

Ethnography involves the study of unique cultural elements of a given culture and the lives of its individual people. It is a type of qualitative research (as opposed to a quantitative research) using participant observation. As a type of qualitative research, advantages of ethnography include a greater depth of information and can lead to a broader understanding of the group and social processes being studied. Disadvantages include that it can only be studied relatively small groups and it is not easily generalizable to other groups. One example of ethnographic research might include female victimization by male partners (i.e., domestic abuse). Based on ethnographic research, we now understand why women who are being abused by their male partners remain in those abusive relationships. Historically, Americans have had little sympathy for female victims of domestic abuse because they believe all an abused woman has to do is to walk out the door. Research has found a significant number of reasons why women remain in those relationships. It takes female abuse victims on average six or seven attempts to leave abusive relationships before they are successful.

Secondary Analysis

Secondary analysis involves making use of data that has already been collected and is accessible for public and scientific use. For instance, the University of Wisconsin has four large datasets that are available for scientific research. If data that has already been collected can be used to study a researcher's interests, secondary analysis saves researchers time and money.

Content Analysis

Content analysis is a research method used to describe and analyze the media in general. For instance, content analysis has been used to study cartoon violence. Researchers would watch children's cartoons and count acts of violence (as previously qualified before the research began). Based on that research, and similar research on other types of TV programming, researchers concluded that children's TV cartoons have the greatest amount of violence in all TV programming. The aforementioned research is important because many psychological and sociological theories suggest that humans learn violence by watching others and therefore children are being taught violence as normative when viewing cartoons.

Variables

Any factor, trait, or condition that can exist in differing amounts or types. Generally, there are three types of variables: (1) independent, which is manipulated, (2) dependent, which means the variable is dependent on how the independent variable is manipulated, and (3) a controlled variable, which is held constant and usually only used in experiments which occur in highly controlled situations. An example of an independent variable would be age, while an example of a dependent variable might be income (which would be dependent on the independent variable of number of years of education).

Operationalization

In research, operationalization is the process of making a variable testable. To do so, researchers need to be highly specific in how they choose to measure that variable. Operationalizing a variable reduces the potential for bias introduced when (1) subjects might be confused by research questions, and (2) researchers are unclear what respondents have reported. For instance, if we wanted to know about someone's income we might ask, "What is your individual, gross, annual income in U.S. dollars?" If income is our variable, we have now fully operationalized it.

Correlation

A statistical tool used to assess the relationship between variables. For instance, as years of post-high school education increases, income increases. A correlation does not necessarily imply cause—simply that a relationship exists between the two variables.

A perfect correlation exists when a one unit rise in the independent variable leads to a corresponding one unit rise in the dependent variable. In other words, a perfect correlation would suggest that if we could know the independent variable, one hundred percent of the time we could predict what the dependent variable would be. There are two types of correlations: those that are referred to as positive and those that are referred to as negative. A positive correlation is one that finds that a one unit rise in the independent variable leads to a one unit rise in the dependent variable. Whereas a negative correlation shows that a one unit rise in the independent variable leads to a one unit decrease in the dependent variable.

Causality

Once two variables are correlated with another, the question of causality needs to be addressed. Correlations by themselves cannot establish causality. To establish causality the independent variable must precede the dependent variable in time and be a necessary or sufficient cause of the dependent variable. For instance, in biology it has been proven that smoking causes cancer. When smokers and non-smokers are compared on rates of cancer, it is obvious that smokers are at significantly higher risk of developing cancer; that is enough to allow us to say smoking is a sufficient cause of cancer. And among our sample of smokers, they started smoking before they developed cancer. Consequently, doctors today would agree with the statement that smoking causes cancer.

Research has found that as family income increases, child S.A.T. scores also increase; this is both a positive and significant relationship. However, it is not causal. It is not family income that would increase a child's S.A.T., but rather income serves as an indication of parental education. Generally, increased education leads to higher income. People with a bachelor's degree earn more than people with high school diplomas only, and people with graduate degrees tend to earn more than people with bachelor's degrees, etc. Since the amount of money people earn seems to be a result of their educational level, we would normally identify education as the independent variable and income as the dependent variable.

Another example would be S.A.T. scores and family income. Research has found that as family income increases, child S.A.T. scores also increase; this is both a positive and significant relationship. However, it is not causal. It is not family income that would increase a child's S.A.T., but rather income serves as an indication of parental education. Generally, increased education leads to higher income. People with a bachelor's degree earn more than people with high school diplomas only, and people with graduate degrees tend to earn more than people with bachelor's degrees, etc. Since the amount of money people earn seems to be a result of their educational level, we would normally identify education as the independent variable and income as the dependent variable.

Spuriousness

There are two conditions where there may appear to be an association between an independent and dependent variable but in fact doesn't provide accurate data. The first is where there is an accidental association between the independent and dependent variables and would not occur if the research was repeated elsewhere. For instance, what if a researcher found an association between shoe size and GPA among college students. Clearly, if his research was repeated in other classes or with other groups, the same association would not be found because there is no logical reason the two should be associated. The other cause of spuriousness is where there is a third unknown variable involved and is the true independent variable. The classic example is where it has been proven there is an association between the number of fire trucks at the scene of a fire (i.e., the independent variable) and the amount of fire damage (i.e., the dependent variable). But in reality the true independent variable is size of the fire and both the number of fire trucks at the scene and the amount of fire damage are dependent variables.

Research Validity

This is the degree to which a measure (e.g., an index or scale) really reflects what is being studied. It is largely associated with the process of operationalizing variables. Does the measure really measure what it is supposed to measure?

Research Reliability

Reliability is the degree a measure (e.g., an index or scale) produces consistent results as it is administered to different research groups over an extended period of time.

Statistical Terms

- Mean - When a total sum is calculated and then divided by the number of cases, we have a mean. The mean is what most Americans think of as "average."

- Median - The median is the midpoint of a score distribution; half of all scores fall on side of the median and half fall on the other side.

- Mode - The most common score in a distribution.

Human Subjects Committees (Institutional Review Boards)

Between 1933 and 1945, Nazis murdered 11 million Jews and people from other "undesirable" groups. Fascinated by one the most notorious Nazis responsible for the Holocaust, a social psychologist by the name of Stanley Milgram wanted to know if people in general would be more likely to commit horrendous acts because they would obey authority. To test his theory, Milgram conducted his research on obedience in the early 1960's at Yale University (Milgram, 1963). Milgram found that approximately 2/3s of his male research subjects were willing to administer 450 volt shocks to a victim, despite the fact that the victim wanted to stop participating after receiving a 150 volt shock, simply because they were told to do so by a perceived authority figure (i.e., a male researcher dressed in a white lab coat). Unbeknownst to those administering the shocks, the victim wasn't really being shocked—the victim simply acted the part, using protests and screams of pain. No one was really hurt. Milgram's research has been repeated at different locations throughout the U.S. and around the world, and the results have always been found to be the same.

Milgram was criticized for his work because some of his subjects who administered the pretend shocks complained later of having psychological issues as a consequence of having participated in the research. While Milgram felt the criticism was overblown, his research led to the creation of Institutional Review Boards designed to protect the rights of research participants. Institutional review boards are in place at colleges and universities who deal with research issues related to using human subjects in that research. Committees must adhere to government guidelines that serve to protect human participants in research. Specifically, committees are concerned that there be no harm to participants, that participation is voluntary, that participants are not deceived, and that participants are informed if the information provided by them will remain confidential or anonymous. In cases where there may be a need to violate one of the aforementioned principles, primarily in medical research, committees will evaluate whether the potential for good outweighs the risks or violations.

Concepts, Terms, and Names to Know:

- Stanley Milgram

- Emile Durkheim

- Stimulus

- Response

- Steps of Science

- Presence of a perceived authority figure

- Likert Scale

- Experiments

- Participant observation

- Ethnography

- Sampling

- Random sampling

- Generalization

- Mean

- Median

- Mode

- Population of study

- Sample

- Research validity

- Research reliability

Be Able to Discuss:

- How is a random sample chosen?

- Why can you generalize results back to the population of study?

- How is a random sample generated?

- What is an experiment?

- Stanley Milgram's reseach on obedience to authority

- What is an Institutional Review Board?

References

Asch, S. E. (1951). *Effects of group pressure upon the modification and distortion of judgment.* In H. Guetzkow (ed.) Groups, leadership and men. Pittsburgh, PA: Carnegie Press.

Asch, S. E. (1952). *Group forces in the modification and distortion of judgments.*

Asch, S. E. (1956). *Studies of independence and conformity: I. A minority of one against a unanimous majority.* Psychological monographs: General and applied, 70(9), 1-70.

Bickman, L. (1974, March). The Social Power of a Uniform. Journal of Applied Social Psychology, 4(1), 47-61.

Bushman, B. J. (1984). *Perceived symbols of authority and their influence on compliance.* Journal of Applied Social Psychology, 14, 501-508.

Bushman, B. J. (1988). *The effects of apparel on compliance: A field experiment with a female authority figure.* Personality and Social Psychology Bulletin, 14, 459-467.

Durkheim, E. (1951). Suicide : a study in sociology. The Free Press. Reprinted from 1897.

Milgram, S. (1963). Behavioral Study of Obedience. Journal of Abnormal and Social Psychology, 67(4), 371-378.

Nathan, J., & Nicholas, A. (1972). *The Uniform: A Sociological Perspective.* American Journal of Sociology 77(4), 719-730.

Chapter 4: Culture and Subcultures

Culture

Many times people think of the terms culture and society as synonymous but that's not the case. Culture is the total way of life of a society. The components of culture include values, norms and material goods they manufacture. What are some American values? Can you think of any? What values do we as Americans espouse, whether we live up to them or not? What about our value of freedom of religion? Separation of church and state? A free mass public education? What about our value of freedom of speech? All of these are values that separate us from many other cultures and make use distinct. All cultures are distinct in one way or another from others because of differences in values, norms and material goods.

The second component of culture are the norms that people are expected to follow. They are the ways people are expected to do things. For instance, as Americans we are expected to stand in line in an orderly way and wait our turn, we do not cut in front of people standing in line. However, in many cultures around the world standing in line is not the norm and won't get you the items you need to survive because others will get to the front of the line first. If there is a limited supply of something you need, you're out of luck. In those cultures it's about getting what you need and standing in line is a luxury they cannot afford.

Finally, the material goods that a culture produces are things that are not only manufactured in that culture, but also are used and play an important in that culture. For instance, computers are widely used and to the extent that it would bring about a catastrophe of epic proportions if they all stopped working at once. Like many Western countries, we depend on them for entertainment, business, and government. We also use computers and the Internet for access to information. A friend of mine had his cable go out for a period of about 24 hours. During those 24 hours he had no access to cable TV, the Internet, or his land line. He was literally cut off and isolated from the outside world. While his health and well-being was not necessarily threatened, it certainly put him in the position of not knowing what to do. He was also left with a huge void to fill because he no longer had the Internet as a source of information and something to occupy his time.

Another material good that we as Americans depend upon are our cell phones. Imagine a time not so long ago when there were no cellphones, but instead only landlines. Early phones had no answering machines or caller ID. If you tried to contact someone and they weren't home, you didn't make contact with them until they got home. That's hard for you imagine, isn't it? That is another example of how culture has changed dramatically in a relatively short period of time. We are now dependent upon our cell phones to keep us in contact with the outside world. We depend upon our cell phones for our participation in social media, texting friends, business associates, and other things. Because most phones today are smart phones, they also have computer technology. In fact, the average cell phone has more than enough computer capabilities to have gotten man to the moon in 1969. Cell phones are becoming more common around the world even in third world countries. Even if you own very little, there is a good chance you have a cell phone. Cell phones are not only things we produce and use, but they define us as a nation. The U.S. has the third largest number of cell phones in the world with 328 million, on the heels of China at number one with 1.3 billion, and India with 1.0 billion. Worldwide, there are 69 billion cell phones in use (List of Countries, 2014). Think about how cell phones dramatically affect our lives and in so many ways. Have you ever seen a 1960's comedy called "Gilligan's Island?" If so, that's what life would be like if we lost those technical necessities of modern life. A related material good that we use and produce would be the Internet. We use the Internet for entertainment, information, social media, and communication. We are so dependent on the Internet that according to a recent Gallop poll, approximately one-fourth of Americans get their news from online sources (Saad, 2013).

One final example of technology we depend on is the microwave oven. When the microwave was first invented by accident in the late 1930's, it was as big as your refrigerator and cost thousands of dollars. Consequently very few restaurants could afford them and virtually no private individuals could. The next thing that happened along the lines of cooking revolutions was the advent of the fast food restaurant. Prior to the fast food, mom would spend several hours a day preparing dinner for the family. With the fast food era, Mom's time in the kitchen was reduced allowing her to spend time on other chores.

Still, fast food restaurants were not all that common and so most women had no option but to stay at home and cook for their families, which cut deeply into the time she had to perform other household tasks. In the evolution of cooking technology the next thing to come along was the TV dinner. Back then TV dinners were not microwavable because there were essentially no microwaves in those days. TV dinners were cooked in the oven for 30 minutes.

The next development was the miniaturization of the microwave. By the 1970's microwaves were not much bigger than today's standard microwave. The cost ranged from $300-500 depending upon the options. Still, $300-500 dollars in the 1970's was a great deal of money. However, as prices fell, and more and more families could afford microwave ovens, mom spends even less time in the kitchen preparing meals. While the TV dinner might have taken 30 minutes to prepare in the oven, microwave dinners took about five minutes at most. All of this meant that mom had more time to spend on other activities in the late 1960's and early 1970's. This coincided with a slowdown in the U.S. economy and allowed mom to enter the paid labor force in order to help out the family financially. Even though she worked full-time, she could still have dinner on the table when her husband walked in the door thanks to the microwave oven.

When we look at American culture we can say that microwaves are a central part of our culture and affect us in many different ways, some good and some bad. The price of microwaves has fallen to about $40 at Wal-Mart. This is still beyond the means of people in third world countries, many of which do not have access to electricity. Here in the U.S. 68% of Americans say that having a microwave oven is a necessity, coming in fifth behind a car, clothes washer, clothes dryer, and air conditioning (Pew, 2006).

In the case of culture there is a dominant culture and then there are subcultures. Members of both the dominant culture and subcultures wish to preserve those individual cultures. Culture determines our values, our norms, and the way that we incorporate technology into our lives. Culture is something that we wish to pass down to our children and to their children. It is in this way that we preserve not only those cultures, but the overall society that is made up of those individual cultures. Culture also serves as an important form of conformity. Where do we learn those beliefs and norms? We learn those norms throughout our lives in what are called socializing agents. The most important of those socializing agents is our family.

Generally there are two different types of the overall culture: there is what is called material culture, which is made up of things that we can see and feel such as the houses that we live in, the cars that we drive, the food that we eat. Then there is what is called nonmaterial culture. These are the things that are not tangible like our customs, beliefs, norms. Technology is a part of material culture, yet at the same time technology, even though it is material in nature, has significant nonmaterial effects on culture.

An example here might be one as simple as dinnertime. Dinnertime may not be something that many of you are familiar with. You may understand the concept of sitting down for dinner with your family occasionally, but dinnertime for the Baby Boomer generation meant sitting down for dinner with their family every evening and usually at a specific time. Growing up I knew where I would be at 5 o'clock every evening unless there were some special circumstances. Dinner time was a time that the family used to exchange information so that my parents knew what I was doing and it was also a time that for my siblings and parents to discuss their plans or concerns.

Dinnertime was a wonderfully rich opportunity for family members to exchange information. Because of technology this is changed. It's not nearly as common for young people to experience something called dinnertime as it was in my generation. Because of technological changes such as fast food, and the microwave oven, young people rarely experience dinnertime. It's much common for young people to eat when it's convenient for them rather then and a set time for the family to eat together.

The consequence of this is the loss of genuine quality interaction. Do parents know what's going on in their children's lives? No, not when compared to previous generations. While it is true that the cellphone allows children to stay in touch with their parents over a broader period of time, it doesn't allow for the conversational exchange that occurs around the dinner table.

Society

If you were to drive north and to continue driving north eventually you would get to something called the Canadian border. But imagine that there was no border crossing, no signs in English and French, and you didn't get out of your car to hear the difference in accent. How would you know you were in Canada? Probably, you not would know.

Before the advent of cable TV, people were reliant on broadcast TV through the airwaves. Maybe you've seen old antennas on top of your grandparents' house—those were for broadcast TV. During the time of broadcast TV, 90% of Canadians lived within 100 miles of the U.S./Canadian border. So when Canadians sat down to watch TV at night they undoubtedly watched some American broadcasting--as Americans undoubtedly watched some Canadian TV.

Where did American culture stop and Canadian culture begin? It's a very difficult question to answer because there are certainly a lot of similarities between the two cultures. It's not easy to say where one stops and the other starts. This is very different than with society. Societies are geographically bounded because there are borders. You can see where one society starts and the other stops.

Norms

Norms are expected behaviors and thoughts. There are different types of norms. Some that carry slight or zero sanctions. A sanction is a type of punishment. While some carry extreme sanctions. Think of this as being on a continuum and we'll label the continuum sanctions from two extremes. At the far end of the continuum where there are either no sanctions or slight sanctions, these are called folkways. Folkways are norms that when violated carry no or slight sanctions. For instance, what if you want to a wedding and at the proper time you turned to watch the bride walk up the aisle, but as you did so, you notice that she was wearing a bright red dress. Do you call the police? Do you stop being her friend? No. There are likely no sanctions that you will impose even though it is a violation of norms because the norm says that women should wear white dresses to their weddings. There could be sanctions though minimal. For instance, what if you turn to the person next to you and snickered or made a face? In some sense those are sanctions, but as you can see they are not severe (Sumner, 2007).

Other folkway violations might include picking your nose, passing gas, belching, wearing a hat indoors, or eating with your fingers. Here in the U.S. you're supposed to use utensils for eating with only a few exceptions—sandwiches, French fries, pizza, etc.

But in other parts of the world such exceptions may not be made. It is common for Brits to use a knife and fork to eat pizza.

The next type of norm is called mores. If you think back about that continuum that we called sanctions, mores fall right in the middle. Mores can be divided into two types: the first type is when a norm is violated but the sanctions are not all that severe and not a violation of the law. On the other hand, the other type of more involves violating the law, in which case there will be severe sanctions.

Can you think of some norm when violated because of something you have done or someone else has done but that doesn't necessarily violate the law? For instance, what about a woman who wore a highly revealing dress to work? Breaking a promise to a friend? Wearing a bikini to church? Slurping your food while you eat? Making that hawking noise in a restaurant as you try to clear up your sinus drainage? Appetizing, isn't it? The point is there will be sanctions, but none of those actions violated the law.

The other type of more violation will be sanctioned by the law. Things like running a red light, illegally parking in a handicapped space, abusing a child, robbing a bank, or committing insurance fraud. These kinds of more violations will earn you legal sanctions.

Finally, there are **taboos**. Taboos are at the extreme opposite end of the continuum from folkways. If a taboo is violated, not only will there be sanctions, but they will be severe. The two most common examples of taboos are incest and cannibalism. Why would incest represent a taboo? Because it potentially damages the gene pool which can destroy a society. Cannibalism is also punished severely because it threatens the survival of society. It's not good to eat your fellow citizens when the survival of your people is the ultimate goal.

Towards the end of World War II as The Allies were making their way from one island to the next before finally facing the prospect of having to invade Japan, one of those islands was experiencing severe food shortages for the Japanese troops. A Japanese soldier had been found cannibalizing the body of another Japanese soldier. Japanese on the island were so short of food that they were eating anything that could find. When the Japanese soldier was brought before the Japanese commandant of the island, he was found guilty of a crime, and summarily executed. The Japanese commandant put out a notice to all Japanese soldiers. In the proclamation the commandant stated that if a Japanese soldier was caught cannibalizing the body of a fellow Japanese soldier, he would immediately shot for his actions. However, the commandant went on to state that if a Japanese soldier was caught cannibalizing the body of the enemy, no harm would come to the soldier. The point is that cannibalism threatens the survival of a given society because you are eating your own kind. However, down through history it has not been uncommon for victors to cannibalize the bodies of their captives. Headhunters are notorious for this.

Even where cannibalism is not necessarily punishable by the law, it is still regarded with such revulsion that it is still severely sanctioned. In 1972, a Uruguayan Air Force plane, which was carrying a rugby team from Paraguay to Chile for a competition, crashed in the Andes in the middle of winter. A total of 27 people survived the crash managed to survive for more than two months before they were rescued. After being rescued, they had been asked how they had managed to survive so long on the top of the mountain without food. Survivors reported that there had been a cargo of cheese on board the plane and they survived by eating the cheese.

Within several weeks of the rescue, the survivors found out the press had learned the truth about how they had survived and were about to break the story in the news. So, the survivors granted an interview in which they admitted to cannibalizing the bodies of those that had died from the crash or from their injuries at a later time.

Why did it take several weeks for the survivors to admit that they had survived by cannibalizing the bodies of their comrades? They waited so long because the world thinks of cannibalism as a taboo and barbaric. This was especially true in this situation because South America is largely Catholic and cannibalism is regarded as a mortal sin. Mortal sins are those for which there is no forgiveness and the offenders will go to Hell. Fortunately for survivors, a Catholic Archbishop in Uruguay granted a dispensation for their "crime."

Here in America we have our own example of cannibalism. In the 1800's, as Americans and wagon trains moved from the East to the West Coast to settle California and Oregon, they had to cross the Rocky Mountains. In order to cross safely you had to reach the foothills by October first; to try and cross later than that meant almost certain death. The Donner party's large wagon train of settlers tried to cross Rocky Mountains too late in the season and they became trapped by the heavy snow. Unfortunately the group had split into two, but both were trapped by the snow. One group resorted to cannibalism in order to survive. Again, not legally punishable, but the stigma stayed with the survivors and deeply shocked the American public.

Ethnocentrism and Cultural Relativism

Ethnocentrism is the belief that one's own culture is superior to all others and that belief is used to judge other cultures independently of their unique cultural elements. The converse of ethnocentrism is cultural relativism which advocates objectivity when evaluating other cultures and to do so with their particular cultural elements in mind. Cultural relativism suggests that other cultures should be studied and evaluated within the context of their own culture and not by the culture of the researcher or evaluator.

Subcultures

Within most cultures are many subcultures. Subcultures basically have their own norms and their own ways of doing things that differ in one way or another for the dominant society. Examples of subcultures in large cities might include Italian-Americans, Jewish-Americans, goths, geeks, and other groups. While many see subcultures as a threat to the dominant culture, others see subcultures in a positive way because they foster diversity and creativity. To these latter people, subcultures are a strength. For instance, compare two cultures: the United States and the other Iran. Both countries claim to be democratic, but only one of these countries values diversity to some degree—the United States. Iranian law leaves virtually no room for diversity—no room for diverse thought or action, and anything that is considered non-conformist is often severely punished. Of the two cultures, can you guess which culture has a much higher degree of creativity?

Treatment of Minority Groups by the Dominant Group

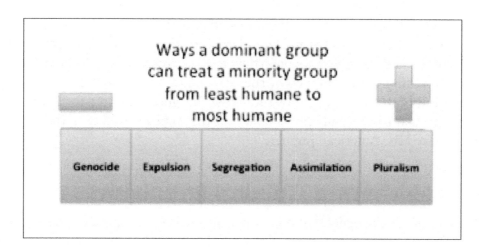

Imagine a continuum and we label that continuum, "Humane treatment of minority groups by the dominant group." We would label one end of the continuum "inhumane" and the other "humane." At the most "inhumane," section we would find genocide.

Genocide

Genocide is the destruction of a people. Imagine the dominant group saying of a group, "They're different than us, we don't like them, can't use them, so let's kill them." There have been many genocides down through the centuries, and while the most famous might be the Holocaust, there have been many more. In recent years, there has been genocide committed by Serbs against Muslim Bosnians, the Tutsi genocide against the Hutu, and the genocide committed by Sudanese militia against civilians in Darfur. Even in our own history we can find instances of genocide—from the first Spanish explorers in the 1400's, to the U.S. military in the 1800's. Some estimate millions of native peoples were murdered.

Expulsion

As we move towards a more humane treatment of a minority group by a dominant group, we come to expulsion. Literally, the dominant group seeks to expel the minority group from its borders. Imagine the dominant group saying, "They're different from us, we don't like them, can't use them, and we don't want them ... but we'd rather not kill them if given a choice." Unfortunately, more often than not expulsion has led to genocide in many instances.

After Hitler came to power in 1933, and the Nazis began to implement more and more laws consistent with their brand of anti-Semitism. The Nazis told the German people that the plan would be to resettle German Jews in Madagascar—an island off the coast of Africa. Though that was never really the Nazis intent, the German populace believed it. That was certainly more civilized than killing them, which the German population probably would not have accepted, but it would rid Germany of the Jews. Even here in the U.S. the Trail of Tears was designed to forcibly remove native peoples from eastern states. They were to be resettled in the Oklahoma territory. Genocide was a result with more than 4,000 dying on the forced march.

Segregation

Next on our continuum is segregation—the mid-point—though to argue that it is devoid of inhumanity would be a mistake. Imagine the dominant group saying, "They're different than us, and we don't like them ... but we can use them." This is the dominant group saying they can benefit from the minority group in some way—their labor being the most common benefit. Segregation literally means to separate members of the two groups; they are not equal. In 1953, the Frontier Hotel in Las Vegas, drained the pool after worldwide African-American singing sensation Dorothy Dandridge dipped her toe into the water of the hotel pool. This kind of treatment of African-Americans existed even into the 1960's—one hundred years after the American Civil War ended in 1865. Rosa Parks was arrested for not giving up her seat on a bus to a white man. African-Americans were still expected to use separate drinking fountains and bathrooms, give way on a sidewalk to whites, and either eat at African-American restaurants or out back of white restaurants. Segregation known as Apartheid was practiced in South Africa until 1994. As you read this, understand that for many of you segregation has existed within your lifetime.

Assimilation

As we move closer to the more humane end of our continuum, we come to assimilation. Imagine the dominant group saying, "They're different from us, but if they will just accept our values and norms ... in other words, be like us, we'll treat them equally." There is a mathematical formula for assimilation: $A + B + C = A$ (where A represents the dominant group and B and C minority groups).

Cultural Imposition. The dominant or controlling culture forces its beliefs and practices on the lesser culture. In a speech delivered in 1907, President Theodore Roosevelt said:

> "In the first place, we should insist that if the immigrant who comes here in good faith becomes an American and assimilates himself to us, he shall be treated on an exact equality with everyone else, for it is an outrage to discriminate against any such man because of creed, or birthplace, or origin. But this is predicated upon the person's becoming in every facet an American, and nothing but an American...There can be no divided allegiance here. Any man who says he is an American, but something else also, isn't an American at all. We have room for but one flag, the American flag... We have room for but one language here, and that is the English language... and we have room for but one sole loyalty and that is a loyalty to the American people."

Roosevelt's view pretty well typifies how Americans think about assimilation: *They need to be like us.*

Pluralism

Finally, at the far end of our continuum is pluralism. This is where the dominant group says, "They're different than us, but we value those differences and see them as strengths, so we'll accept them as different but equal." The formula for pluralism is: A + B + C = A + B + C. Everyone is equal and we don't have to be the same. Many introductory textbooks will cite Switzerland as an example of a pluralistic society, but is that really a good example of pluralism? Switzerland is divided into three regions: the German-speaking region to the north, the French-speaking region to the west, and the Italian-speaking region to the south. The three regions get along well and respect each other's differences. But in reality, who are they? They are all primarily white Europeans. Does that really represent pluralism? Cultural pluralism is where there is coexistence of different subcultures within a society.

In thinking about our continuum of the humane treatment of minority groups by dominant groups, where do you think the U.S. is today? There's no right or wrong answer, but a good question on which to reflect.

Non-Ethnic Subcultures

I could write a litany on subcultures in the U.S. Subcultures in general share different group norms, sometimes these are deviant norms and sometimes they are not. Subcultures often share a language, costumes, and customs—things that help to differentiate them from mainstream culture. Examples could include, but are certainly not limited to, the LGBT community, Trekkies, goths, "cyberlibertarians," Hassid Jews, Italians living in New York, Jews living in New York or Miami, Muslims, Sikhs, skaters, vampires, ravers, mangas, and role-players, and let's not forget furries. Wikipedia lists 99 subcultures.

Nature Versus Nurture

One of the questions that we have to ask is whether or not culture is shaped by biology or by the environment. There is an argument that maybe you've heard of. That argument is called nature versus nurture. Whereas nature represents biology and nurture represents environment. Imagine a continuum where nature was at one end and nurture at the other. There are some things that are completely nature and explained by biology. Height, hair color, or eye color are all examples of biology explaining who and what we are. But with those exceptions there are relatively few things from a biological point of view that completely explain who we are.

On the other extreme of our continuum is nurture. Nurture would suggest that who and what we are is the result of our environment. So when we look at our continuum of nature versus nurture, we understand that most behaviors fall somewhere between nature and nurture. Particular behavior could vary between the two polar opposite ends of our continuum. Behavior sometimes could be more biologically influenced while others may be more environmentally influenced.

There are a number of examples we can draw on. One example is depression. What is the biological reason for some people's depression? The answer for some is low levels of serotonin and/or dopamine. Is there a nature or biological reason for some people's depression? The answer is yes. On the other hand, can there be environmental reasons for people to be depressed? What if someone loses their job? What if a loved one dies? Someone who may have perfectly normal levels of serotonin and dopamine may still experience depression because of those environmental occurrences. What's interesting about this is that researchers tell us that if someone experiences environmental reasons for depression, but who have no biological reasons for depression, if they remain depressed long enough their serotonin and dopamine levels may fall and now they additionally have biological reasons for their depression. So if we were to look at depression on our continuum of nature versus nurture, we would find that it is somewhere in the middle. There are both biological and environmental reasons for depression.

Another example would be schizophrenia. There is a biological link to schizophrenia, researchers don't know exactly what causes schizophrenia. Adults in their early to mid-20s who develop schizophrenia are about ten times more likely to have had a first degree family member with the illness. Some studies point to marijuana use as a precipitator of schizophrenia in adulthood though the exact incidence rate is unknown. Alcoholism and drug abuse have been found to worsen the condition. Because the exact causes of schizophrenia are still unknown, researchers cannot rule out environmental effects on the condition (Long, 2015). Some research finds a link between a history of childhood trauma, including sexual abuse, as possibly precipitating schizophrenia (Moskowitz, 2011).

We can also look at IQ. There is a classic case often cited in introductory psychology textbooks of a young woman given the name Genie. In 1970, an elderly woman appeared in a social services office with a 13-year-old girl. The girl was thin, pale, walked in a very unusual manner and was incapable of speaking. Social service workers began to investigate and discovered a very shocking tale. When Genie was four years old her father was convinced she was mentally retarded. For what he believed was her own good, he locked her in her room for nine years. During the day Genie was kept chained to her potty chair, and at night she was locked in a crib with a wire top to keep her from escaping. The only contact Genie had was when her grandmother brought her food and drink. Social workers tried to estimate Genie's IQ but they were unable to do so because she could not speak. Average IQ is approximately 100 and it was thought the Genie's IQ was significantly and substantially lower than average. For nine years Genie had been deprived of virtually any kind of social interaction.

Further, Genie had been denied any kind of exercise. Genie walked slightly hunched, arms outstretched, and knees bent, and her steps were very tentative. Can you explain why she walked the way she did? You're exactly right if you guessed because that was her position or posture as she sat on the potty chair and physically grew during those nine years. Social workers began to work with her in the hopes of being able to repair some of the damage done. In the beginning they had some initial success and she learned to speak several words. Her walking improved and she could even engage in something resembling play. But after several years of working with her Genie suddenly reverted to her earlier stage and stopped speaking entirely. Genie survives today having lived her life in a nursing home incapable of speaking and living independently. The question becomes why were social workers unable to repair some of the damage done to her intelligence and her ability to socialize?

Genie's case became relevant again to researchers when a similar case occurred in the late 1990's. In California, a neighbor had become suspicious because he had not seen his neighbor's small child for several years. He called the police and they found the child, six years old at the time, locked in her bedroom. She had been locked in her bedroom since the age of two, and during those four years she had been denied of all social interaction. Social workers began to work with the girl and they were able to help her to recover much of the damage done by the loss of interaction for those four years (Schexnayder, 1999). While there were certainly some deficits left in speech and socialization, they were relatively minimal and the girl is now an adult and able to function independently. What was the difference? Why were social workers unsuccessful with Genie but successful in this latter case?

There is a new trend that has developed among young affluent couples with children in need of daycare. In larger cities, and if you are a parent with money to spend, you might well take your child to a daycare center where a foreign language is spoken exclusively. Why? Because the research suggests that we are best able to learn a second language when we are young-generally prior to the age of 10. It has to do with the connections between various parts of the brain, but those connections begin to change at around the age of 10.

Can you see how this applies to the case of Genie and the other girl? Genie wasn't rescued until she was 13 years old and the developmental window that would've allowed social workers to repair some of the cognitive damage had closed, whereas in the case of the other girl who was rescued at the age of six, there was still some time remaining before the window closed, which left rescuers time to repair some of the damage that had been done. In the case of IQ, it is both a result of nature and nurture. Biology sets the predisposition for IQ, but whether it's realized, retarded, or exceeded depends largely on the environment.

Another example of nature versus nurture concerns aggression. While biology (i.e., testosterone) has a strong part to play here, it is not the only thing that can explain why some people are more aggressive than others. Being victimized or treated unfairly might result in a display of aggression.

Finally, we can examine nature versus nurture when investigating gender roles. Based on research by Margaret Mead (1949), and followed by a huge volume of research, there seems to be no evidence that gender roles are biologically determined. The overwhelming evidence supports the belief that gender roles are culturally (i.e., environmentally) learned. Psychologists now tell us that whatever exists in the way of something called a "maternal instinct" also exists in equal strength as a "paternal instinct." While society assumes that women make the most nurturing of parents, the research suggests that's only because society expects them to be and doesn't accept the notion that a father can be just as successful at raising his kids as can a mother. Did you know that women make some of the best snipers? According to several military historians, among the top ten snipers in history, two are female: Sergeant Roza Shanina with 59 confirmed kills and Major Lyudmila Pavlichen with 309 confirmed kills. Both served in the Soviet army during WWII. Nature would suggest that these two women would have made better stay-at-home moms than highly successful killers on the battlefield, but that's simply not the case.

No psychologist or biologist would argue that everything about you is the result of nature (i.e., biology). No sociologist would make the argument that everything about you was the result of nurture (i.e., environment). Psychologists, biologists, and sociologists would agree that most aspects of human behavior are the result of a mixture of both nature and nurture.

To help us study this relationship, researchers turn to twin studies. Since these twins share the same genetic make-up, any differences we find between them as adults are most likely due to environmental differences. Studies involving identical twins separated at birth consistently confirm that environmental factors have significant effects on biological predispositions (Ohlson, 2002). Now that we understand that we are a product of both nature and nurture, let's look at how humans develop and become the unique social creatures they are.

Now, let's come back to the idea of culture. Is culture the result more of nature or of nurture? Is it more biology or the environment? It's an important question because if the answer is that it is more determined by the environment that means the environment (i.e., culture) is capable of evolving and changing. Certainly while there are common characteristics in most cultures, how those characteristics are defined is usually very different. Those characteristics, common to all cultures, are called cultural universals. **Cultural universals** include such things as marriage, the family, language, funeral rites, things considered deviant, prohibitions against incest, and medical practices. For instance, here in the United States a family is generally defined as a mother, father and two children, the so-called nuclear family. However same-sex marriage and single-parent households are changing this definition. In many other parts of the world, families are defined as extended. That means that other family members, more than just parents and their children, live together under one roof.

Also, we tend to deny the term family to spouses who do not have children. In ancient Rome, slaves were often considered part of the family (History Channel, 2006). Companies in Japan are often regarded as a type of family. As Japan modernized in the 1800's factories were built in the cities, but unfortunately people living in the city already had jobs and therefore employers had a labor shortage. What to do? Owners of factories went to the country to try to find workers, but they found that young men were engaged in agriculture and not available as a labor source. However, young women were available. So factory owners went to parents of young girls and made them an offer: in exchange for their labor they would pay them, provide shelter for them, chaperone them, and ensure their safety. They would assume the role of family to the young girls. It is for this reason that many Japanese companies even today are very family-like (Sugiyama, 1988).

Japanese workers put in more unpaid overtime when compared to other countries in the industrialized world, are cross-trained at levels both below and above them so that they can provide quick replacements when necessary, and often tie their identity to their company. For instance, in Japan it would not be unusual for someone to introduce themselves to you by their name and company they work for. There is in fact a blurring of personal and work lives.

We can also look at funeral rites. Every culture has something in the way of funeral rites—it is another cultural universal. While most industrialized countries of the world practicing embalming today, that was not always the case. Embalming actually started here in the United States during the American Civil War. After the war, embalming became a common practice, no doubt because we are such a large country and it would take time for someone to reach a funeral. One of the reasons that embalming became so popular here in the United States was fear of being buried alive. In the 1800's the fear was so great of being buried alive the people who had money had special coffins built for them with ropes, pulleys and a bell on top of the ground that would ring if someone wiggled their toe when mistakenly buried alive. Edgar Allen Poe feared being buried alive and wrote about it. Some cultures of the world do not embalm and in fact religious practices dictate the dead be buried within 24 hours.

Historically, some cultures have expelled their elderly because they could no longer contribute to the survival of the group so that their send-off was more or less a funeral. Cremation as a funeral rite has increased through the centuries. Today, the country with the highest cremation rate is Japan at 99%, whereas the United States approximately 45% of all Americans who die are cremated (International Cremation Statistics, 2011). Historically, cremation was frowned upon by the Christian religion, but religious attitudes are changing about this practice.

Humor is also a cultural universal, however what is funny differs by culture.

Many years ago I was traveling through the heartland and had checked into a hotel. That night I went down to eat dinner at the hotel restaurant. A Japanese car company was in the initial stages of development of what would become a truck manufacturing facility in this particular city. As I sat in the restaurant, the British and American executives of the new manufacturing facility arrived with their Japanese counterparts. As they sat around the table waiting for their meals, the Japanese were very refined as they waited, unlike their British and their American counterparts on the other hand, were loud and boisterous. The British and Americans told jokes and expected their Japanese counterparts to join in the laughter, but were instead met with polite smiles. At one point an American executive told a joke that he thought was so funny that he slapped the Japanese executive sitting next to him on his back. The color drained from the Japanese executive's face and again was met was met only with a polite smile. The British and American executives had failed to study Japanese culture.

Exporting American Culture: Americanism

In the world, Americans are admired, emulated, and hated. However, one thing is certain, American culture has spread throughout the world. Americanization is the spread of American culture or the influence American culture has on the cultures of other countries. Americanization affects the popular culture, media, food, technology, business practices, and political techniques around the world. The term Americanization was first used in 1907.

Even within the U.S., Americanization still occurs. Immigrants to the U.S. assimilate to American culture, which means they accept our customs and values along with all those aspects of culture I mentioned above.

Hollywood has probably done more to export American culture than any cultural component. The American film industry has dominated the world's thirst for media since the 1920's. Even today, regardless where you live, if you want to be an actor or actress, you find a way to get to Hollywood. Movies are the main type of medium by which people from around the world see who we are—our fashions, customs, scenery, way of life (real or imagined), food, cars, and drinks. Everything we are as a culture is desired by someone somewhere (Hoynes. 2011; Pokony & Sedgwick, 2004).

Another component of Americanization is our love for brand named foods. Of the top 10 brands in the world, seven of those are based here in the U.S.. Coca-Cola, which holds the top spot, and fast food is also often viewed as being a symbol of U.S. marketing dominance. Companies such as McDonald's, Burger King, Pizza Hut, Kentucky Fried Chicken and Domino's Pizza among others have numerous outlets around the world (Global Brands, 2006).

Also, let's not forget the computer and software industry. Many of the world's largest computer companies are also U.S. based . Those include Microsoft, Apple, Intel, Dell and IBM, and much of the software bought worldwide is created by U.S. based companies (Carayannis & Campbell, 2011).

In Germany in the 1920s, the American efficiency movement was called "rationalization." The Germans, were very interested in Henry Ford's ideas about the assembly line. The assembly line became the most efficient form of manufacturing in history (Pokorny & Sedgwick, 2004). The process of "rationalization" equated to greater efficiency and consequently greater productivity. The process was adopted by many countries around the world as they sought ways to increase production and profits. Rationalization was used in a number of different areas including businesses, academia, governments, and industry. In a trickle-down fashion, it eventually affected not only the upper class, but the middle and working classes, too (Nolan, 1990). The U.S. had effectively become the model for efficiency and productivity.

Language as well is Americanized. The English language is known to be the business language of the world; if you want to do business with the Western world, English is the most often spoken. Likewise, the official language of the air transportation industry is English; if you are a pilot for a commercial plane flying in any territory outside of your own, you must be able to speak and understand English.

In 2010, the French government appointed a committee to find new words for English words that were being used primarily in technology. When the committee was finished, 2,400 English words were replaced with French words (Jamieson, 2010). Earlier, in 2003, the Culture Ministry of France announced that they were changing the word "e-mail" to "courriel." The move was done because the word "e-mail" was considered "too English" (France officially bans the word email too English, 2003). C'est la vie!

Terms, Concepts and Names to Know:

- "Genie"

- Feral children

- Society

- Norms

- Folkways

- Taboos

- Rationalization

- Material culture

- Nonmaterial culture

- Americanization

Be Able to Discuss:

- Culture and its components

- Ethnocentrism

- Cultural relativism

- Subcultures

- Treatment of minority groups by dominant groups

- Nature versus nurture

- Cultural universals

- Americanism/Americanization

References

Bunnell, D. (2007, August 21). Why Is It Easier for Young Children to Learn a New Language? Retrieved April 1, 2016, from http://www.eldr.com/article/brain-power/why-it-easier-young-children-learn-new-language

Carayannis, E. (n.d.). The USA occupies, also in global terms, a very strong position in the software sector (in Mode 3 Knowledge Production in Quadruple Helix Innovation Systems). (2001). New York, NY 2011: Springer.

DeBres, K. (2005). A Cultural Geography of McDonald's UK. Journal of Cultural Geography. Retrieved March 31, 2016.

France officially bans the word email too English. (2003, July 21). Retrieved April 1, 2016, from http://www.geek.com/news/france-officially-bans-the-word-email-too-english-552584/

History Channel. (2006). Slaves and Freemen. The History Channel: The Roman Empire. Retrieved July 14, 2016 from http://www.pbs.org/empires/romans/empire/slaves_freemen.html

Hoynese, W., Croteau, D., & Milan, Stagfania. (2011). Media/Society: Industries, Images, and Audiences. New York, NY 2011: Sage.

International Cremation Statistics. (Winter 2011). Pharos International, 28-38. Retrieved April 1, 2016, from http://www.effs.eu/cms/fileadmin/members_only/documents/International_cremation_statistics_2010__source_Pharos_-_7_pages_.pdf

Jamieson, A. (2010). French government picks new words to replace English. The Telegraph, March 31, 2010, retrieved July 13, 2016 from http://www.telegraph.co.uk/news/worldnews/europe/france/7540588/French-government-picks-new-words-to-replace-English.html

Long, P. Schizophrenia. Internet Mental Health. Retrieved July 14, 2016 from http://mentalhealth.com/home/dx/schizophrenia.html

Moskowitz, A. 2011. Schizophrenia, Trauma, Disassociation, and Scientific Revolutions. Journal of Trauma and Dissociation, 12(4).

Nolan, M. (1990, October). Housework Made Easy: The Taylorized Housewife in Weimar Germany's Rationalized Economy. Retrieved from http://www.jstor.org/stable/3178019?seq=1#page_scan_tab_contents n, M. (1990, October).

Pew Research Center. (2006, December 14). Things We Can't Live Without: The List Has Grown in the Past Decade. Retrieved July 13, 2016, from http://www.pewsocialtrends.org/2006/12/14/luxury-or-necessity

Pokorny, M. & Sedgwick, J. (2004). Economic History of Film. Trenton, NJ: Routledge.

Saad, L. (2013, July 8). TV Is Americans' Main Source of News. Retrieved March 30, 2016, from http://www.gallup.com/poll/163412/americans-main-source-news.aspx

Schexnayder, C. (1999, September 9). Neighbor's missing-child call led to chained Norco girl. The Riverside Press-Enterprise. Retrieved July 14, 2016, from https://groups.google.com/forum/#!topic/alt.true-crime/rbaXJwsM2ZY

Sugiyama, S. (1988). Japan's Industrialization in the World Economy: 1859-1899 Export,

Trade and Overseas Competition (1st ed.). New York, NY: Bloomsbury Academic.

Sumner, W. (2007). Folkways: A Study of Mores, Manners, Customs and Morals. New York, NY: Cosimo Classics. (Originally published in 1906).

The Global Brands Scorecard 2006. (2006, August 2). Business Week.

Unknown. (2014, January 14). List of countries by number of mobile phones in use. Retrieved March 30, 2016, from https://en.wikipedia.org/wiki/List_of_countries_by_number_of_mobile_phone

Chapter 5: Socialization

What is Socialization?

Socialization is the term we use to describe the life-long process of passing down or teaching norms, customs, values, and beliefs to members of the groups to which we belong. Essentially, it is the teaching of the do's and don'ts of the groups to which people belong. Sometimes they may even be necessary skills needed for a person to function in the group—and groups can range from your family to your nation. So while socialization would involve someone learning the do's and don'ts of their family, they may also be learning about the do's and don'ts of society at large.

Socialization also strengthens the continuity of society, which is why your beliefs and behaviors are probably more similar than dissimilar to those of your parents. Likewise, because your beliefs, values, and behaviors are likely more similar rather than dissimilar to those of your parents, your attitudes towards things such as prejudice, the value of diversity, the value of honesty and hard work, and many more societal values are learned and passed down through the process of socialization. The way you were and are socialized creates your mind-set for how you view individual issues. For instance, your political and/or religious views are more likely to be similar to those of your parents rather than dissimilar.

Not too long ago I had a student in one of my classes who threatened to spank his future child if he or she ever made the statement they would vote for a Democrat. I thought he was joking, but he was not. I genuinely believed him. Whereas the dad who supported the Chicago Bears was teaching his young daughter to hate and despise any other team but the Chicago Bears, my former student will teach his yet future unborn child to despise Democrats. While these issues may seem funny, they tell us a great deal about the power of the socialization process.

While socialization is thought of as only being experienced by the young, reality says we are socialized into the beliefs, values, and behaviors of the groups to which we belong during our entire life course. Socialization provides the tools necessary for a young child to begin to function within the family and then later into school. While some animals, especially lower forms of life do not need social interactions to help them learn how to survive and function, humans do. Our behaviors are mostly not biologically determined. We need social experiences to learn the ways of those groups to which we belong in order to function in them and survive.

Socialization is a key process in the survival of mankind, but we cannot eliminate the role that biology plays in determining how or if we survive. Aristotle believed that man was born as a blank slate, table raza, and that we lead our life discovering "facts" we already knew thanks to biology, but no modern scientist would advocate such a position.

Instead, most researchers admit that who we are as socialized creatures is both the result of biology and our environment—the so-called "nature versus nurture" argument.

Theoretical Understandings of Socialization and the Development of the Self

As a sociological concept worthy of study, socialization is a relatively new concept. The study of socialization first became popular as a sociological research subject as a result of the work by C. Wright Mills (1916 – 1962). Prior to his work, socialization was simply part of work that theorized the development of the social self. Because of this, the understandings of socialization have varied through the years. Each associated with particular theoretical approaches.

Role Theory

Role theory, which will be discussed later when we learn about the development of the self, suggests that socialization is the response by humans to their social world in which everyone has a role or roles to play. It is during the socialization process that people begin to adapt the norms, values, attitudes, and behaviors associated with the specific roles they are expected to hold. Role theory, which is associated with George Herbert Mead's development of the self and the "generalized other," is also a key component of another topic we will discuss later, social reproduction.

Internalization Theory

Largely formulated by Talcott Parsons (1902 – 1979) internalization theory suggests that people internalize a system of rules to be used in their association with others. Very much associated with theories of cognitive development, internalization theory holds that people construct a cognitive framework in stages and with which they use to guide their interactions at the various levels of social organization (e.g., the family, school, the community). For instance, internalization theory would suggest that children learn "expressive symbolism," in other words, norms and role behaviors that are used in their interactions with others. Parsons believed that it is during this period that children learn moral codes (i.e., the development of a conscience).

Symbolic Interactionism

A major tenant of symbolic interactionism is that (a) we use symbols in our daily interactions with others, and (b) those symbols have shared meanings; without shared meanings the symbol has no agreed upon meaning. While many theories associated with socialization, and by default theories that explain the development of the self, are more concerned with socialization during childhood, symbolic interactionism does not limit itself to that framework, but instead sees socialization as a life-long process. The key process here is that the individual situations people find themselves in are interpreted in order to define their meaning, and socialization is the process by which they learn appropriate norms or ways to act within those situations.

Reinforcement Theory

Borrowing a little from psychology and Homans' Social Exchange Theory, reinforcement theory suggests that as we begin to assume new roles we seek to negotiate that role to our advantage. In approaching new roles, we evaluate our costs and benefits in order to enhance our position as the one being socialized.

As we've already learned, socialization is the process of learning the dos and don'ts of the groups to which people belong. Socialization is a life-long process. Through socialization we learn about the social roles that we are expected to occupy. Consequently, we develop a sense of self and a sense of self-knowledge that is shaped over our lifespan and in turn shapes how we see and interact with the world.

We are unique from one another in a number of ways, and those differences influence the process of socialization as it applies to us. This uniqueness can be referred as our self, in other words, are unique identity. So, before we begin looking at the overall process of socialization, let's begin with some ideas about how the "self" is formed. The "self" is what George Herbert Mead (1863 – 1931) referred to as self-awareness. Mead was a sociologist credited for being the main contributor to the development of social interactionism. He believed that we developed our self-identity through interactions with other people. Further, Mead proposed that we develop our self as we progress through three stages of development. Those stages are:

- **Preparatory Stage:** This stage occurs during the first several years of life. This is when the child begins to mimic the actions of others in his social world. Children in this stage are unable to understand what the actions mean, but by mimicking the actions of others, they begin to develop as actors in a social world.

- **Play Stage:** In the play stage, occurring between the years of two and six, children begin to model the roles of others who are close to them (e.g., parents, siblings, grandparents). It's at this point that they begin role-play, which allows them to see themselves as others might see them.

- **Game Stage:** In the final stage, the game stage, occurring in children aged seven years and older, children have mastered the ability to mimic the behaviors of others for given roles and the ability to act out those roles with an understanding of what those roles mean. Also, in this final stage, children learn their roles while continuing to act out the roles of others much as someone would when playing a game. During this stage the child takes on the role of the generalized other and thus learn the "rules of the game" when that game refers to the values, beliefs, and rules of their culture.

Charles Cooley proposed another prominent theory that explains the development of our social self. In his theory, called the looking-glass self, which he outlined in his book Human Nature and the Social Order (1902). Cooley was a prominent philosopher and social psychologist who believed that our sense of self develops from interactions with others in our social world. Cooley emphasizes the importance of feedback from those interactions. Using that information or feedback, humans begin to modify their self-perceptions. Cooley identified three stages that are involved in the development of the self. Those are:

- **Stage 1: We imagine how others see us.** In this first stage, humans imagine how they appear to others,

- **Stage 2: We imagine how others are judging us.** In this second stage, humans evaluate the feedback they get from others about who they are, and compare that feedback with how they view themselves.

- **Stage 3: We react accordingly.** In the third stage, if humans accept the imagination that others have of them, they will react positively or negatively and act accordingly. In other words, if people imagine others in their social world look at them positively in regard to some aspect of their self, that component of the self will be reinforced and internalized; on the other hand, if he/she imagines people think about them negatively in regard some component of their self, they might feel ashamed that others feel about them in that way and that might change that part of their self in order to avoid negative feelings.

Klaus Hurrelmann. In his book titled, Social Structure and Personality Development, Hurrelmann proposes that socialization is entirely tied to a person's personality development. The theory suggests there are two "realities" to the self: (1) the inner reality, which is composed of mental traits, and (2) external reality, which refers to the social and physical environment. In his theory, Hurrelmann proposes that the developing self wrestles with the developmental tasks particular to the groups to which he or she belong. Whether a person is successful in self development is dependent on the social, physical, and personal resources that are available to him or her. Within all the developmental tasks the self is expected to perform, is the need to work out a personal fit between personal individuation and social integration. If successful, the individual has developed what Hurrelmann called the "I-Identity." (Hurrelmann, 2009).

Erik Erikson (Erikson, 1950) developed his psycho-social stages of development and noted that these changes occurred throughout the life course.

- **Stage 1:** In infancy children learn to trust.

- **Stage 2:** Children struggle with autonomy versus doubt (i.e., of their abilities).

- **Stage 3:** Preschool children attempt to work out the difference between initiative and guilt (i.e., was I wrong to have done what I did?).

- **Stage 4:** In pre-adolescence, children must work out the difference between industriousness and inferiority (i.e., can I master what I set out to do?).

- **Stage 5:** In adolescence, teenagers must work out the conflict of identity versus confusion (i.e., who am I? Do I know who I am?).

- **Stage 6:** In young adulthood struggle to work out the relationship between intimacy versus isolation.

- **Stage 7:** In middle adulthood people work to make their mark—to make a difference in some way.

- **Stage 8:** In later life people must work out the challenge of integrity versus despair.

Lawrence Kohlberg's Stages of Moral Development (Snarey et al., 1985). Kohlberg developed a theory of moral development.

- **Stage 1: Pre-conventional stage.** In this stage children see the world in terms of pain and pleasure; moral decisions are largely worked out as children wrestle with their experiences.

- **Stage 2: Conventional stage.** Adolescents and adults work to accept society's definitions of right versus wrong. It is during this stage they begin to explore the consequences for obedience or disobedience.

- **Stage 3: Post-Conventional stage.** The highest stage of development and not everyone reaches it. This is when a person is able to think more abstractly and make judgments about right or wrong regardless of how society has done so. Abstract ethical principles are used when making decisions involving morality.

Socialization and Interaction

Many people think that socialization is a process that only applies to children, but that's not true. Socialization is a life-long process. Through socialization we learn about the social **roles** that we are expected to follow. Consequently, we develop a sense of self and a sense of self-knowledge that is shaped over our lifespan and in turn shapes how we see and interact with the world.

One of the most famous studies that investigated the relationship of socialization and interaction, was done by the husband-and-wife team of Harry and Margaret Harlow. The Harlow's took baby monkeys and divided them into two groups, one group was left with their biological mothers the other group was given to a surrogate mother constructed out of wire. The latter group of monkeys was given all the necessities that they needed to survive, such as food, water and warmth. When the experiment concluded, the research was indisputable: the monkeys that have been raised by wire mothers developed a significant range of abnormal behaviors.

Another example on the long-term consequences of social isolation is research done by rate René Spitz in 1945. René Spitz looked at children who have been removed from the biological families for one reason or another. Some children were placed in foster care, but because of a lack of room, some children had to be placed in nursing homes. You can imagine the very unhealthy environment in which those children were raised. Care was provided by nurses whose primary job was to take care of elderly patients and not to provide care to infants. Approximately one-third of the children raised in nursing homes died and another one-third lived in mental institutions for most of their lives, as they were incapable of functioning physically and mentally on their own. The research concluded that a lack of social interaction has significant and long-term consequences on the infants.

A very famous case of poor or absent socialization and the lack of interaction happened in 1797 when a so-called "feral child" was captured in France. He was incapable of speaking, had numerous scars on his body, and lacked any social graces. A medical student by the name of Jean Marc Gaspard Itard took an interest in Victor and began to work with him and even allowed him to live in his house. Gaspard believed that there were two characteristics that separated animals from humans: empathy and language, neither of which Victor demonstrated. After working with him for quite some time Victor was able to learn one word. It was the word for milk. Itard was disappointed with this outcome. However, one day Itard had come home to find Victor attempting to comfort his housekeeper who had recently lost her husband. Itard saw this as an example of empathy. In the end, Itard was not able to demonstrate that Victor was in fact human as opposed to a feral animal. Victor died in 1828 in Paris. Controversy still exists about the case. Some researchers believe that Victor was not a feral child, but rather he was the victim of an abusive father and had run away. The existence of a feral child, raised by animals, has never been proven.

Severe social isolation contributes to poor social development. Depending on the severity and duration of the isolation, long-term consequences can be severe and even lead to death. For example, in 1970 an elderly woman walked into a social services agency with a 13-year-old girl. The girl was emaciated, pale, walked in a strange manner, and was unable to speak. Workers got suspicious and began asking questions. What they found out astonished them. At the age of four, Genie's father was so convinced she was mentally retarded that he confined her to her room. During the day she was chained to a potty chair, and at night she was put into a crib with a chicken wire top that kept her from climbing out. Genie remained in that state of isolation for nine years—from the age of four until the age of thirteen.

Social workers began working with her intensely to repair the emotional and intellectual damage done by the years of isolation. They named the girl "Genie" in order to keep her real identity confidential. At first clinicians were successful when working with Genie and she learned a few words she could speak, and her walking greatly improved. However, after several years Genie stopped learning and in fact regressed to an earlier stage. As of this writing, Genie is still alive, but because she is incapable of living independently, she has lived in a nursing home since shortly after she was rescued.

In another similar case that occurred in 1999, a man grew suspicious and called the police because he had not seen his neighbor's young daughter for several years. When the police investigated, they found the girl, who was age six at the time, chained to her bed and confined to her bedroom, which she had been since the age of two. The girl used the corner of her bedroom as a latrine. Conditions were appalling. Once removed from the home, clinicians began working with the girl in an effort to repair the emotional and intellectual damage that had been done by the social isolation. Unlike with Genie, results were much better, and while the girl is capable of living independently, some emotional and cognitive damage remain. Psychologists believe the reason they were successful in the latter case, but not in Genie's, is because of the age difference when rescued. Significant brain changes occur in children around the age of 10, and those changes affect the way we learn. Genie had gone past that developmental window, whereas the other girl had not.

Agents of Socialization

Socialization is a lifelong process occurring in many different arenas. Those arenas are referred to as agents of socialization. Generally, there are seven regarded as agents of socialization. They are: family, the educational system, friends, the mass media, work, religion, and the military. Each has its own role to play in teaching the do's and don'ts of the particular group to its members.

Family

Of all the agencies of socialization, perhaps the most important is the family, if for no other reason than because for the first few years of life that is where the child spends most of its time. Therefore it has the potential to learn a great deal about membership in the family because the child is often isolated from the outside world. Families teach children many things. Families teach children how to dress, how to eat, to obey orders, and generally what is considered right or wrong within the family unit and also of the larger culture in which the live.

After learning "mama" and "dada," the next word many young children learn is "no." As a very young child, I remember trying to stick what must have been a paperclip into an electrical outlet in the wall. My mother, who was in the kitchen, saw me and screamed, "NO!" Later, as I grew up, the word "no" became something to challenge, as it does for virtually all children as they go through the stages of development.

Unfortunately, families can also teach things that are destructive. While there are many reasons that people become prejudice towards one group or another, one not so uncommon reason is because of the way children are raised. Research shows that children can learn prejudice within the family setting from parents and that prejudice may be life-long.

The Educational System

The next agency of socialization is the educational system. Schools teach us what you're supposed to teach us. For instance, you expect to learn math in a math course, English and grammar in an English course, and physical activity in the PE course. But the educational system also has what's called a hidden curriculum. The hidden curriculum has to do with teaching us things about our society rather than about particular disciplines. For instance, if a child in the third grade math class needs to use the restroom that child is expected to raise their hand and ask for permission that is a social norm and not one tied to learning math. Learning to raise their hands to ask questions in class also as part of the hidden curriculum, it's teaching order and also respect for teachers.

Gender socialization also occurs in the educational system. Essentially, girls or talk to be girls and boys or talk to be boys. I like to ask my female students how many of them had auto shop, or metal shop, or woodshop, in high school. Have a class of on average 100 students typically no more than three or four will raise their hands. I will then ask my male students how many had home economics in high school. A few more hands are raised, but when I ask Male students why they took Home economics in high school the vast majority of them will answer that's because that's where all the girls were. Why wouldn't more girls being in wood shop, metal shop, or auto shop that apparently are? The best answer is because society, which in this case really means family and friends, directs them elsewhere. Generally girls in high school are not encouraged to take what are typically regarded as male shop classes. In other words, there is one track for girls and another track for boys. Family, friends, and high school guidance counselors still direct women to typically female professions such as teaching, nursing, and social work.

The question has to be asked is whether or not women are capable of performing in some occupations that are typically male. For instance, only approximately 28% of all engineers are female. Does that suggest that females are incapable of performing duties as an engineer? There is a ratio that I want you to become familiar with and that is 48 to 52. For every 48 males there are 52 females. So any point during the life course there are more females than there are males. All things being equal, I should expect to find that ratio in virtually anything I want to study. Therefore, if all things were equal I should expect to see that 52% of all engineers in the United States were female, but as I've just said, only 28% are female. Why is this? Another example we could look at would be the proportion of male to female physicians in United States. If all things were equal 52% of all doctors in the United States should be female, but statistics revealed that only 33% of all doctors in the United States are female (Distribution of Physicians, 2016).

Again, why is this? At some point you have to ask whether or not all things are equal, and if they're not, Why not? Is it prejudice? Is it society trying to replicate traditional roles? Generally, women score lower on the math component of SAT tests then do men. Why is this? Is it because women simply have less cognitive skills when it comes to math then do men? Are men and women's brains really that different? While the research suggests that there are some differences between men and women's brains those differences are judged to be slight and generally cannot be used to explain these differences in math scores on SAT exams. So now her back to our question why do men perform better on average on the math component of SAT exams when compared to women? While there can be no one answer to this question one possibility has to do with what's called the self-fulfilling prophecy. The self-fulfilling prophecy suggests that if people believe what society says they are they may become that very thing. So in this case imagine a girl growing up in the American educational system. From the first grade on she may come to learn from her teachers the boys are supposed to be better at math than girls. Perhaps this is demonstrated by something as simple as teachers calling on boys more often than girls to solve math problems in class. If this continues through elementary and even into secondary education, is it possible that a girl might say to herself, "Why should I try to be good at math when I'm not expected to be good at math?" And if her conclusion was that she was not supposed to be good in math in comparison to boys why should she continue to try to be good at math? Why should she continue to try to learn? If that's the case, we have an example of the self-fulfilling prophecy.

Friends

The next socialization agent are friends. We learn a great deal from our friends. Friendships are important especially when we are younger and being socialized by our families, the media, and the educational system. Friends teach us about what it means to be a member of the friendship group. Friends also answer questions that we may not find answers to from other agencies and socialization. For instance, whereas approximately 50% of young girls will turn to their mother for answers about sex, only about 45% of young boys will turn to their father for answers about sex. Aside from the quality or lack thereof of those conversations in which children turn to their parents, where do the rest of those young people go for answers to questions about sex? The research says there are two primary places: the first their friends and the second the Internet. There is a problem with both sources. First, friends are not likely to know more about sex than the person asking. Something akin to the blind leading the blind. And in these days of STDs, this lack of accurate information can be dangerous at least. The second place that young people go for information about sex is the Internet, and that can be equally dangerous. Anyone can publish anything on the Internet. Accuracy of information is far from guaranteed. One thing I tell my students is how to initially judge the credibility of online sources and the first thing I tell them to look for is the container: EDU, GOV, ORG, and COM. Credibility is generally awarded in that order, But that is certainly not the only things that people should look for when trying to assess the quality of an online source.

The Media

Another agent of socialization is the mass media. The mass media can have both positive and negative effects on socialization. Certainly recent developments in social media have positive consequences for some people-In particular, expanding their social connections. Bringing people together who might not otherwise be brought together increases their interaction and like when the group becomes a socializing agent. On the other hand, the Internet can certainly have negative consequences when it provides in accurate information, deliberately one-sided information design to play on the part of less aware people, and less face-to-face interaction. The media, which would include television magazines books social media games played either alone or online with others, may again have positive or negative consequences. Violent video games are associated with a greater tendency towards aggression (Strasburger, 2009), aggressive thoughts, reductions in help others (Anderson et al., 2012), and it can increase depression in preadolescent youth (Tortolero, 2014).

The average American spends 32 minutes a day on time-shifted television, an hour using the Internet on a computer, an hour and seven minutes on a smartphone and two hours, 46 minutes listening to the radio. Children aged 2-11 watch over 24 hours of TV per week, while adults aged 35-49 watch more than 33 hours, according to data from Nielsen that suggests TV time increases the older we get (Hinckley, 2014).

Also, TV viewing has been associated obesity (Dietz, 1985).

Eating Disorders

The media can actually have lethal potential. One of the best examples concerns eating disorders. Think about who we see in the media. Who do we see on television, in movies, in magazines? Do we see average looking people? No, of course not. We see good-looking people. We see "the beautiful people." This can lead to an incorrect perception of society. People may come to believe that everybody but himself or herself is beautiful and that the level of beauty displayed in the media is the standard for our society. It is thought that anorexia and bulimia, both eating disorders, come from the development of body distortion and poor self-image largely resulting from comparing themselves to this false standard of beauty that exists in our society and the media perpetuates it. Anorexia is basically someone who chooses not to eat or not to eat enough to survive and stay healthy. In my generation there was a brother and sister singing team called The Carpenters--Karen and Richard. Karen developed anorexia. When she looked in the mirror she saw someone who was fat and unattractive. In the months preceding her death, Karen's weight had ranged from a low of 80 pounds to a high of 120 pounds. But even when she weighed 80 pounds it was said that she was displeased with her weight. Anorexia is not a well-understood disease by the American public. Americans believe that all someone has to do is to eat and they'll be fine. It's that simple. But it's far from simple to cure eating disorders in a society that still holds up a false standard of beauty in the media.

Imagine this: your instructor passed out some chocolate candy to you in class and you ate the chocolate. After passing out the candy, your instructor continued to lecture for five or 10 minutes. Then suddenly he/she stopped lecturing and stated: "by the way class, I want to tell you that I put arsenic in that candy that I gave you." What would be your reaction? Undoubtedly, you would stick your finger down your throat and force yourself to vomit continuously until you felt that you had managed to get rid of every last molecule of the arsenic. What do you suppose food is too an anorexic? It's poison.

Another eating disorder that is largely the result of the media is called bulimia. Bulimia is binging and purging. Someone who has bulimia will stuff himself or herself, get up from the table, go to the bathroom, stick their finger down their throat, and vomit until they believe they have vomited up all the food they have eaten.

Like anorexia, it can be lethal because people who suffer from anorexia or bulimia are nutrients they need to survive. Additionally, they are damaging their esophagus, mouth, and teeth because of the acid from the vomiting. Many years ago I had a student come up to me after class and confess that when she was in high school she was bulimic.

Because she had been a cheerleader, and all of her friends were cheerleaders, she said they were all bulimic. She went on to say, they all followed the "carrot rule." I didn't understand so I asked her what she meant by the carrot rule. She then proceeded to explain it to me. "Let's say," she said, "that my friends and I went to a restaurant. We knew we had to have a little bit of meat and little bit of vegetables to stay healthy, so we would order the least we could from the menu. We would then pick at the meat and vegetables, and when we'd had enough we'd take our carrot and eat it. Next, we would order the cheese covered fries, ice cream, cake, cookies, onion rings, and all the junk food that we could order. We would stuff ourselves until we could eat no more. Then," she continued," we'd all get up go to the restroom, stick our finger down our throat, vomit until we saw carrots and then we'd stop."

I was speechless. Do you understand how they thought the stomach worked? They thought the stomach worked in layers-so that the first layers would be the meat and vegetables, the second layer would be carrots, and the third layer would be the junk food. They would simply go to the restroom and vomit until they saw carrots, leaving the meat and vegetables in the bottom of their stomach. Does the stomach really work that way? No, it mixes food up as we eat-there is no layering. So here was this simple little belief that these bulimics had that was putting their health in serious danger-all because they had a distorted view of their own bodies. They had no idea how were they were endangering their health all because they had developed a distorted body image that made them see themselves as fat because they weren't like all the beautiful people in the media. Only recently has the media responded by beginning a gradual and slight change so that more normal and average people are being presented in the media. Time will tell what effect these subtle changes will have on these eating disorders.

The Workplace

The next agent of socialization is work. When you graduate with your Bachelors degree, you will have the necessary foundation to perform your future job, but you will still need to be trained in how to do the specifics of that new job. One of the first things that you will probably do after being hired is to attend an orientation. The orientation is designed to teach you about the company's culture; in other words, the do's and don'ts of that company. For instance, one of the first things that you will be taught in this orientation is what constitutes sexual harassment. Companies need their employees to know what constitutes sexual harassment so that they can (a) provide a harmonious workplace, and (b) protect themselves from litigation should someone sexually harass an employee. After this initial orientation you will be trained in the particular aspects of your new job. So, while the socialization for your particular skilled career starts in school, it continues once in the job, and because organizations are always changing, so will the socialization process continue in your workplace as long as you work there.

The Military

The military also represents an agent of socialization. One of the first things that a new recruit experiences after joining the military is going through a process of de-socialization; in other words, new recruits unlearn certain aspects of our democratic culture. After de-socializing new recruits they are then socialized into the ways and culture of the military. This process is functional. Democracy doesn't belong in a battle zone. So, while recruits are desocialized in traditional American values, they are socialized into military values, which include following orders rather than discussing issues. One problem that is surfaced is how to re-socialize or reintegrate former military back into society? Research indicated the psychological trauma many returning vets bring with them, yet many are afraid to discuss the issues or see it in non-clinical terms. One soldier when asked if he thought he suffered from PTSD responded to a clinician, "No, because I don't think it's a disorder ... you can't expect them [returning vets] to be the same right away when they come back. It's not PTSD, it just takes time" (Brenner et al., 2015).

Anticipatory Socialization

While not an agent of socialization, people can be taught or prepared for certain roles in which they will occupy. This process is called anticipatory socialization. In other words, there are situations that prepare us for occupying those roles. For instance, marriage. Anticipatory socialization suggests that there are things that we can do to help prepare us for occupying the role of marital partner. Can you think of some acts in advance of marriage that can help prepare people for marriage and the rolls it will have to perform as part of a married couple? One obvious act would be that of dating. The process of dating allows people to get to know each other. It allows them to discuss how they will carry out the future marriage-for example, the division of household tasks. Who will perform what around the house? Another example would be that of parenthood. How does one prepare for the role of parent? For women, often time baby-sitting serves as anticipatory socialization. While there are many roles that we may occupy in our lives, anticipatory socialization helps us prepare for many of those roles.

Life Stages

As I've mentioned, socialization is a continual process. It is not one confined simply to childhood. We are socialized over our entire life course. Today generally speaking there are five stages of socialization: childhood, the teenage years, young adulthood, mature adulthood, and old age. However, it is not always been so. After the time of the Industrial Revolution infants essentially went from where they were just another mouth to feed to where they were expected to help the family out by labor or financially. In other words, there was no such thing as childhood. There was no time to play games, play with dolls, or sit around idly. The same is true of the teenage years. They simply didn't exist. Someone at the age of 13 would be expected to be out in the fields or helping the family in someway. So the definition of childhood 150 years ago is very different from our definition today. Yes, there were children, but children beyond the age of five or six were expected to work and help the family. Additionally, old age exists today as the final life stage, as it always has, however, today there is a stage between adulthood and old age, and this is later life.

While old age existed as a life stage in previous centuries, today old-age as a category is even difficult to define. The aging process is completely unique to each person. As Americans we have gotten in the habit of using numbers to indicate someone's age, but that is largely the result of the arbitrary age of 65 that was adopted President Roosevelt when he created Social Security Retirement in 1935. To the left you will see a 90-year-old British woman skydiving, something I'm willing to be most of you reading this book have not done. In 2011, Fauja Singh, a British citizen, and 100-years-old completed a 26.2 mile marathon. Do you think that's something you could do? In 2015, 70-year-old Gunhild Swanson became the oldest woman in history to complete 100-mile Western States Endurance Run. Could you run 100 miles? Or in 2013, Diana Nyad, a 64-year-old American woman swam from Cuba to Florida, a distance of 90 miles. Today, people are living longer, they are healthier overall, and more independent. A loss of independence may best define old age today, whereas that time period between adulthood and old age may best be called later life. A significant question emerges from these older athletes: should age be measured in numbers or by functional abilities?

Stages of the Life Course

- **Infancy**. Traditionally, infancy was that period from birth to the point where the child was old enough to work.

- **Childhood**. Childhood is a relatively new stage. Generally, young people went from infancy to adulthood. Historically, children were valued for their ability to contribute to the family's survival and were therefore a liability until they could do so. Changes in cultural attitudes towards children, resulting from both child labor laws, which restricted children in the workplace and lower infant and child mortality rates, have contributed to this stage in the life course.

- **Teenager.** Like childhood, the teenager as a life course stage didn't exist until recently. Historically, young people went from infancy to young adulthood. Some have argued that the teenage years as a life stage is functional for society because it delays the entry of young people into the paid labor force, which doesn't have room for them,

- **Young adulthood.** In young adulthood, people are expected to have a job, marry, have children, and raise those children.

- **Mature adulthood.** The stage that many would refer to as "midlife." This is the time people can focus on themselves and their relationships after the children have left the nest.

- **Old age.** Historically, the old had great status among earlier types of societies. As story-tellers and keepers of the history of the society, and as landowners, they were revered and held in esteem. The invention of the printing press in the 1500's devalued their status as the keepers of their society's history, and the industrial revolution devalued their status even more by the movement of adult children to the city.

Social Reproduction

Marx saw social reproduction has the passing down of wealth and power from one generation to the next thus perpetuating social inequality. However, it has a broader meaning as well. Society replicates itself down through time by using the process of socialization. Generally, there are no dramatic changes that take place in the values, norms, and behaviors esteemed from one generation to the next. So, the socialization process passes those values, beliefs, and norms down from one generation to the next relatively unchanged. So, while we might see a change in the rights of women between 1919 and 2016, we will see a smaller change in the current parent/child generation (e.g., a parent that was born in 1973 and their 21 year old child born in 1995).

Terms, Concepts and Names to Know:

- C. Wright Mills

- Talcott Parsons

- George Herbert Mead

- Charles Cooley

- Jean Piaget

- Klaus Hurrelmann

- Erik Erikson

- Lawrence Kohlberg

- Rene Spitz

- Gaspard Itard

- "Victor"

- "Genie"

- Harry and Margaret Harlow

- Anticipatory socialization

- Life course stages

Be Able to Discuss:

- Nature versus nurture

- How the self develops

- Mead's stages of the development of the self

- Cooley's looking glass self

- Jean Piaget stages of development

- Lawrence Kohlberg's Stages of Moral Development

- Erik Erikson Stages of Psychosocial Development

- Process of socialization

- Agents of socialization

- The dangers of social isolation

- Social reproduction

References

Ahmad, J. (2015, February 18). 5 Paths to Islamic Radicalization. Retrieved February 18, 2016, from http://nationalinterest.org/feature/5-paths-islamic-radicalization12269?page=2

Anderson CA, Gentile DA, Dill KE. Prosocial, antisocial, and other effects of recreational video games. In: Singer DG, Singer JL, eds. Handbook of Children and the Media. 2nd ed. Thousand Oaks, CA: Sage; 2012:249-272.

Palmer, L. (2002). Bonding Matters: The Chemistry of Attachment. Attachment Parenting International News, 5(2).

Ballas, D. (2010). Prisoner Radicalization. Retrieved March 21, 2016, from Federal Bureau of Investigation, https://leb.fbi.gov/2010/october/prisoner-radicalization

Cooley, C. (1983). Human Nature and the Social Order. Piscataway, NJ: Transactions. (Original work published 1902).

Dietz WH, Jr., Gortmaker SL. Do we fatten our children at the television set? Obesity and television viewing in children and adolescents. Pediatrics. 1985;75:807-12

Erikson, E. (1950). Childhood and Society. Norton: New York, NY.

Federal Bureau of Investigation. (2015, February 26). Statement Before the House Judiciary Committee, Subcommittee on Crime, Terrorism, Homeland Security, and Investigations, Washington, D.C.. Retrieved March 21, 2016, from FBI.gov: https://www.fbi. gov/news/testimony/isil-in-america-domestic-terror-and-radicalization

Federal Bureau of Investigation. (2016, September 20). House Homeland Security Committee Subcommittee on Intelligence, Information Sharing, and Terrorism Risk Assessment. Retrieved March 21, 2016, from FBI.gov: https://www.fbi.gov/news/testimony/islamic-radicalization

Federal Bureau of Investigation. (2006, September 19). Senate Committee on Homeland

Security and Governmental Affairs and Related Agencies, and Investigations, Washington, D.C.. Retrieved March 21, 2016, from FBI.gov: www.fbi.gov/news/testimony/ prison-radicalization-the-environment-the-threat-and-the-response
Georgia Public Broadcasting. (2016, December 16).

The Henry J. Kaiser Family Foundation. (2016, January). Distribution of Physicians by Gender. Retrieved March 20, 2016, from http://kff.org/other/state-indicator/physicians-by-gender/

Hinckley, D. (2014, March 5). Average American watches 5 hours of TV per day, report shows. NEW YORK DAILY NEWS. Retrieved from http://www.nydailynews.com/life-style/average-american-watches-5-hours-tv-day-article-1.1711954

Hurrelmann, K. (2009). Social Structure and Personality Development. New York. Cambridge University Press.

Luhrmann, T. (2012). Beyond the Brain. Woodrow Wilson International Center for Scholars, 36(3), 28-34.

Mead, M. (2001). Male and Female. Harper Perennial, 1st ed., New York. (Original work published 1949).

Media Violence Commission. International Society for Research on Aggression. Report of the Media Violence Commission. Aggress Behav. 2012;38:335-341.

Ohlson, K. (2002). It Takes Two. New Scientist, 176(2363), 42-50.

The Psychology Of Radicalization: How Terrorist Groups Attract Young Followers. Retrieved March 21, 2016, from http:// www.npr.org/2015/12/15/459697926/the-psychology-of-radicalization-how-terroristgroups-attract-young-followers

Sheffield, J., Williams, L., Blackford, J., & Heckers, S. (2013). Childhood sexual abuse increases risk of auditory hallucinations in psychotic disorders. Comprehensive Psychiatry, 54(7), 1098-1104.
Snarey, J., Reimer, J., & Kohlberg, L. (1985). Development of social-moral reasoning among Kibbutz adolescents: A longitudinal cross-cultural study. Developmental Psychology, 21(1), 3–17.

Strasburger VC, Council on Communications and Media. Media violence (policy statement). Pediatrics. 2009;124:1495-1503.

Tortolero, S. (2014). Daily violent video game playing and depression in preadolescent youth. Cyberpsychology, Behavior And Social Networking, 17(9), 609-615.

United Nations High Commissioner for Human Rights, General Assembly, Report on the Protection of Civilians in Armed Conflict in Iraq: 6 July – 10 September 2014. Retrieved from: http://www.ohchr.org/Documents/Countries/IQ/UNAMI_OHCHR_POC_Report_FINAL_6July_10September2014.pdf

Chapter 6: Social Interaction

Social interaction involves the shared experiences through which we relate to other people. How we relate to other people to a large degree is shaped by a perception of who they are in relation to us. It is also affected by the meanings that we attach to other people's actions. Social interaction is affected by status, the normative actions we expect from others, and even our cultural values.

Types of Social Interactions

There are different types of social interactions. They are:

- Exchange

- Cooperation

- Conflict

- Coercion

Let's look at each of these individually. When two or more people exchange something–for example, material goods, advice, and affect, it is a type of social interaction. Of all the reasons for social interactions, exchange is by far the most common. People interact with each other because they have things to exchange, tangible or intangible. Next, when two or more people work together to reach some shared goal, that's an example of cooperation. In other words, people feel that they must cooperate to achieve their mutual ends, but by so doing they are interacting. When two or more people compete for the same goal, or reward, or scarce resources, that type of interaction is called conflict. Finally, coercion is using illegitimate authority to get something from others. If I were to demand that a student get me coffee, and threatened to fail them if they didn't, that would be an example of coercion because I have no legitimate authority to demand a student get my coffee.

Focused Versus Unfocused Interactions

As we move further into talking about interactions we need to talk about two specific types that have to do with our situational awareness. Unfocused interaction is that mutual awareness that people have of one another in large gatherings even though they may not directly be involved in conversation. For instance, let's say you walk into a party, there are many people at the party and most are talking to other people. The room is filled with conversation, but you are not directly involved in any of those conversations—you simply know that they are occurring. That would be an example of an unfocused interaction. On the other hand, a focused interaction is when two or more people are directly attending to what others are saying. So let's say that you are now at that same party and you see a friend. You walk up to the friend and begin to talk to them—you are now engaged in a focused interaction because your attention is now on the conversation occurring between you and your friend.

Erving Goffman, a great sociological writer, wrote a great deal about interactions (Goffman, 1959). If you read Goffman, he could even help you find a date. For instance, let's say John is at a party and he is engaged in a focused interaction with a friend. Jane is engaged in focused interaction with one of her friends. As John interacts with his friend he notices Jane from across the room. John has never met her, but finds her attractive. John and Jane conclude their focused interactions with their friends at about the same time. Jane wanders over to John and says, "Hi. I couldn't help overhear what you said to your friend about ..." What has happened? Jane was supposed to have been completely engaged in her focused interaction with her friend, but in fact has been eavesdropping from across the room to the conversation John had with his friend. In other words, Jane paid more attention to what John was saying than what her own friend was saying. If Goffman was alive he would probably say, "John, you need to put a big checkmark there. Jane likes you. She paid more attention to you, from across the crowded and noisy room, than she did to what her own friend was saying. That's a clear indication she's interested in you." Social convention dictates that when Jane was talking to her friend she should have been entirely focused on that interaction, but she wasn't. Yep, put a big checkmark up there under the column that reads, "Girls that like me."

Encounters

Erving Goffman called focused interactions an encounter. Encounters are separated by what Goffman called brackets (Goffman, 1961). Brackets help us understand when a focused interaction begins and ends. For instance, can you think of ways that you would acknowledge the beginning of an interaction with a friend? One of the most common ways is to simply say, "Hello." Likewise, one of the most common ways to end the interaction is to say, "Bye." These would be examples of brackets. There could be many examples of brackets. However, not everyone says hello and goodbye, but usually people have something symbolic in either their words or actions that signal to the other party that the interaction is over. Along with this are the subtle nonverbal cues that we may give people we are interacting with that we wish to end the interaction. A good example might be, "I've got to go study for an exam." It would be expected that the person with whom you are engaged in conversation understands that you need to end the interaction, which then would leave it up to them in most situations to say something to the effect of, "Okay, I'll talk to you later." But sometimes that doesn't happen. Sometimes you could be engaged in interaction with a friend that doesn't pick up on those subtle cues that you want to end the interaction. Have you ever been in that kind of situation? How have you handled it? Another good example would be that of telemarketers. When a telemarketer calls, and because we don't know who it is when we answer the phone, we say "Hello," and by doing this we have signaled that the interaction (i.e., a bracket) has began. After they begin their spiel, and you realize he or she is a telemarketer, you look for a way to end the interaction. Unfortunately, you realize they have a script so they can counter your trying to end the interaction. You want to end the interaction, but you have been taught that it would be rude to just hang up the phone. So, you keep repeating, "I'm sorry, but I'm just not interested." At some point one of two things will happen:

- either they finally accept your desire to end the conversation, or

- you say to yourself, "To hell with manners," as you press the button on your cellphone to end the call.

So this latter situation would be a good example of differences in brackets—saying "hello" was a bracket indicating the beginning of the interaction, but hanging up the phone while the telemarketer was still talking served as a bracket saying that the interaction was over.

Impression Management

Erving Goffman is considered to be the father of what is called impression management. Simply put Goffman believed that we work to manage the impression others have of us when we're in public and we use symbols to do it. Let's say that you think of yourself as a courteous person. Because you want others to think of you as you think of yourself, a courteous person, you work to manage your impression by saying, "Please," "Thank-you," "You're welcome," or "After you." Here's another example. Let's say a friend of yours named Jake gets a job interview for an assistant manager position at the local bank. Jake asks you what he should wear. Knowing that banks are conservative institutions, you tell Jake he should wear a dark suit, dark pants, a light colored tie, and dress shoes. You're a little concerned about his pony-tail and nose ring, so you suggest that he might want to have his hair cut and lose the nose ring. Knowing what you do about banks, you have helped Jake "dress the part," in other words, to help him give off the impression that he is professional and conservative. Jake calls you later and thanks you because he got the job. Pat yourself on the back, you have just helped Jake manage his impression. Likewise, there are impressions you want to give called expressions given. Impressions we would rather not give are called expressions given off.

Symbols

Next we need to talk about symbols. There are three primary things we need to mention about symbols. First, a symbol is anything that conveys meaning. For instance, let's say I was sitting at my desk. If I were to pound on my desk, my hand would hurt. The desk is real, it is made of wood and wood is real. But my use of the words "desk" and "wood" are symbolic. A tree is real but the word" tree" is symbolic. Words are great examples of symbols, but certainly not the only ones.

Second, symbols are interpreted contextually. Because symbols always represent something else, they are contextual. In other words, they are interpreted with the situational context in mind. For instance, let's use tears as our symbol we need to interpret. Tears are real but the act of crying is symbolic. For instance, imagine going to the wedding of a good friend of yours. As you sit in the pew waiting for the wedding to start, you notice a woman several rows up who is obviously crying because she is dabbing her eyes with her handkerchief. While her tears are real, they are symbolic because now we have to ask the question why is she crying? In that situation or context, which in this case is a wedding, we would likely interpret her tears to be tears of joy. She is excited for her friend who is getting married. So we interpret symbols, but because we interpret symbols interpretations can sometimes be wrong. What if the reason this young woman is crying isn't because she's happy about her friend getting married but rather unhappy that her former boyfriend is the one getting married? So the tears again are real but the act of crying is symbolic and therefore up for interpretation. To take this example one step further what if after the wedding you were walking across the park to get to your car. As you walked across the park you noticed a young woman sitting on a park bench who was crying. Just like the woman at the wedding, she is shedding tears. Would you interpret her tears in the same way that you interpreted the tears of the woman at the wedding? Of course not, because the context has changed. Now, in the latter case, you would be far more likely to interpret the young woman's tears as an indication she was sad or unhappy, but certainly not as tears of joy. So symbols are interpreted contextually.

Third, symbols define the situation. A symbol can be anything that conveys meaning, and that meaning is derived from the context, symbols may define a situation.

Channels of Communication

Channels of communication use symbols to help define and interpret the meaning behind the situation. Let's start with verbal symbols. There are two types:

- Language - words and spoken language represent language.

- Para-language - the **way** that words are spoken.

Para-language

Are the words spoken quickly or slowly? Are the words spoken with a shaking or quivering voice? What about if someone speaks with a thick accent? If you wanted to work as a news anchor at the national level you would learn very quickly that a deep southern accent or a thick New York/New Jersey accent has to go. Why? Because our society does not interpret those accents positively. On the other hand, Americans love the British accent (Kitching, 2014).

Also, people who speak quickly often do so because they are stressed (Siegman et al., 1990), and that stress is something others can pick up on, and when combined with a loud voice, can produce anger or fear in a listener. On the other hand, someone who speaks slowly projects a calming effect on others who are feeling anxious. If you were a car salesman, would you rather speak softly and slowly or loudly and quickly? So while pace of speech, accent, or whether someone shivers and shakes as they deliver a sentence may not necessarily tell us anything by themselves, when combined with spoken words, they may be used to define the situation, whether that situation is defined correctly or not.

Verbal Communication

Social interaction involves nonverbal communication as well as verbal communication. Verbal communication requires both language and para-language, whereas nonverbal communication involves such things as body language, eye contact, and facial expression. When we speak of nonverbal communication, the first thing we need to identify is called channels of communication. Channels of communication has to do with the way that symbols are communicated.

Non-Verbal Communication

Nonverbal symbols include two categories the first is body language and the second is physical characteristics. Body language includes such things as:

- Body movement

- Eye contact

- Civil inattention

- Interpersonal distance

- Marking our territory

Physical characteristics include our biological image and our made image.

Body Movement

Body movement is often interpreted in our society. The way someone stands, folds their arms, crosses their legs, or even slouches, all represent actions that are interpreted. As an example, in our culture, how would we interpret someone talking to us with his or her arms crossed? Generally, we would regard that action as indicating the person is on the defensive or resistant to questioning.

Eye Contact

Eye contact is also very important in our culture. We expect others to maintain eye contact with us when we are engaged in focused interactions. For instance, Sue who is friends with Sally, is curious whether or not there is something between Sally and her boyfriend. One day Sue asks Sally, "Sally, did you sleep with my boyfriend?" Where should Sally's eyes be as she responds to Sue's question? Imagine Sally staring at the ceiling as she says to Sue, "No, of course not. What a crazy idea."

Civil Inattention

Erving Goffman said that there was something called civil inattention that we use in our daily lives. As we enter into each other's interpersonal space, we acknowledge the other person briefly with eye contact. So imagine walking in one direction on a sidewalk and someone is walking towards you in the other direction. Goffman suggests that for one brief part of a second both parties will acknowledge each other by making eye contact.

Why is this symbolic? Imagine the same situation where you're walking on the sidewalk in one direction and someone is walking towards you in the other direction and as you lift your eyes to make eye contact with the other person you notice that their eyes are glued to the sidewalk. As you get closer and closer to each other you notice in your peripheral vision that the other person never looks up from the sidewalk as they pass you. If eye contact is the symbol we are interpreting, how might you interpret the fact that they never made eye contact with you even as you entered their space? Distracted? Depressed? Low self-esteem? What if as they walked toward you on the sidewalk you noticed that not only did they make eye contact with you, but they also continued to stare at you the entire time you entered each other's space? How would you interpret that? Aggressive? Sexual interest? Potential serial killer who pees the bed and hurts small animals? One way or another you will interpret the meaning of that eye contact or lack thereof.

Marking Our Territory

The final component of body language is marking our territory. Dogs may mark their territory by peeing on things, but fortunately humans do not. However, we do still mark our territory just in different ways. As I stand in front of my students when I teach in the classroom, I notice that sometimes students will have their books, notebooks, computers, and purses scattered left and right of them on the desk beside them. By doing this they are marking their territory; in other words, they are keeping others from sitting next to them. It's as if they have a sign that says, "This is my territory. Keep away!"

Another example, imagine a friend of yours needs a place to crash for the night and you volunteer they can stay with you. The next morning, you climb out of bed and make your way to the bathroom only to find them brushing their teeth with your toothbrush. OMG! "That's disgusting!" you say to yourself. Why? Because it's YOUR toothbrush and your territory.

Interpersonal Distance

Interpersonal distance refers to the distance we like to keep others based on their relationship to us (Hall, 1966; Moore, 2010). Research suggests that we Americans like to keep strangers at about six feet, friends around four feet depending on the friendship, and then intimate others at around two feet or less. When this distance is violated we may feel threatened and find a way to increase the distance.

Sometimes increasing our distance as a reaction to someone getting too close to us might be automatic, you don't have to think before acting. However, sometimes there are occasions where you might have time to think about what to do if your interpersonal space is violated. If you have time to think about it before you react to the intrusion, you might want to increase the distance in a subtle way because otherwise they will know that they have made you uncomfortable and that's something you may not want them to know. Remember, their action and your reaction are both symbolic and will be interpreted. Can you imagine some situations in which you'd rather not let them know they've made you uncomfortable? Another example would include elevators. There are "unwritten" rules when we ride an elevator with strangers. When you're riding an elevator with a stranger do you stare at them? Do you sing? Do you talk to yourself? No. The most common behavior while riding on an elevator with a stranger is staring at the control panel with the floor numbers or even staring straight ahead at the doors. If Goffman was still with us he would probably make the argument that we do this so we can "pretend" our interpersonal space isn't being violated by being in an enclosed environment with a stranger. Finally, again Goffman might help you find out if someone likes you or not. Is there someone you want to know if they like you or not? Violate their interpersonal space and see what happens. If they don't increase the distance between you, that's a huge checkmark that they might like you! On the other hand, they could just be too scared to walk away from the nutcase that's standing too close to them! You'll have to figure that one out for yourself.

Physical Characteristics

The second component of channels of communication are physical characteristics. Again, these are symbols that are interpreted. The first is our biological image. Our biological image represents those characteristics about us over which we have no control, we are born with those characteristics. Height, eye color, skin color, facial features, gender, and weight to some degree. These are things that we have no control over, but they are interpreted by others. Tall people are generally perceived to be more competent than our short people. Likewise, the research also suggests that attractive people are more favored in the workplace than lesser attractive people. Overweight people, according to the research, are often victims of discrimination. Research also suggests that married males are more likely to be promoted and are paid more than single males. The reason for all of these research findings is that these characteristics are interpreted and people treat us according to those interpretations.

The number one characteristic that is associated with discrimination in the workplace may surprise you: it's gender. The ratio of males to females in the United States is 48 to 52. As I've mentioned before, all things being equal, we should expect to see that ratio in anything we study. If we have had 44 presidents, approximately 23 or 24 of those should have been female. As we all know we have not had one female president to date. What does that suggest? Think about the last time you went to a car dealership to buy a car. How many of those sales people were female? Why would there be more males than female car sales people? Again, because gender is interpreted-women are not supposed to know about engines or anything mechanical. Would it surprise you to know that when the typewriter was first invented secretaries were males and not females, but as wages in other occupations increased males left the secretarial positions and females filled them.

Made images are those things that we have control over. We can change your hair color, we can control the type of clothes that we wear, we can choose the type of car that we want to be seen driving, or the house we live in. Again, those are all symbolic and therefore all interpreted. When symbols are interpreted and often acted upon, prejudice and discrimination may be involved. Sometimes it may seem trivial, but sometimes it is not. What is the stereotype we have about blonde women? Not overly blessed with intelligence says the stereotype. And thinking about the new car market, and without naming names, there is a particular car that you can buy new for about $14,000. If the point of a car is to get you from point A to point B safely, and the $14,000 car will do just that, why are we not all driving $14,000 cars? Why? As you sit next to a $70,000 Mercedes waiting for a light to change, how do you explain the difference between your driving a $14,000 car and they're driving a $70,000 car? Undoubtedly, you will reach the conclusion that the $70,000 car is to be interpreted as a sign of their success. So, even the cars that we drive are symbols and interpreted differently.

Nonverbal Communication

Nonverbal Communication, in other words, what we communicate with symbols, includes expressions of intimacy or lack thereof. The first would involve intimacy with words. As examples: Bbl versus tbl, Sie versus du, and Usted versus tu. Do you recognize any of those word pairs? All of them represent the formal form of the word "you" versus the informal form of the word "you"—first in Russia, then German, and finally Spanish. Here in the U.S. we make no such distinction—which therefore deprives us of information that could be used to help us interpret an interaction.

For instance, imagine you were in Germany and you overheard two adults conversing on the street and they frequently used the word "Sie" as they spoke to one another. If we understand not one more word of German than the word for "you," and its formal versus informal distinction, how might we interpret the interaction between these two Germans we hear conversing on the street? How would we likely interpret their relationship? More than likely we would conclude they were either strangers or one was perhaps a superior from their mutual workplace. In other words, that they chose to use the formal form for the word "you" was symbolic and therefore something that could be interpreted and add meaning to the situation. What if instead of two adult Germans interacting we overheard a German child and an adult speaking and the adult kept using the informal form of the word for "you," in other words "du?" How might be we interpret that? Generally, that would suggest it was either a parent talking to his or her child or a stranger talking to a child. Again, the form of the word, a symbol, adds meaning to the situation. But "you" is not the only word for which there are formal or informal designations.

There are also special words that are symbolic and convey meaning—words that are meant for particular others but not for the general public. Being from up north, I was shocked the first time a relatively young Southern waitress referred to me as "honey." The "rules" up north are different—only older waitresses are "allowed" to use such a special word to a customer. Other special words would be "darling," or "sugar," or "sweetie." These are words generally reserved for significant others and therefore are supposed to hold special meaning. Imagine seeing a man and a woman in a grocery store, and the woman turns to the man and says, "Oh, honey, I forgot, could you go pick up a loaf of bread?" Because the word "honey" is symbolic, how would we likely interpret the relationship between them? Husband and wife? Boyfriend and Girlfriend? It's not likely we would think of them as strangers who just met minutes earlier while on their mutual excursions to the grocery store.

And while there is intimacy with words, obviously there is intimacy without words. Touching is the best example, but have you ever really given any thought to touching being symbolic? Imagine this scenario. You are at a party and stationed so that you have a view of the door and can see newcomers arriving at the party. In walks a man and a woman arm-in-arm. You've never seen them before, can't hear anything being said between them, but how are you likely to interpret their touching one another? Most likely you would interpret their symbolic act of walking in arm-in-arm as an indication they were together romantically. What if instead they walked in together without touching and then went their separate ways after entering the room? Strangers? Friends at best? What if after walking into the room arm-in-arm, they kissed, and as she went in one direction he went the other, but while he walked away from her you noticed he slid his wedding ring off and put it in his pocket? How would you interpret that? Sleazebag!

And while not quite touching, what about interpersonal space violation? What does it say when a man and a woman are seen sitting closely together while having lunch or dinner? Is that not interpreted as intimacy? Interestingly in Europe when a couple sits at a table or booth while having a meal, they sit side by side, but here in the U.S., couples are more likely to sit across from one another.

Words can also symbolically represent status. Imagine a famous cardiologist who wants to reserve a table at a crowded restaurant that evening. After introducing himself as "Dr. Smith," the maître 'd accommodates him, "Well, of course Dr. Johannsen we can reserve you a table tonight at 8 p.m." even though he has just got off the phone with another potential customer who he told they had no openings at 8 p.m. What happened? Status. That's what. In our culture status can be conveyed with works: e.g., sir, Dr., Judge, Mr. President, etc. Unfortunately, because as a Ph.D. I'm not a "real" doctor, I don't have much luck getting reservations in crowded restaurants!

Status

As status can be conveyed by words, research has found that people with higher perceived status tend to talk more frequently, talk longer, talk louder, and interrupt more. Statuses are the positions we occupy in society. Positions are always going to be relative to others. For instance, your boss occupies a status or position higher than you and you may hold a status or position higher than a subordinate. At any point in our life we hold multiple statuses. For instance, if you're reading this you are obviously are a student, which is a status, on a status hierarchy you rank higher than someone who is not a student, but you would rank lower on that hierarchy than someone who has already graduated. What other statuses might you hold? Are you male or female? Married or unmarried? Young or old? Are you a parent? Are you Hispanic, African-American, Asian, or Caucasian? All of the aforementioned are statuses and undoubtedly several of the above apply to you—hence you occupy a number of statuses at one time. Ascribed statuses are those that are given by society—you have no control over an ascribed status. In a monarchy, a title that is passed down from generation to the next is a great example of an ascribed status, but we are not a monarchy.

On the other hand, if you are born with the last name of Kennedy, Rockefeller, or Gates, you are "given" ascribed status—people treat you differently because you are born to a recognized family name usually associated with wealth. Other ascribed statuses include race, gender, and age. Age is an ascribed status because young people rank lower on the status hierarchy than do people in their 50's, but people in their 60's or older tend to rank lower in status than people in their 50's or younger people.

The other way status is awarded is through effort. Whereas ascribed status is simply handed to someone based on certain characteristics, the other way status is awarded is through effort. For instance, while Bill Gates' children will have ascribed status, Bill Gates himself achieved his status through his own efforts. When you graduate college, that would be an example of achieved status—your position on that status hierarchy will be positively affected because you hung in there and earned your degree whereas other people may not have done so. Other examples of achieved status would include employee, friend, club member, etc.

Master Status

Is one status more important than others? Yes. Everyone has what is called a master status. While master statuses are the most important, a master status is determined by society and not by the individual. As I mentioned earlier, the number one reason discrimination is experienced in the workplace is because of gender. And even though gender is an ascribed status and you had nothing to do with whether you are a male or female, and though society is changing, it still places women lower on the status hierarchy than men, therefore gender may be a working woman's master status. On the other hand, the research says that married males climb to the top of the work world faster than do unmarried males—in which case marital status could be a man's master status. Again, master statuses are decided by society and not the individual.

Social Roles

Social roles are expected behaviors for people occupying specific statuses. If I were to use the example of your status as a student, I would expect that your role as student includes coming to class, taking notes, and staying awake in class. Another example might be if you were a policeman. As a policeman I would expect your role to include obeying the law and not running red lights on your way home from work, parking in handicapped spaces, or threatening your neighbors because you didn't like the way they mowed their yard. Because we occupy a number of statuses at one time, and therefore fulfill multiple roles at the same time, we might experience role conflict.

Role Conflict

Role conflict occurs when we struggle with situations that put our roles in conflict. For instance, as a married woman with a child, you are expected to buy groceries, cook dinner, transport your children, take care of them if they are sick, and so forth. But can you see several of those roles coming into conflict? What if you have a hungry husband, a hungry child, a sick child, a clothes dryer that has just finished its cycle, and your best friend is on the phone in tears because her husband of 20 years has just left her? You certainly can't perform all the duties associated with the associated roles at one time. That's role conflict.

Role Strain

There is role strain which occurs when in a particular status there are different expectations that come into conflict with each other. For instance, what if you are a police officer and you pull someone over for speeding. Your radar gun shows the violator traveling 15 miles per hour over the speed limit. All you have to do is hand out a speeding ticket, but as you approach the violator's car you realize it's your best friend. OMG! Unfortunately, because it's on the radar, you have no choice, you have to issue the ticket, but that's not going to make your friend feel good about the friendship—in this case you are experiencing role strain.

Role Exit

Role exit is the process where you end or exit one role and start another. Divorce or widowhood would be great examples. As a newly single person someone would have to create an entirely new identity—in other words, moving from the "we" to the "I." For some this process can be difficult and lengthy.

Sapir-Whorf Hypothesis

Edward Sapir and Benjamin Wharf hypothesized that language is used to shape our perception of reality (Sapir, 1929; Whorf, 1956). Words as symbols shape our interpretations of reality.

Culture uses language to shape itself, and in turn is shaped by language. The Sapir-Wharf hypothesis suggests that language is how we perceive the world. Edward

Sapir and Benjamin Whorf were interested in explaining the connection between language and culture. Specifically, they wanted to investigate how our view of the world is shaped by our thoughts and how language influences our thoughts. They believed that language shaped the way we think and how we perceive the reality of our world. The most important feature of their hypothesis was that because language shapes the social reality of our world, people who speak different languages would have different views of their social world (Kennison, 2013).

As an example, let's look at how a culture's language can influence gender roles. John and Mary are best friends and have been so for most of their lives. Both of them decided they wanted to be pilots and fly for commercial airlines. So, both went to pilot school and both put in the required training. They graduated at the same time and both found jobs almost immediately with the same airline. John and Mary are still very close and will often see other at parties. Mary has noticed that when fellow party-goers talked about John they referred to him as a "pilot," but when people talked about her, they referred to her as a "female pilot." Mary wondered why people tied her gender to her job, but they didn't do the same thing to John. They performed the exact same job, so why would people refer to them differently? Mary concluded that When others referred to her as a "female-pilot" and her friend as just a "pilot," their friends were using sexist language created by their culture and this suggested that Mary was not in accord with societal views of gender roles by being a female pilot, because after all according to society, males are pilots and women are housekeepers.

Terms, Concepts and Names to Know:

- Sapir-Wharf hypothesis

- Social interaction; types of social interactions

- Focused versus unfocused interactions

- Role conflict

- Role strain

- Encounters

- Brackets

- Impression management

- Symbols

- Channels of communication

- Language and para-language

- Social roles

- Status

- Master status

- Verbal symbols

- Non-verbal symbols

- Body movement

- Eye contact

- Civil inattention

- Marking our territory

- Interpersonal space

- Physical versus made images

- Non-verbal communication

- Expressions of intimacy

- Expressions of status

- Ascribed versus achieved status

Be Able to Discuss:

- Explain what a master status is and give examples.

- Explain Erving Goffman's concept of impression management

- Know encounters and the use of brackets

- Explain how symbols are interpreted contextually

- Know the difference between focused and unfocused interactions

References

Goffman, E. (1967). Interaction Ritual: Essays on Face-to-Face Behavior. Anchor Books, New York, NY.

Goffman, E. (1961). Encounters: Two Studies in the Sociology of Interaction – Fun in Games & Role Distance. Indianapolis, Bobbs-Merrill.

Goffman, E. (1959). The Presentation of Self in Everyday Life. University of Edinburgh Social Sciences Research Centre. Anchor Books, New York, NY.

Hall, E. (1966). The Hidden Dimension. Anchor Books, New York, NY.

Kennison, S. (2013). Introduction to Language Development. SAGE Publications, Thousand Oaks, CA.

Kitching, C. (2014, October 5). Brits? You're all uptight, obsessed by tea, the royals and family trees, say Americans... and no, we can't understand Geordie accents either. Retrieved March 3, 2016, from http://www.dailymail.co.uk/travel/travel_news/article-2781088/What-Americans-think-Britains-revealed-survey.html

Moore, N. (2010). Nonverbal Communication: Studies and Applications. Oxford University Press, Oxford, England.

Sapir, E. (1929). The status of linguistics as a science. Language 5:207–214.

Whorf, B. (1956). Language, thought, and reality: Selected writings of Benjamin Lee Whorf. Edited by John B. Carroll. Cambridge, MA: MIT Press.

Chapter 7: Social Stratification

What is Social Stratification?

It occurs when individuals or groups occupy unequal positions in society based on socioeconomic factors. It is sometimes referred to as social inequality. Members of a particular society are awarded power and privilege by where they fall in a hierarchy that is divided into layers. This layering leads to an unequal distribution of rewards available within that society. The three key components of social stratification are class, status, and power.

The Evolution of Social Stratification and Inequality

Systems of stratification, or social inequality, have evolved over time as mankind progressed through different types of societies:

Hunting and Gathering Societies

Hunting and gathering societies had little stratification. Men hunted for meat while women gathered edible plants, and the general welfare of the society depended on all its members sharing what it had. The society shared food more or less equally. Research has found that hunting and gathering societies in recent times tend to be fully nomadic, live in small communities, have low population densities, have little wealth differentiation (i.e., stratification), and divide labor by sex, with women doing the gathering and men doing the hunting (Ember, 2014). Some hunting and gathering societies still exist though they are few in number. This includes the Kalahari bushmen of Africa, the Spinifex of the Great Victorian Desert in Australia, and the Piraha of the Maici River in the Brazilian Amazon (Czartoryski, 2011).

Horticultural, Agricultural, and Pastoral Societies

Horticultural Societies

For the first time in human history, societies had stable sources of food. Horticultural societies cultivated plants, like corn and wheat. Horticultural societies were so successful at cultivating crops that they began to accumulate more foodstuffs than was necessary for their survival. Because of this surplus of food, some tribal members began to specialize in certain jobs or crafts, and the surplus itself became a commodity that gave them more power and privilege. Also, the division of labor led to stratification. Some jobs or crafts became more valuable than others, which again meant more power and privilege.

Agricultural Societies

As pastoral societies transitioned to agricultural societies, manual laborers became the least valued members of a society. Those who job or craft was valued and esteemed by others, such as art or music, became the most respected of the society. As basic survival needs were met, people began trading goods and services they could not provide for themselves. It was at this time that members of a society began to accumulate possessions. Some were able to accumulate more than others, which led to greater stratification or inequality between societal members. Accumulated wealth was passed down from father to son, or one generation to the next, and the inequality that had been created by some amassing more than others stayed in the hands of a select few.

Pastoral Societies

Pastoral societies shepherd cattle, goats, and other livestock. The Maasai of Africa are considered a pastoral society as they shepherd their cattle and goats around southern Kenya and northern Tanzania. While the Kenyan and Tanzanian governments have worked to change the Maasai lifestyle, it is interesting to note that OXFAM (Oxford Committee for Famine Relief) suggests that the world adopt the practices of the Maasai as a response to climate change because of their ability to farm in previously unfarmable areas like deserts. Newly defined park boundaries of both countries have forced the Maasai to grow more of their own food, which is a significant change from their nomadic past.

Industrial Societies

The Industrial Revolution began in Great Britain in the late 1700's after the invention of the steam engine, which ran the machines necessary for the manufacturing of goods (though water power was successfully used in a smaller scale prior to the invention of the steam engine). With the accumulated wealth that had been passed down from their forefathers, wealthy individuals began building factories to harness this newly found energy source. Most factories were built in urban areas, like London or Manchester. Former farm workers who craved for a better living migrated by the thousands to the cities to work in these factories. Workers were usually paid poor or inadequate wages. It is at this time in history that the gap between what Marx referred to as the "haves" and "have-nots" grew even larger. Essentially, a new generation of nobility was created.

As technology evolved, there was a need for more specialized workers. These skilled workers earned more than the unskilled. Inequality widened. Those specialized or skilled workers often knew how to read and write, and earned them substantially more money, because it was necessary to practice their skills, but the unskilled likely didn't know how to read or write. The U.S. was the first country to provide free mass public education. Thomas Jefferson, who urged for the creation of schools, believed that a true democracy depended on an educated populace. However, Jefferson's idea of free education for the masses really only applied to the sons of rich property owners. Eventually this changed so that education is available to most Americans. In fact, before the American Civil War, America was the most literate country in the world. Unfortunately, today we are the 7th most literate country in the world with Scandinavian countries and Switzerland coming in ahead of us.

Post-Industrial Societies

In today's postindustrial societies, industry has given way to information-based economies. The decrease in industry led to a drop in average wages in the U.S. as the information-based companies pay less because technology can be used to perform a great deal of the work and specialized or skilled workers are less valued by society. This process of de-industrializing has increased stratification and widened the gap between the rich and the poor. The majority of workers either work in service industries or in jobs that require few skills and training.

Four Major Types of Stratification

Four major types of stratification are caste, estate, slavery, and class.

Caste Systems Caste systems depend on legal or religiously sanctioned inequalities. Caste is not "officially" recognized and stems from economic factors. Position is bestowed for life at birth, rather than achieved through personal accomplishment. Social status is based on personal characteristics such as race, parental religion, or parental caste. The "purity" of the caste is maintained by rules of marriage required by custom or law. Globalization is challenging the few remaining caste systems.

Rigid restrictions of the caste system interfere with freedom and flexibility necessary for modern industrial production. These are systems based on ascription—status handed down from generation to generation. Ascribed statuses can include race, gender, family name, and age. People are born into castes, and whichever caste into which they are born, they will die—there is no potential for mobility. The best example of a caste system was the system that existed in India prior to 1949. Though the system has been outlawed by the Indian government, there are still some surviving features. In the Indian system, there were essentially four castes:

- Brahman, which usually consisted of priests or scholars who enjoyed a great deal

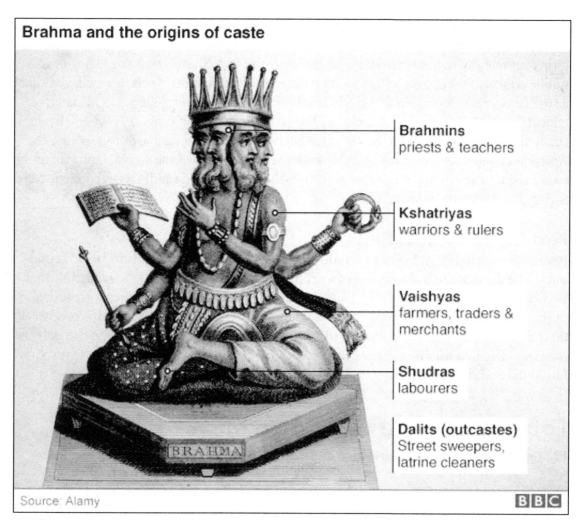

Brahma and the origins of caste

Brahmins
priests & teachers

Kshatriyas
warriors & rulers

Vaishyas
farmers, traders &
merchants

Shudras
labourers

Dalits (outcastes)
Street sweepers,
latrine cleaners

Source: Alamy

BBC

of prestige and wealth.

- Kshatriya, or warrior caste, was composed of those who distinguished themselves in military service.

- Vaishva which consisted of business-people and skilled craftspeople.

- Shudra consisted of those who made their living doing manual labor.

- Harijan, or Untouchables, were thought of as inferior and repulsive to touch.

Estate Systems

Estate systems are stratification systems that were made up of nobility, the clergy, and peasants or commoners. Most of Europe lived under estate systems during the middle ages. The Nobility inherited the wealth of their fathers and lived off of the sweat of the commoners who farmed their land and paid rent, taxes, and gave a share of their crop to their lord.

The Catholic Church was powerful and nearly as wealthy as it is now. It had a strong influence on European culture until the Protestant Reformation in the mid-1500's. At the top of the hierarchy in these estate systems was the nobility, with Catholic clergy in the middle, and commoners at the bottom. The commoners had no power and no matter what the land owner wanted to do, they had no recourse. Commoners worked their entire life for their lord, and ended their life with about as much as they had when they came into it, nothing. There was no chance for upward mobility or to better their lot in life. This is why so many people migrated from Europe to North America in the past several hundred years—to have control of their own life and reap the benefits from their work.

Slavery Systems

Slavery systems are an extreme form of inequality in which certain people own other people as property. Slave labor is not an efficient use of labor as slaves usually resist the work they are assigned to do without compensation. In a slavery system, one man owns another man. The slave is literally his property and he may see fit to do anything he likes with the slave. Historically, the reasons for slavery included the survivors of one societies victory over another in battle (e.g., the enslavement of the Greeks by the Romans), for unpaid debt, indentured servitude (i.e., where a person would agree to essentially be a slave for a specific amount of time in order to "pay" back their expenses), and racial inferiority.

America was founded with the institution of slavery intact and it was largely based on the belief that Africans were less intelligent. Therefore slavery was seen as a way to protect them much as a parent does for his or her child. By the early 1800's, both England and France had outlawed slavery, northern America soon followed. By the 1830's, importation of slaves into North America was illegal. Slavery in the American south was dying, as the cost for maintaining the slaves was more than what the slaves produced. The use of the cotton gin changed that. Though Eli Whitney didn't create the cotton gin, he made it more efficient and revitalized the institution of slavery. Between 1830 and 1850 cotton production went from 750,000 bales to 2.85 million bales (Pierson, 2009). During the American Civil War, white southerners often defended slavery by saying that freed slaves were not intelligent or resourceful enough to support themselves. In most parts of the world, slavery was not usually permanent nor was it based on racism—though here in the U.S. it was. Often slaves could work themselves to freedom by paying off their debt or literally paying for their freedom, but this was rarely so in the United States.

Class Systems

Class Systems are based on the control of information (i.e., service industry) and material goods (i.e., resources). This sets up a tiered system of stratification with those who own and/or control the most of the aforementioned at the top, those who own and/or control some of the aforementioned, in the middle, and those who have no assets, skills, or control of information at the bottom of the pyramid.

Class systems differ from caste, estate, or class systems in four ways:

- Class systems are fluid (i.e., people can move in or out of their class),

- People can move in or out of their class through their achievements (i.e., social mobility may occur),

- Class is based primarily on the economy and the economic resources people own or control,

- Class systems are impersonal. In the days of monarchies, the peasants would work the land and pay their lord what he is owed either in taxes or as his share of the crop.

Monarchies

Monarchies were in some sense paternal—monarchs felt they had some sense of obligation to care or protect those under them—though their definition of care and protect might be very different than ours. Essentially, that obligation to care for their inferiors is called **noblesse oblige**. The poor were often looked after (this was before industrialization). Scholars suggest that one of the reasons for such inequality in modern industrialized societies, especially in the U.S., is because we never had a monarchy, there was never any "obligation" on the part of the rich to help the poor. If you like history, you should know that the "men who built America" were generally not very caring or considerate of their workers. That seems even stronger today as there is a growing gap between the rich and poor. Though most people are more affluent today, the distribution of wealth and income is still highly unequal. Between the early 70's and the late 90's, the gap grew wider—globalization caused sharp increases at the top while working families saw a drop in income. Ordinary workers, minorities, and single-parent families have been the hardest hit.

Social Inequality and Mobility

Social mobility refers to how people can change their class position. They can:

- Move upward, by climbing to a higher class position, or

- Move downward, by falling to a lower class position, or

- Not move at all, to stay in the same class position.

How do we know whether someone has moved up, or down, or stayed the same? How do we measure social mobility? Generally, there are two ways:

- Intragenerational mobility. We can measure where you are in terms of your class position at one point in your life and then measure your class position again at some later point in time to see if your class position has changed.

- Intergenerational mobility. We can measure where you are in terms of your class position and then measure where your parents are in terms of their class position. If there is a difference in class position between you and your parents, then we can say that there is evidence of mobility of class positions.

Social Mobility

Social mobility is of limited range. Most people remain close to the level of their family. But expansion of white-collar jobs has allowed for short-range upward mobility. Some sociologists believe lifestyle choices (how we dress, what we eat, where we relax) are important influences on class position. In a class system, status is based on achievement, not ascription.

The effect of education on mobility opportunities has declined some in recent years due to:

- Globalization

- The spread of new technologies

- And more competition for top-paying jobs as more people acquire degrees

Socioeconomic Status

Socioeconomic status (SES), is the chief indicator of class in the U.S. Components of socioeconomic status are:

- Education,

- Wealth (assets),

- Income,

- Occupation and occupational prestige.

Prestige

Prestige is how highly an occupation is valued by society and esteem is the honor that we give to people who have a particular occupation. The amount of money people earn may not necessarily correspond to the status we give them. For instance, in the 1700-1800's, the most important people in a town (i.e., had the highest status) were the sheriff, the minister or priest, and the doctor. Today the sheriff and priest have relatively low status and doctors have more. While the president of the United States may have incredibly high status and prestige, his income isn't all that great in comparison--$400,000 per year. However, even among doctors there can be a difference in status and income; compare your local podiatrist to the world-renowned cardiologist who just bought a house in Malibu for $25 million.

Classes

Upper Classes. There are two upper classes:
- The upper upper class, in which membership is based on ascription, wealth – 'old money,' have close social ties with others of the same class, and usually have a recognized name (e.g., Kennedy, Rockefeller),

- The lower upper class in which people work to achieve their status, typically is 'new money' people, and are the "working rich."

Middles Classes. There are two middle classes:
- The upper middle class, which is made up of working professionals in relatively prestigious occupations, making 100—250K per year, and have college degrees (usually graduate work), and

- The lower middle class, which is made up people who have less education (may not have attended college), attended public institutions, have fewer assets, and are dependent on a job.

Lower Classes. There are two lower classes:
- The upper lower class, which is the working class, have few if any assets, and do not have a college degree (and may not have even graduated high school),

- The lower lower class, which are those people who lack virtually any formal education, have few, if any skills, and lack steady employment.

Social Exclusion

What Is Social Exclusion? Social exclusion is when people are cut off from society; excluded because they are poor, live in substandard housing, attend inferior schools, have an old car, and on and on. Essentially, social exclusion refers to the people we don't notice and don't want to notice as a society. I would equate them to what Marx called the lumpen proletariat. The homelesswould be a good example. We know they're out there. We even think we see them sometimes, but in reality we are seeing the one percent who usually have a mental illness like schizophrenia. The "real" homeless that we don't see are the ones who live in their cars, or spend the night in homeless shelters and their days walking the streets looking for a job they'll be lucky to find. Would it surprise you to know that 25 percent of all homeless in the U.S. are children under the age of 18 years and they're not living on the streets by themselves. We work so hard not to see them, because if we did see them, we might fell guilty that we have so much and they have so little. So, what do we do? Before the 1996 Olympics held in Atlanta, GA Fulton County officials gave one-way bus tickets to the homeless if they promised never to return. Even more recently, the Mayor of New York, Michael Bloomberg, "defended a city program to send homeless families out of New York on planes, trains, and buses..." (Bosman & Barbaro, July 29, 2009).

The Myth of Horatio Alger

In a class system, the argument is made that there is a carrot that is dangling in front of us. The belief is that everyone can succeed in life if they just work hard. Picking up on this idea, a man by the name of Horatio Alger wrote a series of books that are described as rags to riches stories, illustrating how down-and-out boys might be able to achieve the American dream of wealth and success through hard work, courage, determination, and concern for others.

Horatio Alger's books put forward a vision of America (often referred to as the American dream) that is still esteemed today. No matter how you started life, if you work hard enough, you too can get to the top. All that matters is that you work hard and you have some degree of intelligence.

Let's put this to the test. We're going to go out and randomly select members of the middle class (upper or lower middle class) and ask them several questions. First, we ask our middle class sample, "Are you working hard?" To which the vast majority will probably answer, "Hell yes, I'm working hard! In fact, I don't think I've ever worked harder in my life!" Knowing that the American dream says that all you have to do is work hard to have it all, we ask these same people, "Well, if you're working hard, harder than you've ever worked in your life, why are some people doing better than you? Why do some people have so much more than you?" Do you know how the research says they answer that question? With this, "Some people are just lucky. They have a rich daddy. They were just in the right place at the right time." The middle class says that the reason some people are doing so much better than them is because they are lucky.

Next, we ask our middle class sample, "Why do you suppose some people don't have as much as you?" This is an example of blaming the victim. Do you know how the research says the majority answer that question? With this, "Well, they're just not working as hard as I am," or, "they just don't have my values and work ethic," in other words, "they're lazy" something is wrong with them. Is it really just hard work? The middle classes say of those doing better, they're lucky, and of those doing more poorly, they're lazy. Now, if we were to go out and ask the wealthy, the upper classes, why some people didn't have as much as them, how do you suppose they'd answer? With the exception of a few who might credit inherited wealth as a reason for their success, don't you think the majority would say of those who don't have as much didn't work as hard as they did? The question becomes then is the carrot really out there? And if the carrot really is out there, is it held out at different distances between people?

Donald Trump, who ran for president in 2016, was held up as the model of American success. Through his hard work he had climbed to the top. He epitomized Horatio Alger. Unfortunately, that's not true. Donald Trump didn't pull himself up by his bootstraps in the way that Horatio Alger did. Donald Trump started off with a $200 million inheritance from his father (Washington Post, February 29, 2015). Think of what Horatio Alger would have done with $200 million!

Poverty

There are two types of poverty measures: relative and absolute. A relative measure of poverty would examine how much any one person or household had in comparison to the average individuals or households had in that society. However, relative poverty might identify someone as poor with an income of $50,000 per year if the mean income for the community or society is $75,000 per year. But can an individual live on $50,000 a year? Of course, and in relative comfort. So that doesn't seem to be the best measure of poverty. What is needed is something that measures how much individuals and families need to survive and that is what an absolute measure of poverty does—it takes into account the costs of those things necessary for survival. Survival items would include food, shelter, medical costs, transportation costs, clothing, and other items. The condition of having too little income to buy those necessities is called absolute poverty.

Cycle of Poverty

The cycle of poverty occurs when a family has been impoverished for three or more generations. They therefore lack any familial "memory" of anything other than poverty. The family members cannot bring to the family any intellectual, social, and cultural capital necessary to change their economic situation. In the cycle of poverty members of poor families do not have someone to look to as an example of being able to climb out of poverty. They

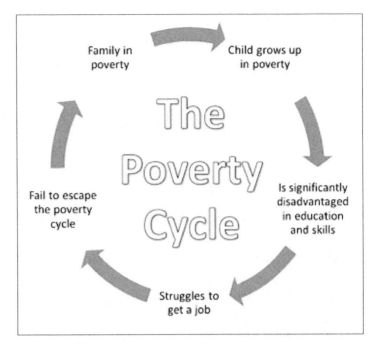

have no model for improving their position and thus may not believe that they can climb out of poverty. Such families may not believe that education is key to climbing out of poverty because no one in their family has been able to do so.

Parents who are poor are likely to have little education. Often they have to put in long hours to keep the family afloat. They may not have the time or ability to help their children with school work, so their children are less likely to graduate high school. With little education they can only find low wage jobs and the whole cycle starts over again. This is why it is so crucial that people who manage to climb out of poverty serve as role

2016 Federal Poverty Levels

Size of Household	Household Annual Income					
	138%	150%	200%	250%	300%	400%
1	$16,105	$17,505	$23,340	$29,175	$35,010	$46,680
2	$21,708	$23,595	$31,460	$39,325	$47,190	$62,920
3	$27,311	$29,685	$39,580	$49,475	$59,370	$79,160
4	$32,913	$35,775	$47,700	$59,625	$71,550	$95,400
5	$38,516	$41,865	$55,820	$69,775	$83,730	$111,640

If your total annual household income is within these levels you may qualify for premium subsidy (discounted health insurance premium)

models for those left behind in poverty. Also, scholarships like the Pell Grant, which is designed to help lower income people pay for a college education, may not help if:

- The parents need the young person to help them out financially by getting a job,

- Are not likely to fill the young with ideas of college through their teenage years.

Poverty Threshold

In 2016, the Department of Health and Human Services established its poverty guidelines for a family of four at $24,300. What's covered? Some examples of federal programs that use the guidelines in determining eligibility are: Health and Human Services programs like Head Start, Low-Income Home Energy Assistance, Food Stamps, Women, Infants and Children (WIC) Supplemental Nutrition Program, legal services for the poor, and the National School Lunch and Breakfast programs.

Imagine how difficult it is for a family of four to live on or near the poverty level (i.e, at or near 2,025/month). The median price for a 2-bedroom apartment in the U.S. currently is $1,300, while 1-bedrooms are at $1,140 (Woo, 2016). Below are some average costs associated with the cost of living in the U.S. in 2014 (Cost of Living in the U.S., 2014):

- Groceries for four people can run from $80 to $160 for one week, depending on what you diet consists of.

- A gallon of milk costs approximately $3.50,

- A loaf of bread is about $2.50,

- Rice is about $1 per pound, and

- Eggs are about $2.00 per dozen.

- Fresh produce costs quite a bit and will fluctuate depending on which fruits and vegetables are in season.

- Gas costs approximately $2.50 per gallon.

- If you are lucky enough to be in an area that has public transportation, you can get a monthly pass for approximately $50-$60 (some areas have discounts for students).

- Clothes are relatively expensive unless you go to a large chain department store (Walmart, etc). A pair of jeans can cost you around $20.

- Electric: $50 to $100 per month, depending on the size of your apartment and if there are energy efficient appliances and lights used. If your heating is electric, it can make your costs up to $150 per month.

- Gas: Not in all apartments. If used for cooking, it will only run from $10 to $15 a month, depending on how much you cook. If used for heating, it can run upwards of $50-$100/month.

According to the U.S. Census Bureau (2015), in 2014, 46.7 million people were poor (14.8 percent of the population), Mississippi had the highest poverty rate in the nation (21.5%), which translates to 3 million people, New Mexico comes in second place with 2.1 million living in poverty (21.3%). The state with the lowest number of people living in poverty was New Hampshire at 9.2%. The report also noted that 21.1% of children (under 18 years of age) were poor (Pew Research Center, 2015).

The Power Elite

In his book The Power Elite, C. Wright Mills argued that there was an elite in America, which is made up of organizations that "dominate industrial societies" (Mills, 2000). Mills believed that these power elite could be found in three key institutions:

- The economy,

- The government, and

- The military.

These elite are in leadership positions within the aforementioned institutions which have more power than at any time in recorded history. The elite get their power through historical authority resulting from bureaucratic organizations that has resulted in centralized decision making.

Running these massive bureaucratic organizations is in the hands of a few people who have a similar background and vision for America. Mills went on to state that these elite came from the upper class, attended Ivy League schools, socialize with one another (e.g., a country club), belong to the same organizations, and there is a high degree of marital relationships that tie theses families together. Using their power and influence, the power elite actively work to get the average American citizen to accept their vision of America.

During the American Civil War, most Confederate soldiers were spurred to fight for "state's rights." To this day many Americans still believe that was the case, but that's just an attempt to glorify the war in order to justify the deaths of 490,309 Confederate soldiers. The state's right to what? To own slaves. The overwhelming majority of Confederate soldiers didn't own slaves, so why should they be so willing to die for something they didn't have and couldn't be taken away from them? Using Mills' perspective, Southern politicians, plantation owners, and military leaders wanted to preserve slavery (i.e., that was there view of the South) and using their power and status were able to convince Southerners that their way of life was in jeopardy of being destroyed by a North that had as its mission to destroy that way of life. But take away the slaves, the average southerner's way of life was no different than the average northerner's way of life. One Confederate soldier summarized it all when he wrote, "a rich man's war and a poor man's fight" (Kolb, 2000).

Today similar arguments can be made about the power elite actively working to get Americans to share their vision of America. In 2011, the Occupy Wall Street protests began with the goal of changing social and economic inequalities. Their slogan, "We are the 99%" comes from the fact that the richest one percent have more money and assets than all other money and assets in the world combined. "Power and privilege is being used to skew the economic system to increase the gap between the richest and the rest," wrote Stephen Lendman (January 20, 2016) for the Centre for Research on Globalization. According to Lendman, Louis Brandeis, a former Supreme Court Justice, once commented "we can have democracy in this country, or we can have great wealth concentrated in the hands of a few, but we cannot have both."

If C. Wright Mills were alive today, my guess is that he would have been there in New York City right along side of the protestors. Who were the protestors? The largest percentage of protestors said they did not identify themselves with either political party, more than one-third had incomes of more than $100,000 per year, 76 percent had Bachelor's degrees and 39 percent had graduate degrees. These people didn't fit the stereotype of your average run of the mill protestor.

Theories of Stratification: Conflict Perspective

Karl Marx, known for the conflict perspective, emphasized class, in which he saw a fundamental split between the owners of capital and the workers who do not own capital. Marx believed maturing of industrial capitalism would increase gap between rich and poor. He believed that the wages of working class could never rise far above subsistence level.

Keeping the powerful on top. The conflict perspective sees inequality as the result of the differential power between the haves and have-nots. People are either the owners (of the means of production), haves, or they are the workers (those that work for the owners of the means of production), have-nots. The haves use their power (which elor's degrees and 39 percent had graduate degrees. These people didn't fit the stereotype of your average run of the mill protestor.

Theories of Stratification: Conflict Perspective

Karl Marx, known for the conflict perspective, emphasized class, in which he saw a fundamental split between the owners of capital and the workers who do not own capital. Marx believed maturing of industrial capitalism would increase gap between rich and poor. He believed that the wages of working class could never rise far above subsistence level.

Keeping the powerful on top. The conflict perspective sees inequality as the result of the differential power between the haves and have-nots. People are either the owners (of the means of production), haves, or they are the workers (those that work for the owners of the means of production), have-nots. The haves use their power (which results from income and assets) to keep the status quo—in other words, they use their power to keep themselves at the top and everyone else at the bottom. The conflict perspective says that the haves are able to do this because their power gives them the ability to shape laws and policies that benefit them.

Max Weber, known for the structural functionalist perspective, had ideas similar to Marx, but two main differences:

- He believed class isn't just about who controls labor and who doesn't. There are other economic differences besides property such as people's skills and credentials, and

- He distinguished another aspect of stratification—status refers to the esteem, or "social honor," given to individuals or groups.

Rewarding the Best People. Functionalism suggests that social stratification and inequality has some positive benefits and outcomes for society. Some statuses are more important than others for the survival of a society. To attract the best qualified (i.e., the best people), there have to be rewards (e.g., money, prestige, power, etc.). Structural functionalism also suggests that people whose job skills make them highly irreplaceable, are more valuable to society and therefore receive more money (which then gives them more status and power); conversely, people who don't have a lot of skills are considered less valuable to society and more easily replaceable—which then leads to lower incomes and less status and power.

Terms, Concepts and Names to Know:

- Social inequality
- Stratification
- Horatio Alger
- Mobility
- Occupy Wall Street
- Absolute poverty measure
- Relative poverty measure
- Noblesse oblige
- Intergenerational mobility
- Intragenerational mobility
- The Maasai

Be Able to Discuss:

- Four systems of stratification
- Different types of societies historically
- Social exclusion
- Poverty threshold
- Power elite
- The conflict perspective as it relates to inequality
- The structural functional perspective as it relates to inequality
- The cycle of poverty
- The class system in the U.S.

References

Bosman, J., & Barbaro, Michael. (2009, July 29). Mayor Defends One-Way Tickets for Homeless. The New York Times. Retrieved from http://cityroom.blogs.nytimes.com/2009/07/29/mayor-defends-one-way-tickets-for-homeless/?_r=0

Czartoryski, A. (2011, May 27). Amazing Hunter-Gatherer Societies Still In Existence. Retrieved April 12, 2016, from http://www.huntercourse.com/blog/2011/05/amazing-hunter-gatherer-societies-still-in-existence/

Ember, C. (2014). Hunter-Gatherers (Foragers), in C. R. Ember, Explaining Human Culture. Human Relations Area Files, http://hraf.yale.edu/hunter-gatherers-foragers. Retrieved April 12, 2016, from http://hraf.yale.edu/resources/faculty/explaining-human-culture/hunter-gatherers-foragers-2/

Henderson, T. (2015, September 18). Poverty Rate Drops in 34 States, DC. Retrieved April 12, 2016, from http://www.pewtrusts.org/en/research-and-analysis/blogs/stateline/2015/09/18/poverty-rate-drops-in-34-states-dc

Kolb, R. (2000). Thin Gray Line: Confederate Veterans in the New South. Retrieved April 12, 2016, from http://vaudc.org/confed_vets.html

Lendman, S. (2016, January 2-). Economy for the One Percent: Unprecedented Global Wealth Disparity. The Richest 1% have More Wealth than the Rest of the World Combined. Retrieved April 12, 2016, from http://www.globalresearch.ca/economy-for-the-one-percent-unprecedented-global-wealth-disparity-the-richest-1-have-more-wealth-than-the-rest-of-the-world-combined/5502320

Mills, C. (2000). The Power Elite. Oxford University Press, Oxford. Reprinted from 1956 edition.

Pierson, P. (2009). Seeds of Conflict. America's Civil War, 22(4), 25. Retrieved April 12, 2016.

Swanson, A. (2015, February 29). The myth and the reality of Donald Trump's business empire. The Washington Post. Retrieved from https://www.washingtonpost.com/news/wonk/wp/2016/02/29/the-myth-and-the-reality-of-donald-trumps-business-empire/

U.S. Census Bureau: Poverty 2014 Highlights. (2015, September 16). Retrieved April 12, 2016, from https://www.census.gov/hhes/www/poverty/about/overview/

Chapter 8: Race & Prejudice

Ethnicity

Ethnic background is simply the cultural heritage of our forefathers. It is those cultural practices of that particular cultural heritage that sets people apart and serves to bond them together. For instance, if you were to go to New York you would find "Little Italy," "Chinatown," or "Little Odessa" (Brighton Beach), and other parts of the city that are often divided geographically by ethnic group. Or, go south to Miami and you will find "Little Havana," or to Chicago and you'd find Chicago's "Polish Village." In Chicago, to maintain their ethnic identity, Polish-Americans will change the name of certain parts of the city to more closely correspond to a Polish town. They do this by adding "owo" to the names of Catholic churches in particular areas of the city. For instance, the area around St. Joseph's Catholic Church is referred to as "Jozefowo" or "Stanislawowo" to refer to the area around St. Stanislaus Kostka church. So, these groups often share special rituals and ceremonies while many still speak the language of the "motherland." Doing so increases the cohesion of these ethnic groups.

Next, for the definition of a minority group we're going to build on our previous definition of ethnic background, which is the shared cultural heritage of our forefathers, and add the following: a peoples who view themselves as targets of collective prejudice and discrimination. The U.S. government generally recognizes four categories of minority groups: African-Americans, Hispanic-Americans, Native-Americans, and Asian Americans. Minority groups feel as if they are singled out for discrimination on the basis of physical or cultural characteristics. These minority groups are not one cohesive unit because to say minority group implies cultural differences, even between the general categories. For instance, African-Americans in the North might not feel they share special bonds with African-Americans in the South, or Puerto Ricans may not feel they share special bonds with Mexican-Americans. These four general categories of minority groups should not be thought of as blending cultural differences. To say someone is Hispanic could mean their cultural heritage is Cuban, or Puerto Rican, or Mexican, or to say someone is Asian American could mean their cultural heritage is Japanese, Chinese, Vietnamese, or Pilipino. Each and every group is unique from the others.

Race refers to physical characteristics that are treated by the community or members of society as signaling distinct cultural characteristics. However, there are no cultural characteristics associated with race; race is not cultural. There are many popular but incorrect beliefs about what the word "race" means. Anthropologists and biologists cannot even agree as to how many "races" there are in the world. More than 70 years ago, a famous anthropologist, Ashley Montagu, concluded there were four "races:"

1. Negroid,

2. Archaic white or Australoid,

3. Caucasoid or white, and

4. Mongoloid.

However, Montagu concluded that all of these "races" were mixed; there was no such thing as a "pure" race (Montagu, 1946). In speaking of Ashley Montagu's work, Alfred Werner, another anthropologist, wrote:

> "Some clever mathematician once computed that, theoretically, every person now alive had one billion ancestors in the generation of the year 1000 A.D.; while each of the latter had a billion in the generation of Jesus Christ. The logical conclusion is simple: there exist no pure races. If mankind preferred to think logically, there would be no need for Professor Montagu's book. Unfortunately, this is not the case" (Werner, 1946).

Hermann Rauschning, a former Nazi Party leader in referring to a meeting he had with Adolf Hitler, reported that Hitler once told him, "I know perfectly well," he said, "just as well as all these tremendously clever intellectuals, that in the scientific sense there is no such thing as race ... with the conception of race, National Socialism will carry its revolution abroad and recast the world." Though debated by historians, there is other evidence to suggest that even Hitler realized the concept of race was flawed. Hitler, in developing his political skills, used several falsifications on which he built his Nazi agenda. The first was that Germany lost World War I because they were "stabbed in the back" by Communists and Jews, and the second, that there was a Jewish race. Ashley Montagu specifically responded to this latter claim of Hitler's by writing, "membership in Jewish culture" is what makes a Jew a Jew. In other words, Montagu acknowledged that Judaism was a religion and not a race.

The term "race" wasn't even first used until 1749 when a French scientist used the term to distinguish species of animals. Slave owners in referring to slaves as they attempted to justify the institution of slavery then applied the term "race." Montagu and others have vehemently argued there is no such thing as race. According to Dr. Andrea Manica of Cambridge University, Africa is "the source of all human genetic diversity" (Manica, 2015). Scientists believe that mankind came out of Africa, though there was a "backflow" of Eurasian peoples back into the horn of Africa about three thousand years ago; in other words, we all the descendants of one initial genome. So, if there is no real meaning to the word "race," why do we still use the term?

The reality to "race" is not that there is such a thing, but rather that people believe there is such a thing, and treat people differently because of those false beliefs. In other words, the reality to "race" is prejudice and discrimination based on a false concept. The reason "race" is a social reality is because people routinely make assumptions about other people they do not even know on the basis of their stereotypical beliefs. And on those assumptions people classify others into "racial" groups, and treat them according to those stereotypical beliefs and assumptions.

Racism is prejudice based on socially significant distinctions. Racists cling to the concept of "race" to justify their superiority to what they deem as inferior minority groups. Harrell (2000) found that racism be found at four different "levels." Those levels are cultural, institutional, individual, and internalized racism. Cultural racism is when the false beliefs and assumptions about a people are widespread among a dominant group and that the dominant group's culture and traditions are superior to that of the minority group (Helms, 1999).

Institutional racism refers to state-sponsored discrimination and unequal treatment of minority groups. As a nation, we don't have to look far to see institutionalized racism. In the U.S. South, laws were passed in the late 1880's that legalized discrimination and the segregation of African-Americans from White Americans. These laws are collectively referred to as the Jim Crow laws. The name Jim Crow came from a minstrel act that featured a song titled, "Jump Jim Crow." Though the laws were said to treat African-Americans as "separate but equal," that was far from the case. Jim Crow laws made legal the segregation of public transportation, public schools, public restrooms, restaurants, drinking fountains, and other aspects of public life. Even the military was segregated. The system was challenged and in a landmark decision, in 1954 the U.S. Supreme Court ruled, in Brown v. Board of Education, that school segregation was illegal under federal law. However, it wasn't until the passing of the Civil Rights Act of 1964, and later the Voting Rights Act of 1965, which officially made institutional racism in the South illegal. Even so, discrimination continued on. In the 2000 state elections, Alabama residents were asked whether they wanted to strike down a state law forbidding interracial marriage. Alabamians did vote to strike down the law by a vote of 60/40. In other words, 40 percent of Alabama voters said they wanted to keep a state law that forbids the marriage of an African-American to a white person.

Individual racism happens when stereotypes, or assumptions, beliefs and behaviors result in discrimination against someone (Henry & Taylor, 2006). Stereotypes are highly associated with prejudice. Generally, individual racism that is tolerated by the larger group, implies **systemic prejudice**. Antiracism refers to any thoughts or behaviors to reduce or eliminate racism.

Finally, internalized racism is defined as "the acceptance, by marginalized racial populations, of the negative societal beliefs and stereotypes about" the minority group to which they belong (Williams & Williams-Morris, 2000; Taylor & Grundy, 1996). In other words, members of a minority group begin to believe they are what they are painted to be by the dominant group. Self-stereotyping occurs when these negative self-beliefs are accepted and internalized (Hogg & Turner, 1987; Simon & Hamilton, 1994).

Dorothy Dandridge was a talented African-American actress & singer in the 1950's. In some of her later movies, she was able to showcase her talents as a singer. She often appeared in some of the nation's finest hotel nightclubs in New York, Miami, Chicago, and Las Vegas. She was even featured on the cover of Life magazine—the first African-American to do so. But while she may have been allowed to sing in these fine hotels, because of racism, she couldn't stay there, nor could she enter through the front door. In fact, it was reported that one hotel drained its swimming pool because she had put her toe in the water. She died at the age of 42. Halle Berry played her in the 1999 movie, "Introducing Dorothy Dandridge."

Rosa Parks (1913-2005) lit the match that finally brought down racial segregation in the South. African-Americans were required by law in Alabama to give up their seat on the bus if was needed by a white person. On December 1, 1955, Ms. Parks was riding in the "colored" back of a Montgomery city bus when she was ordered to give up her seat to a white man because the white section was full. She refused. For this act of civil disobedience, she was arrested and jailed. Her arrest led to the Montgomery bus boycott, which was an important part of the Civil Rights Movement in the U.S. led by the Rev. Martin Luther King, Jr. Though she was not the first African-American to be arrested for refusing to give up their seat on a bus, she will forever be known for her defiance of institutionalized racism in the South.

Racism leads to prejudice and prejudice leads to discrimination. If you'll remember, prejudice is an irrational, rigid, and usually negative attitude that is generalized to an entire group of people. To say that all Polka-Dot people are lazy, or that all Green people are dumb, are generalizations in which the prejudice is obviously negative, but to say that Triangular people make the best doctors, well, that's prejudice, too. It may seem positive, but it's still a generalization. Likewise, if you'll remember, prejudice is the attitude, and **discrimination** is the behavior. Discrimination is being singled out for unfair treatment based on personal, physical, or cultural characteristics. For instance, age, "race," ethnicity, sex, sexual orientation, height, weight, religious beliefs, and anything else that makes one person different from another can lead to discrimination.

Treatment of Minority Groups

There are different ways the dominant group or society can treat minority groups. Imagine we had a continuum and called it "the humane way a dominant group can treat a minority group." At one end of the continuum we would have something called genocide. Genocide is when the dominant group says of the minority group, "we don't like them, we don't need them, let's get rid of them." Genocide is the deliberate destruction of a peoples or culture. Have Americans ever used genocide as way of dealing with minority groups? "Genocide ... also appropriately describes White policies toward Native Americans in the nineteenth century. In 1800 the Native American population was about 600,000; by 1850 it had been reduced to 250,000 through warfare with the U.S. cavalry, disease, and forced relocation ..."(Kidwell, 2010). Native American villages were literally wiped out – men, women, and children murdered by U.S. cavalry. At one point in the 1800's the U.S. and Canadian military deliberately distributed smallpox infected blankets to Native American villages with the intent of killing them off.

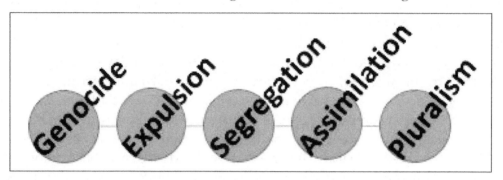

As we move right towards a more humane treatment of minority groups, we have expulsion. This is when the dominant group says of the minority group, "we don't like them, we don't need them, but we'd prefer not to kill them unless they resist." Expulsion is the forced relocation of a peoples or culture. Have Americans ever used expulsion as a way of dealing with minority groups? During the nineteenth and early twentieth century, the United States government forcibly drove and relocated Native Americans from one settlement area to the next. Thousands of Native Americans died as they were forcibly marched to these 'reservations.' Between 1838 and 1839, the U.S. government forcibly removed the Cherokee Nation from all lands east of the Mississippi River. This was part of President Andrew Jackson's Indian removal policy. Of the 15,000 Cherokee that were forced to march 2,200 miles of trails that finally settled them in present-day Oklahoma, more than 4,000 died. This forced expulsion is referred to as the Trail of Tears.

Moving right on our continuum, we have segregation. Segregation is when the dominant group says of the minority group, "we don't like them, but we need their labor, so let's keep them, but separate them from us." Have Americans ever used segregation as a way of dealing with minority groups? The institution of slavery was in place when America declared her independence from Great Britain. By the early 1800's, both Britain and France had banned the slave trade, and the U.S. followed suit. The importation of slaves into the U.S. was formally banned in 1808. This latter act was largely directed at the American South since by 1804 all Northern states had abolished slavery. Vermont has the right to hold its head up high, as it was the first state in the newly independent United States to ban slavery in 1777. Even though the American Civil War brought an end to the practice of slavery in the South, for the next one hundred years segregation was alive and well in the South.

Does segregation still exist? Well, it's illegal, so no, right? Wrong. Though illegal, there are practices that skirt the law and that result in segregation. For instance, residential segregation is the practice of minority groups living in particular areas of a town or city and the dominant group in another part of the town or city. Why? For one, people want to live where they feel comfortable and secure. Often times that means they feel safer living amongst themselves.

There is also the practice of "steering," which is when real estate agencies direct minority groups away from one part of town to another. Imagine a real estate agent who is sponsoring an open house in an affluent part of the city. He or she has built up a reputation among the more affluent people of the city, especially in the more expensive part. The doorbell rings, the agent opens the door, and the smile slowly leaves his or her face as they see a minority couple standing at the threshold. The real estate agent realizes that if he or she sells the house to the minority couple, he or she will lose affluent clients and have their reputation damaged; that's money out of their pocket. So, what can the agent do? Well, flip the situation around. Let's say a couple shows up to look over the house, they're from the dominant group, and are driving an expensive car. The real estate agent will show them the best parts of the house and will talk about all the new appliances, the new roof, or the new water heater. But what if the real estate agent doesn't want a couple to buy the house? What parts of the house will the real estate agent show the couple? The agent might show the couple the 'problem areas' of the house. "The roof is original, so it will probably need to be redone in the next few years. Oh, and the water heater works ok, but it's old and that's something else you'll probably need to replace in the future." Steering is illegal, but trying to prove it in a court of law would be difficult.

Still moving to the right on our continuum to most humane way a dominant group can treat a minority group, we have assimilation. Assimilation is the dominant group saying of the minority group, "we don't like or dislike them particularly, but as long as they will accept our values, beliefs, and behaviors, we'll let them in." At the bottom of the Statue of Liberty, there is a plaque inscribed with a poem written by Emma Lazarus titled "New Colossus." There is one passage in the poem that has become synonymous with Ms. Liberty: "Give me your tired, your poor, your huddled masses yearning to breathe free." Imagine the dominant group saying to these huddled masses, "well, we'll let you in, but we have conditions....you've got to be like us." There is a formula for assimilation: A + B + C = A, where A is the dominant group and B and C are minority groups.

Finally, we've reached the end of our continuum. This last way a dominant group can treat a minority group is called, pluralism. The formula for pluralism is: A + B + C =

A + B + C, where A is the dominant group and B and C are minority groups. This is the dominant group saying to the minority group, "Welcome! We appreciate diversity. To each his own." That may be oversimplifying it, but the bottom line is that the dominant group isn't threatened by the minority group's beliefs and behaviors. Maybe the dominant group realizes just how boring life would be if everyone acted and looked the same. Pluralism implies tolerance and respect between the various groups of a society, acceptance of differences between groups, and prejudice based on group membership is non-existent. Some sociologists will refer to Switzerland as an example of pluralistic society because it is made up of three parts that manage to function well together: there is the southern Italian-speaking part, the northern German-speaking part, and the western French-speaking part. Switzerland has one of the highest standards of living in the world, so they're doing something right. But do they really epitomize pluralism? One way you could look at it is to say they're pretty well all white Europeans. I'm not sure that best characterizes pluralism.

The U.S. has a great deal of cultural diversity today. Each group has a number of characteristics. As I've already written, the U.S. government recognizes four categories of minority groups: African-Americans, Hispanic-Americans, Native-Americans, and Asian Americans. However, remember that within each minority group category there sub-groups. For instance, among Native Americans there are Cherokee, Sioux, Apache, Navajo, and others, each with their own language and customs. It is a mistake to think all Native Americans are the same, as it is for any minority category recognized by the U.S. government.

Gender and Race

Discrimination

The Equal Employment Opportunity Commission reports that the number of times in which employees have filed claims against employers for discriminatory practices have been declining in the past decade. The second most common complaint is racial discrimination followed by sex discrimination and/or sexual harassment. Women of racial or ethnic minorities are already facing discrimination because of their "race" or ethnicity and being female just increases their odds of being discriminated against.

Functions of Stereotypes

Stereotypes can have positive functions:

- They allow people to quickly process new information about an event or person.

- They organize people's past experiences.

- They help people to meaningfully assess differences between individuals and groups.

- They help people to make predictions about other people's behavior.

Dangers of Stereotypes

Stereotypes can lead to distortions of reality for several reasons:

- They cause people to exaggerate differences among groups.

- They lead people to focus selectively on information that agrees with the stereotype and ignore information that disagrees with it.

- They tend to make people see other groups as overly homogenous, even though people can easily see that the groups they belong to are heterogeneous.

Theories on the Development of Prejudice

Prejudice is an attitude whereas discrimination is the behavior. Prejudice involves holding preconceived views about an individual or group. Stereotypical thinking is thinking in inflexible terms. Prejudice is a rigid, irrational generalization and is usually negative. Prejudice as a negative attitude is based on stereotypes. Prejudices are usually negative statements finding fault with the group at which the prejudice is directed though the person may know little or nothing about the group of which they are prejudice. It is easy to be prejudice towards people you don't know. For instance, Aging Watch, is a website setup to inform the public about elder stereotypes, identifies five characterizations of the elderly in the media:

1. elders are portrayed as helpless victims,

2. elders who defy negative stereotypes are presented as bizarre and comical,

3. growing old is equated with inevitable deterioration and decline,

4. elders are demonized as a group, and

5. elders are underrepresented and ignored (Aging Watch, 2010).

While sometimes the elderly are portrayed in the media either as frail and needing help getting off the floor, or as leading an active but well-to-do lifestyle. The reality is somewhere in between for many seniors. While the elderly may be shown as weak and needing help with activities of daily living (e.g, the walk-in tub), younger people are targeted for many products (e.g., car commercials, real estate commercials, and others).

Prejudice can sometimes appear as positive when in fact they're still prejudices because they are based on stereotypes. For instance, if you live in Miami or New York your family might suggest that you go to one of those "Jewish doctors" because they're so smart and make the best doctors," or you would want to hire an Asian for a computer or science related job because the stereotype says their smart and studious.

Prejudice is rigid. Once learned or adopted, prejudice is very difficult to eliminate or often even reduce. Stereotypes are not easily changed because when people encounter instances that disconfirm their stereotypes of a particular group, they tend to assume that those instances are atypical subtypes of the group. For example, Ben stereotypes gay men as being unathletic and not into sports. When he meets Dave, an athletic gay man who loves football, he assumes that Dave is not truly representative of gay people. Or, Frank stereotypes Mexican-American males as heavy drinkers who love their cerveza, but Juan doesn't drink, and therefore he thinks Juan is different. In other words they make exceptions. He or she is "different." They're not like the "rest."

Prejudice is irrational as people's perceptions are influenced by their expectations. For example, Liz has a stereotype of elderly people as mentally unstable. When she sees an elderly woman sitting on a park bench alone, talking out loud, she thinks that the woman is talking to herself because she is unstable. Liz fails to notice that the woman is actually using the hands-free device on her cell phone.

Prejudice is a destructive phenomenon, and it is pervasive because it serves many psychological and social functions. Prejudice allows people to avoid doubt and fear. For example, Rachel's parents came from a working-class background but are now wealthy business owners. Rachel might develop a dislike of the working class because she does not want to be identified with working-class people. She believes such an association would damage her claim to upper-class social status. Prejudice also provides people scapegoats to blame in times of trouble. For Example, Glen blames his unemployment on foreign nationals whom he believes are incompetent but willing to work for low wages.

Prejudice can boost self-esteem. For example, a poor white farmer in the nineteenth-century South could feel better about his own meager existence by insisting on his superiority to African-American slaves. Evolutionary psychologists suggest that prejudice allows people to bond with their own group by contrasting their own groups to outsider groups. For example, most religious and ethnic groups maintain some prejudices against other groups, which help to make their own group seem more special.

Prejudice also legitimizes discrimination because it justifies one group's dominance over another. For example, pseudoscientific arguments about the mental inferiority of African Americans allowed whites to feel justified in owning slaves.

People commonly hold prejudices about individuals of a particular social class, sex, sexual orientation, age, political affiliation, race, or ethnicity (Adorno & Frenkel-Brunswik, 1993). Researchers are interested in knowing what prejudices are held by people, the intensity of those prejudices, and how they were learned or adopted. With this information social policy makers can work to develop programs that will reduce prejudice.

How do we measure prejudice? Imagine coming to this statement on a survey designed to measure prejudice:

I am prejudice. (Circle one)   YES or NO

How would you answer it? Do you suppose anyone would answer, "Yes?" Probably not. Even members of the KKK or Aryan Nation would not think of themselves as prejudice, but as "realistic" or "justified," but not prejudice. Ok, so there might be a problem in trying to measure it directly. There might be a few people who would answer yes, but most people aren't going to think of their attitudes as prejudice. So, we still haven't come on an effective way to measure. How about we use the following to measure prejudice?

I would marry someone of a different race. (Circle one)   YES or NO

Couldn't we say that someone was prejudice if they answered "no?" The logic here being that we select people for dating based on how attractive we find them as individuals and not as members of a group. For instance, John is 22 years old, single, and white. Let's say I lined up 10 single white women in front of him. Should I assume that John would want to date them all of because they were white? Of course not. Some of them may be too old for John. Some may be too short or too tall. Some may have a prettier smile than others. In other words, John will choose to date someone he finds attractive ... and attraction is an individual appeal. For John to say that he would only date someone of the same race, whatever that means, negates the importance of individual attraction. John would literally have to say that all members of a 'race' look alike to him and that all members of that 'race' are not attractive to him. Which is simple nonsense.

Maybe, we could measure prejudice by asking people with which of the following statements they agree. This is an adaptation of the Bogardus Social Distance Scale (Bogardus, 1947), a way of measuring how close or accepting of another group we are. The general idea is that the more prejudice we are, the more distance we want to keep between ourselves and members of the other group. Can you figure out how it works?

Personality Dynamics

A despised and hated outgroup promotes a desire to belong to an ingroup and increases the cohesiveness of the ingroup. Ingroup: those people we think of as being like us in some way (usually based on very superficial characteristics). Outgroup: those people not in our 'ingroup.' The best way to increase the conformity and cohesion of a group is to find an outgroup that can be made a 'threat.'

Adorno's Authoritarian Personality

Theodore Adorno's theory on the authoritarian personality suggests personality needs or deficits that exist within people can precipitate the development of prejudice. Adorno believed that children raised in authoritarian homes where there is an absence of love, harshness of discipline, discussion, and freedom of thought, are often insecure. Further, Adorno suggested that these children, and later as adults, often repressed their hostilities and impulses and projected them to outgroups. Adorno believed that such people tended to be inflexible and have a rigid way of thinking about life; i.e., they found ambiguity difficult to tolerate (Adorno & Frenkel-Brunswik, 1993).

Adorno's research suggested that people who tended to be prejudice against one outgroup, were more likely to be prejudice against other outgroups. There does appear to be research supporting Adorno's theory when looking at the prejudices held against Blacks, gays and lesbians, women, AIDS victims, the homeless, and even fat people (Bierly, 1985; Crandall, 1994).

Social Identity Theory

Social identity theory suggests that people:

1. categorize others - in that we find it useful to put people, ourselves included, into categories,

2. identity with others - in that we associate ourselves with certain groups (our ingroups); and

3. compare - in that we contrast our groups (ingroups) with other groups (outgroups) and we are favorably biased towards our own group.

Cognitive Sources

A cognitive source of prejudice, categorization involves the way that people categorize or organize the world by clustering objects into groups. Essentially, it is easy and "efficient" for people to use stereotypes (a form of categorization) when:

- they don't have a lot of time to think about a present encounter (Kaplan et al., 1993),

- they are preoccupied (Gilbert & Hixon, 1991),

- they are physically and/or emotionally tired (Bodenhausen, 1990),

- they are aroused or upset emotionally (Esses et al., 1993), and

- when they are too young, inexperienced, and egotistical to appreciate diversity (Biernat, 1991).

Race, gender, and sexual orientation are powerful ways of categorizing people. By itself, categorization is not prejudice, but it does provide a foundation for prejudice.

Conformity

Another source for the development and maintenance of prejudice is associated with our desire to conform. If prejudice is socially accepted, if it is the norm of an ingroup, the group to which you identify, members of the group will tend to conform to group norms. Whether out of a need to hate or simply a need to conform, people want to be liked and accepted by other ingroup members (Pettigrew, 1958; Campbell & Pettigrew, 1959; Agnew et al., 1994).

Social Learning Theory

Perhaps the simplest explanation of the development of prejudice centers on social learning theory. Social learning theory suggests that prejudice, just like any other value, belief, or norm, can be learned through the process of socialization. Children raised in families where there is expressed attitudes of prejudice, are likely to themselves have prejudiced attitudes towards outgroups. Likewise, peer relationships are another socializing agent where attitudes of prejudice can be transmitted and learned.

Psychological Interpretations of Prejudice

Displacement and scapegoating are psychological mechanisms associated with prejudice and discrimination. In displacement, feelings of hostility are directed against objects that are not the real origin of anxieties. People **project** anxieties and insecurities onto scapegoats.

Reducing Prejudice

Research shows that prejudice and conflict among groups can be reduced if four conditions are met:

- the groups have equality in terms of legal status, economic opportunity, and political power,

- authorities advocate equal rights,

- the groups have opportunities to interact formally and informally with each other, and

- the groups cooperate to reach a common goal (Allport, 1979).

Communication is another way to reduce prejudice, but it has its strengths and weaknesses. Strengths include persuasive communication refers to any form of communication (written, verbal, visual) specifically intended to influence attitudes. Anti-prejudice communications are successful depending on who is giving the message (i.e., credibility of the communicator). The message must be understood and remembered. Its limitations are that people who receive and understand anti-prejudiced messages tend to be people who are already anti-prejudiced (Farley, 2000), and people who are highly prejudiced tend to not "hear" the messages. Further, prejudiced people tend to not view themselves as prejudiced. Therefore, when the message is heard, it is assumed that it applies to someone else.

In addition to communication, education can help to reduce prejudice, but again like communication, it has its strengths and weaknesses. Strengths include that education is most successful when it causes the least amount of stress and not put people on the defensive. One way to facilitate a positive environment is to make students feel that they are participants in the process (Farley, 2000). But education by itself has difficulties reducing prejudice, in part, because there is some self-selecting taking place in that the most prejudiced people probably do not take the courses designed to increase the understanding of majority/minority issues. On the other hand, required courses in inter-group relations might avoid the problem of self-selection. If a person is prejudiced as a result of social learning, then education (combined with change of environment) may be successful in reducing prejudice.

Allport's Theory of Contact suggests that contact between groups will reduce prejudice if the two groups meet on the basis of equal status and pursue common goals. Intergroup contact appears more effective in reducing prejudice than communication and education. This "contact hypothesis" receives support in public housing projects where people have to live in close proximity to each another. It also receives support in the military. It appears, for example, that school desegregation is associated with decreasing levels of prejudice (Farley, 2000). This is the philosophy behind school busing. The contact has to be more than superficial. Casual contact will have little impact on reducing prejudice.

Communication, education, and intergroup contact are not effective when a prejudiced person suffers from personality problems. Many argue that personality problems are best dealt with through therapy (either individual or group therapy). The goal of therapy is to resolve the problem that caused people to be prejudiced in the first place and convince prejudiced people that prejudice is not an appropriate way of dealing with one's insecurities or problems (Farley, 2000). However, for instance, the authoritarian personality is an example of prejudice that results from personality disorders. People with a prejudice deeply rooted in their personality are more likely to reject self-analysis; and if they don't think they have a problem, they won't seek therapy.

A Final Word on Prejudice

There is no one theory that can exclusively be used to explain the development of prejudice. However, taken together, these many theories presented above, because of their basis in research, suggest some possible explanations. If we know why prejudice attitudes are developed we can implement procedures and public policies to reduce or eliminate them in the future.

Terms, Concepts and People to Know:

- Ethnicity

- Ethnic background

- Minority group

- Race

- Racism

- Cultural racism

- Institutional racism

- Individual racism

- Systemic racism

- Internalized racism

- Dorothy Dandridge

- Rosa Parks

- Segregation

- Genocide

- Expulsion

- Assimilation

- Pluralism

- Prejudice

- Discrimination

- Stereotypes

Be Able to Discuss:

- Personality dynamics and prejudice

- The Trail of Tears

- Adorno's Authoritarian Personality and prejudice

- Allport's Theory of Contact

- Social Identity Theory

- Conformity as a cause of prejudice

- Social Learning Theory and prejudice

References

Aging Watch. (2010, October 30). Elder Stereotypes in Media and Popular Culture. Retrieved April 12, 2016, from http://www.agingwatch.com/?p=439

Adorno, T., & Frenkel-Brunswik, E. (1993). The Authoritarian Personality (Studies in Prejudice). Norton, New York, NY. Originally published in 1951.

Allport, G. W. (1954). The nature of prejudice. Cambridge, MA: Perseus Books

Biernat, M. (1991). Gender stereotypes and the relationship between masculinity and femininity: A developmental analysis. Journal of Personality and Social Psychology, 61, 351-365.

Allport, G. (1979). The nature of prejudice. New York, NY 2011: Basic Books. Originally published in 1954.

Bierly, M. (1985). Prejudice Toward Contemporary Outgroups as a Generalized Attitude. Journal of Applied Social Psychology, 15(2), 189-199.

Bodenhausen, G. V. (1990). Second-guessing the jury: Stereotypic and hindsight biases in perceptions of court cases. Journal of Applied Social Psychology, 20, 1112-1121.

Bogardus, E. S. 1947. "Measurement of Personal-Group Relations," Sociometry, 10: 4: 306–311.

Bryant, W. (2011). Internalized Racism's Association With African American Male Youth's Propensity for Violence. Journal of Black Studies, 42(4), 690-707.

Crandall, C. (1994). Prejudice against fat people: Ideology and self-interest. Journal of Personality and Social Psychology, 66(5), 882-894.

Esses, V. M, Haddock, G., & Zanna, M. (1993). Values, stereotypes, and emotions as determinants of intergroup attitudes. In D. M. Mackie, & D. L. Hamilton (Eds), Affect, Cognition and Stereotyping: Interactive Processes in Group Perception (pp. 137–166). San Diego, CA: Academic Press.

Gilbert, D., & Hixon, J. (1991). The Trouble of Thinking Activation and Application of Stereotypic Beliefs. Journal of Personality and Social Psychology, 60(4), 509-517.

Henry, F., & Tator, C. (2006). The Colour of Democracy: Racism in Canadian Society (3rd). Nelson Press, Toronto, CA.

Hogg, M., & Turner, J. (1987). Intergroup behaviour, self-stereotyping and the salience of social categories. British Journal of Social Psychology, 26(4), 325-340.

Kidwell, C. (2010, September). The Effects of Removal on American Indian Tribes. Retrieved April 10, 2016, from http://nationalhumanitiescenter.org/tserve/nattrans/ntecoindian/essays/indianremoval.htm

Manica, A. (2015, October 8). Ancient genome from Africa sequenced for the first time. Retrieved April 13, 2016, from http://www.cam.ac.uk/research/news/ancient-genome-from-africa-sequenced-for-the-first-time

Montagu, A. (1997). Man's Most Dangerous Myth: The Fallacy of Race. Alta Mira Press, New York, NY. Originally published in 1942.

Simon, B., & Hamilton, D. (1994). Self-stereotyping and social context: The effects of relative in-group size and in-group status. Journal of Personality and Social Psychology, 66(4), 699-711.

U.S. Equal Employment Opportunity Commission. (2016). Enforcement and Litigation Statistics. Retrieved April 12, 2016, from https://www.eeoc.gov/eeoc/statistics/enforcement/index.cfm

Werner, A. (1946, April 1). Book review. Man's Most Dangerous Myth, by M. F. Ashley Montagu. Commentary Magazine. doi:https://www.commentarymagazine.com/articles/mans-most-dangerous-myth-by-m-f-ashley-montagu/

Williams, D., & Williams-Morris, R. (2000). Racism and Mental Health: The African-American Experience. Ethnicity & Health, 5(3/4), 243-268.

Chapter 9: Conformity and Deviance

Conformity

In 2013, approximately fifty-four percent of adult Americans (i.e., 18 years and older) were married according to a Gallop poll (Newport & Wilkie, 2013). Today, twenty-three percent of adult males and seventeen percent of adult females are single. However, 5% of adult Americans say they are not married and don't want to marry (Goodwin et al., 2009). The conformist thing to do is to marry, but not only marry, but to have kids, too. In fact, we tend to deny the term "family" to spouses who have no children. The conformist thing to do in America, and has been since its founding, is for a man and a woman to marry and have kids; to do anything less, is deviant. And in this case, someone who doesn't marry and/or have kids is "broken."

Marital Status and Desire to Get Married in the U.S.	%
Currently married	54
Never married and want to get married	21
Never married and do not want to get married	5
Previously married/Other	20

June 20-24, 2013

GALLUP

Another example would be someone at a party who wasn't drinking. How do we think about people who don't drink? Something must be wrong with them. Maybe they're an alcoholic. What about vegetarians? Society often wants to label them "health nuts." In short, the conformist things to do are to get married, have kids, drink alcohol, and eat meat.

Before we can adequately discuss deviance, we have to define and investigate conformity. Why? Because deviance is simply non-conformity. Nothing more, nothing less. Deviance represents violations of the do's and don'ts of society. Conformity is going with the values and actions of the groups to which we belong. Just because we are expected to conform, doesn't give those overarching groups the right to insist we conform—unless conformity is tied to specific laws that those groups have put in place.

Obedience is the idea of conforming to higher authorities who in theory have the legal right to enforce that obedience. But even then, the question becomes are we obligated to conform to all rules and laws put in place by the conforming majority? A good example of this would be the military. Today, U.S. "military personnel have an obligation and a duty to only obey Lawful orders and indeed have an obligation to disobey Unlawful orders, including orders by the president that do not comply with the UCMJ (Uniform Code of Military Justice, (UCMJ) 809.ART.90 (20). We will return to these topics later in the chapter.

Deviance

What is deviance? Deviance is action or thoughts that differ from the groups to which you belong. While deviance can be found in all groups and cultures, including subcultures, we will be focusing on those thoughts and/or actions that differ from the dominant group.

Every group has standard practices members are expected to adhere to—whether they are thoughts or actions. When members of the group do not adhere to those standards, they are given the label deviant. I use the word "label" because deviance doesn't really exist because it is a social construct—what is considered deviant varies by culture and time. And because it can vary by time and culture, and therefore change, our understanding must also be flexible. For instance, most drugs were perfectly legal in the U.S. until the early part of the last century. Opium and marijuana were made illegal in the 1920's/1930's; opium remains illegal while marijuana laws are shifting towards decriminalization for medicinal use in 19 states

and for recreational use in four states and the District of Columbia. Other examples include prohibition, which made alcohol illegal in 1919 but was then reversed in 1933 to make it legal again, and divorce—with a divorce rate of somewhere around 45% today, it's hardly a deviant thing to do, but 50 years ago, divorce would have been considered highly deviant and earn the divorced woman a label that I dare not repeat in this text.

Deviance also varies by culture. In Japan, not bowing to someone of higher rank or status would be disrespectful and deviant. In Turkey it would be deviant to have your hands in your pocket while talking to another or offering your left hand when attempting to shake someone's hand. In some countries it is deviant to show the sole of your feet to another, or sitting with your legs crossed when conversing with another. Being on time is something else that varies significantly by culture. In South America and some parts of the Middle East, being late is rarely seen as deviant—twenty, thirty minutes or more is considered normal. On the other hand, being even a minute or two late for a meeting in Japan is seen as significantly deviant and disrespectful.

Who are deviants? We are all deviants in one way or another. At some point in our lives we have all broken rules or laws and therefore fall on a continuum of conformity versus deviance. Can you think of things you have done in your life that have violated normative expectations? Have you ever run a stop sign or red light? Worn a hat inside the house? Failed to pay a parking ticket? Cohabitated with someone with whom you had a romantic relationship? Failed to report every dollar you have earned on your tax return? Spoken out against a popular political view? Used an illicit drug? Driven after having too much to drink? These could all be considered deviant actions. On the other hand, does deviance necessarily conflict with the law? Let's go back and look at one action—running a stop sign. At one point in all of our lives we have run a stop sign. If most people have done it, can it still be deviant or is it conformist? Keep in mind that just because a majority of people do something, so that it becomes the new norm, doesn't mean it's legal. Even though I suspect most Americans fail to report every dollar they earned through the year on their income taxes, I doubt the IRS would shrug it off just because it was the conformist thing to do. Even if it is the conformist thing to do it might still be illegal. This is a list of few things, ranging from formal to informal, that are deviant in India. Which do you think are deviant in the U.S.?

1. Cannibalism.

2. Dyeing your hair purple and wearing a spike cut.

3. Shoplifting.

4. Smoking marijuana.

5. Using hallucinogenic drugs or narcotics.

6. Selling illicit drugs.

7. Cheating on an exam.

8. Cheating on your taxes.

9. Seeing someone else cheat and not reporting it.

10. Premarital sex.

11. Gay or lesbian sex.

12. Marrying your sister/brother or first cousin.

13. Having sex with an animal.

14. Watching a pornographic movie.

15. Making a pornographic movie.

16. Extramarital sex.

17. Polygamy.

Deviance Can Lead to Innovation

Emile Durkheim believed that deviance was necessary for society. He felt that deviance would spur innovation and encourage different methods of problem solving. Therefore, he advocated that society be more tolerant to certain types of deviance, not crime, but rather a deviance that allowed people to move away from social norms to some degree that is not a threat to society nor will the action violate laws. Grant (2016) expressed that notion in an article published in Harvard Business Review. He wrote that innovation is essential for business growth and that most people, given some degree of freedom, are capable of being innovative. Grant goes further by actually suggesting that organizations work towards "creating a culture of non-conformity." He proposes the following steps in the process of creating a culture of non-conformity:

- Give employees the freedom to nurture and encourage their imagination.

- Encourage employees to see things from the eyes of a competitor.

- Resist having people work in groups when generating new ideas as group brainstorming tends to encourage conformity to group ideas.

- Once ideas are generated, have "visionaries" evaluate and give feedback on which ideas to pursued. These visionaries should be "other innovators with a track record of spotting winners."

- Value the support and maintenance of programs designed to encourage non-conformity and imagination.

- Perform a delicate balancing act between the important elements of the organization: cohesion between organizational members with "creative dissent."

Dangers of Conformity and Obedience

Like Durkheim, Eric Fromm believed that deviance was necessary for society. Fromm wrote, "Human history began with an act of disobedience," referring to Adam and Eve's disobedience to God. "Man has continued to evolve by acts of disobedience. Not only was his spiritual development possible only because there were men who dared say no to the powers that be in the name of their conscience or their faith, but also his intellectual development was dependent on the capacity for being disobedient to authorities who tried to muzzle new thoughts and to the authority of long established opinions which declared a change to be nonsense" (Fromm, 1981).

The Events of Salem

A classic example of the dangers of deviance can be found in the Salem Witchcraft Trials of 1692. Allegations of witchcraft snowballed from three accusers to seven. Nineteen people were convicted of witchcraft and executed. In Salem Village, in February 1692, Betty Parris, age 9, and her cousin Abigail Williams, age 11, the daughter and niece, respectively, of Reverend Samuel Parris, 12-year-old Ann Putnam, Jr., and Elizabeth Hubbard, began to have fits that the Rev. John Hale said couldn't be caused by epilepsy. The girls screamed, threw things about the room, uttered strange sounds, crawled under furniture, and contorted themselves into peculiar positions. The doctor was called and he could find nothing physically wrong with the girls. Accusations of witchcraft were leveled against Sarah Good, Sarah Osborne, and Tituba (a slave).

In the case of Ann Putnam, she was probably accused because the Putnam and Porter families were feuding and the whole community of Salem had taken sides; it was a way to get even. Sarah Good was a beggar and homeless—things that didn't go well with the ideas of the Protestant work ethic and Calvinist thought, which had affected all non-Catholic Christianity. Sarah Osborne attended church infrequently, which was interpreted as a sign that she rejected Christian beliefs, and it didn't help matters when she married an indentured servant—someone perceived beneath her class position. Tituba was a slave from the Caribbean who would tell stories of black magic to young girls as they sat around a fire at night. These girls accused her of telling them stories of demons, black magic, and witchcraft.

In March of 1692, more townspeople were accused of witchcraft. Martha Corey had stated that she didn't believe the girls' accusations, but this was problematic because she was seen as a devout Christian who attended church regularly as was Rebecca Nurse, also accused. The charges against her and Rebecca Nurse were compounded by the townspeople's belief that if such upstanding people could be witches, then anybody could be a witch.

The trials began on June 2, 1692 with Bridget Bishop's case first. Bishop was described in testimony as not living a Puritan lifestyle, wearing black clothing, which was not allowed by the Puritan faith. She was convicted and sentenced to hang. She was executed by hanging on June 10, 1692. Trials immediately followed for 36 others accused of being witches and in league with the Devil. By the time the trials were ended by the Governor of Massachusetts, 19 people had been found guilty and hanged, despite pleading their innocence. Giles Corey was pressed to death with stones because he would not plead one way or the other.

The Use of Spectral Evidence

During the trials, spectral evidence was allowed in the testimony of those accusers who were "afflicted" by the Devil. Spectral evidence is when someone claims to see an apparition, which could be anything, that was interpreted as the Devil. The apparition was enough to accuse the defendant of voluntarily having allied themselves with the Devil. Only after Cotton Mather, a highly respected minister, argued against the use of spectral evidence, and the governor's own wife was accused of witchcraft, did the trials begin to lessen.

The Aftermath

There are a number of explanations for the events that occurred in Salem between February 1692 and May 1693:

- Old feuds with disputes between the two congregations in Salem, and the new minister, Rev. Samuel Paris, was incapable of acting as a mediator between the two sides;

- Native Americans continued to attack many English settlements up and down the East coast, resulting in a climate of fear;

- A stage for young women to gain the attention they were denied as part of Salem's cultural values;

- A belief that Satan was the cause of instability affecting their community— i.e., natural disasters, Indian attacks on nearby settlements, smallpox;

- Mass hysteria;

- A belief that Satan recruited people to work for him.

In 1695, reacting to Mather's statement, "it were better that one hundred Witches should live, than that one person be put to death for a Witch, which is not a Witch." Doubt began to increase throughout the American colonies, and in particular, Salem. Between 1700 and 1703, the Massachusetts government demanded that the convictions be overturned for three accused witches who not yet been executed. In 1711, 22 people who had been tried, convicted, and executed of witchcraft, had their convictions reversed. Martha Corey was posthumously restored to the Salem church. In December of 1711, the Governor of Massachusetts authorized compensation to the families of the 22 people who had been executed. Today, Salem is known as Danvers, Massachusetts. A number of memorials were erected by the townspeople of Salem who honestly were repentant for their actions.

In the end, one thing stands out: each of the women accused of witchcraft were on the fringes of Salem society. This was enough to make other members of the community suspicious of them because of their unusual actions. For most, their greatest crime was that they were seen as deviant by other members of Salem society. The world is not often kind to those seen as deviant like Martin Luther King, Jesus Christ, Malcolm X, Joan of Arc, Mahatma Ghandi, and others.

The Holocaust

While those labeled deviant can have sanctions directed at them, there are potential dangers to conformity, too. I've already mentioned the military's policy where soldiers are not obligated to follow "unlawful orders." The policy was created largely as a result of the Holocaust. Between 1933 and 1945, Nazi Germany had murdered over six million Jews and five million other civilians. After the war ended, the U.S. , Britain, France, and the Soviet Union convened the Nuremberg Trials in which high-ranking Nazis were put on trial on one or more of four charges, the most famous being crimes against humanity. As Americans listened on their radios every night to the summary of the day's events at the trial, they were astounded to hear one Nazi after another proclaim their innocence to the charges leveled against them. "Nicht Schudig!" (not guilty) they would utter defiantly. When asked why they participated in the mass murder of innocent men, women, and children, they all responded that they were just following orders supposedly issued by Hitler—who had long since committed suicide.

It was determined that even though they were following orders, they had a personal responsibility they failed to exercise. The orders to commit the murders was unlawful, most were found guilty and hanged for their crimes. Nazi Germany represents a good example of the dangers of both conformity and obedience. A significant number of German military personnel carried out atrocities in the name of obedience. By our standards and even those of the time were judged to be unlawful.

Most scholars agree that the Holocaust happened because Germans conformed to Nazi rule. They were motivated because they believed in Hitler's vision of a Greater Germany, or they feared the consequences of not conforming to Nazi doctrine. German citizens stood by and did or said nothing as rights were taken away from Jews one by one. As their Jewish neighbors began to disappear in the dead of night Germans looked the other way.

When one U.S. soldier was asked after the liberation of Buckenwald, a Nazi concentration camp, if the German citizens of the nearby town of Weimar knew what had been going on at the camp, he responded, "They saw the trains going in but no one saw them leave. If they say they didn't know what was happening, they were lying." As Stanley Milgram said, "Behavior that is unthinkable to people acting on their own, may be executed without hesitation when we believe we have legitimately been ordered to do so" (Milgram, 1974).

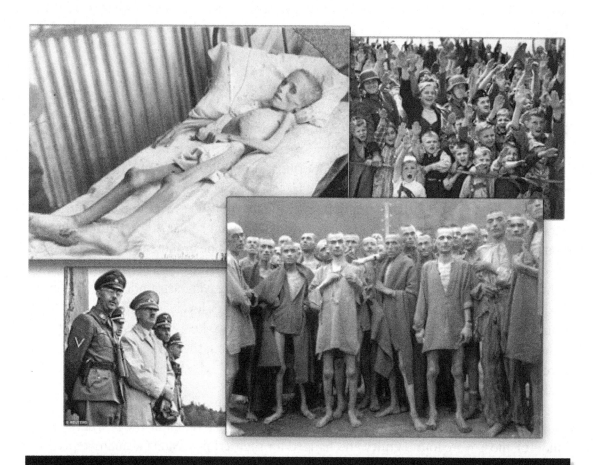

Make the lie big, make it simple, keep saying it, and eventually they will believe it." -Adolf Hitler

The Native American Genocide

One of the dangers of conformity is the idea that unthinkingly go along with the crowd or the public sentiment of the time. What if going along with that public sentiment leads to a call for genocide like what happened in Germany under the Nazis?

> "The proud spirit of the original owners of these vast prairies inherited through centuries of fierce and bloody wars for their possession, lingered last in the bosom of Sitting Bull. With his fall the nobility of the Redskin is extinguished, and what few are left are a pack of whining curs who lick the hand that smites them. The Whites, by law of conquest, by justice of civilization, are masters of the American continent, and the best safety of the frontier settlements will be secured by the total annihilation of the few remaining Indians. Why not annihilation? Their glory has fled, their spirit broken, their manhood effaced; better that they die than live the miserable wretches that they are" (Gitlin, 2011).

The above was taken from an editorial written in the 1890s after the death of Sitting Bull. Who was the author of the editorial? L. Frank Baum. He wrote, "The Wonderful Wizard of Oz." Strange how the author of one of the most beloved children's books ever written would call for the cold-blooded murder of an entire people ... or is it?

Milgram's Research

The world was outraged by the Holocaust as the details were revealed in the post-war months. Americans, listening to daily summaries of the Nuremberg trials on their radios in the evenings, were horrified and angered by the cold-blooded murder of 11,000,000 innocent men, women and children (i.e., Jews, Gypsies, Russian civilians, Russian POWs, people with disabilities, homosexuals, political dissidents, Jehovah's Witnesses, clergy, Masons, union members, communists, and many, many more). Though shocked, we said it could never happen here! But one man, Stanley Milgram, wasn't so sure and decided to experiment on the issue of obedience to authority, and specifically on illegitimate authority.

In 1961, Stanley Milgram, a Yale university professor, published an ad in help wanted column of the local New Haven newspaper. In exchange for $4.50, (a lot of money back then) males who agreed to participate would work on a research project investigating the effects of punishment on learning. They arrived at the laboratory in pairs at a specified time. After drawing straws, one subject would be designated "teacher" and the other as "learner." They were then taken to a room where the "learner" was strapped into a chair and wired to a shock generator in an adjacent room. The researcher explained that the "teacher" would be taken into another room where he would read a list of word pairs over an intercom system.

After reading the word pairs, the teacher would give one word of the word pair and ask the learner for the matching word. When the learner was incorrect, the teacher would administer a shock. At this, and in front of the teacher, the learner would state that he had been diagnosed with a slight heart problem and ask if that would be a problem. Again, in front of the teacher, the researcher stated that while the shocks may be painful, they were not harmful. After that the teacher was taken to the room that housed the shock generator. The shock generator consisted of 30 toggle switches each marked with a corresponding voltage which ranged from 15 volts to 450 volts. The researcher positioned himself behind and to the right of the teacher. The experiment began with the learner getting the first few questions correct, but at some point he answered incorrectly, to which the teacher responded by stating, "That is incorrect. Fifteen volts," before pressing the corresponding switch. The question and answers continued and at some point the teacher could hear the learner verbally reacting to the pain of the shocks. After administering a 150 volt shock, the learner screamed in pain before demanding the experiment be stopped. "I told you I had a heart problem," he yelled. At this point, the teacher stopped and asked the researcher seated behind him for instructions. The researcher replied by reminding the teacher that while the shocks may be painful, they are not dangerous. If there was resistance on the part of the teacher, the researcher would state the following to gain compliance:

- Please continue.

- The experiment demands that you continue.

- You have no choice, you must continue.

The average household voltage is 120 volts and that therefore 450 volts could well be lethal, yet in the end, approximately 2/3s of the teachers took the voltage to 450 volts simply because they were told to do so. In researching differences between the 1/3 that refused to administer voltage past 150 volts (if they made it that far) and the 2/3s that did, Milgram found that the 2/3s were willing to let others assume responsibility for their actions whereas the 1/3 were not.

In later research, Milgram found that the closer the learner was physically to the teacher, the less the maximum amount of voltage the teacher was willing to administer, and the closer the authority figure (i.e., researcher) was to the teacher, the greater the maximum amount of voltage the teacher was willing to administer. Milgram's research shook America—he showed that something that could have never happened here like the Holocaust could in fact happen here. Milgram concluded, "Human nature cannot be counted on to insulate man from brutality at the hands of his fellow man when orders come from what is perceived as a legitimate authority."

Solomon Asch's Conformity Experiment

Solomon Asch was a social psychologist who is known for his research on conformity and for his belief you had to study the whole to understand the part. He wrote: "Most social acts have to be understood in their setting, and lose meaning if isolated. No error in thinking about social facts is more serious than the failure to see their place and function" (Asch, 1952).

In a 1951 experiment, Asch designed an experiment to test whether people would go along with the group even though there was an obviously correct answer; if the subject gave an incorrect answer it would be clear that they did so because of group pressure (i.e., a desire to conform to the group). Asch put eight college-aged males in a room. Seven of the eight had been coached on what they were expected to do. The eighth person was unaware that the other seven men were different than him or had been instructed to answer in specified ways. As the eight men sat around a table, the real subject of the experiment was deliberately sat in the last position around the table. Asch handed the first subject the first subject two placards: one with three lines of different length, labeled A, B, or C, and one with a single line, which Asch called the target line. Asch then proceeded to ask the first subject the following: "Of the three lines, A, B, and C, which is the target line closest to in length?" The seven subjects had been coached to give an incorrect answer. One after the other, each of the seven subjects gave an incorrect answer. Finally, Asch handed the placards to the eighth subject, the real subject of the experiment. Asch repeated his question: "Of the three lines, A, B, and C, which is the target line closest to in length?" Asch found that about one-third of the real subjects went along with the group and gave the incorrect answer though there could have been no doubt that it was the incorrect answer.

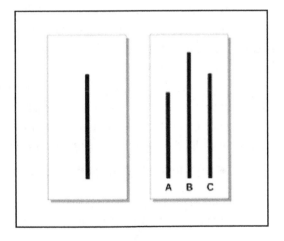

Why did the participants conform even though they must have known they were giving the incorrect answer? When the real subjects were debriefed after the experiment, most said they knew they were giving an incorrect answer but did so to go along with the group out of fear they would be ridiculed by the group. Only a few subjects believed they were giving the correct answer.

Asch concluded that people conform for two main reasons:

- they want to fit in with the group (normative influence),

- they believe the group is better informed than they are (informational influence).

Asch found other factors that influenced group conformity. He found that group size affected conformity. Conformity is decreased as the presence of deviance is increased. This is true up to five acts of deviance. In other words, as the number of people deviate from a group norm increases, the less likely someone will conform to group norms simply for the sake of conforming. "The most robust finding [of Asch's research] is that conformity reaches its full extent with 3-5 persons, with additional members having little effect" (Hogg & Vaughan, 1995). Other factors Asch found that influenced conformity include:

- difficulty of the task (the more difficult the task, the more people will conform largely because of self-doubt),

- the presence of high status group members (i.e., people are more likely to conform with someone they perceive as having high status), and

- answering in private when subjects were allowed to answer in private, conformity decreased dramatically.

Research by Heerdink et al. (2015) wanted to revisit Asch's finding that people will conform because they don't want to stand out and/or be ridiculed. The researchers wanted to investigate whether anger could influence people to conform. So, where Asch found that subjects were more likely to conform when the presence of deviance (i.e., other group members who disagreed with the group) was low, Heerdink et al. found that as the degree of anger increases in the group to deviants, the greater the likelihood the real subject feels rejected. The authors believe that the rejection felt on the part of the subject will lead to anti-conformity unless:

- the deviant or deviants seek forgiveness from the group and seek reacceptance, and

- re-conforming becomes a "strategic behavior aimed at gaining reacceptance from the group."

In summary, we have studied the nature of conformity, the dangers of conformity, and the dangers of deviance. Most importantly, we have studied why people conform. It should be noted that most Germans who actively participated in the genocide of 11 million people, were good Germans. They went to church, they helped their elderly neighbors when needed, they smiled, and they loved their wives and children. You wouldn't know in 1943 by looking at a German you see standing on a street corner holding his young son's hand as they wait to cross the street had only days before put a gun to a women's head and pulled the trigger because she was Jewish. You wouldn't know by looking at him that he would laugh as he looked down at the woman's body after shooting her. You wouldn't know that he had given orders to shoot 100 gypsies in one place, 500 Jews in another, and a few Russian prisoners of war on occasion. You wouldn't know any of that by looking at him. He was a normal German. But it was normal Germans who murdered 11 million people in cold blood. But why shouldn't they just be normal Germans? After all, they were simply obeying orders, conforming, weren't they?

Now that we have a good understanding of conformity, why we conform, the dangers of conformity, and the dangers of deviance, we will move on to crime. Crime is when someone violates formal norms that are prohibited by law and therefore carry sanctions.

Terms, Concepts and Names to Know:

- Deviance

- Conformity

- L. Frank Baum

- The Holocaust

- Spectral evidence

Be Able to Discuss:

- Dangers of conformity

- The Salem witchcraft frenzy

- The Nazi Holocaust

- The Native American Holocaust

- Stanley Milgram's research on conformity to authority

- Solomon Asch's research on conformity

References

Asch, S. (1952). Effects of group pressure on the modification and distortion of judgments. InH. Guetzkow (Ed.), Groups, leadership and men(pp. 177–190). Pittsburgh, PA: CarnegiePress.

Fromm, E. (1981). On Disobedience and Other Essays. Harper & Rowe, NY.

Gitlin, Marty. The Wounded Knee Massacre. 2011. Greenwood Press, Denver, CO.

Goodwin, P., McGill, B., & Chandra, A. (2009). Who Marries and When? Age at First Marriage in the UnitedStates: 2002.National Center for Health Statistics, Centers for Disease Control. Retrieved July 23, 2016 fromhttp://www.cdc.gov/nchs/products/databriefs/db19.htm

Grant, A. (2016). How to Build a Culture of Originality. Harvard Business Review, 94(3), 86-94.

Herding, M., Van Kleef, G., Homan, A., & Fischer, A. (2015). Emotional reactions to deviance in groups: The relation between number of angry reactions, felt rejection, and conformity. Frontiers in Psychology, 6 (June 15).

Hogg, M. & Vaughan, G. Social Psychology (6th ed.). (1995). Pearson, London.

Kumar, 2015. Quora. What are some examples of "deviant" acts? Retrieved July 30, 2016 fromhttps://www.quora.com/Whataresomeexamplesofdeviantacts/answer/AmitKumar100

Milgram, S. (1974). Obedience to Authority. New York: Harper & Row.

Newport, F., & Wilkie, J. Most in U.S. Want Marriage, but Its Importance Has Dropped. Gallop. June 2024,2013.

Chapter 10: Crime

Life is Like a ... Cookie Jar

If our society says that life is like a big cookie jar, and that we should all want cookies, why don't we just take the cookies rather than earning enough money to pay for them? Because we are socialized into believing that stealing is wrong and we are threatened with punishment should we violate that norm.

Social control mechanisms are those things that every culture has to keep people in line. These are techniques to ensure that people are following the norms and not acting in deviant ways. Like conformity, what is criminal varies by time and culture. For example, in the 1920's it was illegal for women to show cleavage when wearing a bathing suit, smoke in public, in some places, to drive a car. All of these things are legal today. On the other hand, in the U.S. the age of consent for marriage was elevated from age 12 in 1880 to age 16 in 1920, but in many parts of the world the age of consent can be less than 10 years of age.

Social control mechanisms also have penalties, sanctions, or rewards attached to them. For instance, if you're waiting your turn orderly in line, what happens if someone cuts to the front of the line? Is there a sanction? Almost certainly someone will either say something to the offender or worse. Social control falls into two types: informal and formal. Informal social control includes the process of socialization and sanctions not imposed by the law whereas formal social control involves the application of sanctions by agents like the law, school administrators, and employers.

So why don't you steal if society says you should want something for various reasons you can't have? For one thing, you have probably been brought up by family members to understand that stealing is wrong. You might have also been taught the same value in church or Sunday school. You've also probably watched enough TV to receive the same message through the media: stealing is wrong. Those are all informal social control mechanisms. On the other hand, as you contemplate robbing your local convenience store, you remember that it's against the law to do so and if you are caught and convicted, you will almost certainly go to prison. The law represents one formal social control mechanism. Another example might include plagiarism. Plagiarism is taking someone's ideas or work and claiming it as your own by not citing the work in papers you might write for school. The punishment for plagiarism can be severe—being dropped from a class with an F or worse. Both of the aforementioned would be examples of formal social control mechanisms. Often formal social control mechanisms are found in society as laws because their violations can pose a threat to society or an institution.

Biology and Crime

Though the United States has a number of active informal and formal social control mechanisms, it has one of the highest crime rates in the world—even higher than Russia and we put more people in prison than any other country (2.2 million) (Ye He Lee, 2015). Countries with fewer informal social control mechanisms, in addition to their formal social control mechanisms, generally have significantly lower crime and incarceration rates. Here in the U.S., we have socialization, religion, and laws (with their attached sanctions), and we have a high crime rate. In societies like China where religion has a relatively minor role in social control, they have a significantly lower crime rate. Is our system broken?

Since the 1800's, there has been a desire to prove there is a link between biology and crime. In the mid-1800's, an Italian physician by the name of Cesare Lombroso (1835 – 1909) decided to investigate that link. Many considered him to be the father of modern criminology. He was an Italian physician who researched criminals in Italian prisoners in the 1870's. After studying inmates in prison, primarily by performing autopsies on the bodies of convicts, Lombroso concluded there were something he referred to as "born" criminals—in other words, criminals were born with physical characteristics, and distinguishable features that separated them from the general population (e.g., low foreheads, prominent jaws, protruding ears, hairiness, emaciated, walked bent over with unusually long arms that dangled at their sides). He referred to a "born" criminal as the atavistic criminal (Lombroso, 1911).

Lombroso had significant methodological problems with this early research. The largest methodological fault was that he had no control group—in other words, he didn't investigate the physical characteristics of the non-institutionalized general population. Had he done so, he would have found the same features or physical characteristics. However, after publishing his initial research, he became world-renowned because he gave the world what they wanted—the ability to look at someone and know if they were a "born" criminal but his conclusions were false because of the methodological flaws in his research.

Sociological Theories on Crime

Emile Durkheim, a structural functionalist, believed that adhering to norms at the expense of tolerating deviance was dysfunctional to society. Deviance is necessary for a society to evolve and grow; adherence to norms with no acceptance of tolerance causes a society to stagnate in a world that is not standing still. The status of women might be a good example here. While women fought for the right to vote since the country's birth, and were thus labeled as deviant and fanatical, it wasn't realized until the passage of the 19th Amendment to the Constitution in 1920. There are some countries in the world where women have virtually no rights and certainly no right to vote—Saudi Arabia and the Vatican. Durkheim argued that deviance is positive function because it can bring about change—and any society, culture, or system must deal with change or risk dying.

Differential Association Theory

Differential association is a theory used to explain crime as developed by a man named Edwin Sutherland (1924). Sutherland believed that people could adopt deviant norms by associating with people who possess deviant norms. A gang member will learn the gang's norms, judged as deviant by the dominant society, once he/she joins the gang. Similar to deviant attachment theory, both theories maintain that deviant norms are learned as a result of association with others who hold those deviant norms. Another example would include deviant families. Research clearly shows that adults who grew up in households where one or both parents spent time in prison have a significantly higher chance of ending up in prison themselves. While it's unlikely that offending parents teach their children how to steal and rob, the research has found that felons tend to commit crime spontaneously and therefore have poor impulse control—something that can easily be taught to children through the socialization process.

Labeling Theory

Labeling theory is used to explain crime by first explaining deviance. The theory suggests that people are labeled based on some action or attitude, which is perceived as deviant. Those labeled as deviant then internalize the attitudes of others and this reinforces the deviance. There are two stages in the labeling process: (1) primary deviance is the initial act that is labeled as deviant by others, and (2) secondary deviance which happens when the individual accepts the deviant label (Becker, 1973).

Labeling theory suggests that people can become victims of a self-fulfilling prophecy. People can come to be seen as deviant because the rest of society puts a deviant label on them. Imagine you are sitting in a class with your car keys on the desk beside you. Just as your professor begins to lecture, they stop as a young man enters the classroom. "Glad to see you, John!" your professor says. "Why don't you have a seat right there," as he/she points to the seat beside you. "Oh, by the way class, I want you to make John feel welcome—he was just released from prison for grand theft auto." Tell me, would you leave your car keys on the desk beside you? If you're like most students, you would quickly move them as far from where John will be sitting as possible. Why? Because you have convinced yourself that "once a car thief, always a car thief." You have labeled him. Do you suppose you are the only one to label him? No. If everyone applies that deviant label to John, he could internalize the label and become the very thing society said he was to begin with even though there's a good chance he wouldn't have become that way if he had not been labeled.

Another example of labeling theory: Mom takes her little four-year-old son Frankie with her to the grocery store. They finish shopping and are on their way home when she realizes she has forgotten something, so she stops at the local convenience store. She and little Frankie go into the store, she gets what she wants, and they get back into the car. Just as she starts to put the key in the ignition, she looks over to see little Frankie with a candy bar in his hand. "Where did you get that?" asks Frankie's mom. Shyly little Frankie answers, "In the store." Furious his mom screams at him, "Why you little thief!" She marches little Frankie back into the store and tells the clerk, "My little thief of a son has something he stole from you that he needs to return." Once home, Frankie's mom calls his father and says, "You'll never guess what your little thief of a son did today." A month later at the family reunion, someone asks about Frankie, "You mean my little thief of a son?" asks Frankie's mom. While an exaggerated example that I hope would never happen, I've tried to illustrate how little Frankie could have a label put on him that might end up contributing to him becoming the very thing his mother said he was all along, a thief.

Strain Theory

Robert K. Merton (1910 – 2003) was an American sociologist who believed that we are all taught by our shared culture to want the same cultural goals, but he argued that some people feel that they don't have access to those goals using legitimate and approved means...such as going to college or experience. Some people he said use inappropriate and illegitimate means to get those toys. Cultural goals are those things that we are taught to be valuable in our culture and to which we should all aspire. For instance, having a nice car, a nice house, and money in the bank, being able to take nice vacations, etc. In other words, we are taught to want these "toys." So, to acquire these "toys," Merton (1932) argued that we used approved and unapproved modes of adaptation. Merton identified five modes of adaptation:

Robert K. Merton

- Conformists who accepted the cultural goals and the institutionalized means to obtain those goals.

- Innovators who accepted the cultural goals but used non-institutionalized means to obtain those goals.

- Ritualists who rejected the cultural goals but accepted the institutionalized means.

- Retreatists who rejected the cultural goals and the institutionalized means to obtain goals.

- Rebel who may or may not accept the cultural goals and who may or may not accept the institutionalized means to obtain the goals.

So, as you a student read this, I'm going to say that you wouldn't be a student unless you wanted the "toys" and by being a student you are using an approved method to acquire them—i.e., getting a degree. Therefore, you would be called a conformist—you want the cultural goals, the "toys," and you are using social approved means to get them, going to school and getting a degree. On the other hand, let's say that you want the "toys," but choose to get them by selling illegal drugs. You would be what Merton called an Innovator—someone who wants the "toys" but chooses to use illegitimate means to get them. Generally, criminals are regarded as innovators.

Social Control Theory (social bond theory)

Based on Travis Hirschi's book Causes of Delinquency (1969), Hirschi (1935 – present) proposed that social bonds play a large part in encouraging conformity through the socialization process and inhibiting deviance—especially criminal deviance. He identified those bonds as:

- **Attachments** (to the group to which the person belongs). So, imagine the costs should we commit a crime. Are there attachments we might lose? Are there friends, family members, co-workers, club associations, etc., that we might risk losing if we were found guilty of committing a crime? Would we ever be able to recreate those attachments or would those relationships be forever changed or dissolved? Hirschi suggests that out of fear of losing some if not all of those bonds (i.e., attachments) keep us in line and from committing crime.

- **Investments** (e.g., financial resources, higher education). What are the social losses we might incur if convicted of a crime? In the United States, felons can be legally discriminated against in the labor market. So, let's say that you graduate with your B.S. from college, but lose your way and commit a crime. Good luck finding a job utilizing your college degree when you get out of prison. The four long years you spent taking notes, listening to lectures, and taking exams is now all for naught—no one will hire you.

- **Involvements** (i.e., being active and engaged in the community). The next component of Hirschi's bond theory is involvements—easily remembered as, "Idle hands are the Devil's workshop." The idea is that the more involved people are in their social world, the less time they have to get into trouble and commit crime. Research shows that crime rates are significantly higher in areas of high unemployment.

- **Beliefs** (i.e., religious values, knowing something is a violation of the law). Beliefs represent the last component in Hirschi's social bond theory. This involves those beliefs held in esteem or in contempt. For most of us, we are taught from the earliest age that stealing is wrong. Considering ourselves as honest is an integral part to our psyche. On the other hand, research has found that when thieves are asked why they stole or robbed from someone they often blame the victim for being "a fool."

Hirschi also believed that the strength of these four elements would contribute to whether they prevented deviance; the stronger the elements, the less likely someone will deviate from social norms and commit crime. While primarily developed to explain juvenile delinquency, Hirschi's theory has been expanded to include crime among all ages.

Techniques of Neutralization

Techniques of neutralization (Gresham Sykes and David Matza, 1957) are statements that allow perpetrators to maintain a relatively high sense of self-esteem while justifying their behavior. These techniques or excuses are made by adults and children who have been caught committing illegal activities. Those techniques include:

- denying responsibility,

- denying harm and injury,

- blaming the victim,

- denouncing authorities, and

- invoking higher principles or authority.

The first technique of neutralization is denial of responsibility. "She made me hit her," or, "yes, I did it, but I'd been drinking," or maybe, "yes, I held up the convenience store, but I needed the money for gas." Next is denial of harm or injury—something akin to 'no harm, no foul.' "Yes, I hit them officer, but they won't be in the hospital long," or, "Yes, I know I broke out her car window with a baseball bat, but that'll be easy to fix." Blaming the victim is next and is where the perpetrator lays the blame for what happened on the victim—it's their fault, not the perpetrator's. "I wouldn't have forced her to have sex with me if she hadn't worn that short dress," or, "She shouldn't have agreed to have dinner with me unless she knew I'd want sex later that evening."

Next is denouncing the authorities, sometimes referred to as condemning the condemners or, two wrongs make a right. In 1995, Timothy McVeigh left a bomb in a rental vehicle parked in front of the Oklahoma City Federal Building. At 9:10 AM, the bomb blew up killing 168 men, women, and children. When asked why he did it, McVeigh said he did it to get even with the federal government for their siege of the Branch Davidian complex in Waco, Texas in 1993. In McVeigh's eyes, he was a hero for bringing the federal government to account. McVeigh was executed for his crimes on June 11, 2001.

Finally, the last technique of neutralization is invoking higher principles or authority. Perpetrators feel greater obligation to a higher authority or moral code. For instance, on May 31, 2009, Scott Roeder murdered Dr. George Tiller, a physician who performed abortions, at his church. When interviewed by the police about his crime, Roeder defended his action claiming a greater authority than man's law—in other words, he had a greater loyalty to God than to man's law.

Confessions

Americans strongly believe that no innocent person would confess to a crime they didn't commit. It's illogical. On the other hand, research suggests that in some cases it is distinctly possible that innocent people confess to crimes they didn't commit. Why would an innocent person confess to a crime they didn't commit? There are number of reasons: mental impairment, coercion, alcohol impairment, threats, and even the use of physical violence. In fact, in about 25% of cases where DNA evidence was used to exonerate people wrongly convicted of a crime, many had pled guilty and/or gave a confession (The Innocence Project, 2015). Yet, Americans hold firm to the almost sacredness of a confession.

Researchers wanted to investigate further the idea of why people would confess to a crime they didn't commit. Using a sample of college students, Kassin and Kiechel

(1996) researched the validity of confession by constructing an experiment where student volunteers would simply take dictation on a standard computer. When they would individually arrive for their appointment with the researcher, a female researcher wearing a white lab coat would meet them. They would then be led to a desk with a desktop computer. The researcher explained that as she read sentences, sometimes fast and sometimes slow, they were expected simply to type what she read. One thing they were clearly told was not under any circumstances to hit the ALT key. She then began reading aloud and the student volunteers took dictation using the computer keyboard. Sometimes she would read at a fast pace, and then sometimes she would slow it down and read at a slow pace.

At some point in during the session the researcher would stop reading and loudly accuse the volunteer of having hit the ALT key. Sixty-nine percent of the sample volunteers confessed to hitting the ALT key after being accused of doing so. In fact, and unbeknownst to the student volunteers, their computer was attached to a computer in another room that monitored keystrokes, and according to the data collected by the other computer, not one student volunteer actually hit the ALT key. Why would 69% of them confess to having hit the ALT key when in fact none did? Even more shocking was that 10% who had confessed to having hit the ALT key, but who really hadn't, were able to show the researcher how their violation had occurred! Granted the greatest risk these college students faced by falsely confessing to a crime was probably the loss of their pay for participating, but it does further the case for asking if we should accept confessions as "proof" of someone's guilt.

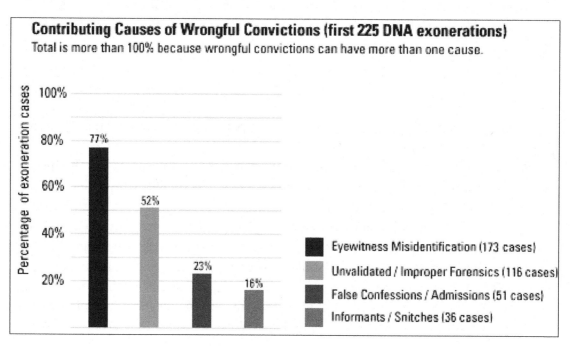

Contributing Causes of Wrongful Convictions (first 225 DNA exonerations)
Total is more than 100% because wrongful convictions can have more than one cause.

Percentage of exoneration cases

- 77% — Eyewitness Misidentification (173 cases)
- 52% — Unvalidated / Improper Forensics (116 cases)
- 23% — False Confessions / Admissions (51 cases)
- 16% — Informants / Snitches (36 cases)

Hate Crimes

Hate crimes are those crimes committed against another person because of their race, religion, sexual orientation, ethnicity, gender, or nationality.

On June 7, 1998, three white men offered to give a ride to James Byrd, 49, a local African-American resident. After driving him out of town, the three men stopped the vehicle and attacked Byrd slashing his throat. Still alive, they chained Byrd by his ankles to the bumper of their truck and dragged him for several miles. According to the autopsy, Byrd died after his head hit a drainage culvert and was severed from his body. The three perpetrators then dumped what remained of Byrd's body in the black cemetery before going to a barbeque. When police investigated the crime scene, they found 75 pieces of Byrd's body along a three-mile stretch of a dirt road. The three men, Shawn Berry, Lawrence Brewer, and John King, were arrested and because Byrd was African-American, charged under hate crime statutes.

All three men who participated in the murder of James Byrd were found guilty— John King and Lawrence Brewer, who were self-avowed racists, were sentenced to death and Shaw Berry to life in prison because the jury couldn't find solid evidence he was in fact a racist though his participation in the murder was without question. John King, arguably the leader of the three men, had multiple racist tattoos—one of an African-American man hanging from a tree, swastikas and other Nazi symbols. In a letter to one of his fellow murderers, King bragged about what they had done by writing, "Regardless of the outcome of this, we have made history. Death before dishonor. Sieg heil!" 'Sieg heil!,' is a Nazi-era term for 'hail victory.'

Another example of a hate crime is that of the murder of a gay man by the name of Matthew Shepard. On October 7, 1998, two men, Russell Henderson and Aaron McKinney, kidnapped Matthew Shepard from a campus bar. They lured him from the bar by telling him they were gay like him. He was driven to the outskirts of Laramie, WY where he was tied to a split-rail fence, beaten and pistol-whipped by Henderson and McKinney. Matthew was found unconscious and suffering from hypothermia by a passing bicyclist the next evening and taken to the hospital where he died from his injuries four days later. As a result of plea deals, both Henderson and McKinney were sentenced to two consecutive life sentences without the possibility of parole.

Matthew Shepard

White Collar Crime

Edwin Sutherland (1883 – 1950) was the first to coin the term "white collar crime." Crimes committed by people in a position of authority and high social status within an organization. Because they are trusted, and have a great deal of autonomy, it is much harder to expose white-collar crime than other types of crime. White-collar crimes include fraud, bankruptcy fraud, bribery, insider trading, embezzlement, computer crime, medical crime, public corruption, identity theft, environmental crime, pension fund crime, RICO (i.e., Racketeer Influenced and Corrupt Organizations Act) crimes, consumer fraud, occupational crime, securities fraud, financial fraud, and forgery. Generally, white-collar crimes can be divided into two types:

- those committed on behalf of the company and

- those committed against the company.

> White collar crime refers to financially motivated nonviolent crime committed by business and governmnet professionals. In criminology it was first defined by sociologist Edwin Sutherland in 1939 as "a crime committed by a person of respectability and high social status in the course of his occupation.

Crimes committed on behalf of the company can include activities like bribes, knowingly selling defective products, or faking test results. Examples of bribery include the case where Johnson and Johnson bribed "government-paid doctors and health officials to promote sales of medical devices in Greece, Poland and Romania" (Goozner, The Fiscal Times, December 13, 2011). Halliburton bribed Nigerian officials to win construction contracts for natural-gas production facilities. And the case of two army corps of engineers who received kickbacks for steering government contracts to a specific contractor.

Probably the best example of knowingly selling a defective product is that of the Ford Pinto. The Ford Pinto, introduced in 1970, was a small four-cylinder car competing with other small cars of the time like the VW Beetle and the Chevrolet Corvair. Unlike the Corvair and the Beetle, the Pinto had the engine in the front but was rear-wheel drive. Cars that have the engine mounted in the front but are rear-wheel drive use a differential to send power to the rear wheels of the vehicle. Differentials have a bolt that can be removed so that lubrication can be changed or added and on the Pinto that was located between the main body of the differential and the fuel tank. At some point, Ford executives began to receive data suggesting that in the case of a rear-end collision, the head of the bolt on the differential would puncture the fuel tank and fuel would be directed upward into the cabin of the car—resulting in serious burn injuries or death to occupants of the vehicle. When this became an issue that Ford executives could no longer ignore, they chose to explore their options with a cost-benefit analysis. Discovered by the federal government in its investigation, the memo, titled, "Benefits and Costs Relating to Fuel Leakage Associated with the Static Rollover Test Portion of FMVSS 208," Ford calculated the costs of fixing versus the costs of not fixing the design flaw. Ford calculated to recall the vehicles and fix the problem would cost approximately $138 million. To not fix the problem and simply pay out on wrongful death and injury lawsuits would cost the company an estimated $50 million. Ford chose not to recall and fix the vehicles.

Another type of white-collar crime is faking test results. In 2000, a husband and wife team was seeking FDA approval for a new cancer drug they were developing. The company they owned jointly had gone public and they believed that with successful drug trials and approval

Annie Dookhan tested more than 60,000 drug samples involving 34,000 defendants during her 9 years in the lab. She admitted identifying narcotics "by looking at them". It's estimated that dozens of drug defendants already back on the street because of her misconduct. Dookhan also lied about having a master's degree in chemistry.

by the FDA the stock evaluation would skyrocket and they would make millions of dollars. However, the FDA investigation revealed that the husband and wife had faked test results in their bid to gain approval from the FDA. Imagine what would have happened had the FDA approved the drug based on false test results—some cancer patients would have received a worthless drug that did nothing to help them win their battle against cancer and remain alive.

Research by Carlson and Chaiken (1987) found that white collar criminals were:

- less likely to have their cases dismissed (40% vs. 26%),

- not to have to put up bail (13% vs. 37%),

- be given probation (54% vs. 40%), and

- be given a shorter sentence (29 months vs. 50 months).

So, there seems to be a clear moral: if you're going to commit crime, commit white-collar crime. Maybe that's not the message we should be sending.

Crimes committed against the company typically include crimes like theft, sabotage, and embezzlement. According to the FBI, employee theft is the fastest growing crime in America, and in 2010, the average amount stolen by employees was $640 (National Retail Federation, 2010).

Sabotage

Sabotage is another type of crime committed against the company, but more often than not people think of sabotage as something that occurs during wartime: the enemy agents sneak into a factory, plant a bomb, and flea before being caught. And while wartime sabotage has happened in the U.S., one of the most common arenas for sabotage today is the workplace. Disgruntled workers have the capacity to throw the proverbial "monkey wrench" into the works because of grievances they may hold. Have you ever had the misfortune of watching a fellow employee being laid off from their job? If so, you probably remember that from the time they were informed of their lay-off until they walked out the door they were escorted by security. Employers are afraid that newly fired or laid-off employees will want to 'get back' at them through some act of sabotage.

Embezzlement

Embezzlement is theft of money from a company. According to recent research (Marquet Report on Embezzlement, 2012) increased 11% since 2011. Most likely hit by embezzlers are financial institutions and surprisingly, not-for-profit organizations (including churches).

The most common method for embezzlement is forgery or illegally writing a company check. There are four factors associated with embezzlement:

- embezzlers tend to be in a position of trust in the company—i.e., they have a large degree of autonomy with no one watching over their shoulders,

- they tend to have financial problems (with gambling losses being the most common),

- they tend to have the technical knowledge to pull off the embezzlement without getting caught

- and they tend to rationalize their theft—i.e., they intend to pay the money back.

Federal Crimes

White collar crime appears to be increasing. In a 2011 report, the FBI released data to show an increase in the number of corporate fraud cases being investigated. Between 2007 and 2011, there was an increase in corporate fraud investigations from 529 to 726.

On the other hand, insurance fraud investigations by the federal government seem to be falling. The FBI reported that the Coalition Against Insurance Fraud estimated that the cost of insurance fraud could be as high as 80 billion dollars per year (FBI, 2011).

Types of insurance fraud investigated by the FBI include:

- diverting insurance premiums (i.e., insurance agents embezzling insurance premiums,

- misuse of customer insurance premiums for operational use of the company,

- workers's Compensation, fraud,

- disaster fraud (i.e., the fraudulent filing of a claim),

- staged auto accidents, and

- property insurance fraud (i.e., when someone files an insurance claim for an amount greater than the amount of damage warrants).

Terms, Concepts and Names to Know:

- Norms

- Social control mechanisms

- Sanctions

- Plagiarism

- Atavistic criminal

- 19th Amendment to the Constitution

- Timothy McVeigh

- James Byrd

- Matthew Shepard

- Edwin Sutherland

Be Able to Discuss:

- The link, if any, between crime and biology

- Who was Cesare Lombardo and what did he contribute to criminology?

- Explain the differential association theory of crime

- The social bond theory

- Labeling theory

- Merton's strain theory

- The techniques of neutralization

- Explain the research on confessions

References

Albrecht, A. (1910). Cesare Lombroso. Journal of Criminal Law and Criminology I (2): 71.

Becker, H. (1973). Outsiders: Studies in the Sociology of Deviance. New York: The Free Press.

Carlson, K., & Chaiken, J. (1987). White Collar Crime. Bureau of Justice Statistics Special Report, Washington, D.C., Government Printing Office.

Federal Bureau of Investigation. Financial Crimes Report to the Public, Fiscal Years 2010- 2011. Retrieved May 11, 2016 from: https://www.fbi.gov/stats-services/publications/financial-crimes- report-2010- 2011

Gartner, Rosemary (September-October 2004). Book Review. Canadian Journal of Sociology Online. Retrieved 10 March 2016.

Gresham M. Sykes and David Matza. (1957). Techniques of Neutralization: A Theory of Delinquency. American Sociological Review, 22(6), 664-670.

Goozner, M. (2011). The Ten Largest Global Business Corruption Cases. The Fiscal Times. December 13, 2011. Retrieved MAY 11, 2016.

Hirschi, T. (1969). Causes of Delinquency. Transaction Publishers. (Reprinted December 24, 2001).

Hirschi, T. (2001). Causes of Delinquency: Criminology and Criminal Justice Research. Transaction Publishers, Piscataway, New Jersey. Original edition published in 1969.

Kassin, S., & Kiechel, K. (1996). The Social Psychology of False Confessions: Compli- ance, Internalization, and Confabulation. American Psychological Review, 7(3), 124-129.

Lombroso, C. (1911). Crime: Its Causes and Remedies. Boston, Little & Brown Co. Marquet, C. (2014). A WHITE COLLAR FRAUD STUDY OF MAJOR EMBEZZLE-MENT CASES ACTIVE IN THE U.S. IN 2013. THE 2013 MARQUET REPORT ON EMBEZZLEMENT. December 19, 2014. Retrieved May 11, 2016.

Merton, Robert K. (1932). "Social Structure and Anomie". American Sociological Review 3 (5): 672–682.
Rafter, Nicole Hahn (2004). Criminal Woman. Durham, NC: Duke University Press.

Sutherland, Edwin H. (1924) Principles of Criminology, Chicago: University of Chicago Press.

Ye He Lee, M. (2015). Yes, U.S. locks people up at a higher rate than any other country. Washington Post, July 7, 2015. Retrieved July 23, 2016 from https://www.washington-post.com/news/fact-checker/wp/2015/07/07/yes-u- s-locks- people-up- at-a- higher-rate-than-any- other-country/

Chapter 11: Religion

Most likely at some point in your life, maybe when you were younger, your parents took you to church. Maybe you still attend church. Why do people attend church? Why do parents often want to see their children raised in a particular church? Who or what is God? What are the differences between the major world religions? Why do some people worship the God of Abraham (e.g., Christians, Jews, and Moslems), while others worship Buddha or other gods and goddesses (e.g., Hinduism). Overall, is religion a good thing or bad thing for man? These are some of the issues we will be studying in this module.

So let's begin by coming up with a general statement on the definition of religion. Religion is a shared system of beliefs that explain how and why man and God exists, provides some meaning or purpose to life, structure that includes norms and beliefs, and offers an explanation as to why the world is as it is, and serves as a means to integrate members and increase cohesiveness. In the movie "Signs" with Mel Gibson, a news commentator talks about people flocking to churches, temples, and Mosques because of an imminent alien invasion. So, another aspect of religion is that in times of crisis it provides comfort and hope.

Sociology and Religion

An important point to remember is that sociology as a discipline is not interested in advocating for or against religious beliefs or any religion. Sociology studies religion objectively, without offering subjective judgments about which religion is right or wrong or the existence of a heaven or hell. Sociology is interested in finding out why people believe as they do, how those beliefs shape their lives, and how religion serves both as an organizational unit and social bond.

Marx and Religion

Marx believed that religion served to mollify the masses by holding out an afterlife as a reward for good and obedient behavior. Marx is famous for his quote about religion being the "opiate of the people," but few realize he was specifically addressing the issue of slavery in the U.S. He believed that slave owners deliberately indoctrinated slaves into religion, specifically Christianity, so they would accept their second class position in society (if you can call slavery a second class position). To run away would be a violation of the eighth commandment: thou shalt not steal. To rise up in the middle of the night and slay their master, would be a violation of the sixth commandment: Thou shalt not kill. To want what your master had, would be a violation of the tenth commandment: thou shalt not covet what thy neighbor has.

In Marx's view, acceptance of religion was false consciousness - accepting an ideology that is contrary to a person's best interests. Likewise, the Biblical saying, "the meek shall inherit the earth" also tells people not to challenge the status quo and they will be rewarded in an afterlife. Whether slaves or the proletariat, Marx believed that religion was used in a way so that those under them would resign themselves to their miserable conditions in exchange for a heavenly reward.

Durkheim and Commonalities of Religions

If you'll remember, Émile Durkheim was the first to use scientific principles in the relatively new science of sociology. He used those principles to study people and groups. Durkheim was the first to advocate that the social world affected people's behaviors.

Durkheim believed there were five commonalities of religions. They include beliefs, the sacred and profane, rituals and ceremonies, moral communities, and personal experience.

- **Beliefs**. Beliefs explain what we are unable to explain and understand. For instance, what does it mean to say that space is infinite? There is nothing in our lives that is infinite and therefore we have problems grasping the concept. However, religion responds to that by saying that God, who is eternal, knows the answer and mankind need not concern themselves with the question.

- **The sacred and profane**. The sacred are things central to the religion and are to be revered and are above the corruption of mortal life. For instance, for Catholics things like Communion chalices and plates, statues, and holy water would be examples of things sacred. Likewise, prayer beads used by Catholics, Buddhists, and Moslems would be examples of things sacred. Things that are part of our normal daily life represent the profane. Things like driving to work, watching TV, selfishness, or adultery would all be examples of things profane. The idea is that we need to rise above those mundane parts of our daily lives to those things deemed sacred.

- **Rituals and Ceremonies**. These are behaviors exhibited by members of religious organizations that are routinized. This routinization allows for the reinforcement of religious beliefs through rituals or ceremonies. Examples include baptism, confirmation, prayer, chants, crossing oneself after dipping their fingers in holy water.

- **Moral Communities**. When people who hold similar beliefs and values come together and form bonds, these are called moral communities.

- **Personal Experience**. The personal experience a religious person has might give purpose and meaning to their life.

Max Weber and Religion

Building on Calvinist beliefs, Weber coined the term "Protestant work ethic." Weber described the ethic as a dedication to hard work because it was thought to please God. Calvinism espoused the belief that there were elects who were blessed by God and that success was an earmark that one was an elect. Though success was seen as pleasing to God, frugality was expected and it was frowned upon for people to flaunt their success or to spend money lavishly. Because Calvinist thought idealized simplicity and living a plain life, being successful but not living a life of opulence was seen as a measure of a person's devotion to God. In turn God would reward those who were successful but led simple and frugal lives.

Durkheim believed that capitalism evolved from the religious seeking wealth as a symbol of work and therefore pleasing to God. Eventually those who had money, but had always tried to be frugal with it, began to spend more on themselves. This was contrary to Calvinist thought and probably why religious doctrine and capitalism separated, yet many consider capitalism to be a religion in itself. Weber believed that the idea of rationally pursuing economic was the essence of capitalism, but without religion to constrain those activites by advocating the wealthy seek simple and frugal lives, rationality became the norm: make as much money as you can with the least effort.

Unlike Marx who had predicted all societies would become capitalistic before the inevitable classless society would be formed, Durkheim believed that some religions were just not suited for capitalism. Weber believed that while the Protestant work ethic was ideally suited to industrialism, some Asian religions were not. This was largely because Asian religions stressed community and a sense of belongingness, whereas Protestantism essentially believed that man approached God as an individual accountable for his or her actions.

Weber noted that Capitalism was not a necessary or inevitable thing. For instance, in China, where the main religion was Confucianism, held that the pursuit of wealth was wrong. In studying in India, Weber noted a fatalism that led to their acceptance of the caste system. Hinduism, and to a lesser degree Buddhism, held that Nirvana came from karma resulting from good deeds and not making money at the expense of others. Hindus and Buddhists both believed that there was no heaven that awaited the common people who had accepted their class position.

The Functionalist Perspective on Religion

The functionalist perspective on religion argues that religion fulfills a number of positive roles for society. Those functions are:

- For some people, religion provides meaning and purpose to people which are two things that humans desire in order to live a good and content life.

- Religion also provides emotional comfort. At the funeral of small child, the minister, priest, or rabbi might say that "God has a plan and that's why he took little Jimmy or Jane," or he/she might say, "Little Johnny or Jane has been called home to Jesus." These kinds of statements or explanations can offer great comfort to grieving religious people.

- Social solidarity is something else that religion supplies. With the use of rituals and ceremonies, religions bond members together and form a community of believers.

- Religion also provides rules for daily living. It tells us what we should or shouldn't do. For instance, one study found that those who attend church regularly are less likely to have problems with alcohol, drugs, and cigarettes than are non-church goers (Gillum, 2005; Wallace et al., 2007; and Newport et al., 2012).

- Religion also acts as a social control mechanism. People obey laws because they fear God. And some states enforce religious laws, such as no alcohol sold on Sunday or before a certain time of day.

- Social change can also be the result

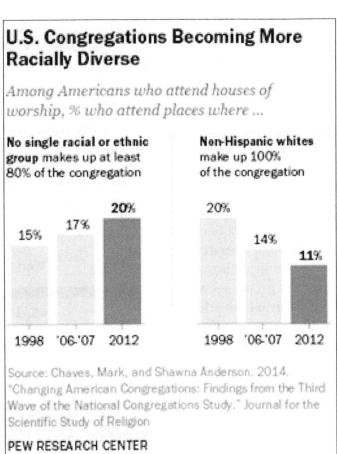

U.S. Congregations Becoming More Racially Diverse

Among Americans who attend houses of worship, % who attend places where ...

No single racial or ethnic group makes up at least 80% of the congregation

15% (1998)
17% ('06-'07)
20% (2012)

Non-Hispanic whites make up 100% of the congregation

20% (1998)
14% ('06-'07)
11% (2012)

Source: Chaves, Mark, and Shawna Anderson. 2014. "Changing American Congregations: Findings from the Third Wave of the National Congregations Study." Journal for the Scientific Study of Religion

PEW RESEARCH CENTER

of religious doctrine. For instance, liberal churches supported the right for women to vote, some churches supported the civil rights movement, and some religions advocate for the poor trying to change social policy to benefit those affected.

Negative Features of Religion

Objectively, religion has both positive and negative features. Throughout history, man has fought man in the name of God. Each side believes that God is on their side and not the other's. Even today as terrorism is a fact of life, Al Qaeda, ISIS, or Boko Haram, invoke the name of God (Allah) as they commit brutal acts of terrorism. In a scene from the remake of Flight of the Phoenix, one of the characters says of religion, "Spirituality is not a religion. Religion divides people."

Religion is highly associated with intolerance towards others who are different from them in some way or have different religious beliefs. In 1616 the astronomer Galileo was tried by the Catholic Church on charges of heresy because of his belief that the sun was the center of the universe and not the earth as taught by the church. For seventeen years Galileo backed away from the argument and chose not to speak of his beliefs, but then in 1633, again he was brought before the church on the same charges. He was found guilty and sentenced to house arrest where he remained for the rest of his life.

Another negative feature of religion is that it segregates people —even today. Martin Luther King Jr. referred to 11a.m. on Sunday morning as the most segregated hour in America. While racial segregation within religious bodies is still high, churches have become more diverse in recent years

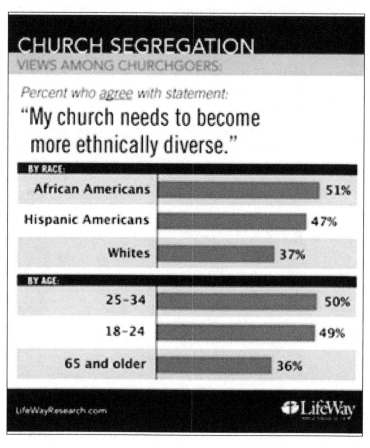

(Lipka, 2014). Today about 80% of Americans still attend religious services where 80% of church members represent one dominant racial or ethnic group, whereas the other 20% of Americans attend religious services where there is no one single and dominant racial or ethnic group. This represents a growing trend since 1998 where only 15% of Americans worshiped at a church where there was no one single dominant ethnic group to 17% in 1998 and, as stated above, to 20% as it is today (ibid).

In a national phone survey done by LifeWay (Smietana, 2015), respondents indicated that they agreed with the statement, "Churches in America are too segregated." Researchers also reported that 82% of those respondents interviewed said that overall social diversity was a good thing, 74% said the country has made significant progress on improving race relations in the country, but 81% said that the U.S. still has a long way to go before we reach racial parity.

When researchers questioned only Protestant ministers, the picture was different. Of those pastors interviewed, almost 90% stated that "racial reconciliation is mandated by the gospels." Further, pastors reported that more than two-thirds their church was involved in racial reconciliation.

Researchers concluded that though the majority of churches are slowly moving toward reconciliation, and most ministers are doing their part to help that movement, however a sizeable percentage of American Protestants felt that enough was or had been done already towards that movement. So, while things are changing, Rev. King was right, 11 a.m. Sunday morning is still the most segregated time in America.

In an article published by Dr. Clay Routledge in Psychology Today (2009), Dr. Routledge points out an additional three negative features of religion.

- First, religion can cause a person distress. The idea is that when confronted with scientific research that contradicts religious teachings, such as the earth was created in six days, it can create cognitive dissonance in someone who is religious. Cognitive dissonance is a state of discomfort, and it exists when two sets of values, or information, or behaviors are in opposition to one another. Routledge believes that this kind of cognitive dissonance can lead to a negative emotion about the information that contradicts what they want to believe.

- Second, that religion can direct people away from conventional (and modern) medical treatment. Some religions advocate against medical treatment. These religions believe that if healing is to be done, it will be done by God, and if a person dies for lack of treatment it surely must be God's will. Routledge and some of his colleagues conducted an experiment where they created two scenarios related to faith healing versus modern medical treatment. They found that those subjects identifying themselves as religious fundamentalists were far more likely to choose faith over medicine, whether that treatment was for themselves or others. This would explain why we still read in the newspapers from time to time about children dying because their parents refused to seek medical treatment for them.

- Third, religion can be a type of avoidant coping. Routledge defines avoidant coping as when people "engage in efforts to avoid dealing with unpleasant situations."

Positive Features of Religion

Research on religion and health find that religious people on average are in better physical and mental health (on self-report surveys) than non-religious people. Other research found that death rates were lower among the religious as opposed to non-religious and the authors suggested this was most likely the result of lower stress levels (Kark et al., 1996). Further, one study found that church attendance increases life expectancy. Researchers reported that it raised life expectancy by an average of eight years for study participants (Hummer et al. 1999).

Also, religion acts as a social control mechanism. While religion promotes cohesiveness, by default it condemns deviance. Religion also provides a social control mechanism in addition to the law. Why shouldn't you steal? Because religion and the law both say it is wrong—and God or man will punish you. Finally, religion can provide answers that science cannot to four of the most central questions to man's existence:

- The existence of God. Science can neither prove nor disprove the existence of God.

- The purpose or meaning of life. Science is unable to offer anything in the way of a meaning or purpose to life.

- An afterlife. Science can neither prove nor disprove the existence of an afterlife.

- Morality. As one author put it, "...that science cannot even prove whether loving your family and neighbor is morally superior to hurting or killing them" (Henslin, 2016).

Types of Religious Organizations

Churches are over-arching organizations that are usually supported by the state, merge religious doctrine with state policy, expect subservience by the masses, and tolerates no competition. In the past, Catholicism served as a good example of a church, but this has changed as more religious denominations compete for membership.

Denominations are basically sub-groups that exist within a specific religion. For instance, Christianity constitutes a religion but Christian denominations include Methodist, Lutheran, Southern Baptist, etc. Islam constitutes a religion but Islamic denominations include Sunni (the majority), Shia, and Khawarij. Generally, denominations have resulted from schisms or differences in the interpretation of religious doctrine.

Christian denominations can trace their roots to the Protestant Reformation that occurred during the 1500's. At the same time King Henry VIII was setting himself up as head of the Church of England, Martin Luther, a German priest, was challenging the Catholic Church's authority and teachings. The result was the birth of the Protestant Church and then Lutheranism, Reformed Protestant, Anabaptist, and Anglican. Today there are more than 217 Christian denominations.

Ecclesia are churches that are formally allied with the state. For instance, Islam would be both a church and ecclesia in Iran. Likewise, the Church of England is an ecclesia because it is the official state religion of England.

Sects are religious groups that have recently broken away from the parent denomination. Most denominations started as sects. An example of a modern sect would be the Amish. The Amish reject much of modern life in America and isolate themselves physically from non-believers whom they refer to as "English." The Amish are a sect based on traditional beliefs founded by Jakob Ammann. Bringing with them their

The Protestant Reformation

On October 31, 1517 a Catholic priest named Martin Luther posted his Ninety-Five Theses on the door of Schosskirch (Castle Church) in Wittenberg, Germany.

His theses essentially contained grievances leveled at the Catholic Church. This began a schism in the Catholic Church that led to the formation of the Protestant religion. In 1521, King Henry VIII of England decided to annul his marriage to his legal wife, Catherine of Aragon. However the Pope denied the King's request. Angered, Henry decided to break away from the Catholic Church and set himself up as the head of the newly formed Church of England. The Church of England was a hybrid Protestant religion taking practices and beliefs from both Lutheranism and Calvinism. Protestantism, as comprised of Lutheranism, Calvinism and the Church of England became the starting point for every Christian denomination in existence today.

Half of 'nones' left childhood faith over lack of belief, one-in-five cite dislike of organized religion

Reasons for disaffiliating among those who were raised in a religion and are currently ...

	NET Unaffiliated %	Atheist %	Agnostic %	Nothing in particular %
Don't believe	49	82	63	37
Disenchanted/don't believe	36	71	46	25
Not interested in/don't need religion	7	3	8	7
Views evolved	7	7	12	5
Went through a crisis of faith	1	2	1	1
Dislike organized religion	20	10	19	22
Anti-institutional religion	15	2	17	16
Religion focuses on power/politics	4	5	1	6
Religion causes conflict	1	3	2	1
Religiously unsure/undecided	18	5	12	22
Unaffiliated but religious	7	1	1	10
Seeking/open-minded	6	3	5	7
Spiritual but not religious	3	2	4	3
Uncertain about beliefs	2	0	4	2
Inactive believer	10	0	3	14
Non-practicing	8	0	2	11
Too busy	2	0	1	3
Other	<1	0	<1	1
Unclear/no answer	6	3	7	6

Note: Excludes those who said they had been misclassified and were still affiliated with a religion. Figures do not sum to 100% or to subtotals indicated because multiple responses were permitted.
Source: 2014 U.S. Religious Landscape Study recontact survey conducted March 17-May 6, 2015. QC13.
"Choosing a New Church or House of Worship"

PEW RESEARCH CENTER

traditional values, their Swiss-German language, strict adherence to tradition, their plain and simple way of life, and separation from non-believers (referred to as "English"), settled in parts of Pennsylvania and Indiana. The Amish reject modern technology as it relates to telephones, automobiles, and electricity. Amish men have complete say in the affairs of the community and women's roles are reserved for homemaking and helping with chores. The Amish abide by a strict code of behavior, and if violated, they are shunned or excommunicated.

Cults are usually sects that have either split away from the parent denomination or constitute an entirely new religion. Usually smaller than sects in members, cults are characterized by:

- being viewed as deviant,

- having a charismatic leader,

- having a doctrine that is radically different from other sects and denominations, and

- living a way of life significantly different from mainstream society.

We'll go into greater about the specifics and characteristics of cults in a later chapter.

Cult leader Jim Jones and hundreds of his People's Temple followers commit mass suicide in Guyana. Jones, an American pastor, led his followers to South America in 1977 and set up an agricultural commune called Jonestown in remote northwestern Guyana. On November 14, 1978, U.S. Congressman Leo Ryan arrived in Jonestown with a group of journalists to investigate the commune. Four days later, Jones—who some Temple members believed was God—ordered Ryan and his companions ambushed and killed at the airstrip as they attempted to leave. The congressman and four others were murdered. Later that evening, Jones directed his followers in a mass suicide. Hundreds drank a cyanide-laced fruit-flavored concoction in a clearing in Jonestown. Those who tried to escape were chased down by Jones's lieutenants and shot. The final toll was 913 dead, including 276 children. Jones died of a gunshot wound in the head, possibly self-inflicted.

World Religions

Christianity

It's the world's largest religion with approximately 2.5 billion followers. Approximately 70% of Americans self-identify as Christian—a percentage down from 78% in 2007 (Pew Research Center, May 7, 2015) Christianity, an Abrahamic religion and monotheistic, began as a sect with Jesus as the leader.

Islam

Islam is the world's second largest religion with approximately 1.5 billion followers. Also an Abrahamic and monotheistic religion, Islam is centered on the Prophet Muhammad (born around 570 C.E.) and holy writings are recorded in the Koran. Islam is the fastest growing religion in the world today.

Hinduism

Primarily found in India and has almost 900 million adherents. It is the world's third largest religion. Hindus adhere to the principle of dharma—laws that dictate what is right and wrong. Hinduism is based on the principle of reincarnation—living a correct life will result in being reborn in a more advanced position (i.e., caste) as one moves towards Moksha (i.e., essentially it is the Hindu equivalent of Nirvana, the difference being that in Hinduism only the upper caste, the Brahmins, could reach Moksha or Nirvana).

Judaism

Judaism is one of the world's smallest religions with about 15 million Jews around the world—approximately six million reside in Israel and another six million reside in the U.S. An Abrahamic and monotheistic religion like Christianity and Islam, it is the parent of both other religions.

Buddhism

Primarily an Asian religion with approximately 300 million followers worldwide. Buddhism centers around Buddha or the "awakened one." The central tenants of Buddhism are: (1) lead a moral life, (2) to be mindful and aware of thoughts and actions, and (3) to develop wisdom and understanding. Abiding by these actions people are reborn time and time again until finally they reach Nirvana, or "nothingness."

Changing American Religious Landscape

Atheism is not a disbelief in gods or a denial of gods; it is a lack of belief in gods. It is a belief that there is no god.

Agnostic people believe that nothing is known or can be known of the existence or nature of a god or of anything beyond material phenomena; a person who claims to neither believe nor disbelieve in god.

Studies have found a gradual increase in the number of people identifying themselves as not affiliated with a particular religion since the 1950's (Roof, 1999). In fact, research reports the fastest growing religious affiliation is no affiliation (Kosmin et al., 2001). In 2007 there were approximately 37 million Americans that reported being unaffiliated with any religion, but by 2014 that figure had risen to 56 million (Pew Research Center, 2014.

As a whole, 70% of Americans identify as Christian, 5.9% as members of other religions, and 22.8% cite not being affiliated with any religion—and of those, 3.1% say they are atheist (Statistical Abstract of the United States, 2014).

Research on religious affiliation and the importance of religion in everyday life shows that a majority of Americans reported that religion was very important to them in a poll done by the Pew Research Center (2012). Further, they reported that 69% of poll respondents stated they believed in God and 55% said they prayed on a daily basis. Other findings include that 80% of those polled reported believing in an afterlife (Roof, 1999), 69% said they believed in God, and 81% said they had believed in God since childhood. Based on the religious landscape study (2014), mainline Protestant religious affilia-

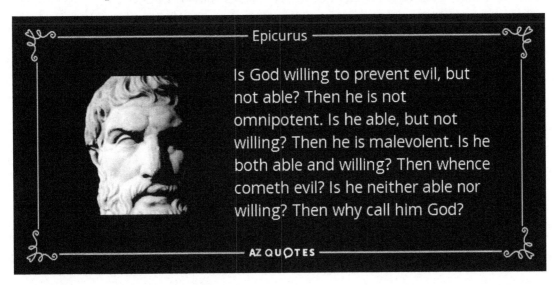

Epicurus

Is God willing to prevent evil, but not able? Then he is not omnipotent. Is he able, but not willing? Then he is malevolent. Is he both able and willing? Then whence cometh evil? Is he neither able nor willing? Then why call him God?

AZ QUOTES

tion declined from 18.1% to 14.7%, Catholics decreased from 23.9% to 20.8%, while the unaffiliated increased from 16.1% to 22.8% between 2007 and 2014. Also of note is the increase in the percentage of non-Christian religions from 4.7% in 2007 to 5.9% in 2014. All told, that is an increase of almost 8% in non-Christians during that period and that almost one-quarter of Americans do not identify as Christians. Also, the Pew Research Center (2012) reported that one-third of those Americans under the age of 30 identify themselves as having no religious affiliation. These are important facts since many Americans still fail to recognize the extent of religious diversity in the U.S. It is the case in the U.S. that though religious liberty is praised and held up as a standard to other nations, it is common to hear someone wish a stranger a "Merry Christmas" or "Happy Easter" without giving any thought to religious diversity.

While a majority of Americans say they believe in God, a recent poll by the Pew Research Foundation (Lipka, 2016) reported that nearly 25% of all Americans identify themselves as atheists, agnostics, or not affiliated with a religion—up dramatically from the previous generation. Researchers referred to the latter group as "nones." Approximately 80 percent of "nones" left the religion in which they were raised. Reasons for leaving the church in which they were raised include not believing in church doctrine anymore, a dislike for organized religion, a belief in the logic of science over religious doctrine, and just general apathy.

Religion in America is the most stratified part of American life. Looking at three measures by social class, the research reports that Jews and Episcopalians rank the highest on education, income, and occupational prestige. Southern Baptists and Jehovah's Witnesses rank the lowest on those same three measures.

Terms, Concepts and Names to Know:

- Christianity
- Islam
- Hinduism
- Buddhism
- Churches
- Denominations
- Ecclesia
- Sects

- Cults

- Anomie

Be Able to Discuss:

- The goal of sociology in regard sociology

- Marx on religion

- Opiate of the masses

- Durkehim's research on anomies

- Durkheim's five commonalities of religion

- Weber on religion

- Functionalist perspective on religion

- Negative effects of religion

- Positive effects of religion

References

Gillum, R. (2005). Frequency of Attendance at Religious Services and Smoking. Preventive Medicine, 41, 607-613.

Hummer, R. (1999). Religious involvement and U.S. adult mortality. Demography, 36(2), 273-285.

History.com Staff. (2010). Jonestown. Retrieved March 27, 2016, from http://www.history.com/topics/jonestown

Kark, J., Shemi, G., Friedlander, Y., Martin, O., Manor, O., & Blondheim, S. (1996). Does religious observance promote health? mortality in secular vs religious kibbutzim in Israel. American Journal of Public Health, 86(3), 341-346.

Kosmin, B., Mayer, E., & Keysar, A. (2001). American Religious Indentification Survey. December 19, 2001. NY: CUNY Graduate Center.

Newport, F., Agrawal, S., Witters, D. (2012). Religious Amricans Enjoy Higher Wellbeing. Princeton Univesity Press, Gallop Poll, Febrary 16.

Pew Research Center. (2016, August 24). Why America's 'nones' left religion behind. Pew Research Center retrieved September 5, 2016 from http://www.pewresearch.org/fact-tank/2016/08/24/why-americas-nones-left-religion-behind/

Pew Research Center. (2012, October 9). Nones on the Rise. Pew Forum on Religion and Public Life. Retrieved March 26, 2016 from: http://www.pewforum.org/2012/10/09/nones-on-the-rise/

Pew Research Center. (2015, May 7). America's Changing Religious Landscape Christians Decline Sharply as Share of Population; Unaffiliated and Other Faiths Continue to Grow. Retrieved March 26, 2016, from http://www.pewforum.org/2015/05/12/americas-changing-religious-landscape/

Roof, W. (1999). Spiritual Marketplace: Baby Boomers and the Remaking of American Religion. Princeton University Press: Princeton, NJ.

Routledge, C. (2009, September 15). Is religion bad for your health? Retrieved March 27, 2016, from https://www.psychologytoday.com/blog/more-mortal/200909/is-religionbad-your-health)

Smietana, B. (2015, January 15). Sunday Morning Segregation: Most Worshipers Feel Their Church Has Enough Diversity. Retrieved March 27, 2016, from http://www.christianitytoday.com/gleanings/2015/january/sunday-morning-segregation-most-worshiperschurch-diversity.html

Wallace, J., Yamaguchi, R., Bachan, P., O'Malley, P., Schulenberg, J., & Johnston, L. (2007). Relifiosity and adolescent substance Use: The Role of Contextual and Individual Influences. Social Problems, 54(2), 308-327.

Chapter 12: Cults and Radicalization

Cults

Cults are usually sects that have either split away from the parent denomination or constitute an entirely new religion. Usually smaller than sects in members, general characterizations of cults include:

- being viewed as deviant,

- a charismatic leader,

- a doctrine that is radically different from other sects and denominations, and

- a way of life significantly different from mainstream society.

Sociological Characteristics of Cults

- Cults use deception to recruit new members. Cult members mislead potential members as to the real beliefs or agenda of the cult when first talking with a potential member.

- Cults have a dynamic and authoritarian leadership. There is one leader who holds all power and control. That control is not challenged nor is the cult leader's right to lead the cult challenged. Cult leaders are almost always highly charismatic and much of their power comes from that charisma. This charisma makes them easier to follow, to obey, and to accept the cult's belief system.

- Cults always set themselves above others. They have some inner knowledge that allows them to see the "truth" or "reality" of something related to human existence. In effect, they alone have the secret that can only be shared among other cult members and true believers. In some way they believe they are superior to others.

- Cults have a specific vocabulary known only to cult members. For instance, Heaven's Gate members referred to their bodies as "vessels," Jim Jones' the People's Temple members knew that "code red" referred to the cult being overran by enemies and that they should take their own lives rather than being captured by these enemies. One way cults enhance their solidarity is to impose an external threat—something in the environment wants to see their demise.

- One of the first things that cults do is to isolate new members from their family and former friends. This assures the cult that members will not hear or be swayed by information from outside the group, which would almost always be negative—in other words, counterarguments. This is also a component of spouse and elder abuse. Abuse victims are almost always cut off from friends and family members to prevent victims from being urged to leave the abusive relationship. Outsiders are a threat to abusers and cult members. This process is referred to as "social implosion."

- Cult members are usually subjected to sleep deprivation. When do you think you would best be able to think critically about a professor's lecture in college when you were tired or awake and alert? It is the same principle here. It is easier to get cult members to accept the goals and beliefs of the cult if they are not at their best cognitively. Induced fatigue leads the inability to think critically and come up with counterarguments to the cult's message.

- Mind control results from induced fatigue combined with members being cut off from outside informational sources (e.g., family and friends).

- New cult members are expected to sign over all financial assets to the cult. Not only does this support the cult's ability to survive, but it also makes it much more difficult for cult members to try and escape the cult—they have no money and maybe no place to go.

- Cults use punishment to keep members in line and this is largely accepted by cult members as proof they are cared for by the cult. Again, common to domestic abuse, abused children are almost always asked during an investigation who they love more, mommy or daddy. The parent that is identified as the one loved the most is more often than not the abuser. Why? Because they are indoctrinated by the abusive parent that they are being punished because the parent loves them. So it is with cults.

- While most people approached to join a cult refuse, the attraction of a cult manages to successfully recruit some percentage of those approached. One technique is to "love bomb" the new or potential member. The group might literally surround the potential member while promising protection, love, and belongingness. This technique is very effective considering that a significant number of new recruits are alienated from society and possibly family and friends. That isolation is used against the potential member as a recruiting tactic.

- Clergy, or cult leaders, are rarely professionally trained. They develop the doctrine the cult will follow. Mainstream religion and its doctrine is shunned as naïve or untrue to the true reality whatever it may be. Cults are therefore anti-intellectual. Literalism, and that literalism is determined by the culture leader, is the name of the game.

- Cult doctrines are often in flux. Many cults will make predictions about the "end days" or something similar, but are forced to re-prophesize when the previous prophecy failed to materialize. In this latter case errors in calculations are always used as an excuse for the original prophecies failure to materialize.

Jonestown

On November 18, 1978, in what became known as the "Jonestown Massacre," Massacre," more than 900 members of an American cult called the Peoples Temple died in a mass suicide-murder under the direction of their leader Jim Jones (1931-78). The mass suicide-murder took place at the so-called Jonestown settlement in the South American nation of Guyana. Jones had founded what became the Peoples Temple in Indiana in the 1950's then relocated his congregation to California in the 1960's. In the 1970's, following negative media attention, the powerful, controlling preacher moved with some 1,000 of his followers to the Guyanese jungle, where he promised they would establish a utopian community. While the religious doctrine is complicated, the political motives on Jones' part was not: Jones was a Communist and wanted to found a religious communal.

Family members back in the U.S. said they were receiving mail from relatives saying they wanted to leave the cult and return home, but were prevented from doing so. On November 18, 1978, U.S. Representative Leo Ryan, went to Jonestown to investigate claims that members were being held against their will. After meeting with Jones, Ryan along with cult members who wanted to return home, were escorted to the local airfield where they were to fly back to the U.S. However, Jones had sent a few cult members on ahead and they ambushed the congressman and his entourage. Four were killed, but some managed to escape into the jungle.

After hearing that the congressman had been killed, Jones got on the loud speaker and announced a "code red," which was the signal that the compound was under attack and cult members needed to commit suicide. A large barrel of Kool-Aid and cyanide had been mixed and one by one cult members drank the poison. Some were forced to do so at gunpoint. Jones himself died of a gunshot would to the head. In all 918 people died. Only a few managed to escape into the jungle.

Branch Davidians

The Branch Davidians are a religious group that splintered away from the larger Davidian Seventh-Day Adventist Church, which itself was an offshoot of the Seventh-Day Adventist Church. The Branch Davidians was eventually headed by David Koresh. The Branch Davidians had a location in Waco, Texas and it was there that Koresh took control after a power struggle with another head of the cult. In February of 1993, as a result of information that stated that Koresh has amassed a number of illegal weapons, the Bureau of Alcohol, Tobacco, and Firearms attempted to serve a search warrant. Telling followers that the end was near, the Branch Davidians were prepared for the ATF as they had been tipped off. They armed themselves with automatic weaponry. When the ATF attempted to serve the warrant, a gun battle ensued. Wishing to avoid as much bloodshed as possible, the Attorney General, Janet Reno, ordered a siege of the Waco compound. The siege lasted for 51 days before the decision was made to breach the main building. During the breach fire was seen coming from several parts of the building. It was later determined that the Branch Davidians themselves started the fires. In total 74 men, women, and children died in the inferno that ensued. Koresh himself died in the shootout—whether he committed suicide or was shot is still debated.

Koresh was referred to as the Messiah according to followers, had multiple wives, and was accused of having sex with underage minors.

Warren Jeffs

Warren Jeffs a Mormon elder, headed a faction of the Mormon church in which polygamy was allowed. After his father died, he married all 20 of his father's wives. The cult flourished in Colorado City, Arizona and Hilldale, Utah. Men living in these towns were required to have multiple wives. Jeffs defended this with a fundamentalist doctrine that stated all faithful men must follow the rule of plural marriage in order to enter Heaven. Amidst allegations of polygamy and sexual misconduct, the FBI arrested Jeffs and originally charged with sexual assault on a minor. Jeffs is known to have taken a number of underage girls as a wife before his final arrest and conviction on charges of rape. By the time of his arrest he is reported to have been married to 70 women with whom he had 60 children.

Nazi Germany

Adolph Hitler

Many believe that Nazi Germany had all the characteristics of a cult. First, there was a charismatic leader. Hitler for all his evil tendencies, was a highly skilled and effective speaker. Ironically, some research suggests that he underwent training in public speaking from a Jewish magician. New members to the party were surrounded by like-minded Germans who considered themselves part of a large Nazi family that stood for the greater good of Germany. Nazis were superior to other Germans because they had a greater vision for

Germany; certainly they believed themselves superior to Jews, Gypsies, Communists, the physically and mentally challenged, Slavs, particular religious and secular groups, and many more.

The Nazi party itself was largely started by uneducated thugs who beat people up in the street if that's what it took to gain their compliance. It had a doctrine that was largely concocted (e.g., the myth of an "Aryan" race and mythical heritage), therefore Nazis were anti-intellectual. Top Nazis were usually not highly educated. But that's not to say they were stupid, Hitler himself knew that the way to build the Nazi party was to impose an external enemy—thus the Jews and Communists primarily. They were a threat to the German people and therefore had to be eradicated from German society; this is a very typical characteristic of a cult.

As cults impose doctrine on members, and prevent counterarguments, so did the Nazis. Joseph Goebbels held the title of Propaganda Minister. Today calling someone "propaganda minister" would be negatively interpreted, but not so with Nazi Germany. The job of propaganda was to impart knowledge about Nazi party doctrine to the masses by simplifying it; in other words, propaganda destroyed freedom of thought—"you don't need to think, that's why we have Dr. Goebbels telling us what to do and what not to do."

Hitler ruled as an authoritarian. No one challenged the Fuehrer. Germans who stepped out of line, were severely punished, just like cult members who fail to follow cult rules. Countless thousands of non-Jewish Germans died in concentration camps because they refused to "follow the rules." I personally knew a man whose grandmother was forcibly sterilized by the Nazis because she was overheard one day referring to Hitler as "crazy." For many Germans, the punishment was much worse.

The Nazis also set up the German people as superior to all other peoples. In particular, the Nazis believed that their Aryan race, though there is no such race grounded in history, as being superior to the Slavs of Central and Eastern Europe, Africans, Chinese, and the "mongrelized" Americans. While the first stanza from the German national anthem was created before the Nazis came to power, Deutschland, Deutschland uber alles" (Germany, Germany over all), the meaning was elevated during the Nazis reign to literally refer to the superiority of the German nation. Again, this belief in their superiority is characteristic of cults.

Nazis also isolated its citizens from the influence of outsiders. Once World War II began, the Nazis made it a crime to listen to foreign radio stations—the punishment was death. Like cults, they didn't want outside information affecting the German people and possibly hindering the war effort. Finally, Germans were thoroughly indoctrinated into Nazi doctrine. Slogans were painted on buildings praising the Fuehrer, Nazi flags hung from windows—woe to you if you failed to hang out your own flag. Germans, like cult members, were encouraged to report speech or activity that was contrary to official doctrine, and those who were denounced were often punished severely—often with their life. Even German children were taught in school to report anything said by their parents that was deemed as anti-Nazi. Many German children did just that.

Heaven's Gate

Founded by Marshall Applewhite Jr., also known as "Bo" and Bonnie Nettles, also known as "Peep". They were referred to as the "two." In the 1970's, cult members believed that mankind was a descendent of alien beings who had visited earth several millennial before. Bo and Peep took over their human bodies in their 40's; other ancient ones had come before and "tagged" them when they were younger. Bo and Peep were from the "evolutionary level above human." Many of those who had been "tagged" in staged spaceship crashes and occupied human bodies before gaining their earthly "containers." Before their human incarnation, they were "briefed by older beings with details about how to take over the human vehicle."

Members led strict lives avoiding sex, drugs, and alcohol. They were also expected to severe all ties with former friends and family members. Members had to wear their hair short, wear "androgynous clothing," and to participate in a regimen of training for their eventual travel to their home planet. Once they had successfully fulfilled all the requirements of cult membership they shed their human "containers," which they believed were just vessels needed while on earth. Bo and Peep told cult members they would need their containers to enter "God's kingdom." At an appointed time, they would shed their earthly containers in order to rise to a higher level to be with God.

Cult members believed there were evil aliens on earth that enslaved humans "through worldly concerns like jobs, sex, and families." These were called Luciferians. After having been persecuted and put to death by Luciferians, and their bodies laying in the open for three days, they believed that they would ascend into heaven through a biblical "cloud" that was actually a spaceship.

Sensing the arrival of the spaceship in the trail of the Hale Bopp comet, which was about to be at its closest to earth in many years, they all went to the movies to watch Star Wars. They even bought a small telescope to try and see the spaceship, but were unable to do so. As the comet drew to its nearest point to earth, cult members dressed in black track suits and Nike shoes, took a combination of phenobarbital and alcohol, and placed a plastic bag over their head. On March 26, 1997, police discovered the bodies of 39 cult members as described in the previous sentence.

While having all the characteristics of a cult, it is interesting to note that the age range of cult members was from 26 to 72 years of age. Do you suppose that everyone believed the stated doctrine of the cult? If not, why would they commit suicide? Think about it.

Charles Manson

By the time Charles Manson turned 13, Charles Manson had already been convicted of a series of crimes including robbery. In the 1960's, Manson started a cult that became known as the "Manson family." Made up of nine people, five of which were female, Manson lauded over the other family members. Manson believed that there would be an impending race war, which he coined as Helter Skelter, a name he took from the Beatles' song. He believed that the way to begin the race war was to go on a killing spree, which he did. In total nine people were murdered including actress Sharon Tate who was pregnant at the time. In 1971, Manson was found guilty of conspiracy to commit the murders of seven people—Manson himself did not participate in the murders, but ordered them. Manson was sentenced to life in prison with the possibility of parole. As of 2012, Manson has been denied parole for the 12th time. During that parole meeting it was decided not to allow Manson to petition for parole for another 15 years.

Christianity

Christianity started as a cult, largely because of its singular charismatic leader, Jesus. Cults can advance to denominations and finally to a church. Today, Christianity is the largest religion in the world.

The Moonies

The "Moonies" are followers of Sun Myung Moon. Followers believe him to be divine and he is worshipped as God. The Reverend Moon wields complete control over his followers. The cult actively works to recruit young members, separate them from former friends and family members, has its own doctrine, and adheres to the other characteristics of cults in general. Moonies are banned in Germany because the German government considered them to dangerous for young people because they are so easily influence. Moon believes that Korea is his chosen realm, by virtue of the fact he is considered God, and routinely speaks out against the Christian church.

Ku Klux Klan

Originally started by General Nathan Beford Forest, an infamous Confederate commander during the American Civil War, he was very charismatic and could get his followers, and soldiers when he war was in progress, to do whatever he asked them to do. At their foundation were Christian principles that were as perverted then as they are now. However, at seeing what the KKK had become, Bedford Forest withdrew from the Klan in 1872. The Klan reformed and at one point the KKK had over four million members in the U.S. Their hatred and terror tactics extends to Jews, Blacks, Catholics, foreigners, and other minorities; in other words, everyone who is Protestant, born in America, and white is welcome. The Klan has always operated anonymously though this has changed in recent years. Thomas Robb is the current "Director" of the KKK (a title that replaced Grand Drgaon), and therefore is essentially head of the KKK cult.

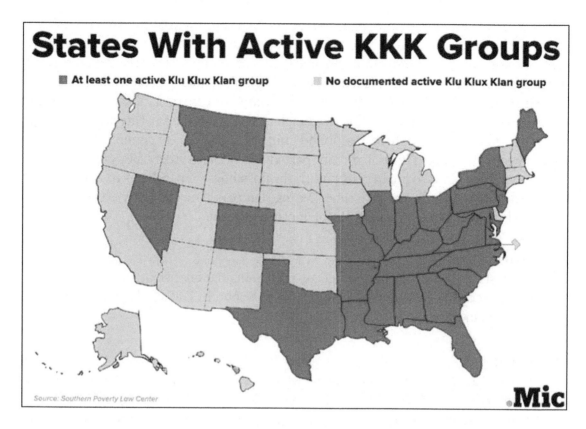

Aum Shinrikyo

A Japanese cult whose meaning translates as "Supreme Truth." The cult was founded by Shoko Asahara in 1984. Starting as an innocuous cult, the group gradually became more vocal and were accused of forcing people to donate to the cult, fraud, and murder. In 1995, his paranoia winning out, Asahara ordered the release of nerve gas in the Tokyo subway system. A total of 12 people died in the attack. The police captured Asahara and discovered he had amassed a huge stockpile of arms and explosives capable of producing more deaths than had the gas attack on the subway. A raid by police not only found the aforementioned arms, but hostages as well. Police were horrified when they began to identify all the weapons Asahara had: poisonous gas that was capable of killing four million people and other nerve agents like anthrax. After his arrest, the cult was formally banned, but even today followers still gather and practice a modified religious doctrine.

Order of the Solar Temple

The cult advocates that the Knights Templar still exist and the only way to ascend to heaven is to convert to their brand of Christianity. In 1994, cult members murdered an infant in the belief the child was the anti-Christ. The cult imploded at that point and there were many murders of members by other members and mass suicides. In the end, more than 100 people died—either murdered or by suicide.

Conclusion

In conclusion, it is estimated there are hundreds if not thousands of cults existing in the U.S. today. Many under FBI scrutiny, but many go underground and are only discovered when former members come forward. Close social ties with family and friends makes recruiting new members much more difficult for cults.

Radicalization

President Obama referred to the actions of ISIS as nihilistic (The Psychology of Radicalization, 2016), which is a value system that disregards the sacredness of human life and rejects worldwide definitions of moral standards. ISIS, otherwise known as Da'ish, is not a new phenomenon, instead it is a religious disagreement that has existed since the 14th century. In the 1300's, a Muslim scholar named Taymiyyah wrote about those whose practices offended Allah. Another scholar, Abd al-Wahhab, who lived in the 18th century, believed that those whose practices offended Allah were imposters and not true Muslims. Abd al-Wahhab "demanded conformity" to a Caliph who would be established to represent Islam on earth. The writings of Abd al-Wahhab called for the death of those he didn't consider to be Muslims: Shia, Sufis, and other Muslim denominations. Wahhabism, as those who followed the doctrines of Abd al-Wahhab were called, at one point controlled most of the Arabian Penninsula, and large parts of Syria and Iraq. In the early 1800's, the Wahhabists committed many atrocities in their capture of those aforementioned territories. By 1815, Wahhabist forces were finally defeated once and for all by the combined forces of Egyptians and Turks from the Ottoman Empire. The war by Sunni Muslims against Shiites and other Muslim denominations seemed to be at last at an end. But the religious and philosophical differences remained, simmering until the Middle East was de-stabilized by the second Iraqi war.

Today, Abu Bakr al-Baghdadi is the leader of the religious faction that advocates a return to Wahhabist doctrine, and was made Caliph of the self-proclaimed Islamic State in June of 2014.

The targets of ISIS include any and all who don't share the rigid doctrines associated with Abd al-Wahhab: Shiites, Sufis, Middle Eastern Christians, Jews, and Westerners in general. While it is impossible to know exactly how many people have been killed by ISIS, a United Nations report from September 2014 reported that at "least 24,015 Iraqi civilians had been murdered by ISIS just in the first eight months of 2014" (United Nations High Commissioner on Human Rights, 2014).

With the attacks by members of ISIS on Paris, twice, Belgium, Britain, Turkey, and San Bernardino, California, ISIS represents a serious threat to the world. While the majority of ISIS members are from Iraq and Syria, a significant number are being recruited from Western countries. What would cause someone raised in France, Belgium, England, or the U.S. to become "radicalized," in other words, socialized into the radical goals and means associated with ISIS?

In a speech to the House Homeland Security Committee Subcommittee on Intelligence, Donald Van Duyn reported to the committee: "Although the most dangerous instances of radicalization have been so far been overseas, the Islamic radicalization of U.S. persons, whether foreign-born or native, is of increasing concern." (Federal Bureau of Investigation, 2006). In his speech, Van Duyn went on to report that the two primary arenas for recruitment were prisons and the Internet. In both cases, "radical imams" are actively involved in the process of recruitment. Also, he reported that, "Although radicalization can occur without overseas travel, the foreign experience appears to provide the networking that makes it possible for interested individuals to train for and participate in operational activity." This is almost certainly the case in the 2015 in San Bernardino, CA in which a radicalized Muslim husband and wife shot and killed 14 people attending a holiday party at the Public Health Department. The wife, Tasheen Malik had spent some time living in Pakistan before marrying her husband, Syed Farook, and authorities believe that it was during her time in Pakistan that she was radicalized.

Radicalization is a process involving socialization, in many ways like cults. Both teach their newly recruited members the norms, values, and beliefs of their deviant group. Others believe that members of such radical groups with violence on their agenda, do so because of mental illness or religious fanaticism, the latter which is shared with cult membership. However, while we would like to easily explain the actions of such barbarous groups like ISIS as the result of madmen, researchers report that most ISIS fighters have no such tendencies. The most commonly reported characteristic of ISIS members is their desire to belong to something bigger than themselves and to form brotherly-like connections with others who share their same purpose in life. This latter finding is also consistently found in research on cults.

In one study by (Georgia Public Broadcasting, 2016), researchers identified 16 "key mindsets" associated with membership in terrorist groups. Among the more important of those beliefs was:

1. the world was a disaster,

2. it was too late for peaceful change,

3. self-sacrifice is honorable,

4. that the ends justify the means, and

5. that a religious or secular utopia is possible. Researchers reported that members of terrorist organizations do truly believe that they are working to make the world a better place and many feel victimized by the U.S. government (Ballas, 2010).

The process of radicalization is a complex one. One research study found that ISIS recruiters spent hundreds of hours on social media sites working to convince young people that the problems of the world are exactly the problems that ISIS is fighting (Georgia Public Broadcasting, 2016). There are a number of indicators associated with radicalization.

First, religious beliefs do play a key role and this is amplified with members of a religion, in this case Islam, are marginalized or shunned by society. The effect is to increase the cohesiveness of these young men seeking their identity through these extreme religious beliefs. However, the vast majority of radicalized members of ISIS do not understand the Koran well, and therefore are easily led or misled by others; in point of fact, Islam at its heart advocates peace and humaneness.

Second, recruits are led into seeing the situation as a war between Islam and the West; the killing of civilians, albeit accidental, angers potential recruits and leads them to believe that the West doesn't care about innocent victims of bombings and drone attacks. This results in young men taking action by doing something meaningful like joining ISIS.

Third, social media is used to form networks of radical extremism. In these social media networks, disgruntled young people can share their frustration with events and those social media connections are usually led by so-called clerics and who are able to influence these young men with personal charisma. Uneducated, isolated, and gullible young men are easy prey for these charismatic clerics.

Fourth, these disenfranchised young men, who powerless to effect change through the democratic process, see violence as an effective way to bring about change and are willing to die for it.

Lastly, as is always the case with such extreme ideologies, poverty and unemployment play a key role in recruiting. Typical characteristics of radicalized young are that they are between 17 to 25 years of age, uneducated, and unemployed (Ahmad, 2015).

Radicalization occurs in social media, too. In January 2015, ISIS used a social media site to release a video that encouraged supporters to attack particular sites in the U.S. and Western Europe (Federal Bureau of Investigation, February 26, 2015). ISIS uses to social media to incite supporters to the point of violence. When an individual carries out an act of terrorism by themselves, they are called "lone wolves."

In addition to social media as an arena for radicalization, the prison system serves as another. Prisons literally provide a "captive" audience. Targets of radical Muslims, or radical imams, are those incarcerated young men, more often minorities, who feel they have been victimized by the system, and in many, cases feel as if they have been victimized their whole life by the U.S. Donald Van Duyn, Deputy Assistant Director, Counterterrorism Division Federal Bureau of Investigation, stated, "...for Muslim converts, but also for those born into Islam, an extremist imam can strongly influence individual belief systems by speaking from a position of authority on religious issues" (Federal Bureau of Investigation, September 19, 2006). However, even though we know radicalization occurs in the prison system, and that radicalization is almost always led by an imprisoned radical imam, one study found that the U.S. prison system simply doesn't have the ability to accredit which Imams are allowed to serve as chaplains (Ballas, 2010).

Lone Wolves

Recently, there have been more attacks in the name of ISIS where the attacker had no direct contact with radical Imams or other radicalized Muslims. A lone wolf is someone who commits a terroristic act without the aid of others. When there is a conspiracy to commit an act of terror, there is greater chance the FBI or other foreign secret service agencies can plant an agent in their midst. In such cases, most attacks are thwarted as law enforcement agencies move in before the planned attack. The danger of lone wolves is that single individuals do not constitute a conspiracy because they are not directly working with others. Radicalized by listening to radical speeches, reading radical material, coupled with some characteristics of cults (e.g., feeling isolated and alienated, following the will of the cult leader, seeing external threats), these lone wolves carry out their attacks without warning. Examples of lone wolf attacks include the attack by Omar Mateen on the Pulse gay nightclub in Orlando, Florida. Forty-nine people were killed. In July 2016, Mohamed Lahouaiej Bouhlel, drove a semi-truck through a crowd of people walking down the Promenade des Anglais killing 84 people and wounding more than 200 others. Both Mateen and Bouhlel had no prior history associating them with radicalism, yet both committed their acts of terror in the name of ISIS.

Lone wolves are not unique to ISIS, they have been around for some time. In "Laws for the Lone Wolf," white supremacist Tom Metzger wrote: "The less any outsider knows, the safer and more successful you will be. Keep your mouth shut and your ears open. Never truly admit to anything" (Anti-Defamation League, 2013). Researcher Michael Becker defines it this way: "Ideologically driven violence, or attempted violence, perpetrated by an individual who plans and executes an attack in the absence of collaboration with other individuals or groups" (Becker, 2014). Although you wouldn't know it at the moment in America, the motivation for such attacks can run the gamut from religiously inspired anti-abortion beliefs to white supremacism, from animal rights to an al-Qaeda-inspired worldview (Harwood, 2015). To date there have been 62 lone wolf attacks in the U.S.

Because the lone wolf acts alone, they are usually off the radar of counter-terrorism organizations. In research done by Sara Teich (2013), she found five "emerging trends in Islamist lone wolf terrorism" in the US, Canada, and Western Europe. She found:

- An increase in the number of countries targeted by lone wolves from the 1990's to the 2000's.

- An increase in the number of people injured and killed by lone wolves.

- Increased effectiveness of law enforcement and counter-terrorism.

- Consistency in the distribution of attacks by "actor types" (loners, lone wolves, and lone wolf packs).

- An increase in the number of attacks against military personnel.[5]

But it is wrong to think that the majority of lone wolf attacks are ISIS inspired; they are not. The Christian Science Monitor reported, "With the exception of the attacks on the World Trade Center, experts say the major terrorist attacks in the United States have been perpetrated by deranged individuals who were sympathetic to a larger cause – from Oklahoma City bomber Timothy McVeigh to the Washington area sniper John Allen Muhammad," both native-born Americans (Marks, 2003).

There are many groups that advocate lone wolf actions. Anti-abortion groups are a good example. Some like the Army of God encourages lone wolf activity (Gonnerman, 1998). Prior to the Boston Marathon bombings, an Al-Qaeda activist, Samir Khan, advocated lone wolf activities directed at Americans in Inspire magazine and even published detailed information about how to build bombs (Shane, 2013).

Terms, Concepts and Names to Know:

- The Sociological Characteristics of Cults

- ISIS

- Lone wolf

- Abu Bakr al-Baghdadi

- Mohamed Lahouaiej Bouhlel

- Omar Mateen

- Tasheen Malik and Syed Farook

Be Able to Discuss:

- Radicalization

- Jonestown

- Branch Davidians

- Heaven's Gate

- Moonies

- KKK

- Why Christianity was a cult at one time

- Order of the Solar Temple

- Aum Shinrikyo

- Charles Manson

- Warren Jeffs

References

Ahmad, J. (2015, February 18). 5 Paths to Islamic Radicalization. Retrieved September 21, 2016, from http://nationalinterest.org/feature/5-paths-islamic-radicalization-12269?page=show

Anti-Defamation League. (2013). Extremism in America: Tom Metzger. Retrieved July 16, 2016, from http://archive.adl.org/learn/ext_us/tom-metzger/default.html?LEARN_Cat=Extremism&LEARN_SubCat=Extremism_in_America&xpicked=2&item=7

Ballas, D. (2010) Prisoner radicalization. FBI Law Enforcement Bulletin 79(10): 1–9.

Becker, M. (2014). Explaining Lone Wolf Target Selection in the United States. Studies in Conflict & Terrorism, 37:11, 959-978.

Federal Bureau of Investigation. (February 26, 2015). Statement Before the House Judiciary Committee, Subcommittee on Crime, Terrorism, Homeland Security, and Investigations. Retrieved September 30, 2016 from https://www.fbi.gov/news/testimony/isil-in-america-domestic-terror-and-radicalization

Washington, D.C.: ISIL in America: Domestic Terror and Radicalization

Gonnerman, J. (1998). "Villagvoice.com". Retrieved July 14, 2016 from Villagevoice.com.

Harwood, M. (2015, February 5). Lone Wolf Terrorists Are Exceedingly Rare, So Why Does Everyone Keep Talking About Them? Retrieved July 16, 2016, from http://www.motherjones.com/politics/2015/02/government-using-fear-lone-wolf-terrorist-justify-police-state

Marks, A. (2003). Lone wolves pose explosive terror threat. Christian Science Monitor. Retrieved July 14, 2016 from csmonitor.com.

Shane, S. (2013). "A Homemade Style of Terror: Jihadists Push New Tactics". The New York Times. Retrieved July 14, 2016 from http://www.nytimes.com/2013/05/06/us/terrorists-find-online-education-for-attacks.html?_r=0

Teich, S. (2013). Trends and Developments in Lone Wolf Terrorism in the Western World. International Institute for Counter-Terrorism. Retrieved July 14, 2016 from http://www.ict.org.il/Article.aspx?ID=691

United Nations High Commission for Human Rights. (2016). Report of the United Nations High Commissioner for Human Rights on the protection of human rights and fundamental freedoms while countering terrorism. Retrieved September 30, 2016 from http://www.ohchr.org/EN/HRBodies/HRC/RegularSessions/Session28/Documents/A_HRC_28_28_ENG.doc.

Chapter 13: Dating and Marriage

What is Dating?

At some point, you will probably marry. Fully 95% of Americans will marry at some point in their life and that number will probably increase now that same-sex marriage is legal in all 50 states (Obergefell v Hodges 2015). In some cultures, children's parents choose your spouse for you. That is called arranged marriage and while practiced in many countries worldwide, the most widely known example is India, though even there it is changing. But in the Western world, the number one reason people marry is because they fall in love (Pew Research Center, 2013). So, how do we fall

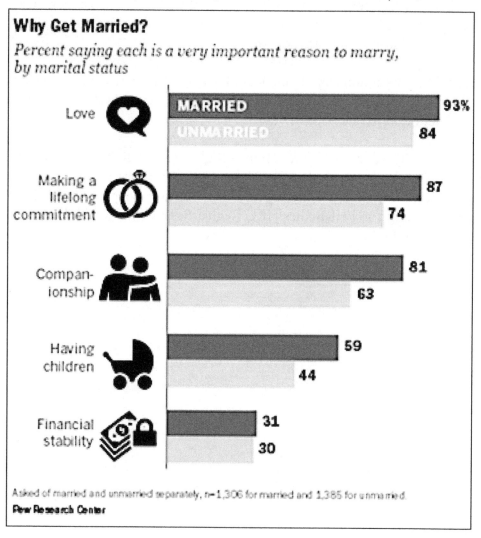

Why Get Married?

Percent saying each is a very important reason to marry, by marital status

Love
- MARRIED 93%
- UNMARRIED 84

Making a lifelong commitment
- 87
- 74

Companionship
- 81
- 63

Having children
- 59
- 44

Financial stability
- 31
- 30

Asked of married and unmarried separately, n=1,306 for married and 1,385 for unmarried.
Pew Research Center

in love with someone? The answer is through the process of dating.

The first thing we need to do is to define dating. Though it might sound very clinical, sociologists are essentially in agreement over a basic definition of marriage: The process by which we select a mate based on physical attraction and other more intangible qualities for the purpose of companionship, sex, and/or marriage. The older definition used to limit dating purposes to finding someone to marry, but as times have changed, so have the reasons people date. It is not solely about finding a prospective spouse anymore.

If we were to break the dating process down into more elemental components, we could ask what are the functions of dating? Research shows they fall into two general categories: manifest and latent. Remember the structural functionalist perspective. Manifest functions are intended functions and latent functions are unintended. Though even unintended functions can be beneficial. Manifest functions of dating would included components like:

- **Recreation**. Most people find dating fun, adventurous, and entertaining,

- **Companionship**. I like to say there are three "L" words associated with courtship and dating:

  - **Love** - which we use so much we throw it around like candy, diluting it to the point that it has lost meaning;

  - **Lust** - which we feel during the dating process but don't necessarily like admitting to—one person saying to another, "I lust for you" may or may not go over well;

  - **Loneliness** - Most dating partners would probably find it pathetic if one said to the other, "I want to date you because I'm lonely"—though the research finds that is a major reason we date.

- **Mate selection**. Sounds nice and clinical, doesn't it? Almost like the act of dating needs to occur in a laboratory. However, marriage is still a popular institution and therefore dating an integral part of the process leading up to marriage.

- **Sex**. Most researchers specializing in family studies would identify sex and sexual experimentation as a latent function of dating. I disagree. I think people dating today, especially younger generations, expect to have sex while dating. If the intended goal of dating for many is to ultimately find that perfect soul mate to marry, they need to be simpatico in as many ways as possible. To some it seems logical that similarity in sexual needs and preferences be a part of that similarity.

Latent Functions of Dating

Socialization. Socialization is the process of learning the do's and don'ts of the groups to which people belong. Dating is a process that occurs between two people immediately and much more than that when the extended family comes into play. So it is necessary to learn the norms of the dating partner and also of their family. It is a learning process.

Gaining social status. We are often judged by our associations with others— guilt or esteem by association. When you get up in the morning and look into the bathroom mirror, you will make a judgment about how you look – a kind of self-statement. On a scale of one to ten, with one being highly unattractive and ten being highly attractive, maybe we look in the mirror and see a seven. The research suggests we will look to date someone we judge to be a seven or slightly better. Why? First, because it is human nature to want to get as much of a valuable commodity as we can get, and second, because if we're a seven and we're dating an eight or nine, the esteem people have for us will increase— esteem by association. The whole idea of a man acquiring a "trophy wife" captures the idea that we gain social status when we date someone judged to have high social status whether the result of looks, celebrity, or money.

Ego needs. Even though there are more than seven billion people in the world, one of the things we expect to hear from the person that we are dating is, "Ah, honey, you're so special." Other statements might include, "You're so unique," "your boss just doesn't appreciate what a great worker you are," or "no one can cook like you can." Psychologists tell us that it is important for our self-esteem to have our ego needs met (Baumeister, 2003), and those we are romantically involved with are expected to fill that role.

Who Do We Date?

Generally, there are three primary factors involved in whom we choose to date:
1. propinquity, (those found nearby in our social world)

2. those we perceive to have important factors that are derived from our values.

Propinquity. Historically, we have been more likely to date people who are physically proximate to us. Most people date people from the same geographical area—i.e., from the same city or nearby. And while this has been the case for hundreds of years, recently it has been changing rapidly because of the Internet.

Our social world. Our social world, which consists of those places we go—to school, church, parties, friends, the gym, and even the grocery store on a weekend morning, provides a very small arena for meeting people to date. In a 2015 survey conducted by Mic using Google Consumer Surveys, researchers found that 39% of those surveyed said they met their significant other through mutual friends, while 22% said "in a social setting" (Liebowitz, 2015).

Values we hold important. Generally, we choose to date people who are attractive, healthy, have a good personality, and are emotionally mature.

Endogamy

Endogamy represents a preference for groups within which people are supposed to date (and marry). For instance, we are expected to date/marry people within our own ethnicity, race, religion, social class, and close to our age. So, what happens when people violate the rules of endogamy? In 1994, a former Playmate of the Year, Anna Nicole Smith, married the oil tycoon Howard Marshall. She was 26 and he was 89. While they were married, Smith would state emphatically that she loved him. After he died, Smith maintained that she never made love with him and they rarely kissed. Did she love him? What did America say? For Americans, she was a gold digger—only interested in his money. On the other hand, his friends probably said something like, "Way to go, Howie!" We'll talk about "double-standards" when we get to gender inequality.

Exogamy

Whereas endogamy represents a preference for groups within which people are expected to date & marry, exogamy represents groups that people are expected not to date and marry within. For instance, we are expected to date & marry outside of our nuclear family. Likewise, most states have laws prohibiting marriage to nieces, nephews, first cousins, aunts, uncles, etc.

Historically, another example of exogamy was applied to gays and lesbians. Laws existed preventing people from marrying within their own sex. While gays and lesbians were free to date, though it was never recognized in the same way as it was for straight couples, they were prohibited from marrying in the U.S. Over time some states passed legislation permitting same-sex marriage, but the majority of states continued to resist. The problem for those resistant states was the issue of reciprocity. All states are obliged to recognize marriages performed in other states, but some states refused to recognize same-sex marriages that were conducted outside of their state and thus violated this law of reciprocity. However, on June 26, 2015, the United States Supreme Court ruled that states cannot keep same-sex couples from marrying and must recognize their unions.

The Role of Physical Attraction

We discussed why we date, what we look for in whom to date, and the groups we expected to marry within or without. But, we haven't yet discussed one important feature of dating: the role of physical attraction. Physical attraction has a huge role to play in whom we date. For instance:

- Physical attraction has the greatest effect on first impressions.

- When looking at what's important to a woman in deciding what man to date, she is most likely to identify his physical attractiveness to be the first criteria. However, after physical attractiveness, women are likely to identify other more intangible factors as being important—e.g., sense of humor, would he make a good provider, would he make a good father, would he make a good husband, and many other things.

- Like women, men are just as likely to identify physical attractiveness as being the first criteria in identifying someone to date. However, and unlike women, other more intangible criteria are much less important. It would be like asking a man what's most important in deciding to date a woman and he answers, "Her looks." So, we respond by asking, "Ok, what next?" He responds by saying, "Her looks." "Ok, ok," we say, "but what after that?" After pausing for a second he says, "Her looks." Eventually the research suggests he would identify those intangible criteria like women have named, but again, they tend to be given much less importance by men.

- Generally, we want to date people we judge to be about as attractive as we are or better. Further, research suggests that we are attracted to people who we perceive as similar in values and behaviors. There is little evidence that "opposites attract" and no evidence that suggests "opposites" stay together in the long run.

- Research has found that the more in love a woman is with a man, the better looking he gets. Why? Because she has gotten to know him and discovered that he possesses many of those intangible criteria identified above. Unfortunately, the research does not support that the same holds true for men.

- Research shows that there is an expectation that males look for females to date who are slightly shorter than them. The "male taller bias" has been supported in the literature time and time again (Gillis and Avis, 1980; Graziano, Brothen, and Berscheid, 1978; and Berscheid and Walster, 1974).

What is the Role of Appearance in Falling in Love?

Studies have found that humans, especially men, are attracted to people who have symmetrical faces. Facial symmetry would be where the two sides of a person's face are in proportion to each other. Women seem to value facial symmetry a little less than do men. Research has also found that men are more attracted to women with a waist to hip ratio of 0.7. To calculate your hip to waist ratio, measure your waist and divide that by your hip measurement. It seems men subconsciously still prefer women with "child-bearing hips" for biological reasons: women with wider hips are less likely to die during childbirth and thus the man's genes are passed down to a large number of offspring (BBC Fisher, 2014).

Other research by David Perrett (2012) found that humans have a subconscious preference for their own face when it comes to mate selection. Perrett used a system of facial morphing to turn a subject's face into the face of an opposite sex person. His research found there was a preference for his or her own face as morphed into someone of the opposite sex. While Perrett admits he doesn't know the reason for this, he suggests it might be because the morphed faces remind us as how we looked in childhood.

Pheromones and Falling in Love

Biologists have found that pheromones are associated with falling in love. Pheromones are chemicals secreted in urine and sweat and can be picked up by a vomeronasal organ in the nose. It had been studied in rats, but wasn't until 1985 before researchers discovered that most humans have that same organ in their nose. In rats, the chemical is used to both attract and reject other rats. In 1995, Claus Wedekind found that a group of women were asked to smell sweaty t-shirts worn by men. He discovered that the majority of women chose t-shirts of men whose immune systems were different than their own. From a biological view, this makes sense for both rats and humans because we want a broad immune system. On the other hand, when Martha McClintock performed a similar experiment, she found that women chose t-shirts that, unbeknownst to them, had been worn by their fathers. McClintock concluded that a father's genes, as detected in the pheromones in the sweaty t-shirts, would be "similar enough that her offspring would get a tried and true immune system," and different enough to provide a wider range of genes for purposes of immunity (BBC Fisher, 2014). In other words, women preferred the sweaty t-shirt worn by their father. Yikes!

Types of Love

The word "love" is so often used and in so many situations, it has little meaning. Generally, there are three types of love we can investigate while studying courtship and dating: passionate love, companionate love, and romantic love.

Falling in love is most closely associated with passionate love. Passionate love is a physical and emotional state. We pine for the person with whom we are in love when they are not around, and encounter significant chemical and personality changes when we are around them. "When lovers claim they feel 'high' and as if they are being swept away, it's probably because they are" (Miller & Barnes, 2015).

"Love is addictive, akin to cocaine and speed" (Vaknin, 2013). Because of the all the chemicals dumped into the bloodstream when people are "in love" (e.g., dopamine, serotonin, norepinephrine, and phenylethylamine), some researchers see a parallel between being "in love" and psychosis and substance abuse.

The BBC, when writing about Helen Fisher of Rutger University wrote, "events in the brain when we are in love have similarities with mental illness" (BBC Fisher, 2014). Finally, it might surprise you to know that the research has found that men fall in love more quickly and out of love more slowly when compared to women. Women always seem surprised at that finding. I think the most likely explanation is that men don't like talking about their feelings, and so while they may be falling in love more quickly than a woman, they are less likely to express they are feeling the emotion.

To say that romantic love has an agreed upon fixed period in which it emerged on the scene, would be false. However, most scholars agree that the concept has achieved its greatest evolution as a form of love and unity between people since medieval times. Historically, arranged marriages were always more common, but love-marriages still occurred from time to time. Romantic love means more than just marrying for love or because some arrangement made parents. Romantic love refers to the emotional bonding of two people who are sexually attracted to each other and they anticipate a long-term sharing of that emotional, physical, and sexual attraction—elements that were not expected or usually present in arranged marriages.

Companionate love is a more stable, longer-lasting type of love and less dependent on sex and sexual attraction—which is not to say that sex and sexual attraction don't exist in companionate love, but rather they are simply less important than in other forms of love. As the chemical effects of falling "in love" wear off, and as oxytocin (the "cuddling chemical") levels increase in the bloodstream, the intensity of passionate love gives way to the more steady companionate love because the effects of the chemicals released when falling "in love" tend to last only up to two years in most people. One way of looking at companionate love is to say that couples have two years to convert passionate love to companionate love or the relationship has a good chance of ending.

Fisher (2014) identified three stages of falling in love. They are:

- **Stage 1: Lust**. Driven by the hormones testosterone and estrogen, people are

- more or less pushed into getting out and looking for someone to have sex with.

- **Stage 2: Physical attraction**. Chemicals are released into the bloodstream, which drive us. Neuro-transmitters and monoamines flood the brain. Including dopamine, serotonin, and norepinephrine (adrenalin). This results in feeling high or giddy, obsessed with someone, daydreaming about them, feeling sad if they are not around, and affecting our appetite and sleep. We are now "in-love." God help us, we are out of control. Oxytocin, the "cuddling hormone," is released during sex between lovers, and it results in intensifying the bond between the two people. Fisher wrote, "The theory goes that the more sex a couple has, the deeper their bond."

- **Stage 3: Attachment**. Attachment occurs when we have moved beyond the physical attraction stage. If the relationship doesn't move beyond the physical attraction stage, the relationship dies. Attachment involves a much longer-lasting commitment to that special someone, and is an important stage if the couple has children. It keeps them together during a time of extreme stress on the relationship. Research has shown that raising children corresponds to low marital satisfaction during the child-rearing years.

Negative Features of Online Dating

- There are too many profiles from which to choose and it leads people to make comparisons on the basis of these flawed profiles.

- The choices of partners can become confusing and overwhelming. Without a clear plan, online daters can get stuck endlessly "shopping" for the perfect partner, rather than actually starting a satisfying relationship.

- Matching is a difficult process and testing may not be accurate for everyone. In addition, people may present differently in person or change over time. So, matching may overlook potentially good partners in the process.

- Communication through computers is lacking some of the information provided in face-to-face interaction. As a result, it is harder to evaluate a potential match online. Also, some of the cues and features that build attraction (like touching) cannot be accomplished through a computer. So, such computer-mediated communication may have an artificial and unemotional quality.

Positive Features of Online Dating

- Online dating provided individuals with access to many more potential partners than they could often find in their daily lives. This is especially true for individuals interested in partners of a particular type, orientation, lifestyle, or in isolated areas.

- Many online dating sites offer various types of personality testing and matching. Such matching can help guide individuals toward dating partners who may be more compatible.

- Online dating offers a number of ways to get to know a potential date before meeting in person. Such computer-mediated communication allows for safe and convenient interaction, without much risk or time commitment. For the

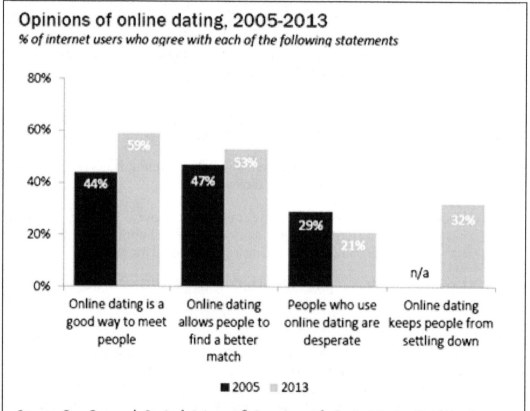

Opinions of online dating, 2005-2013
% of internet users who agree with each of the following statements

Source: Pew Research Center's Internet & American Life Project Spring Tracking Survey, April 17 – May 19, 2013. N=2,252 adults ages 18+. Interviews were conducted in English and Spanish and on landline and cell phones. 2005 survey was conducted September 14-December 8, 2005, n=3,215 adults ages 18+.

Love and Health

Research on the relationship between love and health, both physical and mental, is incredibly clear: being in love is good for your health and not being in love puts your health in serious jeopardy. For instance, the research has found that:

- People who are not in love are more likely to commit suicide (Bhatia et al., 2006),

- People who are in love have a lower incidence rate of heart failure, emotional distress, and ulcerative colitis (Flower, 2011).about having children and how they should be raised

Marriage and the Family

In the U.S., marriage is a popular institution. Most Americans will marry at some point. However, the statistics are difficult to sort out. While 95% of Americans say they have been married or intend to marry, attitudes towards marriage has been falling in the last decade (Newport & Wilkie, 2013).

According to the Pew Research Center, since 1970, each cohort of young adults since then has had a higher proportion of never-married than the previous cohort. If the current trend continues, "25% of young adults in the most recent cohort (ages 25 to 34

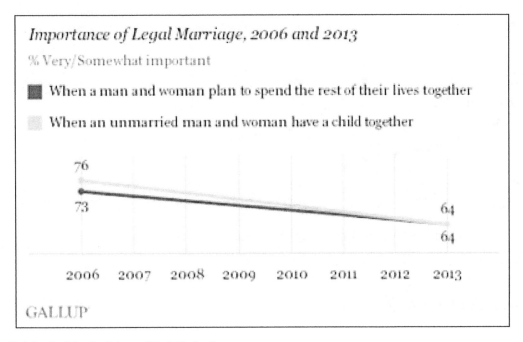

Importance of Legal Marriage, 2006 and 2013

% Very/Somewhat important

■ When a man and woman plan to spend the rest of their lives together

■ When an unmarried man and woman have a child together

76

73

64

64

2006 2007 2008 2009 2010 2011 2012 2013

GALLUP

in 2010) will have never married by 2030" (Wang & Parker, 2014). Factors effecting this dramatic change include:

1. Shifting public attitudes about the value of marriage,

2. What singles look for in someone to marry:
   a. 70% placed the highest priority on women who shared similar ideas
   b. 78% of women said that the highest priority in looking for someone to marry was having a steady job
3. Changing economic conditions (including employment),
4. The value of education (i.e., there is a slight trend for higher education to be less likely to marry).

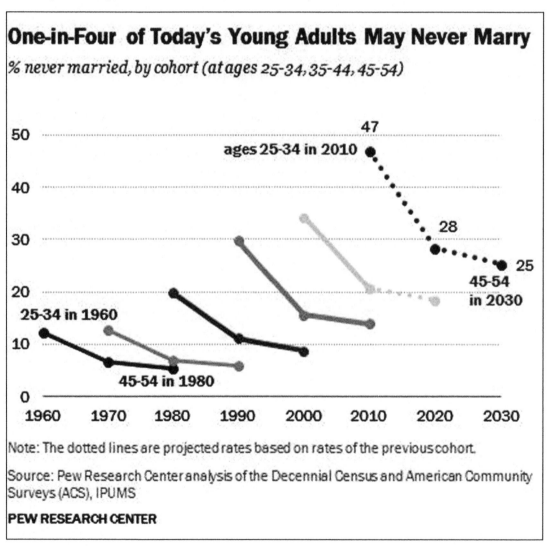

One-in-Four of Today's Young Adults May Never Marry

% never married, by cohort (at ages 25-34, 35-44, 45-54)

Note: The dotted lines are projected rates based on rates of the previous cohort.

Source: Pew Research Center analysis of the Decennial Census and American Community Surveys (ACS), IPUMS

PEW RESEARCH CENTER

A wild card was effectively added to this data with the legalization of same-sex marriage. Prior to same-sex marriage becoming legal in Massachusetts in 1995, and legal in all 50 states, census data may not be correct because of how same-sex couples reported their relationship to census takers.

How Would We Define Family?

In the more recent past, researchers in the U.S. would have included four components in their definition of the family:

1. Members of the family function as an economic unit rather than as individual economic entities;

2. They usually live under the same roof;

3. The parents are expected to engage in sex and therefore have responsibility for child rearing;

4. Are related by blood.

However, and while the aforementioned is the most agreed upon definition of the family in the past, there have been significant problems with that definition. In the modern family, do all members of the family contribute financially to the family as an economic unit? Generally, if teenagers are employed, the money they earn is kept for themselves and not given to the family unit. Next, for economic reasons, sometimes fathers or mothers must leave the area to find

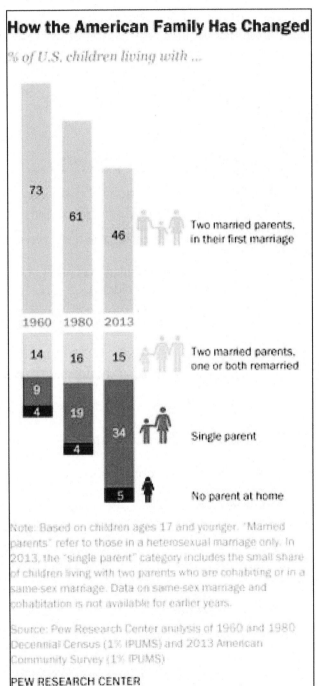

How the American Family Has Changed

% of U.S. children living with ...

73 — 1960
61 — 1980
46 — 2013

Two married parents, in their first marriage

14   16   15

Two married parents, one or both remarried

9   19   34
4

Single parent

4   5

No parent at home

Note: Based on children ages 17 and younger. "Married parents" refer to those in a heterosexual marriage only. In 2013, the "single parent" category includes the small share of children living with two parents who are cohabiting or in a same-sex marriage. Data on same-sex marriage and cohabitation is not available for earlier years.

Source: Pew Research Center analysis of 1960 and 1980 Decennial Census (1% IPUMS) and 2013 American Community Survey (1% IPUMS)

PEW RESEARCH CENTER

work and thus may be absent from the household for some time. A great example of this would be military spouses. Military families become used to being separated for long periods of time. Parents are expected to have sex and provide for child rearing, but not all couples choose to have children. By itself this is a great example of how our definition of family just doesn't fit a large segment of the population: when was the last time you heard a childless couple referred to as a family? I doubt if you have. Finally, the aforementioned definition states that family members must be related by blood, but if that's the case, step-children, adopted children, and foster children would be left out of our definition of family. Even today sociologists are not in complete agreement as to what constitutes a family.

Functions of the Family

What are the functions of the family? William Ogburn (1938) believed that the family performed seven functions:

1. Economic (meeting the basic physical needs of its members);

2. Protection (physical as well as economic protection for children when young and for parents as elders);

3. Prestige and status (providing a sense of place and belonging in the broader society);

4. Education (formal and informal/socialization);

5. Religion (providing traditions and religious identity);

6. Recreation (play and fun);

7. Affection and reproduction.

For more than sixty years, Ogburn's model of family functions was accepted and used to provide information for research on families. However, there were problems with his delineation of family functions particularly in that they were too broad. In 2001 Anne-Marie Ambert offered her model of family functions and it had been reduced to five important functions. Those functions are:

1. Reproduction;

2. Provision of basic needs for growth and development;

3. A sense of personal belonging;

4. Socialization; and

5. Love and affection.

This too is problematic in that a growing number of couples are choosing not to have children though the figure still pales in comparison to those who do have or want to have children which is about 94% of couples (Newport and Wilkie, 2013). When Americans were surveyed and asked about reasons why couples do not have any children, 66% said because of financial issues.

Types of Families

If you were to ask an American what is a family, the most likely answer would be a mom, dad, and their kids. That type of household is called a nuclear family. However, in many parts of the world the most common type of household would include mom, dad, their kids, their elderly parents, and possibly siblings. That kind of arrangement is called an extended family. Another type of family is called the bi-nuclear family. Bi-nuclear family is from the child's point of view—a child whose parents divorced and then remarried, is a member of two nuclear families. A blended or reconstituted family is the "yours, mine, and ours" phenomenon. Spouses and their children from previous marriages live together as one reconstituted family. Other terms related to types of families include family of orientation versus family of procreation. A family of orientation is the family into which one is born. A family of procreation is the family that one begins as an adult.

How Many Spouses?

Historically, monogamy was defined as one male spouse and one female spouse. A more modern definition would suggest two people in love, in a relationship, committed to each other, and sexual relations are limited to between the two partners. Polygamy is a type of marriage where an individual, man or woman, can have several spouses. Polygamy is marriage between one man and multiple women. Polyandry is marriage between one woman and multiple men. Americans are serial monogamists—marriage is limited to one person at a time, but there may be many such relationships over a lifetime. As serial monogamists, we Americans like to date one person at a time, get engaged to one person at a time, and because of law and culture, marry one person at a time.

Arranged Marriages

An arranged marriage is a marriage that is made by parents for reasons other than love. While arranged marriage is still practiced in some cultures around the world, historically nobility practiced arranged marriages to form political alliances. In cultures that still practice arranged marriage today, it is usually done for religious or economic reasons. Which is better—marrying for love or marrying because it has been arranged?

In our culture, it's hard to imagine someone being made to marry someone without being in love with the person they are expected to marry, but supporters of arranged marriage argue that partners can begin their marriage without any expectations of the other and are free to grow together as the relationship evolves and matures. In research done by Pamela Regan (2012), she found that spouses in both arranged and love marriages reported high levels of satisfaction, commitment, and passionate and companionate love. Regan points out that married people tend to be happier regardless of whether their marriage was for love or arranged. Overall, when looking the aforementioned factors, Regan found no differences between spouses in arranged marriages as opposed to those in love marriages. However, it should be noted that all of the couples participating in the study were either American citizens or living in the U.S. What do you think of the idea that spouses can be just as happy and in love in arranged marriages as marriages that follow falling in love?

Authority Patterns

Historically, power has been passed down from father to son. A patriarchy is a culture in which men hold the power and dominate in family decisions. The U.S. has historically been a patriarchal society, though today we are more egalitarian. In egalitarian families, power and decision-making is shared between husbands and wives. Finally, there is the matriarchal society. A matriarchy is a society in which women hold the power and dominate in family decisions. Historically, there have been few matriarchal societies. One example of a matriarchy would be the Mosuo people of Southern China. The Mosuo have what are called "walking marriages." These "marriages" are "based on sex and mutual affection" (Mattison et al., 2014). It is the Mosuo woman who gives permission for a man to visit and have sex with her. The man usually arrives after dark, spends the night, has sex with the woman, and then leaves and returns home in the morning. Mosuo women and men can engage in sexual relations with as many partners as they wish (Shih, 2010).

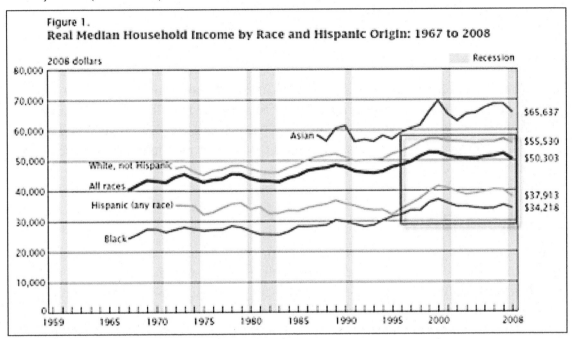

Figure 1.
Real Median Household Income by Race and Hispanic Origin: 1967 to 2008

Diversity and the Family

Cubans, Puerto Ricans, Asian, Native American, and Mexican-American families vary greatly in their economic status, birthrates, and number of family members living under the same roof. Extended families are more common among Asian and Mexican-American families. Asian and Cuban families tend to have the highest incomes with Mexican-American and Native American families coming in with the lowest average household income.

Commuter Marriages

Commuter marriages are when married couples live apart for long periods of time usually for economic reasons. The military is one example, but generally married couples who are in a commuter marriage are college educated and have careers.

Couples either met each other at a distance and built the relationship around that distance, or one spouse was transferred, leaving the other spouse to maintain their career. Separation can be hard on couples in a commuter marriage. Stress and economic strains of maintaining two households can pose problems, as can loneliness and role strain on the custodial parent if there are children. Glotzer and Federlein (2007) reported that successful couples in commuter marriages have an egalitarian relationship, are open in their communication, and agree on the goals of commuting.

Kinship

Have you ever heard the expression kith and kin? Maybe in an old movie set in Scotland or Britain. The phrase dates back prior to the 1300's in medieval Europe and refers to one's acquaintances, friends, and kin (i.e., family). Today, it is an obscure term to most Americans, kin is used to speak about family ties—those resulting from marriage or blood.

Childless Couples

According to the 2015 U.S. Census Bureau, forty-eight percent of women aged 18 to 44 were childless. This represents a slight increase from 2012. Overall, forty-seven percent of women aged 15 to 44 years were childless—up from thirty-five percent in 1976.

The percentage of women not having children has increased dramatically in the past 30 years, most American women still choose to have children. Likely reasons women would choose not to have children include:

- they are unable to put the child's needs ahead of their own (selflessness),

- it's a 21 year commitment,

- studies have found that having children actually decreases marital satisfaction until the children leave the nest,

- children won't make a bad marriage better, in fact, they will almost certainly ma

- children don't respect privacy, so their sex-life might take a hit,

- according to the U.S.D.A. the average cost of raising a child to the age of 18 is estimated to be $245,000. When you factor in inflation, a child was born in 2016, will cost an estimated $304,000 (Lino, 2014). Children are expensive.

The aforementioned are reasons that some women choose not to have children, it should be pointed out that some women want to have children but are not able to. Women are socialized to be caregivers and kin keepers. They are expected to be the ones to take time from their work to raise a child, but even if that is only for a short time, that can damage their careers. Staying out of the paid labor force for more than a couple of years can permanently damage a woman's career. Likewise, if an elderly parent needs care, it is often the adult daughter who provides that care. Taking care of sick loved ones could go on for years, and during that time they are effectively out of the dating pool and therefore having children isn't in the scheme of things at that point. By the time she no longer needs to provide care for a sick loved one, her age may make it difficult to find a husband. Also, when you look at educational attainment and childlessness, it is very clear that the more education a woman has, the less likely it is that she married and has children. Why? First, because she has put off marriage until she has finished her education, which keeps her out of the dating pool for that time. By the time she is ready to re-enter the dating pool, it may be difficult to find a spouse. Second, highly educated women are not likely to be traditional in nature. Highly educated women, with their own careers means that traditional households value go out the window; in other words, highly educated women would not value a husband who expects her to have dinner on the table when they walk in the door at 5:30 p.m. So, this too shrinks the marriage pool for these highly educated women (Newtson & Keith, 1997).

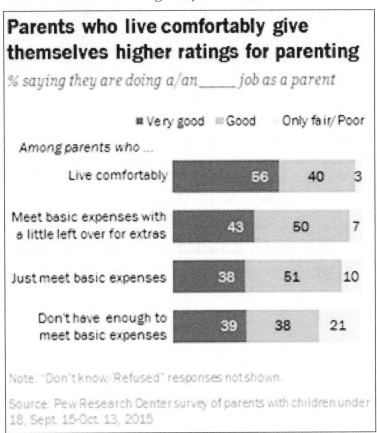

How Many Children?

The desire to have large families prior to the industrial revolution was to ensure there would be enough children who would survive childhood to help with farming and become an heir to the family property. With industrialization, children took on a new role and became more valuable from an emotional standpoint. Children became "little darlings." By 1900, the average number of children in a household was about five. By 1936, that had fallen to 3.6 children and by 2013, 2.6 children. For couples who do choose to have children the single greatest factor in determining how many children they will have is cost. As already stated, children are expensive (Pew

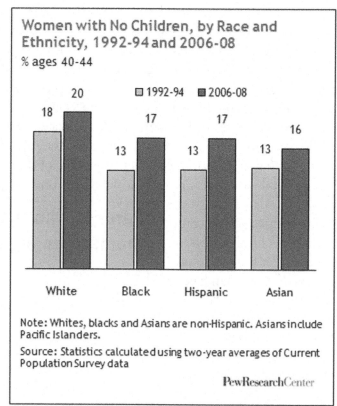

Women with No Children, by Race and Ethnicity, 1992-94 and 2006-08

% ages 40-44

Note: Whites, blacks and Asians are non-Hispanic. Asians include Pacific Islanders.

Source: Statistics calculated using two-year averages of Current Population Survey data

PewResearchCenter

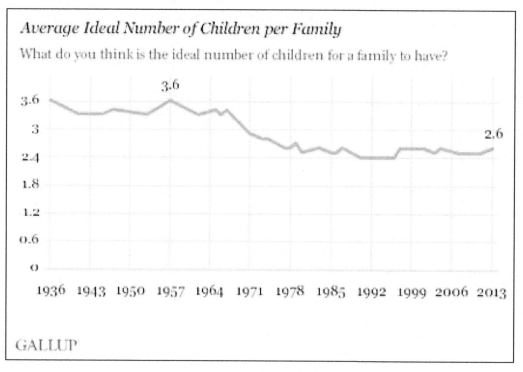

Average Ideal Number of Children per Family

What do you think is the ideal number of children for a family to have?

GALLUP

Education and Marriage

Research by Wang (2015) using data from the Pew Research Center has found that there is a substantial link between having a college education and a successful and long-lasting relationship. The overall divorce rate is somewhere around fifty percent. Eighty percent of college educated women are still married 20 years after marrying. This is consistent with previous research that found that both college educated men and women have a much better chance of remaining married for 20 years or more that non-college educated males and females.

Race and ethnicity to play a part in the likelihood a couple has a long-lasting relationship. For Asian, women seventy percent will stay together with their husbands for at least 20 years. In contrast, White and Hispanic women only have a fifty percent chance of their marriage lasting for 20 years or longer. It is even less so for African-American women as the likelihood of their still being married after 20 years is thirty-seven percent.

Additionally, children are more likely to live with both parents when those parents are more educated (Livingtson, 2013). Of children under the age of 18, eighty-nine percent live with parents who have college degrees, compared to seventy percent who live with parents that have a high school diploma, and only sixty-four percent live with parents who have less than a high school diploma.

Financial Issues and Marriage

Unfortunately, things are not going well for the average American household. Research done by the Pew Research Center (2015) reported that one-third of American households said they able to meet their basic needs with just a little left over for "extras." Twenty-five percent of parents said they were only able to pay for basic expenses, and nine percent don't even have enough to pay basic household expenses. Researchers did find that family type was a good indicator of perceived financial well being. For married parents, a little more than one-third said they lived comfortably. However, of those parents living with an unmarried partner only one-fourth said they lived comfortably and only eighteen of those single parent households indicated they lived comfortably.

Surprisingly researchers found a strong correlation between parents' income and education and how well they thought they were doing raising their children. Fifty-six percent of parents who said their household financial situation was "comfortable" stated they were doing a good job as a parent raising their children. This is in contrast to those parents who said they were barely able to meet basic needs in which fifty percent indicated they were doing a good job raising their children. For those having significant trouble making ends meet, sixty-nine percent stated they were only doing a good or fair job of raising their children (Pew Research Center, 2015).

Division of Household Tasks

Research has consistently found a division of household tasks associated with gender. For all educational and income groups, women are more likely to perform more household tasks than their husbands. As education and income of the wife increases, so does the proportion of household tasks done by husbands. As education and income of the wife falls, so does the proportion of household tasks done by husbands. In more egalitarian marriages, the division of household tasks is more equitable with husbands doing more work than those in marriages with traditional work roles for husbands. It is therefore not surprising that researchers found that mothers were more likely to report that being a parent is tiring rather than fathers.

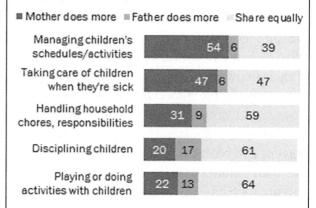

Division of Labor in Households with Two Full-Time Working Parents

% of parents in households where both parents are employed full time saying ...

■ Mother does more ■ Father does more ░ Share equally

	Mother does more	Father does more	Share equally
Managing children's schedules/activities	54	6	39
Taking care of children when they're sick	47	6	47
Handling household chores, responsibilities	31	9	59
Disciplining children	20	17	61
Playing or doing activities with children	22	13	64

Note: Based on respondents who work full time and are married to or living with a partner who works full time and is the parent of at least one of the respondent's children (n=531). Voluntary responses of "Other" and "Don't know/Refused" not shown.

Source: Pew Research Center survey of parents with children under 18, Sept. 15-Oct. 13, 2015

PEW RESEARCH CENTER   Q35a-e

Parenting Advice

Anticipatory socialization, occurs before someone steps into a specific status or role, helps some women prepare for the tasks associated with parenting. Typically, young women may babysit for friends or their parents and are paid a wage. At younger ages, they play with dolls that wet themselves, or I've even seen a doll that sits on a toilet and drops a "poop" into the tiny little toilet bowl so the young child can learn how to wipe a child's bottom. As silly as it may seem, even those socializing acts help prepare female children for what will probably be their future as a parent. No similar type of anticipatory socialization exists for males. So whom do parents turn to for advice about parenting? In addition to watching television or movies, mothers are more likely to turn to family and friends than are men. Approximately one-third of mothers reported turning to a family member compared to only nineteen of fathers, and while twenty-one percent of mothers turned to friends for advice, only 8% of fathers did so. One important finding was that both mothers and fathers equally turned to each other for advice with parenting issues. Among college-educated mothers, about half turn to the media (e.g., magazines, websites, and television) for advice on parenting as opposed to only thirty-nine percent of non-college educated women who do so.

Marriage, Parenthood and Happiness

% saying they are ... with their life

	Married		Not married	
	Parent	Non-parent	Parent	Non-parent
Very happy	36	39	23	22
Pretty happy	49	51	46	62
Not too happy	13	9	25	15

Note: Parents include those with children of any age. "Don't know/Refused" responses not shown.

Source: Pew Research Center survey Nov 28-Dec 5, 2012, N=2,511

Marital Satisfaction and Children

Previous research has reported a U-shaped relationship between marital satisfaction and the presence of children. Marriages start off with high marital satisfaction, but the presence of children lowered that satisfaction until the children left the nest and marital satisfaction climbed back up. New research casts doubt on those findings. In a study by Deaton and Stone (2014), researchers found virtually no difference in the marital satisfaction levels between parents and non-parents. In a study by the Pew Research Center (Parker, 2014), researchers found almost identical results: thirty-six percent of married adults with children and thirty-nine percent of those with no children reported being "very happy" in their marriage. The most notable finding was that single parents indicated the least happiness with their life.

Terms, Concepts and Names to Know:

- Dating

- Manifest functions

- Latent functions

- Propinquity

- Endogamy

- Exogramy

- Types of love

- Types of families

- Functions of marriage

- Arranged marriages

- Monogamy

- Polygamy

- Polyandry

- Polygyny

- Commuter marriages

- Kinship

- Education and Marriage

- Childless couples

- Marital satisfaction

Be Able to Discuss:

- The functions of dating

- Who we date and why

- The role of appearance in attraction

- The role of love and health

- Pheromones and other chemicals in involved in love

- Types of love

- The pros cons of Internet dating

- Defining the family

- Functions of the family

- Arranged marriages and marital satisfaction

- Relationship between marriage and education

- Division of household tasks

References

Baumesiter, R. (2003). Does High Self-Esteem Cause Better Performance, Interpersonal Success, Happiness, or Healthier Lifestyles? Psychological Science in the Public Interest, 4(1), 1-44. Retrieved April 1, 2016.

Bhatia, M., Verma, S., Murty, O. (2006). Suicidal Notes: Psychological and Clinical Profile. International Journal of Psychiatry in Medicine, 36, 163-170.

British Broadcasting Company. (2014, September 17). The Science of Love. Retrieved March 23, 2016, from http://www.bbc.co.uk/science/hottopics/love/

Deaton, A. & Stone, A. (2014). Evaluative and hedonic wellbeing among those with and without children at home. Proceedings of the National Academy of Sciences of the United States of America, 111(4), 1328-1333.

Finkel, E. (2012, February 2). Online Dating: A Critical Analysis From the Perspective of Psychological Science. Retrieved March 23, 2016, from http://www.psychologicalscience. org/index.php/publications/journals/pspi/online-dating.html

Flower, G. (2011). LIFE Support: The physical and emotional benefits of our personal relationships. Alive: Canada's Natural Health & Wellness Magazine., February(340), 1824. Retrieved March 23, 2016.

Glotzer, R. (2007). Miles That Bind: Commuter Marriage and Family Strengths. Michigan Family Review, 12(1), 7-31.

Jay, M. (2012, April 14). The Downside of Cohabiting Before Marriage. New York Times. Retrieved July 14, 2016, from http://www.nytimes.com/2012/04/15/opinion/sunday/the-downside-of-cohabiting-before-marriage.html?_r=0

Liebowitz, L. (2015, March 6). The Way Most People Meet Their Significant Others Is Probably Not What You Think. Retrieved March 23, 2016, from http://mic.com/articles/112062/the-way-most-people-meet-their-significant-others-is-not-what-you-think#.kxs8vcTWT

Lino, Mark. (2014). Expenditures on Children by Families, 2013. U.S. Department of Agriculture, Center for Nutrition Policy and Promotion. Miscellaneous Publication No. 1528-2013.

Livingston, G. (2014, December 22). Fewer than half of U.S. kids today live in a 'traditional' family. Retrieved from http://www.pewresearch.org/fact-tank/2014/12/22/less-than-half-of-u-s-kids-today-live-in-a-traditional-family/Livingston, F. (2013, August 2).

Most in U.S. Want Marriage, but Its Importance Has Dropped. Retrieved from http://www.gallup.com/poll/163802/marriage-importance-dropped.aspx

Livingston, G. (2013, November 27). The links between education, marriage and parenting. Retrieved March 30, 2016, from http://www.pewresearch.org/fact-tank/2013/11/27/the-links-between-education-marriage-and-parenting/

Mattison, S., Scelza, B., & Blumenfield, T. (2014). Paternal Investment and the Positive Effects of Fathers among the Matrilineal Mosuo of Southwest China. American Anthropologist, 116(3), 591-610.

Miller, D. & Barnes, L. (2015). Secrets Of The Mind - Learn About Human Psychology. Seattle, WA: Amazon Digital Services.

Newport, F., & Wilkie, J. (2013, September 25). Desire for Children Still Norm in U.S. Retrieved March 23, 2016, from http://www.gallup.com/poll/164618/desire-children-norm.aspx

Newtson, R. & Keith, P. (1997). Single Women in Later Life. In Coyle, J. (Ed.). Handbook of Aging and Women, pp. 385-399. Westport, CT: Greenwood Press.

Parenting in America. (2015, December 17). Retrieved April 1, 2016, from http://www.pewsocialtrends.org/2015/12/17/1-the-american-family-today/

Parker, K. (2016, February 7). Parenthood and happiness: It's more complicated than you think. Retrieved from http://www.pewresearch.org/fact-tank/2014/02/07/parenthood-and-happiness-its-more-complicated-than-you-think/

Perrett, D. (2012). In Your Face The New Science of Human Attraction. Basingstoke, U.K.: Palgrave Macmillan.

Rauh, S. (2009). 10 Surprising Health Benefits of Love. Retrieved March 23, 2016, from http://www.medicinenet.com/script/main/art.asp?articlekey=97679

Regan, P. (2012, August 1). Arranged vs. Love-Based Marriages in the U.S.—How Different Are They? Not as different as you might think. Retrieved March 23, 2016, from https://www.psychologytoday.com/blog/the-science-love/201208/arranged-vs-love-based-marriages-in-the-us-how-different-are-they

Shih, S. (2010). Quest for Harmony: The Moso Traditions of Sexual Union & Family Life. Standford, CT: Stanford University Press.

Smith, A. & Anderson, M. (2016, February 29). 5 facts about online dating. Retrieved March 23, 2016, from http://www.pewresearch.org/fact-tank/2016/02/29/5-facts-aboutonline-dating/

Vaknin, S. (2013). The Pathology of Love. Rhinebeck, NY: Narcissus Publications.

Wang, W. (2014, September 24). Record Share of Americans Have Never Married As Values, Economics and Gender Patterns Change. Retrieved from http://www.pewsocialtrends.org/2014/09/24/record-share-of-americans-have-never-married/

Wang, W. (2015, March 4). The link between a college education and a lasting marriage. Retrieved 2016, from http://www.pewresearch.org/fact-tank/2015/12/04/education-and-marriage/

Module 14: Alternative Households

How the American Family Has Changed

Fewer than half of U.S. children today live in a "traditional family." Data from the Pew Research Center, Livingston (2014) found that fewer than half (i.e., 46%) of children in the U.S. under the age of 18 live at home with married heterosexual parents. This is down significantly from 1980 when 61% of all U.S. children lived in intact households and down even more from 1960 when 73% of all children lived in intact households. Explanations include more Americans are delaying marriage into their late-20s and many are choosing not to wed at all. Further, children born outside of wedlock were relatively few in 1960, about 5%, but they represent 41% of all children born in the U.S. today.

Growth of Single-Parent Households

Between 1970 and 2003, according to the Pew Research Center (2013) single-mother headed households increased from 3 million to 10 million. At the same time, the number of single-father headed households increased from about half a million to 2 million during that time period. In terms of proportions to all households during that time period, single-mother headed households increased to 26 percent of all households and the proportion of single-father headed households grew from 1 percent to 6 percent though Livingston (2014) reports that 35% of all children in the U.S. today live in single-parent households—slightly higher from the 2013 data reported. What the research is telling us is that almost one-third of all households in the U.S. do not consist of a mother and father instead living in single parent headed households.

Of all the alternative types of households in the U.S. today, the single parent headed household is by far the largest.

Cohabitation

Between 1970 and 2003, the marriage rate in the U.S. decreased dramatically. Fewer people are getting married today than at any time in U.S. history. That decrease in the marriage rate could be interpreted as a lowered value of marriage as both a sacred institution and rite of passage. Though marriage has declined in recent years, the practice of cohabitation (i.e., living together romantically as a couple without being married) has increased. In fact, cohabitation prior to marriage has become a common practice for people in their 20's and 30's. Such couples view cohabitation as something along the lines of a trial marriage. The idea is that cohabitating couples will live together, explore their ability to live and love as a couple, and if they feel they are successful, they will then decide to tie the knot and marry. The research has found that about half of all currently married couples state that they cohabitated prior to marriage. In total, 6.3% of all couples in the U.S. are currently cohabitating.

When two people live together romantically, they are cohabitating. The number of cohabitating couples is thought to be around 6%. As a social experiment, cohabitation came from Scandinavia in the 1960's as sort of a trial marriage. The idea was that two people, in love, could live together for a trial period to see if they were right for each other; if they were, they would then marry and have a happy and successful marriage because their trial marriage was successful.

Research indicates that the growth in cohabitation has increased in all segments of the population. The increase in cohabitation has increased in 30–44-year-olds at the expense of marriage. In 2010, approximately 56% of all U.S. adults without a college degree were married, but that represented a decline from

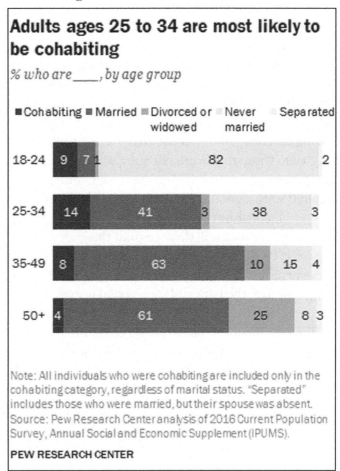

Adults ages 25 to 34 are most likely to be cohabiting

% who are ____, by age group

■ Cohabiting ■ Married ■ Divorced or ░ Never ░ Separated
widowed married

Age	Cohabiting	Married	Divorced or widowed	Never married	Separated
18-24	9	7	1	82	2
25-34	14	41	3	38	3
35-49	8	63	10	15	4
50+	4	61	25	8	3

Note: All individuals who were cohabiting are included only in the cohabiting category, regardless of marital status. "Separated" includes those who were married, but their spouse was absent. Source: Pew Research Center analysis of 2016 Current Population Survey, Annual Social and Economic Supplement (IPUMS).

PEW RESEARCH CENTER

63% in 1995. So, more and more non-college educated couples were choosing to cohabitate rather than to marry (Fry and Cohn, 2011). Research has also found that approximately 70% of women in their early 30's had cohabitated at some point. And in fact, it would seem that for many cohabitation is the norm before deciding to marry. Approximately 58% of women aged 19–44 years old who marry for the first time had lived with their husbands before the wedding (Kennedy and Bumpass, 2008).

The idea of cohabitating prior to marriage made its way to the U.S. from Scandinavia in the 1960's and was accepted here as a 'trial marriage.' It made sense and still makes sense. If you go shopping for a car, you test-drive the car before buying it. Many feel that cohabitation should be viewed in the same way. The idea is that if a couple manages to work through their troubles and build a relationship on trust and communication, marriage is the obvious end and cohabitation the means.

Unfortunately, while the idea makes sense, the reality is that couples that cohabitate prior to marrying are significantly more likely to divorce than couples that did not cohabitate prior to marriage. In fact, the research has found that 40% of cohabitating couples that marry will eventually divorce; that is twice the rate of divorce for the general population (Luscombe, 2015).

The National Marriage Project (2001) found that about half of people in their 20's said they would only marry someone if they could live (i.e., cohabitate) with them first. Two-thirds said that living together prior to marriage was a good way to avoid divorce. The problem is that the research finds that couples cohabitating prior to marriage not only have a significantly higher divorce rate than those who didn't cohabitate prior to getting married, but for those that are not divorced they are less satisfied with their marriage than those that were not cohabitating. There are various theories as to why couples cohabitating prior to marriage have higher divorce rates with the most likely reason associated with a greater tendency towards deviance.

If cohabitation is effective as a trial marriage, why is it more likely that cohabitating couples will divorce than those that don't cohabitate prior to marriage? The answer is two-fold. First, couples that cohabitate without being married are going against traditional social norms. In regard to their feeling about living together without being married, they are violating social norms and are in some sense deviant. If that's the case, and that they are comfortable with breaking away from traditional norms, what is marriage to them? Some might argue that it is just a piece of paper once stripped of the traditional and sacred aspects. Seeing marriage as just a piece of paper certainly would make divorce easier for couples who have failed at their marriage though they cohabitated prior to marrying.

The second reason starts with a question: should we assume that cohabitating couples that marry are in fact ready for marriage? The answer may be no. It is possible that one or both partners set a time limit on the period of their cohabitation. In other words, "we'll live together for a year, if it goes well, we'll marry, but if it doesn't, we'll each go our separate ways." If things aren't going as well as they should, cohabitating couples could still end up getting married simply because they fear losing the partner who issued the ultimatum, or it's just easier to get married. Being single and in the romance market can be a horribly and emotionally draining situation. Most people don't like being single, and the prospect of having to go "shopping" all over again is scary. So, the end result is that some couples that are cohabiting still decide to marry even though things are rocky in their relationship and the last thing they should do is to marry one another. Also, no doubt some couples who cohabitating, but in a shaky relationship, feel that marrying might decrease their problems, when if anything, it will almost certainly do the opposite. It's much like married couples who decide to have children because they are not getting along well; having a child in that situation will only make the marital situation worse and the poor child will pay the price.

Finally, it should be noted that one-third of all children spend some time living with a mother and her cohabiting partner, and to a lesser extent with a father and his cohabitating partner.

Remaining Single/Ever-Single

To refer to someone as "never married," implies they lack something important—a spouse. The term "ever-single" is a judgment free term that refers to people who have remained single. Excluding young people who have not yet married, ever-single people are more likely female, educated, have a large social support network of friends, be better off financially than divorced and widowed women, and generally are in better health than divorced and widowed women. Ever-single women are often found in higher education where they've had to make a choice between family life and their career. Another reason ever-single are more likely female is because they are also care-givers. If an elderly parent needs care, they often remove themselves from the dating pool to care for their loved one, and by the time they return to the dating pool, there are few eligible bachelors (Newtson & Keith, 1997).

Today a record number of Americans are choosing to remain single. In a 2012 survey, 20% of U.S. adults 25 years and older had never been married (Wang & Parker, 2014). Remaining single represents a clear departure from societal expectations and some people can feel lonely in a society that presumes marriage is the source of all happiness. However, women don't necessarily need to marry to enjoy a satisfying life. Society has always been tougher on women who remain single than men. The double standard has always applied. The man who remains single is called a "playboy," and that has a positive connotation in the male world. On the other hand, a woman who remains single is referred to as a "spinster" or "old maid," neither of which are flattering terms.

There is a greater trend toward maintaining a single lifestyle for a longer period and it is related to the growing economic independence of young people. Research also shows that for all age groups, 15% of American adults have used online dating services. However, among the ever-single that climbs to 30%. That means that the ever-single are the biggest users of online dating of all age groups. However, for all U.S. adults only 5% report having found their current partner through in online dating service (Anderson, 2016).

Marriage Without Children

There has been a significant increase in the number of women who do not have children childlessness in U.S. (Livingston & Cohn, 2010). While historically the more highly educated women had a greater likelihood of being childless, and spouseless as well, this has changed in recent years. In 2008, 24% of women between the ages of 40 – 44 with a graduate degree had not had children, but this represents a decline from 31% in 1994. Further, about 16-17% of women will complete childbearing years without children, compared to 10% in 1980. More couples, of all age and economic groups, are choosing not to have children with economic reasons being the most cited reason for not having children.

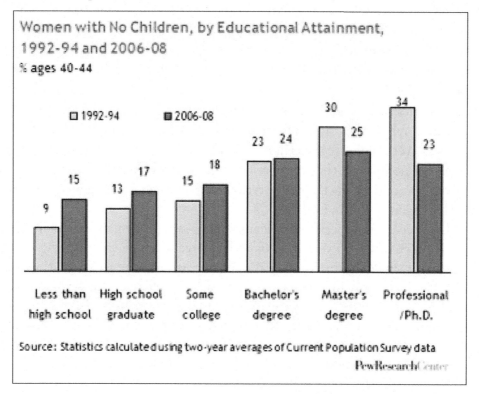

Women with No Children, by Educational Attainment, 1992-94 and 2006-08
% ages 40-44

Source: Statistics calculated using two-year averages of Current Population Survey data

PewResearchCenter

Commuter Marriages

Commuter marriages are when married couples live apart for long periods of time usually for economic reasons. The number of commuter marriages has risen 30% to 3.6 million between the years 2000 and 2005. Military would be one example, but generally married couples who are in a commuter marriage are college educated and have careers. Couples either met each other at a distance or built the relationship around that distance, or one spouse was transferred leaving the other spouse to maintain their career. Physical separation can be hard on couples in a commuter marriage. Stress and economic strains of maintaining two households can pose problems, as can loneliness and role strain on the custodial parent if there are children. Glotzer and Federlein (2007) reported that successful couples in commuter marriages have an egalitarian relationship, are open in their communication, and agree on the goals of commuting. While military deployments, migratory jobs and economic need have long forced couples around the world to live apart, in America today, it is more often the woman's career that drives the separation. Finally, the research finds that divorce in commuter marriages is no more frequent than in those where the couple is under the same roof.

Non-Marital Childbearing

Data from the National Center for Health Statistics reports that the number of non-marital births has decreased by 7% in recent years. Non-marital births totaled 1,605,643 in 2013, which accounts for about 40% of all births between the years 2007 and 2013. While non-marital birth rates fell for women under 35 years since 2007, the rate increased for non-marital women aged 35 and older. The number of children born out of wedlock is increasing among the poor of all races (Curtin et al., 2014). Why do women have children out of wedlock? For many it's because they stop using contraception and are confident about their ability to raise a child, and for the poor, they place more value on having children.

Gay Marriage

On April 1, 2001, Helene Faasen and Anne-Mrie Thus were legally married in the Netherlands. It was the first legally recognized gay marriage in the history of the world. The next country to allow same-sex marriage was Belgium, which came under intense attack from the Vatican. European countries began to fall like dominoes to overwhelming support for same-sex marriage. After Belgium came Spain, Norway, Sweden, Portugal, Iceland, Denmark, and France. And along that timeline a few countries outside of

"Same sex marriage isn't gay privilege, it's equal rights. Privilege would be something like gay people not paying taxes. Like churches don't.

Europe also jumped on the bandwagon—Canada in 2005, South Africa in 2006, Argentina in 2010, Uruguay and New Zealand in 2013 (Andersson & Gunnar, 2006). Some countries like the United States and Mexico, allowed states to decide for themselves as to whether same-sex marriage should be legalized. Allowing individual states in the U.S. to decide for themselves as to the legality of same-sex marriage became problematic because of the rule of reciprocity. The rule of reciprocity mandated that states must recognize marriages performed in other states as legal within their own state. Consequently, a number of states passed laws forbidding same-sex marriage—the so-called defense of marriage laws. Appeals were made and eventually the issue found its way to the U.S. Supreme Court.

In 2011, the federal government stated that it would support a bill proposed by Senator Dianne Feinstein, from California, to repeal the Defense of Marriage Act. (The Defense of Marriage Act had been voted into law in order to prevent same-sex marriage.) The U.S. Justice Department was then ordered to stop defending the act. In 2013, the U.S. Supreme Court struck down part of the Defense of Marriage Act as it related to California's Proposition 8, which denied gays and lesbians the right to marry. This effectively struck down Proposition 8 and allowed for same-sex marriage in California to resume. In its majority opinion, the U.S. Supreme Court wrote about the "profound cultural shifts" in views of marriage in the past several thousand years. The justices also mentioned that the very nature of marriage had changed from one of having been arranged by parents for financial or political reasons to one based on love, or more correctly, a "voluntary contract."

Even within the past one hundred years, here in the U.S. the nature of marriage has moved from one of male dominance to one of equality or at least equality of "dignity." Rather than weakening the institution of marriage, the justices believed that these changes had strengthened the institution. In one of the most profound statements in their written majority opinion, the justices wrote, "Changed understandings of marriage are characteristics of a nation where new dimensions of freedom become apparent to new generations." From a sociological point of view, this represents recognition that social reproduction can be changed within short period of time when monumental cultural change is present. In the period from 2013 through 2014, the Supreme Court refused to hear appeals effectively from 11 states; by default, this decision by the Court allowed for the legalization of same-sex marriage in those states.

Finally in 2015, the U.S. Supreme Court ruled in the case of Obergefell versus Hodges, which challenged the rule of reciprocity between states and recognition of marriage, that the 14th Amendment to the Constitution requires all states to recognize same-sex marriages. Today, same-sex marriage is legal in all 50 states and its territories.

Income

Some past research claimed that same-sex households earned higher on average incomes than did their straight counterparts, but recent research indicates that's only partially true.

Almost half of same-sex couples have college degrees, substantially more than for heterosexual couples, and this is why some research reported that same-sex couples have higher household incomes. Labor force participation is also higher in same-sex couples. The average household income for same-sex couples was $117,768 and $104,226 for heterosexual couples (Kurtzleben, 2013). When this is broken down further, the mean household income for male/male same-sex couples was $137,149 and $99,681 for female/female same-sex couples (U.S. Census Bureau, 2014).

However, for annual income categories (a) less than $35,000, (b) $35,000 - $49,999, (c) $50,000 - $74,999, and (d) $75,000 - $99,999, the proportion of same-sex couples in each income category is less than for opposite-sex couples. Only for the $100,000 and greater annual household income category do same-sex couples make up a greater proportion in that category than do opposite-sex couples, 43.2% compared to 37.6% respectively (U.S. Census Bureau, 2014). Also, when comparing male-male to female-female same-sex couples using the above annual household income categories, it is interesting to note that for all but the last category, $100,00 or more, female-female couples made up a larger proportion of those categories than did their male-male counterparts. But for the last category, $100,000 and greater, male-male couples made up 49% of that income category as opposed to 37% for female-female same-sex couples. The income disparity in this last category is significant: male-male same-sex households earned an average household income of $137,139 compared to $99,681 for female-female same-sex households.

The myth that same-sex couples out earn opposite-sex couples is misleading and dangerous. With those myths guiding liberal politicians and well doers, they may feel same-sex couples have the financial resources to adequately fend off and deal with hostilities directed at them (e.g., discrimination in the job and housing markets, neighborhood harassment, and as it relates to adoption). Research is needed to discover the risks same-sex couples face because of discrimination, but are at greater risk because they lack financial resources. To be financially well off and gay is one thing, but it is highly likely that being poor and gay is another.

Being poor and gay is likely to significantly increase risks for problems related to discrimination in employment, lack of access to mental healthcare, inability to leave hostile neighborhoods or environments, and financial instability because of a lack of steady employment. For instance, in many states it is perfectly legal to fire someone for sexual orientation (King, 2014). In fact, because of the problems that likely result from being poor and gay, stress, which has already been found in greater levels among gays and lesbians (Mohr, 2016), might lead to greater relationship dysfunction among same-sex couples and in turn lead to a greater likelihood of dissolution of the relationship, whether married, or unmarried. Overall, more research is needed to discover the many aspects of same-sex relationships that are affected by poor financial resources.

Relationship Length

Research on same-sex couples has traditionally shown the past 20 to 30 years that lesbian couples tend to have more stable and longer-lasting relationships when compared to male-male couples. However, more recent research has shown that legally married lesbian couples do not stay together as long as do married gay male couples (Badgett and Hermann, 2011). This will need to be revisited as more data on same-sex divorce becomes available in the next few years.

Infidelity

Another related issue is that of infidelity. While research on this highly sensitive topic varies, most research suggests that as many as 20% of heterosexual couples will experience infidelity in the marital relationship; the rate is higher in unmarried relationships, 30 – 40% (Treas & Giessen, 2000). Among heterosexual males and females, the research is confounded by a number of variables (e.g., degree of commitment, female financial independence, attachment styles, sensation seeking) and so it cannot be stated with certainty who is more likely to commit infidelity. While there is an abundance of research available on the rate of heterosexual infidelity within marital relations, no such parity exists for same-sex couples. As the number of divorces increase for same-sex relationships over time more data on the frequency of infidelity will be available.

What about the effects of infidelity on marital relationships, be they opposite-sex or same-sex? Consistent with previous research, Leeker and Carlozzi (2014) found that emotional and sexual infidelity was more distressing (i.e., stress, anger, anxiety, jealousy, and humiliation) to heterosexuals than to gay and lesbians. Leeker and Carlozzi's research seems to support previous research findings that emotional responses to infidelity seem to be greatest among heterosexual women, followed by heterosexual males, and less so for gay males and lesbians (Bailey et al., 1994).

Why would same-sex couples be less threatened emotionally by infidelity? One possible explanation was offered by Heaphy, Donovan & Weeks (2004). They argued that because gay couples were already in violation of social norms, the significance of social norms either didn't exist or violations were more tolerated. Martell and Prince (2005) suggested that gay and lesbian couples were free to develop their own relationship rules and were therefore not constrained by monogamy, as are heterosexual couples.

This makes studying infidelity difficult because there are no shared rules or boundaries among same-sex couples. Every same-sex couple may have their own boundaries as to what does or doesn't constitute infidelity, and there is likely more diversity in the definition of infidelity among same-sex couples than among their heterosexual counterparts (Newtson, 2011). Also, as addressed by Leeker and Carlozzi, the evolutionary view of infidelity is in every way contrary to the evolutionary history of man. Consequently, infidelity can be seen as a greater evolutionary threat to heterosexuals than to gays and lesbians albeit more subconscious (Den Otter, 2015).

One problem with the aforementioned research in which same-sex couples seem to be less emotionally affected by infidelity hinges on their not sharing societal norms. In other words, same-sex couples are standing on the sidelines looking in, but creating their own rules and definitions of infidelity. However, this research is based on same-sex couples some of whom are married and some of whom are not. With the Supreme Court effectively legalizing same-sex marriage in 2015, it can be argued that married same-sex couples are no longer standing on the sidelines looking in. This fluidity of norms raises many questions:

- Could it be that same-sex couples that are married are adopting dominant social norms that govern monogamy and infidelity?

- What will the outcome of the legalization of same-sex marriage have on societal attitudes towards monogamy and infidelity?

- Will same-sex couples assimilate into dominant social norms of monogamy and infidelity, or will heterosexual couples move to the sidelines and adopt a rejection of social norms on monogamy and infidelity as practiced by same-sex couples?

- If same-sex couples adopt current and dominant social norms in regard monogamy and infidelity, will the emotional effects of infidelity in same-sex married mimic those of opposite-sex couples, which currently they do not?

- Finally, in a recent study of previously married heterosexual couples, 55% identified infidelity as the cause of their divorce (Warren, 2015). If same-sex couples do adopt conventional norms on monogamy and infidelity, which is suggested they had not done prior to the legalization of same-sex marriage, will infidelity be less tolerated and lead to divorce as it does for heterosexual couples now that same-sex marriage is legal?

Divorce and Desertion

Now that same-sex couples have the right to marry in the US, they have the option to legally end their marriage through divorce. Even divorce attorneys are now advising same-sex couples to obtain prenuptial agreements prior to getting married just as they do with opposite-sex couples (Vasileff, 2015). Do they do so? Or, are they like opposite-sex soon-to-be-married couples that think that love and trust are inseparable emotions? Research by Newtson (2000) found that among a sample of undergraduate students, the more recently married respondents had poorer attitudes towards prenuptial agreements.

Prior to the Supreme Court's ruling in 2015, same-sex couples who had lived and married in a state that granted same-sex marriages, and because most states that recognized same-sex marriage did not have laws in place to process same-sex divorce, were left with no choice but to be legally tied to one another. However, because historically marriage as a legal institution has been denied to same-sex couples until recently, research needs to investigate whether same-sex couples will take the same legal path to end their marriage (i.e., legal divorce) as do the majority of opposite-sex couples.

Though same-sex divorces can be somewhat more complicated than for opposite-sex marriages (e.g., couples with children, residency requirements), same-sex couples are enjoying the benefits of both legal marriage and legal divorce. Data on divorce for same-sex couples is incredibly incongruent. The overall divorce rate in the U.S. is estimated to be between 40 – 50% for first marriages and possibly as high as 60% for second marriages (Doherty, 2016). Of the data that is available, some findings point to divorce rates relatively similar to those of opposite-sex couples (Brydum, 2014). Other data suggests the rate of divorce is significantly higher for same-sex couples than their opposite-sex counterparts (Andersson and Gunnar, February 2006), and still more data reports lower rates of divorce for same-sex couples (Jones, 2012). Some countries have no data to report on same-sex divorce. Clearly, research is needed to gather more accurate and consistent data on same-sex divorce.

Desertion is a form of abandonment, and as such, can be grounds for divorce. Desertion among opposite-sex couples without children has fallen dramatically in the past several decades. This is largely because the cost of divorce has dropped dramatically during that period. Today, an uncontested divorce can cost as little as $250 - $500, while a contested divorce can range on average from $15,000 - $30,000 (Magloff, 2016).

However, back beyond 20 or 30 years ago, when uncontested divorces were far more costly, desertion was the poor man's divorce. Now that we have established that same-sex couples generally have lower household incomes than do opposite-sex couples, could desertion reappear as a cheap and quick fix to ending a relationship? To same-sex couples not well up the financial ladder, $250 - $500 could be an unmanageable amount. It could be argued that same-sex couples have not yet fully grasped the concept of formally ending relationships; up until recent court rulings, same-sex couples ended their relationship by simply packing up and moving on.

We know a great deal about marriage among opposite-sex couples, but not much about same-sex divorce. The average age of first marriage for opposite-sex couples is 28 for males and 26 for females (Mundy, 2013). We also know that wives are significantly more likely to instigate a divorce, two-thirds of the time, than are their husbands (Sayer, England, & Kangas, 2011). Proposed explanations for this include greater financial independence for women and less physical and emotional dependence. When investigating survey data obtained from Norway and Sweden, where same-sex partnerships have been legal since 1993 and 1995 respectively, it was discovered that lesbian couples were twice as likely to separate than gay male couples (Mundy, 2013). This finding contradicts previous research, which suggested that lesbian couples, though not legally partnered or wed, were more likely to stay together than gay male couples. Since this research suggests that women take the lead in ending relationships, whether same-sex or opposite-sex, more research needs to be done to discover the reason for this. Is it a case that women are just likely to get bored more quickly with relationships? Or, is it that women expect more out of a partner than is realistic? This could also lend support to previous research that showed marriage to generally be more important to men than to women.

Division of Household Tasks

Within relationships, the division of household tasks still merits study. Researchers long ago gave up talking about the equal division of household tasks and instead began investigating the equitable (i.e., perceived as fair) division of household tasks. Lively et al. (2010) reported that as long as heterosexual couples thought of household chores as "women's work," it would be "women's work" and continue to be so. While things have changed over the past several decades, women still do a disproportionate amount of the household tasks, and this is even more lopsided if the couple has children. Research has found that married men do approximately 21 hours per week in household tasks and childcare compared to women's 32 hours. And while men put in more time at work, averaging 45 hours, to women's 39 hours, men still have more free time (Modern Marriage, 2007). Additionally, the Pew Research Center (2007) identified dissatisfaction over the division of household tasks as the third leading cause of divorce. As of yet, there is no data to show that lesbian same-sex married couples divide household tasks more equally than do opposite-sex couples. Likewise, anecdotally it is believed that gay same-sex couples, married or not, are more likely to practice a more egalitarian division of household tasks.

Marital and Premarital Counseling

While marital counseling exists ubiquitously for heterosexuals, and more sparsely for same-sex couples, it is at least available. Unfortunately, there is little agreement in the literature as to the success of marital counseling. But what about pre-marital counseling? The literature on pre-marital counseling is a little more consistent. Research on premarital counseling for opposite-sex couples reveals that 44% of couples who marry today go through premarital counseling of some kind and the median amount of time opposite-sex couples spend in premarital counseling is about eight hours (20 Significant Premarital Counseling Statistics, 2014). However, previous research has found that self-identified religious couples were just as likely to divorce as the non-religious though religiosity and attendance were confounding variables (McDaniel et al., 2013; Tuttle & Davis, 2015; Village, 2010).

Since most premarital counseling programs are religious based, this might impair the availability of pre-marital counseling for same-sex couples. According to the Murphy (2015), members of a number of mainstream religions (e.g., Evangelical Lutherans, Methodists, Episcopalians, Presbyterians, and members of the United Church of Christ). However, even though a significant number of church members believe that gays and lesbians should be welcomed into their church, only a few churches openly welcome gays and lesbians. This includes Reform and Conservative Judaism, the Episcopal Church, the Evangelical Lutheran Church, the Presbyterian Church, and Quakers (Masci and Lipka, 2015). Do these churches provide premarital counseling to same-sex couples? More research is necessary to answer this question.

Propinquity and Density

South and Lloyd (1995) reported that people living in more urban areas, or what they termed "marrying market," were more likely to divorce. When living in an area where there are many prospective partners, both men and women see remarriage as likely and therefore are more likely to seek a divorce. The authors found this was especially true for married women with a college education. Likewise, in these marrying markets extramarital affairs are more common. South and Lloyd's research found that married couples living in less dense and more rural areas were more likely to stay together. Does this same finding hold true for same-sex couples? Would the divorce rate for same-sex couples therefore be higher in urban areas with larger gay populations (i.e., having a "marrying market") and lower in rural areas without a significant gay population?

In conclusion, it should be noted that gay men and women have waited a lifetime to have the very thing that opponents of same-sex marriage say same-sex marriage will ruin. What have gay men and women wanted more than anything else? To have what their parents have. To have what their married heterosexual friends have. To have what

US culture has always taught every American they should want: to be recognized as a couple with all the rights and privileges that go with it. To live a married life based on the norms that are associated with marriage and that have been passed down from one generation to the next. Those who would say the sky is falling because of the legalization of same-sex marriage might be surprised that same-sex couples may well come to value the institution of marriage in its normative and traditional state more so than do heterosexual couples. The next few years should give us the answers we seek.

Terms, Concepts and Names to Know:

- Propinquity related to same sex relations
- Single-parent households
- Alternative families
- Cohabitation
- Ever-single
- Commuter marriages

Be Able to Discuss:

- The rise of single-parent households
- Non-marital childbearing and hardships encountered
- Gay marriage
- Issues of income, relationship length, divorce, infidelity and the division of household tasks among same-sex households

References

Anderson, M. (2016, February 18). The never-been-married are biggest users of online dating. Retrieved from http://www.pewresearch.org/fact-tank/2016/02/18/the-never-been-married-are-biggest-users-of-online-dating/

Anderson, J., Noack, T., Seierstad, A., & Weedon-Fekjaer. (2006). The Demographics of

Same-Sex Marriages in Norway and Sweden. Demography, 43(1), 79-98.

Badgett, M., & Herman, J. (2014). Patterns of Relationship Recognition by Same-Sex Couples in the United States. The Williams Institute, UCLA School of Law.

Badgett, M., & Mallory, C. (2014). Divorce & Marriage Rates for Same-Sex Couples. The Williams Institute, UCLA School of Law.

Bailey, J. M., Gaulin, S., Agyei, Y., & Gladue, B. A. Effects of gender and sexual orientation on evolutionarily relevant aspects of human mating psychology. Journal of Personality and Social Psychology, 66(1994): 1081–1093.

Barker, M. and Langdridge, D. Whatever happened to non-monogamies? Critical reflections on recent research and theory. Sexualities, 13(2010): 748-772. Web. 28 February 2016.

Brydum, S. (2014, December 13). Same-Sex Couples Less Likely to Divorce. The Advocate.

Curtin, S., Ventura, S., & Martinez, G. (2014, August). Recent Declines in Nonmarital Childbearing in the United States. Retrieved March 29, 2016, from http://www.cdc.gov/nchs/data/databriefs/db162.htm

Den Otter, R. Three may not be a crowd: The case for a constitutional right to plural marriage. Emory Law Journal, 64(2015): 1977-2046.

Doherty, W. (2016). How common is divorce and what are the reasons? Retrieved January 12, 2016, from http://www.divorce.usu.edu

Fry, R. (2011, July 27). Prevalence and Growth of Cohabitation. Retrieved from http://www.pewsocialtrends.org/2011/06/27/i-prevalence-and-growth-of-cohabitation/

Heaphy, B., Donovan, C., & Weeks, J. (2004). A different affair? Openness and non monogamy in same sex relationships. In J. Duncombe, K. Harrison, G. Allan & D. Marsden (Eds.), The state of affairs: Explorations in infidelity and commitment (pp. 167–186). Mahwah, NJ: Lawrence Erlbaum Associates.

Jay, M. (2012, April 14). The Downside of Cohabiting Before Marriage. New York Times. Retrieved July 14, 2016, from http://www.nytimes.com/2012/04/15/opinion/sunday/the-downside-of-cohabiting-before-marriage.html?_r=0

Jones, M. (2012, October 12). Lessons from a Gay Marriage: Despite stereotypes of gay relationships as short-lived, gay unions highlight the keys to success. Psychology Today.

Kennedy, S. & Bumpass, K. (2008). Living Together: The Economics of Cohabitation. Demographic Research, 19(47).

King, Brittany. "Fired for Being Gay: Should Arkansas Ban This Form of Discrimination?" Arkansas Law Review 67.4 (2014): 1019-054. Web. 18 Feb. 2014.

Kurtzleben, D. (2013, March 1). Gay Couples More Educated, Higher-Income Than Heterosexual Couples. U.S. News and World Report.

Leeker, O.; Carlozzi, A. (2012). "Effects of sex, sexual orientation, infidelity expectations, and love on distress related to emotional and sexual infidelity." Journal of Marital and Family Therapy, 40, 68–91.

Lively, K., Steelman, L., & Powell, B. (2010). Equity, Emotion, and Household Division of Labor. Social Psychology Quarterly, 73(4), 358-379.

Livingston, G. (2014, December 22). Fewer than half of U.S. kids today live in a 'traditional' family. Retrieved March 28, 2016, from http://www.pewresearch.org/fact-tank/2014/12/22/less-than-half-of-u-s-kids-today-live-in-a-traditional-family/

Luscombe, B. (2015, March 12). How Shacking Up Before Marriage Affects a Relationship's Success. Time Magazine. Retrieved from http://time.com/20386/how-shacking-up-before-marriage-affects-a-relationships-success/

Magloff, L. (2016). The Average Cost for Divorce (LegalZoom.com). Retrieved February 1, 2016, from http://info.legalzoom.com/average-cost-divorce-20103.html

Marital bliss? Gender gaps in Dutch same-sex divorce rates. (2012). Gender Across Borders.

Martell, C., and Prince, S. "Treating Infidelity in Same-sex Couples." 61.11 (2005): 1429-438. Web. 17 Mar. 2016.

Masci, D. , & Lipka, M. (2015, July 2). Where Christian churches, other religions stand on gay marriage. Pew Research Center. Retrieved January 8, 2016, from http://www.pewresearch.org/fact-tank/2015/12/21/where-christian-churches-stand-on-gay-marriage/

McDaniel, S., Boco, A., & Zella, S. (2013). Changing Patterns of Religious Affiliation, Religiosity, and Marital Dissolution: A 35-Year Study of Three-Generation Families. Journal of Divorce and Remarriage, 54(8), 629-657.

Mohr, J. & Samo, E. (2016). The ups and downs of being lesbian, gay, and bisexual: A daily experience perspective on minority stress and support processes. Journal of Counseling Psychology, 63(1), 106-108.

Mundy, L. (2013, May 23). The Gay Guide to Wedded Bliss. The Atlantic.

Murphy, C. (2015, December 18). Most U.S. Christian groups grow more accepting of homosexuality. Pew Research Center. Retrieved January 8, 2016, from http://www.pewresearch.org/fact-tank/2015/12/18/most-u-s-christian-groups-grow-more-accepting-of-homosexuality/

Newtson, R. (2000). Attitudes towards Prenuptial Agreements. Paper presented at the Southeastern Undergraduate Sociology Symposium.

Newtson, R. (2011). Perceptions of E-Infidelity. Paper presented at the 2011 Annual Meeting of the Georgia Sociological Association.

Pew Research Center. Modern Marriage. (2007, July 18). Retrieved March 17, 2016, from http://www.pewsocialtrends.org/2007/07/18/modern-marriage/

Sayer, L., England, P., & Kangas, N. (2011). She left, he left: How employment and satisfaction affect women's and men's decisions to leave marriages. American Journal of Sociology, 116(6), 1982-2018.

20 Significant Premarital Counseling Statistics. (2014, October 7). Retrieved from http://healthresearchfunding.org/20-significant-premarital-counseling-statistics/

South, S., & Lloyd, K. "Spousal Alternatives and Marital Dissolution." American Sociological Review 60 (1995): 21-35. Web. 17 Mar. 2016.

Treas, J., & Giessen, D. (2000). Sexual infidelity among married and cohabiting Americans. Journal of Marriage and Family, 62(1), 48-60.

Tuttle, J., & Davis, S. (2015). Religion, Infidelity, and Divorce: Reexamining the Effect of Religious Behavior on Divorce Among Long-Married Couples. Journal of Divorce and Remarriage, 56(6), 475-489.

US Census Bureau. (2014). American Community Survey 2014. Retrieved from https://www.census.gov/programs-surveys/acs/

Vasileff, L. (2015, August 27). Start Preparing for Same-Sex Divorce. Money.

Village, A. "Does religion make a difference? Assessing the effects of Christian affiliation and practice on marital solidarity and divorce in Britain, 1985-2005." Journal of Divorce and Remarriage (2010), 51(6), 327-338.

Wang, W. (2014, September 24). Record Share of Americans Have Never Married. Retrieved from http://www.pewsocialtrends.org/2014/09/24/record-share-of-americans-have-never-married/

Warren, Roland. "With This Ring . . . A National Survey on Marriage in America." A National Survey on Marriage in America. National Fatherhood Initiative, 2015. Web. 13 Feb. 2016.

Chapter 15: Divorce

It's Over: The Big "D."

Divorce is the legal dissolution of a marriage. Divorce is more complicated to measure than you might think. It is estimated that between 40 and 50 percent of all marriages end in divorce. However, there are problems with that data. First, that includes people who marry a second time. People who marry more than once are more likely to marry again. Second, the aforementioned data does not take into account cohabitating couples, common-law marriages, and as of 2015, gay and lesbian cohabitators. Of first time marriages, the figure is probably closer to the lower end, but as I say, we do not have accurate data. If you look at the rate of first marriages in the U.S. annually, and then compare that to the rate of divorces and annulments annually, you will see the rate of the latter to be approximately half of the former. However, keep in mind that the latter rate includes all divorces and annulments, which therefore will include people who have already married and divorced before. According to the U.S. Department of Health and Human Services study that produced these findings, one-fifth of first marriages end within five years and one-third end within ten years, across the board (Bramlett & Mosher, 2000).

Uncoupling

In her book "Uncoupling," Diane Vaughan researched divorce and found some common behaviors and attitudes in situations where divorce had occurred. She identifies the "initiator" as the spouse/partner that is most dissatisfied and takes action to end the marriage or relationship. The initiator is the one that plans the divorce. Often, the initiator plans the divorce while the other partner remains in the dark and is totally surprised by the other partner's desire for a divorce.

As time goes by and the initiator moves towards the divorce, they begin spending more time away from home. The cold hard reality is that the initiator would rather be anywhere than with their current spouse. The initiator then begins encouraging their spouse to make new friends or develop new interests and activities outside of the home. This is most likely to help their soon-to-be ex-spouse develop a social support network and at the same time reduce the initiator's feelings of guilt. While the initiator is encouraging their spouse to make new friends, they are making their own. Initiators make new friends, transitional friends, whose purpose is to validate and support their decision to leave their current relationship. During this process it is common for initiators to put down or derogate their soon-to-be ex-spouse so that they can gain the support and sympathy of transitional friends.

Why Do People Divorce?

There are a number of reasons why people divorce. One hundred years ago, only a man could initiate a divorce in the U.S.; today, women are more likely to initiate a divorce than a man. Additionally, changes in the law have made the process easier in all 50 states.

One cultural influence on divorce is that of individualism. While the U.S. was never a collectivist culture, we were far less individualistic in the past. Men and women remained married because they needed each other physically, emotionally, and financially. The source of happiness was more often than not identified as the family. It was the important about which everything revolved. The family came first.

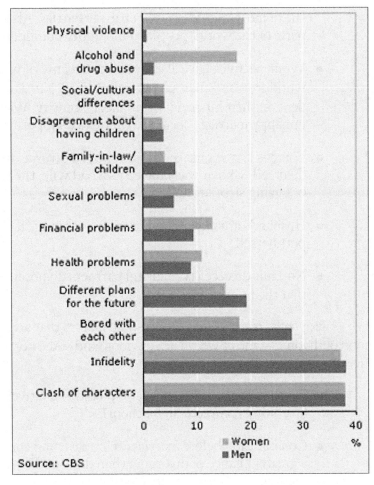

Source: CBS

A move towards individualism has increased rapidly since the 1960's in the U.S. children are taught that the source of all happiness can be found within him or her. Therefore, when a marriage becomes less than what was idealized or becomes work to stay together, the individualist attitudes learned throughout childhood and adolescence have a strong influence on the desire of couples to work at making things better to preserve the marriage. Attitudes towards marriage have therefore changed. Marriage is seen less as a life-long relationship than it is a convenience; in other words, as long as things between the couple are good, the marriage remains intact. Service to self becomes more important than preserving a marital union. Other reasons for divorce include:

- Falling out of love. If you marry because you fall in love, you will likely divorce because you fall out of love.

- Financial problems resulting in stress on both partners.

- Infidelity. While usually this is not a legal justification for divorce, it is an issue in most states for child custody battles. Also, it should be noted in some parts of the world, people found guilty of infidelity are stoned to death.

- Women's roles have also changed. Because of women's greater presence in the workforce, and their greater value in society as a whole, they are less dependent on their husband for financial security. Women no longer have to stay in unhappy marriages because they can't support themselves.

- There is less stigma today attached to divorce. In the not-so-distant past, a divorced woman was labeled as a bad wife, the cause of the marital breakup, or having slept around.

- Husbands are more likely to leave a marriage if they believe their wife can support herself.

- No-fault divorce (i.e., marital partners do not have to prove whose fault it is that the marriage failed).

However, research has found some factors that are associated with a higher likelihood of divorce, some of which are obvious, and some not so obvious. Risk factors for divorce include:

- Highest level of education completed is relatively low (e.g., high school graduate, didn't complete high school).

- Cohabitation before marriage. Couples who cohabitate before marriage have a greater chance of divorcing than do couples who did not cohabitate before marriage. While there are a number theories, the most likely is that the couple already has little regard for social norms by cohabitating prior to marriage. Its

DIVORCE

50% of marriages today will end in divorce.

43% of children will grow up without fathers.

In America, there is a divorce every 13 seconds. That is 6,646 divorces per day.

FACTORS THAT INCREASE CHANCE OF DIVORCE

NO COLLEGE EDUCATION

HAVING A BABY BEFORE MARRIAGE

HAVING AN INCOME OF LESS THAN $25,000

GETTING MARRIED BEFORE THE AGE OF 25

Source:
http://www.divorcestatistics.org/

Burton LAW FIRM

possible that their disregard for social convention might easily translate into them seeing the marriage as "just a piece of paper." Couples who cohabitate prior to marriage are 83 percent more likely to get a divorce than couples who did not cohabitate prior to getting married. However, Teachman (2003) found that women who cohabitate with someone other than the person they end up marrying have anywhere from a 55 to 166 percent increased chance of getting divorced.

- Teenage marriage. If you're a woman who got married before the age of eighteen, you have a 48 percent greater likelihood of divorce within ten years. Study after study shows that the younger the married couple, the greater the likelihood the marriage will not survive. The risk of divorce decreases as the age of the woman. If a woman marries at age 18 or 19, the chance of divorce drops to 29 percent, and if she waits until the age of 25 or older, the divorce rate equals that of the general population (Bramlett & Mosher, 2000).

- One spouse wanting a child more than the other. If you're a woman who wants a child much more strongly than your spouse does, your marriage is more than twice as likely to end in divorce as couples who agree on the number of children, if any, they want.

- Discontented women are more likely to seek a divorce than men. In fact, today the majority of divorces are initiated by women (Kippen et al., 2013).

- Having two sons or two daughters. If you have two sons, you have approximately 37 percent chance of divorce, but if you have two daughters, the chance of divorce goes up to about 43 percent.

- If you're a man with high basal testosterone, you're 43 percent more likely to get a divorce than a man with low testosterone. "Hypermasculinity is neither an evolutionary benefit nor an adaptive trait, especially nowadays, when the best predictor of a successful marriage is not the specialization into two separate roles"—stereotypically male and stereotypically female—"but rather a convergence and a sharing of roles" (Mazur & Lanham, 2005).

- If you have a child with ADHD, you have about a 23 percent chance of getting divorced before the child turns 8 years old. Having a child with ADHD puts a tremendous strain on the marital relationship, and unless marital partners can work out how to cope with the stress, the likelihood of divorce increases (Wymbs & Pelham, 2008).

- If you are currently married but have cohabitated with a lover other than your current spouse, you are slightly more than twice as likely to divorce than someone who has never cohabitated. The same study by Ohio State University sociologists that produced this result also found that even those who cohabitated only with their future spouses "are still 83 percent more likely to experience a marital disruption relative to those that did not cohabit prior to marriage." Cohabitation statistics are hot buttons, used by some pundits to decry premarital sex and "shacking up." A widely quoted 2003 study by Western Washington University sociologist Jay Teachman (2003) found that women who cohabitated with anyone besides their future husbands face a raised divorce risk ranging from 55 to 166 percent, but that those who cohabitated only with their future husbands face no elevated risk at all.

- Believe it or not, if you get out your marriage pictures, if you weren't smiling in the majority of those pictures, you have a five times increased risk of divorcing. It's believed that smiling or not smiling indicates the degree of optimism about the marriage and is also associated with a more resilient personality so they weather life's little bumps more easily (Hertenstein et al., 2009).

- If you're a woman who has recently been diagnosed with cancer or multiple sclerosis, unfortunately your likelihood of being divorced by your husband increased by six times than if the roles were reversed. In other words, husbands are more likely to divorce their wives who have cancer than are women whose husbands have cancer. There are a number of possible explanations including a failure to deal with stress, an inability to tend to a sick wife, and a failure to juggle responsibilities between their work, home chores, and their sick wife (Glantz et al., 2009).

- If you're a farmer or rancher, the likelihood of getting a divorce is relatively low, only about 8 percent. The correlation between occupation and likelihood of divorce is striking. Engineers only have about a 8 percent chance of divorce, nuclear engineers have a 7 percent likelihood of divorce, and the lowest of all, optometrists with a 4 percent chance of getting a divorce. "The differences are most likely due to such non-occupational factors as age, race, income, and personality rather than the occupation itself" (McCoy & Aamodt, 2010).

- If either you or your spouse has suffered a brain injury, your marriage faces a 17 percent chance of ending in divorce. While that may seem high, it is actually lower than for the general population. For some reason spouses are less likely to divorce when one has a brain injury than for the general population (Kreutzer et al., 2010).

- African-American woman in their first marriage have a 47% percent chance of getting divorced within 10 years. Whereas, it is only 34 percent for Hispanics, 34 percent for Caucasian women, and 32 percent for Asian women (Bramlett & Mosher, 2000).

- Military women face a high likelihood of divorce: military women have a 250 percent greater likelihood of divorce than that if their husband was in the military. There are a number of possible explanations, but perhaps the simplest is that military women have learned they don't have to depend on anyone (Karney & Crown, 2007).

- Poverty is a significant risk factor for divorce. While research has found that the poor value the institution of marriage just as much as those in higher income brackets, the poor are still more likely to divorce than do people in higher income brackets (Trail and Karney, 2012).

- People with alcohol or drug problems have a much higher chance of seeing their marriage fail than do people without drug and alcohol problems Wallerstein et al., (2000).

- Financial problems in general (i.e., disagreement about how to handle finances)

Children and Divorce: Custody

The U.S. Census Bureau reports almost 14 million parents who had separated from their spouse or partner had custody of 22 million children (2011). Only about 18 percent of children raised by a custodial parent were fathers, most custodial parents only had one child, and more than one-quarter of custodial parents fell below the poverty line. When it comes to child support, it is often not paid or paid in the amount that was mandated by the court. Only 41 percent of custodial parents received the full amount of child support awarded by the state and the average child support payment was $3,630 per year. Of those custodial parents living below the poverty line, approximately 63 percent of their average income for the year came from child support payments.

When looking at the demographics for custodial parents, the U.S. Census Bureau reported that almost half were 40 years or older, 44 percent were legally divorced, 43 percent had a Bachelor's degree or higher, and 43 percent worked full-time. It is important to note that fully one-third of all custodial parents raising children were African-American.

As previously mentioned, the average child support payment to custodial parents in 2009 was $3,630, or about $300 per month. Almost one-third of custodial parents received no child support payments. Of the nearly 7 million custodial parents, only about half were provided health care for the dependent child or children. Also, of those nearly 7 million custodial parents only about one-quarter contacted a social service agency for assistance, and of those, only about 18 percent requested assistance in getting welfare or public assistance.

Children and Divorce: Emotional Outcomes

McLanahan and Sandefur (1997) reported that children of single parents didn't fare as well emotionally when compared to children raised by two parents. Reasons included a sudden change in lifestyle, often related to decreased income on the part of the custodial parent, less attention by single parents because of work obligations, and the disruption of social ties.

Wallerstein, Lewis, and Blackslee (2001) reported on the 25-year study on the emotional effects of divorce on children. There were a number of important findings. Researchers found that one year post divorce the emotional wounds inflicted on children were "wide open" and even after five years approximately one-third of children were still affected and displayed a number of behavioral traits including poor behavior at school, depression, difficulty in making friends, and sleep disturbances. "The lightning that struck them was the divorce, and they had not even been aware of the existence of a storm" (Wallerstein, 1996).

In general, there are a number of negative effects experienced by children of divorce, but primarily in childhood. Those include:

- Depression

- Poor academic performance

- Difficulty with peer relationships

- Increase in drug and alcohol problems

- More negative self-images

- More conflict with parents

- Greater risk of being a single parent

- Poorer physical health

- Lower standard of living

Further, the research suggests that the effects vary significantly by age group. Divorce effects by age are as follows:

- **The effects of divorce on infants:** They do not understand conflict, but may react to changes in parent mood or energy, may experience a loss of appetite, and often have an upset stomach and spit up more.

- **The effects of divorce on children ages 3 to 5:** Children frequently believe they have caused their parents' divorce, felt fear of being left alone or abandoned, displayed baby-like behaviors, and were in denial.

- **The effects of divorce on children ages 6-12:** Children wee old enough to understand they are in pain, but too young to understand or control their pain, may experience grief, embarrassment, and intense anger, feel rejected by the parent who left, and may complain of stomachaches, or headaches.

- **The effects of divorce on children ages 13-20:** Children may experience fear, anger, loneliness, depression, and guilt, some may feel pushed into adulthood, loss of parental support in handling emerging sexual feelings, doubt their own ability to get married or stay married

Gender Differences in Divorce Outcomes

- Boys more involved in antisocial behavior.

- Boys tend to be less aggressive and have fewer emotional problems.

- Even when parents remain involved and supportive, boys often become depressed due to the departure of their father from the home.

- Boys tend to have more problems dealing with divorce than do girls. Boys develop more antisocial behavior, and greater levels of depression when the father is the absent parent.

- Overall, boys have a more difficult time coping with divorce than do girls.

- Girls become involved in sexual activity at a younger age.

- Girls are more responsible and mature and have fewer emotional problems

- Girls are more likely to engage in sexual experiences at younger agesEven when parents remain involved and supportive, boys often become depressed due to the departure of their father from the homeResearch on the effects of family structure on children living in stepfamilies suggests that girls experience more detrimental outcomes from stepfamily living than boys.

When some of Wallerstein and Blakeslee's subjects were re-interviewed 25 years after their original interviews, some of her subjects spoke about the "sadness" they felt of the "loss" of their childhood because of the divorce, they expressed feelings of having been abandoned, and that these feelings lasted for up to three decades. Wallerstein et al., (2001) found that children of divorce had higher rates of alcohol and drug abuse, limited financial resources for college, and fear of intimacy in adulthood. Because of a low sample size, some researchers despite these findings and report that divorce has relatively minimal long-term effects on children of divorce (Booth & Amato, 2001; Cherlin, 2010; Heatherington & Kelly, 2003).

Chase-Lansdale et al. (1995) reported that most adults whose parents divorced when they were children did have a moderate effect on long-term mental health for some adults, but the majority suffered no long term mental health issues. So, while it may be emotionally traumatizing for children to go through divorce, the research suggests that the trauma subsides over time for the majority of adults whose parents divorced when they were a child.

Finally, while divorce seems to represent a failure, divorce can also have benefits especially for children. Research has found that children living with parents who didn't get along were more likely to feel neglected and humiliated (Kimmel, 2012).

Custodial Arrangements

Almost 1.5 million children go through the divorce of parents each year (Arkowitz & Lilienfield, 2013). The most common custody arrangement in divorce is sole physical custody to one parent (usually the mother) and joint legal custody to both parents.

Custody is shared; there can be joint physical custody, joint legal custody, or joint legal and physical custody. However, studies show that this may not be the best arrangement for the children. Is joint custody the answer? According to the research joint custody is the best way to raise children of divorced parents when:

- There is an amicable relationship between parents

- Parents are able to put children first, instead of the problems between the two of them

- Abuse is not involved on either side of the parents

- Parents are physically proximate to one another, and

- Both parents are willing

Two Parent Versus Single Parent Households

- Parents do not compete for "most loving parent"

- Parents do not denigrate one another to the children

- According to McLanahan and Sandefur (1997), children of single parents don't do as well as children raised by two parents.

- The sudden drop in income following divorce, inadequate parental attention, and lack of social ties affects children adversely.

Overall, joint custody seems to be the best for children if (a) there is an amicable relationship between parents, and (b) parents are able to put their children first instead of the problems between the two of them, (c) when abuse is not present, (d) when parents live proximately to one another, and (e) when parents are willing.

Research suggests that boys are less aggressive and have fewer emotional problems when raised by their father, and girls are more responsible, more mature, and have fewer emotional problems when raised by their mother.

Emotional Support and Divorce

At any point during the life course, women have more close friends than do men. When looking at the quality of interaction in dyadic conversations, the female-female interaction is the highest with the male-male interaction the lowest. Women have close friends with whom they can confide, but men tend to confide only in their wife. Consequently, after a divorce women have a larger emotional support group with whom they can confide their feelings about the divorce and life after divorce. Because men tend to have looser friendships than women, and therefore are less likely to confide in other men, men don't have the emotional support after divorce as to do women. Research reports that this emotional advantage lasts for approximately up to five years after the divorce; at the end of that time, women's emotional state tends to be about what it was shortly before the divorce. While women come out of a divorce initially better off emotionally, men come out of divorce better off financially.

Can Divorce be Avoided?

Are there factors that put couples at greater risk for having a divorce in their future? Every marriage has that risk of divorce to some statistical degree. As noted above, it takes two to make a marriage work, but only one to make it fail. So, despite how much one party loves the other and seeks to remain together, if the other doesn't share that love and commitment, the marriage will almost certainly end and the party still in love can do nothing, but to try and waive goodbye gracefully. Factors associated with preventing divorce:

- Conflict management style. The style in which couples attempt to resolve differences is highly predictive of divorce. Take the conflict management style assessment.

- Communication patterns. Open and honest communication is associated with a significantly lower likelihood of divorce.

- Having a sense of humor about problems that occur in the relationship. People have got to be able to laugh at themselves and others. Not having a sense of humor is associated with a greater likelihood of divorce. So, next time you want to laugh about something between you and your partner, do it.

Conflict Management Style and Divorce

Research by Burditt (2010) found that couples who yell and scream at each other, were more likely to divorce, but that is a fact researchers have known for years. Surprisingly Burditt identified a second conflict tactic that was associated with increased risk for divorce. When one spouse tries to deal with the conflict constructively, rationally, and calmly, listening to the other spouse's point of view, but the other does not reciprocate, puts the couple at increased risk of divorce. This just seems to support my mantra for this chapter: it takes two people to make a marriage work, but only one to make it fail. Burdit says: "This pattern seems to have a damaging effect on the longevity of marriage. Spouses who deal with conflicts constructively may view their partners' habit of withdrawing as a lack of investment in the relationship rather than an attempt to cool down."

Conversely, couples in which both spouses used constructive strategies had lower divorce rates. One interesting finding was that conflict resolution the first year of marriage was not a significant predictor of long-term marital success. Of those who indicated they had no conflicts the first year of marriage, 46% were divorced 16 years later. The research found that husbands were more likely to use constructive conflict resolution strategies in the beginning of the marriage and this held true for the duration of the marriage. On the other hand, women began their marriages using less constructive conflict resolution strategies, including withdrawing, but this changed over time if the couple stayed together (Burditt, 2010).

Self Assessment Test for Conflict Management

To what extent does each statement describe you? Indicate your level of agreement by circling the appropriate response on the right.

Circle the number that indicates how well these statements describe you.	Never				Al-ways
1. If someone disagrees with me, I vigorously defend my side of the issue	1	2	3	4	5
2. I go along with suggestions from co-workers, even if I don't agree with them	1	2	3	4	5
3. I give-and-take so that a compromise can be reached	1	2	3	4	5
4. I keep my opinions to myself rather than openly disagree with people	1	2	3	4	5
5. In disagreements or negotiations, I try to find the best possible solutions for both sides by sharing information	1	2	3	4	5
6. I try to reach a middle ground in disputes with other people	1	2	3	4	5
7. I accommodate the wishes of people who have different points of view than my own	1	2	3	4	5
8. I avoid openly debating issues where there is disagreement	1	2	3	4	5
9. In negotiations, I hold on to my position rather than give in	1	2	3	4	5
10. I try to solve conflicts by finding solutions that benefit both me and the other person	1	2	3	4	5
11. I let co-workers have their way rather than jeopardize our relationship	1	2	3	4	5
12. I try to win my position in a discussion	1	2	3	4	5

13. I like to investigate conflicts with co-workers so that we can discover solutions that benefit both of us.

1   2   3   4   5

14. I believe that it is not worth the time and trouble discussing my differences of opinion with other people.

1   2   3   4   5

15. To reach an agreement, I give up some things in exchange for others.

1   2   3   4   5

Scoring Key for Conflict Management Questionnaire

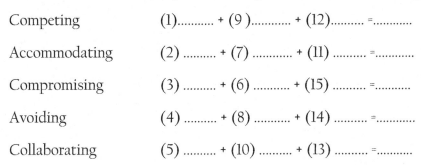

Write the scores circled for each item on the appropriate line below (statement numbers are in the brackets), and add up each scale. Higher scores indicate that you are stronger on that conflict management style.

Competing   (1)........... + (9)............ + (12).......... =...........

Accommodating   (2) .... + (7) .... + (11) .... =...........

Compromising   (3) .... + (6) .... + (15) .... =...........

Avoiding   (4) .... + (8) .... + (14) .... =...........

Collaborating   (5) .... + (10) .... + (13) .... =...........

Competition. High on assertiveness and low on cooperativeness. It is characterized by the win lose outcome where one person sets to achieve their own way almost regardless of the cost to the other involved. In the long run, this is a highly ineffective conflict resolution tactic and has a high chance or resulting in divorce.

Accommodation. Low on assertive behavior and high on cooperative behavior. With this style, a person puts aside her own needs and concerns in favor of others. While this may seem like a healthy and mature way to deal with conflict, the reality is that nothing gets resolved, resentment builds by the accommodating partner, and there is a good chance divorce will occur.

Compromise. Medium on assertive and cooperative behavior. It is associated with splitting issues down the middle and mutual concession thus resulting in middle ground solutions which is mutually acceptable by both.

Avoidance. Low on both assertive and cooperative behavior. This style of conflict resolution tends to avoid conflicts altogether, as the name implies. The style delays the conflict, and the person does not attempt to satisfy his own point of view or that of others. Problems do not get resolved, resentment builds, and divorce is highly likely.

Collaboration. High on both assertive and cooperative behavior. It is characterized by openness, exchange of information and attempts to generate win-win solution where the needs of both parties can be met by placing equal emphasis on their own interests and that of the others. This style of conflict resolution results in the lowest divorce rate for all conflict resolution strategies.

Terms, Concepts and Names to Know:

- Divorce

- Separation

- Dianne Vaughn

- Cohabitation

Be Able to Discuss:

- The process of "uncoupling"

- Reasons for divorce

- Risks of divorce

- The effects of divorce on children

- Emotional effects of divorce on ex-spouses

- Financial effects of income on ex-spouses

- Conflict management styles

References

Akowitz, H., & Lilienfield, S. (2013). The breakup may be painful, but most kids adjust well over time. Scientific American, 26. Retrieved from http://www.scientificamerican.com/article/is-divorce-bad-for-children/

Amato, P., & Booth, A. (2001). The Legacy of Parents' Marital Discord: Consequences for Children's Marital Quality. Journal of Personality and Social Psychology, 81(4), 627-638.

Bramlett, K., & Mosher, W. (2000). First marriage dissolution, divorce, and remarriage: United States, Department of Health and Human Services/National Center for Health Statistics, Advance Data, 23, 7-8.

Burditt, K., Brown, E., Orbuch, T., & McIlvance, J. (2010). Marital Conflict Behaviors and Implications for Divorce Over 16 Years. Journal of Marriage and Family, 72(5), 1188-1204.

Chase-Lansdale, P., Cherlin, A., & Kernan, K. (1995). The long-term effects of parental divorce on the mental health of young adults: A developmental perspective. Child Development, 66(6), 1614-1634.

Cherlin, A. 2010. The Marriage-Go-Round: The State of Marriage and the Family in America Today. Vintage Publishing, 2010.

Glantz, M., Chamberlain, M., Hsieh, C., Edwards, K., Van Horn, A., & Recht, L. (2009). Gender disparity in the rate of partner abandonment in patients with serious medical illness. Cancer, 115(22).

Heatherington, M., & Kelly, J. (2003). For Better or For Worse: Divorce Reconsidered. Norton, 2003.

Hertenstein, M., Hansel, C., Butts, A., & Hile, S. (2009). Smile intensity in photographs predicts divorce later in life. Springer Science and Business Media. Retrieved from: http://www.uvm.edu/~pdodds/teaching/courses/2009-08UVM-300/docs/others/everything/hertenstein2009a.pdf

Karney, B., & Crown, S. (2007). Families Under Stress: An Assessment of Data, Theory, and Research on Marriage and Divorce in the Military. New York, NY 2011: Rand Corporation.

Kippen, R., Chapman, B., Yu, P., & Lounkaew, K. (2013). What's love got to do with it?

Homogamy and dyadic approaches to understanding marital instability. Journal of Popular Culture, 30, 213-247.

Kreutzer, J. (2010). The truth about divorce after brain injury. The Challenge, Winter 2010.

Mammen, K. (2008). The effects of children's gender on divorce and child support. Paper presented at the American Economic Association's annual meeting.

Mazur, A., & Lanham, M. Biosociology of Dominance and Deference. Rowman & Littlefield, 2005, p. 125.

McLanahan, S., & Sandefur, G. (1997). Growing Up With a Single Parent: What Hurts, What Helps. Cambridge, MA: Harvard University Press.

McCoy, M. & Aamodt, M. (2010). A comparison of law-enforcement divorce rates with those of other occupations. Journal of Police and Criminal Psychology, 25 (1), 1-16.

Teachman, J. (2003). Premarital Sex, Premarital Cohabitation, and the Risk of Subsequent Marital Dissolution among Women. Journal of Marriage and Family, 65(2), 444-455.

Trail, T., & Karney, B. (2012, July 10). Why Do Low-Income Couples Marry Less and Divorce More? Retrieved April 5, 2016, from https://www.ncfr.org/press-room/journal-news-releases/why-do-low-income-couples-marry-less-and-divorce-more

US Census Bureau. (2009). Custodial mothers and fathers and their child support. Issued 2013. Retrieved from: https://www.census.gov/people/childsupport/data/files/chldsu13.pdf

Wallerstein, J. (1996). Surviving the Breakup: How Children and Parents Cope with Divorce. Basic Books, New York, NY.

Wallerstein, J., Lewis, J., & Blakeslee, S. (2001). The Unexpected Legacy of Divorce: The 25 Year Landmark Study. New York, NY: Hachette Books.

Wymbs, J., & Pelham, W. (2008). Rate and predictors of divorce among parents of youth with ADHD. Journal of Consulting and Clinical Psychology, 76 (5), 735-744

Chapter 16: Family Violence

The streets can be dangerous places to be sometimes. Filled with crime—sometimes murder. As a nation, we buy guns and then obtain conceal carry permits so we can take them with us onto the streets to provide safety and security. We live in constant fear of street crime, but researchers have clearly and consistently proven that the streets are not the most dangerous places in America—the most dangerous place in America is the home.

In this chapter, we will investigate interpersonal violence in the home, often referred to as domestic abuse. We will look at violence directed at three victim groups: children, spouses, and the elderly.

Child Abuse

According to the Centers for Disease Control, there were 678,932 cases of child abuse or neglect reported to Child Protective Services in 2013. Of those, 1,520 children died from abuse or neglect. Also, of those reported cases in 2013, 27% of reported victims were under the age of three years.

While that is those are the official figures, many researchers believe the number is higher—probably significantly higher. In fact, one study estimates that as many as half of all child deaths reported as "unintentional" are "reclassified" as caused by abuse after cases are reopened for further forensic investigation (Every Child Matters Education Fund, 2012). Research suggests that as many as three million children may be abused each year. Many scholars in the field believe that figure to represent the tip of the iceberg because they believe that a substantial number of child abuse cases go unreported. What figures there are come from police reports, hospitals, and social service agencies, but because young children spend most of their time in the home, hidden from the outside world, they are highly vulnerable to physical abuse. The most likely abusers of children are men, while biological fathers may be the abuser, stepfathers and mothers' boyfriends are statistically more likely to abuse children. The lack of a biological bond between the stepfather or mothers' boyfriend removes an important protective element for child abuse victims.

Further, long-term studies have found that perhaps as many as 80 percent of young adults who have been abused developed at least one psychiatric disorder by the time they turned 21 years. Those disorders were depression, anxiety, eating disorders, and suicide attempts (Silverman et al., 1996). Adults abused as children are 1.5 times more likely to use illegal drugs, more likely to develop alcoholism, and be arrested (Widom & Maxfield, 2001).

Defining Child Abuse

Before we can begin discussing abuse, we need to define it. Defining child abuse falls into two categories: (1) acts of commission, and (2) acts of omission. Acts of commission are intentional acts, but are not necessarily done with the intent to cause serious harm. The C.D.C. explains this by stating, "...a caregiver might intend to hit a child as punishment, but not the extent the child suffers a concussion" (Centers for Disease Control, 2013). Generally, acts of commission involve words or acts that cause harm, potential harm, or threat of harm. Acts of commission include:

- physical abuse,

- sexual abuse, and

- psychological & verbal abuse (making the person feel ashamed, unworthy, threatening, humiliation, deserving of abuse, calling names, shouting, ridiculing the victim)

Acts of omission involves the failure to provide for the needs of the child and/or to protect the child from harm. Again, intent doesn't necessarily mean intent to injure. The following are acts of omission:

- Physical neglect (passive or active)

- Emotional neglect

- Medical and dental neglect

- Inadequate supervision

- Exposure to violent environments

Data Sources

Where does the data on child abuse come from? Generally, data on child abuse comes from two sources: (1) Child Health Statistics, which is the C.D.C.'s National Center for Health Statistics and provides information on the health status of children in the United States, (2) National Violent Death Reporting System, which comes from 18 states funded by the C.D.C. with the intent of gathering, sharing, and linking state-level data on violent deaths. NVDRS provides CDC and states with a more accurate understanding of violent deaths), and (3) W.I.S.Q.A.R.S., which is the web-based Injury Statistics Query and Reporting System, and functions as an interactive database with the intent of providing national statistics on injury-related injury and death among children).

Risk Factors for Child Abuse

The Centers for Disease Control have divided risk factors for child abuse into two categories: (1) risk factors for child victimization, and (2) risk factors for the perpetration of victimization of children.

Risk factors for child abuse include children younger than four years, and children who have special needs. It is thought that special needs children can increase caregiver burden and stress and this in turn leads to victimization.

Risk factors for perpetration include:

- The lack of understanding and education of parents on the needs of children

- The perpetrator is likely to have been victimized themselves as a child (i.e., intergenerational transmission of violence which is a social learning theory)

- Substance abuse or mental health issues (i.e., intra-individual dynamics)

- Parental characteristics such as under 21 years, has little education, is a single parent, poverty, and a large number of dependent children

- Non-biological occupants of the home (e.g., step-father, mother's boyfriend)

- Attitudes that support the idea the child deserved what they got

Who is most likely to kill a child as a result of abuse and/or neglect? The research reports young people in their mid-20s, living in poverty, with little education, and poor coping skills. "Fathers and mothers' boyfriends are most often the perpetrators in abuse deaths and mothers are often at fault in [child] neglect fatalities" (Child Abuse and Neglect Fatalities 2013, 2015).

Family risk factors include social isolation, violence in the home (i.e., victimization of other members of the family like a parent or siblings), parental stress, poor parental attachment to the child, and generally negative interactions between the perpetrator and the child victim. Family protective factors include a supportive family environment (i.e., good parent-child relationship, positive affect), and a social network that serves to provide informational support to parents raising children (i.e., best practices).

While the C.D.C. affirms that the aforementioned protective factors are supported by the research, the following are protective factors currently being researched, but likely to be supported by that research:

- Nurturing parents

- Stable family relationships

- Household rules that are enforced

- Monitoring children's actions

- Parental employment

- Adequate housing

- Access to child health care and child social service agencies

- A supportive family network that can provide useful information about parenting and also act as role models for parental behavior

Community risk factors include a high degree of community violence (i.e., people become desensitized to the violence), poor neighborhood (e.g., poverty, high unemployment, alcoholism and drug addiction), and poor social connections (i.e., the perpetrator has no one to discuss parenting practices). The single best community protective factor is a community that helps and supports parents in need of information while actively working to prevent child abuse.

Long-term Consequences of Child Victimization

In a study conducted between 1995 and 1997, the C.D.C. in collaboration with the Kaiser Permanente Group, released one of the largest studies on child abuse and neglect as it related to later-life well-being of victims of abuse. Over the aforementioned two-year period, over 17,000 patients of Kaiser Permanente HMOs were given questionnaires about incidents of childhood victimization (referred to as ACEs, which stands for **Adverse Childhood Experiences**). Nearly 12,000 respondents reported at least one ACE, and more than 20 percent reported three or more ACEs. Results from the massive study revealed a number of negative outcomes associated with victimization in childhood; generally, as the number of reported ACEs increased, so did the number of late-life outcomes. Some of those outcomes are:

- Alcoholism

- Depression

- Illegal drug use

- Risk for intimate partner violence

- Increased risk for sexually transmitted diseases

- Attempted suicides

- Adolescent or unintended pregnancy, and early sexual activity

- Prevention of Child Abuse

What if anything can be done to prevent child abuse (i.e., ACEs)? Safe, stable, and nurturing relationships and environments within the home and community have the potential to lower the likelihood of ACEs. The goal is to provide resources to parents that reduce the incidence of ACEs and help children grow and develop in a nurturing and supportive home.

Spouse Abuse - Intimate Partner Violence

Defining Spouse Abuse

The term "intimate partner violence" (IPV) describes physical and sexual violence, stalking and psychological aggression by a partner. An intimate partner is someone who is trusted, emotionally connected, has regular contact with, usually has a sexual relationship, who think of themselves and are known to others as a couple. Past boyfriends or girlfriends, lovers, partners are all considered under the category of IPV. There are four categories of IPV:

- Physical violence is the intentional use of physical force to gain compliance of the victim or to serve as punishment for an act. These acts of violence can result in death, disability, injury, or harm. Acts of physical violence includes such things as scratching, pushing, shoving, throwing objects, biting, choking, pinning, shaking, slapping, punching, hitting, burning (usually with a cigarette), and the use of a weapon.

- Sexual violence is divided into five categories. Any of these acts can be considered as sexual violence even if they were not completed. Additionally all of these acts are committed without the consent of the victim—they are not consensual acts.

  - Rape or penetration of victim with the penis or an object. The victim was forced to penetrate someone else with his penis or with an object. Persuasive or coercive taunts or threats to get the victim to agree to penetration.

- Unwanted sexual contact. Touching the victim without permission and usually in specific areas like the groin, breast, and buttocks.

- Forcing the victim to view pornographic material, verbal sexual harassment, threats of sexual violence if the victim doesn't comply with the perpetrators sexual or non-sexual demands, or video recording of sexual acts without the consent of the victim.

- Stalking is more than just a perpetrator following his or her victim. There are a number of behaviors that constitute stalking such as: unwanted and repeated contact with the victim (e.g., physical, phone calls, e-mails, texts), causing the victim to feel threatened, watching, following, spying, eavesdropping, and trespassing.

- Psychological abuse results from verbal or non-verbal acts or speech that demeans, threatens, or intimidates victims. The intent of psychological abuse is to either control or harm the victim. Calling a partner "fat" or stating that "no one but me would want you" are examples of verbal use designed to emotionally and psychologically harm the victim and to make the victim feel they have no choice but to stay in the relationship.

Data Sources

Where does the data on IPV come from? Generally, data on IPV comes from seven main sources:

- Behavioral Risk Factor Surveillance System

- National Violence Against Women Survey

- National Violent Death Reporting System

- National Intimate Partner and Sexual Violence Survey

- The National Survey of Family Growth

- Pregnancy Risk Assessment Monitoring System

- Youth Risk Behavior Surveillance System

Of the aforementioned data sources, the first four contribute the most to understanding IPV. The Behavioral Risk Factor Surveillance System is an on-going telephone survey system that has tracked issues related to health and risk since the early 1980s. This system is used by all 50 states, District of Columbia, and US possessions. The National Violence Against Women Survey uses data from over 8,000 adult men and 8,000 adult women living in the U.S. in 1996. Participants were asked questions in six areas:

- their general fear of violence

- emotional abuse they had experienced by marital or cohabiting partners

- physical assault they had experienced as children by adult caretakers

- physical assault they had experienced as adults by any type of perpetrator

- forcible rape or stalking they had experienced by any type of perpetrator

- threatened violence they had experienced by any type of perpetrator

Risk Factors for IPV

Risk factors associated with IPV can be divided into four categories: (1) individual risk factors, (2) relationship risk factors, (3) community risk factors, and (4) societal factors.

The Centers for Disease Control identify the following individual risk factors for IPV:

- Low self-esteem

- Low income

- Low academic achievement

- Young age

- Aggressive or delinquent behavior as a youth

- Heavy alcohol and drug use

- Depression

- Anger and hostility

- Antisocial personality traits

- Borderline personality traits

- Prior history of being physically abusive

- Having few friends and being isolated from other people

- Unemployment

Emotional Dependence and Insecurity

- Belief in strict gender roles (e.g., male dominance and aggression in relationships)

- Desire for power and control in relationships

- Perpetrating psychological aggression

- Being a victim of physical or psychological abuse (consistently one of the strongest predictors of perpetration)

- History of experiencing poor parenting as a child

- History of experiencing physical discipline as a child

Relationship Risk Factors Include:

- Marital conflict-fights, tension, and other struggles

- Marital instability-divorces or separations

- Dominance and control of the relationship by one partner over the other

- Economic stress

- Unhealthy family relationships and interactions

Community Risk Factors Include:

- Poverty and associated factors (e.g., overcrowding)

- Low social capital-lack of institutions, relationships, and norms that shape a community's social interactions

- Weak community sanctions against IPV (e.g., unwillingness of neighbors to intervene in situations where they witness violence)

- Societal factors are tied to traditional gender norms and misogynistic attitudes. Men who believe that a woman's place is in the home, that she should be subservient to her partner, be submissive, responsible for virtually all domestic chores, are hugely associated with the incidence of IPV.

Long-Term Consequences of IPV

The scope of IPV is staggering. It is estimated that more than one-quarter of all adult women and one-seventh of all men have been victims of severe violence related to IPV. The majority of the aforementioned victims were injured as a result of the violence (Breiding et al., 2014). Further, a study done by the US Department of Justice (Crime in the US: 2010, 2011) reported that 241 males and 1,095 females were murdered by their partner in an act of IPV. Aside from murder, there are considerable consequences of IPV. Those consequences include:

- Physical (e.g., fibromyalgia, G.I. disorders, asthma, migraines, cardiovascular and circulatory problems, and more)

- Reproductive (e.g., sexual dysfunction, STDs, gynecological disorders, and more)

- Psychological (e.g., anxiety, depression, PTSD, suicidal thoughts, low self-esteem, inability to trust others, fear of intimacy, emotional detachment, and sleep problems)

- Social (e.g., sometimes victims of IPV may isolate themselves from supportive networks, their psychological issues may lead to homelessness, and may have problems holding down a job)

- Health behaviors (e.g., engaging in risky sexual behavior, substance abuse, and unhealthy dieting and malnourishment)

Prevention of IPV

Resulting from a study done by the Minnesota Department of Health (Violence Data Brief, 2002), the following were presented as prevention strategies to prevent IPV:

- Increase services available to victims, perpetrators and family members.

- Promote models (specific to cultural norms and sexual preference) of intimacy, coping skills, and community connectedness to prevent intimate partner violence.

- Identify and promote community norms to discourage such violence.

- Help individuals, families, and communities assess and build upon their strengths to understand and deal with risks for domestic and intimate partner violence.

- Collect and analyze data to develop policies and interventions.

- Increase the number of health care providers who routinely ask screening questions.

Of the three victim groups, spouse abuse seems to generate the least sympathy from the American public. Americans believe that all an abused women needs to do is walk out the door. It's that simple. The problem is that it's not that simple for an abused woman to walk out on her husband and her life. In fact it is very complicated. Why? While incomprehensible to most Americans, one of the most significant reasons an abused does not walk out on her abuser is because she is still in love with him. They may have been made to have lower self-esteem and therefore feel they deserve the abuse. They may have been made to have lower self-esteem and that no one else would want them—they fear being alone. Because most abusers are highly controlling, she may have been cut off from family and friends who could provide help and support.

They may have few or no job skills and are afraid they can't support themselves (and children if any). Cut off from the outside world, they may not be aware of the resources available to them such women's shelters. They may fear retaliation. If they are from a traditional family, family members may blame her for the abuse because she's not being submissive.

Increasing Spiral of Violence

It is important to note that there is an increasing spiral of violence associated with spouse abuse. If the violence achieves the end wanted by the abuser, the abuser is rewarded and the behavior reinforced and encouraged. The first phase is known as the "honeymoon phase." It's in this phase that everything seems all right. Relationships usually literally begin in the honeymoon phase, but many men and women experience instances of abuse while dating. Men and women who are abused in any way while dating, verbally, physically, or emotionally and psychologically, should stop dating the abuser: the abuse will not get better, but instead it will get worse. Also, remember you cannot save someone. That's beyond your ability. If the dating turns into a serious relationship, whether that means marriage or cohabitation, there will be an increase in non-physical abusive actions: yelling, threatening, unreasonable jealousy. As the abuser's resentment, dissatisfaction and anger increase, the tension builds. The victim feels like they have to be careful in everything they say or do for fear that it might make the abuser angry, but it's too late, they have already built-up a substantial amount of anger at that point. At some point, some minor action sets off the powder keg and the abuser becomes violent and explodes. The explosive act may be physical, verbal, psychological, sexual, or emotional.

In the beginning, the abuser often shows remorse for his or her actions and apologizes. The victim, who loves the abuser, accepts the apology, and the cycle begins all over again. Because the victim has not left the abuser, the abuser learns that not only will the victim do as they are told, but they stay thereby increasing the control the abuser has over the victim. In other words, the abusive actions have been reinforced and therefore will be used again, and again. Over time, the abusive acts get worse and worse, but even at this point it is probable that the victim is still in love with the abuser and therefore continues to tolerate the abuse, which causes the abuse to continue and intensify. Eventually, the abuser stops showing any remorse, and it's often at this point that victims begin to realize that love, whether it's their love for the abuser or the abuser's love for them, no longer protects them from the violence. The trigger that seems to get victims to start thinking about leaving the relationship is the sudden belief that their life may be in danger.

Most women try unsuccessfully six or seven times before finally being able to leave their abusive partner. Eventually most do end up leaving physically abusive relationships. However, it should ne noted that some women never leave an abusive relationship for the reasons already outlined.

Elder Abuse

Children and the frail elderly represent the two most vulnerable groups to abuse. It is estimated that as many as 10 percent of all elderly over the age of 60 and who lives at home has experience elder abuse (Acierno, et al., 2010). Like other types of abuse, reported cases almost certainly represent only the tip of the iceberg. Estimates of elder abuse suggest the real incidence could be 23 times higher than what is reported (Under the Radar, 2011).

11 Things that Anyone Can Do
to Prevent Elder Abuse

1 Learn the **signs of elder abuse and neglect**

2 **Call or visit an elderly loved one** and ask how he or she is doing

3 Provide a respite **break for a caregiver**

4 Ask your bank manager to train tellers on **how to detect elder financial abuse**

5 **Ask your doctor** to ask you and all other senior patients about possible family violence in their lives

6 **Contact your local Adult Protective Services or Long-Term Care Ombudsman** to learn how to support their work helping at-risk elders and adults with disabilities

7 Organize a **"Respect Your Elders" essay or poster contest** in your child's school

8 Ask your religious congregation's leader to **give a talk about elder abuse** at a service or to put a message about elder abuse in the bulletin

9 **Volunteer to be a friendly visitor** to a nursing home resident or to a homebound senior in your neighborhood

10 Send a letter to your local paper, radio or TV station suggesting that they cover **World Elder Abuse Awareness Day** (June 15) or **Grandparents Day** in September

11 Dedicate your **bikeathon/marathon/other event** to elder mistreatment awareness and prevention

Defining Elder Abuse

Like all types of abuse, the abuse is intentionally designed to accomplish some end, though it cannot be assumed that there was intention to harm. Abuse of the elderly involves actions, physical or verbal, that harms or could harm an older adult. Types of elder abuse fall into five categories. Those are:

Physical abuse is the use of physical force to accomplish some end result and that does or can result in harm to the older adult. These acts include injury, physical pain, functional impairment, striking (with or without an object or weapon), hitting, beating, scratching, biting, choking, pushing, shoving, slapping, kicking, pinning, pinching, burning (usually with a cigarette or candle), or death.

Sexual abuse are forced sexual acts with an older adult. These acts may include penetration of the anus, vulva, or mouth with the penis, finger, hand, or object. Emotional or psychological abuse is verbal or nonverbal acts that can result in emotional harm to the older adult such as engendering fear, anxiety, distress, anguish, and hopelessness. Specific acts include humiliation, threats, isolation, and controlling behavior. Humiliation might include calling the older adult names, berating them, portraying them as worthless. Another tactic might include the caregiver/abuser threatening to leave permanently or to place the older adult in a nursing home.

Neglect and/or self-neglect is when an abusive caregiver fails to protect an elder from harm or meet their needs for medical care (e.g., failing to give the older adult prescribed medications either intentionally or through carelessness), nutrition, hygiene, clothing, and basic activities of daily living.

Financial abuse is when the abusive caregiver illegally uses the victim's money or property for their own gain. Abusers may deprive the abused older adult access to their finances and assets and they may forge documents (e.g., checks).

Data Sources

Where does the data on elder abuse come from? Generally, data comes from four sources: (1) National Electronic Injury Surveillance System, which provides nationally representative data set about types of non-fatal injuries as reported by hospitals, (2) National Hospital Ambulatory Medical Care Survey, which collects data from hospital emergency rooms and outpatient services, (3) National Violent Death Reporting System, which is a CDC funded data base on violent deaths, and (4) WISQARS (Web-based Injury Statistics Query and Reporting System), is a national data base containing information about injuries and deaths in the U.S.

Risk Factors for Elder Abuse

The Centers for Disease Control identify the following Individual risk factors for elder abuse. Risk factors associated with IPV can be divided into four categories. Those categories are:

- Individual risk factors include mental illness and/or past history of mental institutionalization, alcohol abuse, anger management issues, no training in caregiving (though they are the ones providing elder care), resentment if the caregiver has had to start providing care when younger, poor coping skills, and exposure of abuse as a child possibly by the elder for whom they are caring for

- Relationship factors include financial and emotional dependence on the elder abuse victim, poor or inadequate social support network (to turn to for help in developing coping and caring skills), poor or inadequate formal support, and a past history of unusual and disruptive behavior,

- Community factors are usually associated with an inability of the community to offer respite care and other services to help and support the caregiver

- Societal factors include living in a culture where there is tolerance for violent and aggressive behavior, the status of the elderly is relatively low, family members are automatically expected to assume care for their elderly parent without seeking outside help, and people are expected to keep a 'stiff upper lip' and not complain about their pain

Consequences of Elder Abuse

There are two main areas of concern for elder abuse:

1. physical effects, and

2. psychological effects.

Physical effects, other than those resulting in immediate fatality, include bruises, welts, lacerations, broken bones, dental and jaw problems, pain and soreness, malnourishment and/or dehydration, sleep problems, poorly functioning immune system that can make the elder abuse victim more susceptible to new illnesses, the worsening of current medical issues, and increased risk for early death because of inadequate care. Like children, elder abuse victims are more likely to suffer serious injuries as a result of the abuse. Also like children, one reason for this is because they are less able to defend themselves, but additionally elder abuse victims are more likely to be frail and weaker than the abuser.

Psychological effects include depression, anxiety, PTSD, and learned helplessness. Neglect includes failing to care for the elder in the manner that is required for their health and welfare. This constitutes half of all elder abuse cases (Robinson et al., 2016). Neglect can be active, where the caregiver intentionally denies essential care, passive, where the caregiver is careless (for instance, forgetting to give the elder medications as prescribed), and self-neglect. Self-neglect can occur when the elder intentionally fails to care for themselves in a manner that ensures their health and welfare. It is common when a spouse dies after being married 40 to 50 years.

Prevention Strategies

The abuse of older adults is a serious and likely widespread problem that can result in injury or death. Preventing elder abuse is more challenging than preventing child abuse or IPV. The first line of prevention is at the societal level; society must develop a greater respect for the status of the elderly. Community support is imperative especially in making the public aware of elder abuse. Of all three victim groups, the elderly are the least likely to be associated with abuse—largely because the abuse is easier to hide since most victims are frail and homebound and caregivers tend to be adult children. Like child abuse, the public should be encouraged to report suspected elder abuse. It is not an individual's job to determine whether or not elder abuse is occurring, but simply to report suspected elder abuse. Once suspected elder abuse is reported, the social welfare system, along with local law enforcement, are trained in investigating incidents of elder abuse.

Know the signs of elder abuse. Watch for any of the following, and if you suspect elder abuse, call your local authorities. Your only responsibility is to notify your suspicion of elder abuse, professionals will take it from there and conduct an investigation. Your involvement can be anonymous if you fear the suspected abuser might retaliate. Remember, knowing these signs and reporting any suspected cases of elder abuse might just save an older person's life. Here are the warning signs of elder abuse:

- Injuries such as: bruises, welts, broken bones, burns

- Withholding of medication or over medicating

- Untreated injuries/repeated injuries

- Venereal diseases (STIs)

- Intense fear or reaction to certain people

- Mistrust of others

- Extreme reaction to being cared for or bathed

- Regressive or aggressive behaviors

- Malnourished or seeming like they haven't eaten

- Not cared for, not bathed, or wearing dirty clothes

Characteristics of Elder Abusers

Common characteristics associated with elder abuse suggests elder abusers are more likely to:

- be a caregiver

- a husband or middle-aged son

- suffer from stress, depression, alcoholism or drug abuse

- have a dysfunctional social support network

Characteristics of Elder Abuse Victims

Characteristics of physically abused elderly include:

- both male and female victims—men are just as likely to be victims as women, but women are more likely to be injured and also suffer more psychological effects from the abuse

- victims are usually frail and weak

- victims are more likely to have a physical or mental disability

- victims are usually dependent on a caregiver

In Summary: Why Do They Abuse?

There are five precipitants of domestic abuse:

- Intra-individual dynamics include pathological characteristics of the abuser.

- A history of drug or alcohol abuse is present and there is a greater likelihood of mental illness with a past history of institutionalization.

- Intergenerational transmission of violence is a social learning perspective. For instance, children who witness parental violence during childhood are more likely to (a) see the violence as a successful problem solving strategy, and (b) abuse their own spouses in adulthood. Additionally, children who are the targets of parental violence are more likely to (a) suffer from alcoholism and depression, and (b) abuse their own children.

- Dependency is associated with greater risk of abuse for all three target groups. For the elderly, an elderly person may be dependent on the abuser, or the abuser dependent on the elderly person. When elderly are dependent on the abuser, stress can trigger abuse by the caregiver, and when abusers are dependent on an elderly person, an adult child who is acting as caregiver my resent their dependence on the elderly parent, and may also feel ashamed because of the abnormal situation of being dependent on an elderly parent at their age.

- Social isolation is a risk factor that runs through all three target groups. Young children not old enough for school, spend most of their time in the home and therefore are unseen by outsiders. Abused spouses are largely withdrawn because (a) their husbands are controlling and limit his or her outside activities, and (b) they don't want to be seen by outsiders for fear the violence may be discovered. Abused elders are more likely to be socially isolated and withdrawn largely because of physical and/or mental disabilities. Because of this, abused elderly lack a social support network and are seldom seen outside of the house.

Stress can be a reason for abuse in all three target groups. The frustration-aggression hypothesis applies here. Children, spouses, and elderly can be victims of abusers who are under stress (e.g., job, financial, relationship, legal, etc.) and lack the skills to properly manage the stress. However, the fact that some abusers do so because they under stress is in no way excusing the abuse.

Terms, Concepts and Names to Know:

- Misogynistic

- A.C.E.S.

- I.P.V.

Be Able to Discuss:

- Why is the home the most dangerous place in America?

- Child abuse including risk factors and long-term consequences

- Spouse abuse including long-term consequences and prevention

- Increasing spiral of violence

- Elder abuse defining it, risk factors, and prevention standards

References

Acierno, R., Hernandez, M., Amstadter, A., Resnick, H., Muzzy, W., & Kilpatrick, D. (2010). Prevalence and correlates of emotional, physical, sexual, and financial abuse and potential neglect in the United States: The National Elder Mistreatment Study. Amercan Journal of Public Health, 100(2): 292-297.

Breiding, M., Smith, S., Basile, K., Walters, M., Chen, J., & Merrick, M. (2011). Prevalence and characteristics of sexual violence, stalking and intimate partner violence victimization – National Intimate Partner and Sexual Violence Survey, United States, 2011. MMWR. 2014:63(No. SS08); 1-18.

Injury and Violence Prevention Unit, Minnesota Department of Health, Violence Data Brief, Intimate Partner Violence. (2002, November). Retrieved April 8, 2016, from http://www.health.state.mn.us/injury/pub/ipv.pdf

Lifespan of Greater Rochester, Inc., Will Cornell Medical Center of Cornell University, New York City Department for the Aging. Under the Radar: New York State Elder Abuse Prevalence Study. Self-reported prevalence and documented case surveys [Final Report] 2011 [cited 2014 Mar 24]; Available from: http://www.ocfs.state.ny.us/main/reports/Under%20the%20Radar%2005%2012%2011%20final%20report.pdf

National Centers for Disease Control. Injury Prevention & Control: Division of Violence Prevention. (2016, March 28). Retrieved April 8, 2016, from http://www.cdc.gov/violenceprevention/childmaltreatment/index.html

Robinson, L., Saison, J., & Segal, J. (2016, March). Elder Abuse and Neglect: Warning Signs, Risk Factors, Prevention, and Reporting Abuse. Retrieved March 8, 2016, from http://www.helpguide.org/articles/abuse/elder-abuse-and-neglect.htm

Silverman, W., Reinherz, H., & Giaconia, R. (1996). The Long-Term Sequelae of Child and Adolescent Abuse: A Longitudinal Study. Child Abuse and Neglect, 20(8), 709-723.

U.S. Department of Health and Human Services. Child Abuse and Neglect Fatalities 2013: Statistics and Interventions. (2015, April). Retrieved April 8, 2016, from https://

www.childwelfare.gov/pubPDFs/fatality.pdf

United States Department of Justice. Crime in the United States, 2010. Federal Bureau of Investigation, Uniform Crime Reports, Washington, DC, 2011.

Chapter 17: Gender and Gender Inequality

In the chapter on research methods, you were introduced to the survey, which is the most common type of social research method. The modern survey originated in 1824 when an opinion poll was done by a Pennsylvania newspaper to determine who was leading for president, Andrew Jackson or John Quincy Adams. The newspaper showed Jackson leading Adams 335 votes to 169. Jackson won the presidency, but it wasn't until 1916 that surveys first stepped onto the national scene. The Literary Digest conducted a national survey assessing who planned to vote for Woodrow Wilson or his opponent. The magazine correctly predicted the winner based on the survey results.

Since surveys became popular research tools, one standard question on most every survey, whether it was used by a scientific organization or by a marketing com-

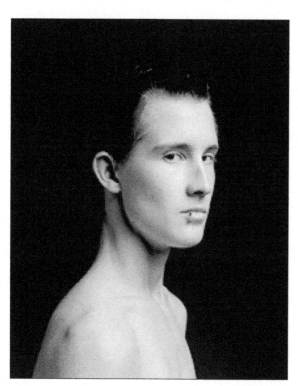

pany, was to simply ask the respondent if they were "male" or "female." Today, we live in a world where the distinction between the words "sex" and "gender" have become important, maybe even essential to educate the public on the difference, though the words are constantly interchanged. The word **"sex"** refers to the biological distinctions between a man and a woman.

Traditionally, there can only be two sexes. However, the argument today is whether there are only two genders, and for that matter, only two sexes. The word "gender" refers to the cultural expectations of a society based on a person's sex. In other words, gender refers to the roles people perform based on their sex. While surveys have always asked whether the respondent was male or female, today maybe that question is too limiting. In a study of 6,450 transgender people living in the U.S., less than 25% of transgender women had underwent genital surgery to make them a man, and less than 5 percent of transgender men had underwent genital surgery to make them a woman (Grant et al., 2010). The question becomes are there now more than two sexes? I will leave this argument to the biologists and the federal government. However, because the words "sex" and "gender" have been used interchangeably, the issue at hand has become not one of how many sexes there are, but rather how many genders there are.

Two court cases set the path for what, as of this writing, has become a hotly contested issue: should transgender people be allowed to use the restroom facility corresponding to their new gender or confined to their old gender? The first court case was Doe v. Regional School Unit in Maine. The Maine Supreme Court ruled that a boy, who was transgender and in the process of becoming a girl, had the legal right to use the girl's restroom. A similar case was heard in Colorado in Mathis v. Fountain-Fort Carson School District 8, with a similar outcome by Colorado's Division of Civil Rights. In both cases, the courts found for the plaintiffs on the grounds it was blatant discrimination. In both cases testimony was given stating that the medical community recognized it was "essential to the health and well-being of transgender people to be able to live in accordance with their internal gender identity in all aspects of life and restroom usage is a necessary part of that existence" (Lambda Legal, n.d.). Employment laws in 18 states recognize the rights of the individual to use the restroom that is in accord with their gender identity.

Are people in the process of changing their gender identity a distinct gender or are they simply the gender they identify with? The legal system and the medical community seem to suggest that a person should be free to live their life in accord with their chosen gender. It is worth mentioning that Facebook recognizes 56 options (plus the two "standard" options of male or female) for users to choose from in establishing their gender. "There's going to be a lot of people for whom this is going to mean nothing, but for the few it does impact, it means the world," Facebook software engineer Brielle Harrison told the Associated Press (Goldman, 2014). The distinctions are not as important as the fact that Facebook now allows users to make a statement about their uniqueness as a human being. So, it would seem that transgender people act out their life in accord with their gender identity. The fact that Facebook users suggested that they identified with one or several of those 56 gender distinctions says that people cannot so easily be "pigeon-holed" into two nice and neat categories of gender (i.e., male and female).

Because society has always interchanged the words "sex" and "gender" it has always been relatively clear and choice was not an issue that could even be comprehended 50 years ago. But today all of that has changed and the distinctions between sex and gender have become very relevant and important to those among us who, in trying to live their life, seek to be the person they feel they are. This is what Facebook is recognizing, and this is the challenge that is given to your generation.

The Social Construction of Gender

The movement to allow transgender people to decide their gender identity and live their lives accordingly is important. We will return to issues of how gender is culturally assigned rather than biologically given. While some would argue that both sex and gender are one in the same, and both assigned at birth, they fail to take into consideration **hermaphrodites**, who are born with both male and female sexual organs. In fact, from a medical standpoint, one could argue there have always been five sexes:

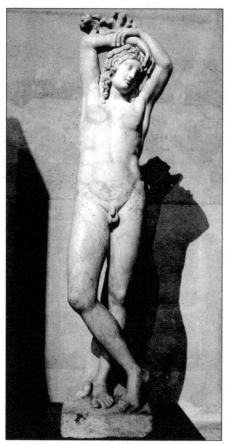

Statue of Hermaphroditus
Roman (200-300 CE)

1. child born with male genitalia,

2. a child born with both ovaries and testicles,

3. a "genetic female" born with male sexual organs,

4. a genetic male born with underdeveloped external sex organs that do not clearly define them which results in female or male/female characteristics, and

5. a child born with female genitalia (Kaneshiro, 2015).

In point of truth, there has never been only two sexes. In some cases where children are born with both sets of sexual organs, doctors will perform surgery to essentially make the infant one sex or the other.

Historically, both Greeks and Romans recognized the god Hermaphroditus who was endowed with both sexes: he had a female body and a male sexual organ.

Is gender biologically determined? No, it is not. Gender is socially constructed. Remember, we use symbols to define meaning—whether it's referring to an attitude or a person's sex. Based on those symbols, people form some kind of consensus in regards the meaning(s) of those symbols. If a group or a larger society interprets and defines situations in the same way, they have socially constructed reality. Once you understand that people and societies may define thoughts, behaviors, and the meaning of tangible objects differently, you should be able to see that each group or society may define "gender" differently.

Gender roles are expectations regarding proper behavior, attitudes, and activities of males and females. Have you ever wondered why your mother is the parent who most likely cooks dinner? Washes dishes? Vacuums the carpet? Stayed home with you until you were old enough to go to daycare or school? The answer is because women are biologically programmed to do those things, and men aren't, right? Sex roles and gender roles are the same and both are entirely created by biology, right? Wrong!

Research has consistently found that gender roles, those tasks and expected behaviors associated with someone because of their sex, are not biologically determined. Women do not cook because of a "cooking gene," they do not wash dishes because of a "dishwashing gene," nor do they stay at home with young children because they are biologically better suited for childcare than are men. Gender roles are entirely culturally determined and biology has nothing to do with it. Some would argue for something called the "maternal instinct," but research shows that to whatever degree some trait exists for women to have that "maternal instinct," men are just as likely to have a "paternal instinct" (Palmer, 2002).

In her book, Male and Female (1949), Margaret Mead, a physical anthropologist, studied tribal culture in New Guinea. Mead found different gender roles in each of the tribes she studied and those gender roles different from those in the U.S. at the time of her research. The most interesting were the Tchambuli. In Tchambuli society women were the more dominant, emotionally distant, and managerial, while men were emotionally dependent. Her research was the first to suggest that sex roles and gender roles are not the same and that gender roles are culturally determined. Gender roles have nothing to do with biology and everything to do with socialization.

Gender Socialization

Gender socialization refers to how males and females are socialized differently. Most textbooks would make the argument that gender socialization begins after birth. Parents will begin to treat that newborn child differentially and socially appropriately depending on the child's sex. My argument is that gender socialization begins before birth. When expectant parents find out the sex of their unborn child (let's say it's a girl), from that day forward that unborn child will be put on a track appropriate for its gender. What color will the receiving blanket be? What dominant color will the walls or wallpaper be? What color clothing will the expectant mother receive as gifts at her baby shower? Will the figures and characters that hang from that mobile above the child's crib be different if the unborn child were to be a little boy? It's my belief that even before birth children are put on tracks that are judged to be socially appropriate based upon their sex.

Once children are born, differential socialization continues. In the U.S., traditional gender-role patterns have a tremendous influence in the socialization of children in. Boys must be masculine: active, aggressive, tough, daring, and dominant, while girls must

Women Outpace Men In College Enrollment

Share of recent high school completers enrolled in college the following October

Hispanic	Women	Men	% point gap, women/men
1994	52%	52%	0
2012	76	62	+13 women

Black			
1994	48	56	+9 men
2012	69	57	+12 women

White			
1994	66	62	+4 women
2012	72	62	+10 women

Asian			
1994	81	82	+1 men
2012	86	83	+3 women

Source: Pew Research Center analysis of the October Supplement to the Current Population Survey. Note: % point gap calculated prior to rounding. White, black and Asian include the Hispanic portion of those groups. Due to the small sample size for Hispanics, blacks and Asians, a 2-year moving average is used.

PEW RESEARCH CENTER

be feminine: soft, emotional, sweet, and submissive. There are number of things that research has found in terms of the different ways that males and females are socialized into their socially appropriate roles.

Research shows that there are differences in playing and games between boys and girls. Generally speaking boys are expected to participate in more active type play whereas girls are expected to play less active types of games or play. However, some research has found that these roles do not remain stable, and in some cases, reverse themselves. For instance, preschool boys are more likely to engage in solitary play while girls are more likely to engage in cooperative play, but boys grow out of the solitary play stage and mimic girls in their desire to play with others (Barbu et al., 2011).

Likewise boys are more likely expected to participate in sports while girls are not. There are also differences in what children are praised for. The research suggests that boys are far more likely to be praised for their physical abilities whereas girls are more likely to be praised for their appearance and academic abilities. There are also differences in parental reactions to identical behaviors. For instance, and while I hope this would never happen, imagine this scenario. Two-year-old little Jane is out on the sidewalk with her father tentatively taking steps as she learns to walk. Suddenly little Susie falls down and starts crying. Immediately dad reaches down, picks her up, cradles her in his arms and says, "Ah, Susie you're going to be okay. Don't cry, sweetheart. It's nothing. Let me kiss your boo-boo." On the other hand, dad is on the sidewalk with two-year-old Johnny who's learning to walk. Johnny stumbles, falls, and begins to cry. Dad reacts by saying, "Come on Johnny, stop crying. It doesn't hurt that bad. C'mon, be a man!" Well I hope I am exaggerating but unfortunately little boys and girls are treated differently for the same behaviors.

Research has also found that there is a significant difference, and largely stereotypical portrayal of men and women in the media. Cartoons also play a large part in gender socialization. Researchers found that even though many cartoon characters are not anatomically correct, children seem to know the sex of the cartoon character by the actions the character performs. That serves to help socialize children into socially appropriate gender roles (Davis, 2003). Further, the process of sexualizing young girls is in-

creasing rapidly. Notice the picture of six-year-old girls performing "All the Single Ladies" at a contest. Do you think it's appropriate for six-year-old girls to be dressed in skimpy attire and performing in a manner more appropriate for twenty-one year-old women? Or what about commercials featuring a sexy green M&M? Is that aimed at least in part to young children? What affects do these things have on the development of gender roles in young children?

As a whole, society wants to take for granted that differences between men and women are "natural," because society has almost a desperate need to treat sex and gender as interchangeable. There is no "natural" gender, and seeing the world in those terms has and continues to lead to differentiation that is unfair at best and outright discrimination at worse. Take into consideration this fact: if I was standing in front of a classroom teaching college students 70 years ago, as I looked out on my audience I would either see no women or several at most. Why? Because 70 years ago the belief then was that women simply weren't as smart as men. So, intelligence is biologically based, right?

First, if you'll remember the chapter on socialization, nature may set the parameters for something called "intelligence," but people have the ability to advance or retard from those parameters.

Second, there are slight differences between men and women in cognitive functions, but research has never found that women are less intelligent than men. In fact, some would argue that because they seem to be praised and rewarded more for their academics when young, they may even be smarter than men on the whole. So, 70 years ago there would be few if any women in my classroom, but today approximately 55 – 60 percent of college students are female.

Further, when you investigate college GPA by sex and age, the results show: non-traditional (i.e., older than the traditional age of college students) females have the highest GPAs, followed by non-traditional males, followed by traditionally-aged females, and then finally traditionally-aged males.

Remember from the chapter on deviance, society has several different social control mechanisms designed to control deviance. Those are the family, religion, and the criminal justice system if the deviance violates a law. Also, our culture socializes us as well. When people "cross the line," social mechanisms are supposed to step in and bring that person back in line with the rest of society. When boys and girls step off the path that is assigned them by society, they are often sanctioned. For instance, a little girl who climbs trees may be called a "tomboy," while a little boy that likes to play with dolls may be called a "sissy." Remember, sanctions are designed to punish a behavior and bring the person back into line with social norms.

Forms of Gender Inequality

Men and women are treated differentially in virtually all societies around the globe, some to a greater extent, and some to a lesser extent. For instance, sadly we read the news about young women who had acid thrown in their face because she was on her way to school in Afghanistan or Pakistan. Malala Yousafzai, a 15-year-old girl living in Pakistan, was shot in the head by radical Islamists because she advocated that girls be allowed to attend school. Miraculously she survived after many surgeries.

Malala became a spokesperson against the unfair treatment of women in Taliban territory and in other places around the globe where women are treated as not much more than slaves. Time Magazine named her as one of their "100 Most Influential People in the World" in their 2013, 2014, and 2015 editions. And in 2014, she was named as co-recipient of the Nobel Peace Prize in recognition of her efforts to provide for the rights of all children to attend school regardless of their gender.

Patriarchy Versus Matriarchy

Patriarchy is simply male dominance in a society. A matriarchy is a society in which women dominate. Not only is there no such thing as a matriarchy in the world today, anthropologists tell us there is no evidence that a matriarchal society ever existed. Many cite Egypt under Cleopatra as a matriarchal society, but that is untrue as males still dominated and that domination passed down in male blood-lines. While women in the U.S. have made tremendous progress in their fight against inequality, they have not reached parity with men.

Around the globe, many countries still practice discrimination against women in draconian laws (Dewey, 2013). For instance:

- It wasn't until 2015 that women were allowed to vote in elections in Saudi Arabia.

- In some parts of India only males are required to wear motorcycle helmets.

- In Yemen, one woman's testimony in court is not equal to that of a man. In Iran there have to be three male witnesses to support a woman's claim in court.

- In Vatican City, women can't vote (yes, there are women in Vatican City).

- In some parts of the Middle East women are punished for leaving the house without a man who is related to her (e.g., husband, father, brother).

Evidence of Patriarchy

Historically women were considered the property of her husband, and in many parts of the world that's still true. There has always been a way of distinguishing between a married or taken woman and an unmarried or available woman. In the U.S., we distinguish between a married woman and unmarried woman by using the terms "Mrs." versus "Miss." Nearly every language has this distinction as part of their language. In German it's "Frau" versus "Fraulein," in Spanish it's "Senora" versus "Senorita," and in French it's "Madame" versus "Mademoiselle." Here in the U.S., if someone is in doubt of a woman's marital status but needs to address her, it is common to either fall back on "Miss" or in some more formal situations, "Ms." (pronounced "mizz").

Another example of evidence of a patriarchy can be found when two people marry in the U.S. If John Smith marries Mary Jones, his name remains John Smith, but her name becomes Mary Smith. In our society it is the accepted norm that a woman take her husband's surname at marriage. In some situations, usually when the woman has a career, she might take her husband's surname while keeping her own. In that case, she would be known as Mary Jones-Smith. While this is more common than in the past, it is not the norm in the U.S. In some societies, for instance Hispanic cultures, there are different practices and meanings associated with names. For instance, the child of Antonio Perez Rodriguez and Maria Quinones Alamo, would have the surname Perez Quinones.

Finally, if a married man takes a mistress, what is the term we use when a married woman takes a ...? What? "Mister?" While mistress is universally understood to be a married man's girlfriend, we have no universally accepted term to refer to a married woman's boyfriend. "Gigolo?" "Boyfriend?"

Another area in which we can see evidence of a patriarchy is in social interactions. In task groups made up of people of different statuses, the research clearly finds that high status people:

- Tend to dominate conversations,

- Are more likely to interrupt, and

- Talk louder and longer.

When researchers look at task groups made up of different sex members, and consistent with the aforementioned research, studies have found that men also tend to dominate conversations, are more likely to interrupt, and talk louder and longer.

Gender Role Socialization

Gender role socialization results from the influences of the same seven agents of socialization that we discussed in the chapter on socialization. Through our interactions with those agents of socialization, we learn normative behaviors for our sex. Again, what constitutes "normative" behavior is determined by society's push to limit gender to two very distinct, and at times, polar opposite genders: male and female. This is changing as society evolves and expands the roles that both men and women can hold without being sanctioned by society and this is largely the result of changing definitions of gender.

Facebook's policy allowing users to select their own gender specific characteristics represents a great cognitive slap in the face to society. The message seems very clear: don't lock us into these very rigid gender categories with their very specific normative behaviors. The traditional vision of heterosexualism as being the source of gender roles is being stripped away little by little in legal contests where allegations of discrimination are being upheld by courts throughout the U.S. But that doesn't mean every American accepts this new freedom for people to define their gender roles for themselves. Discrimination and old value sets still sanction, sometimes seriously, when people cross the line that some still maintain in the U.S. As discussed in the chapter on deviance, society can be very rigid and cruel when it comes to violations of social norms and is labeled "deviant." James Dixon was arrested and convicted for killing Islan Nettles, a transgender woman, because Dixon felt "blind fury" after finding out that the woman he been talking to was in fact transgender. In perhaps one of the most famous cases of transgender hatred was that of the murder of 15-year-old Larry King. Larry, a middle-school student and who liked to dress like a woman, was shot in the back of the head by 14-year-old Brandon McInerney. The day Larry was shot and killed, Brandon McInerney deliberately sat down behind King and shot him point blank. Society is changing, stepping out of line still carries consequences both here and abroad.

Women's gender roles, while changing, still center to a significant degree around her future as wife and mother. They are given toys and dolls appropriate for their gender and that can be argued help prepare them for those adult roles caring for their children and family. While for boys, gender norms still push boys to being active, aggressive, and goal-driven. Even with the Family Medical Leave Act, it is rare for a father to take time off from work to stay at home with young children. While "Mr. Mom" exists, it is far from the norm. Instead, society expects men to "prove" their masculinity by the type of job they hold, the sports they like or can participate in, and their ability to successfully provide for their family. Men who do decide to stay at home to raise young children often face criticism or ridicule because they performing "women's work" and are not doing their job to be the one bringing home the paycheck. In reality, and as society evolves, men are greatly expanding the gender roles they choose to adhere to, even at the expense of ridicule. Women face the same type of gender prejudice, though things are changing. Historically, society has told women they needed to be dependent on a man, be passive, nurturing towards children and their husband, and in need of a strong male to protect them.

I have always argued that the great equalizer in American culture when it comes to prejudice and discrimination was the marketplace. In the 1970's and 1980's, and before, there were few television commercials aimed at minority groups; commercials were full of happy white people enjoying the product the commercial was trying to sell. That's where the market was—well off white people. But the effects of the Civil Right Movement began to elevate the economic status of African Americans in the country and they had money to spend. The marketplace accommodated that emergent market by now promoting African Americans in commercials. The more African Americans on television, even in commercials, led to a greater awareness among white Americans that they were no longer alone. The same can be said for women's greater economic status beginning in the 1970's. Television commercials, which had always tried to sell home products to housewives, found themselves targeting women for clothing, beauty products, and even cigarettes (i.e, Virginia Slims).

Gender Inequality in the Workplace

Sexism is prejudice and discrimination directed at women. It is a belief system that supports the notion that men are superior to women. It is considered institutionalized sexism if the larger group or society supports discrimination against women. Few countries would post a sign as you cross the border into their country, "We are a institutionalized sexist country," though some might as well based on the value of women in those societies. No, instead of looking for a sign that states sexism is an accepted policy of their organization or group, we look for signs of inequality.

Remember this figure, 52/48? It's the ratio of women to men in the U.S. For every age through the life course, there are more women than men. All things being equal, we should expect to see 52% of everything we might want to study in which sex is an issue, this proportion. But we do not. At all levels in the class system, women earn less income, have less wealth, and less overall power than men. One area in which women have caught up and passed men is in education. According to the Pew Research Center (Lopez, 2014) the percentage of women in the U.S. who are enrolled in college is 75% in 2012 up from 52% in 1994. This far exceeds the proportion of men enrolled in college, which is 62%. As the Virginia Slim commercial slogan suggests, "you've come a long way, baby." And while that's true in education, there are still many areas of the economy woman have not made such large advancements. Only 24 of the top 500 CEO positions in the U.S. are held by women; remember if all things were equal, the number of CEOs should be about 260.

We can look at other occupations as well. In 1980, only 6 percent of all engineers in the U.S. were female, but today that figure is 14 percent. If all things were equal, 52 percent of all engineers in the U.S. should be female. Currently, the University of Virginia has the highest proportion of female engineering students in the U.S., 31 percent. However, that's far from the norm. Researchers at Stanford University reported the results of a study that found female engineering students performed as well academically as male students, but had a higher attrition rate. According to the report, "These women switch majors because they don't believe that their skills are good enough and they don't feel like they fit in engineering" as a profession (Crawford, 2012). President Barack Obama is our 44th president of the United States. Not to beleaguer the point, but if all things were equal we should have had 24 female presidents of the United States by this point in our history. Of course, we have not. What does it say when we don't find those proportions when we examine the labor force? While it may not be outright discrimination that limits the proportion of females in the careers mentioned above, it certainly suggests there's something amiss and needs further examination.

One significant life factor that explains why women do not fare as well in the workplace as men has to do with lack of qualifications, which can be used against them. At any point in the life course, women are more likely to leave the paid work force to take care of a child or a sick loved one. Leaving the workforce for any significant amount of time will lead to loss of experience when compared to those who stay in the paid labor force (i.e., men) during that same period of time. Lack of comparable experience has direct and long-term consequences on salary and promotion. When women take time off from the labor force to raise children or tend to a sick loved one, employers will see that as loss of experience as more relevant than whether they can do the job or not. Consequently, men who have stayed in the workforce and therefore did not lose experience are perceived as better candidates for promotion and the associated pay raises that accompany those promotions. The Family Medical Leave Act can give either a father or mother time off to raise a child, but this is limited to six weeks of unpaid time off. Even so it is far more likely that the mother will take time off rather than the father because he almost certainly makes more money.

Networking is another relevant issue when it comes to gender inequality in the workplace. The old saying "it's not what you know, but who you know," unfortunately has a degree of truth to it. In the case of networking, it tends to affect women at higher levels of the corporate world. When we're dealing with top-level executives making organizational business deals, many are not made in the boardroom. Where are they made? One common place for high-level business deals is the golf course. In fact, Forbes magazine offers 19 tips for closing a business deal on the golf course (Conner, 2013). Other places for these top-level business discussions include the racquet ball court, country clubs, and strip clubs. In fact, Goldman Sachs was recently sued over the process. While the venue is not as common as it used to be, largely because of the scrutiny that it came under in 2005/2006, it still goes on. In fact, USA Today wrote in 2006, "Some women on Wall Street want to know how it can be fair — or legal — for their managers and male colleagues to exclude them when they fraternize at strip clubs, often with the women's clients. Strip club clientele is hardly limited to Wall Street. Adult entertainment is enjoyed by men — and some women — in most every industry in the USA, and it's a tax-deductible business expense allowed by the IRS" (O'Donnell, 2006). The idea here is that by excluding women from high-level corporate decision-making processes they are being deprived of experience and networking opportunities. Networking is crucial to success in the business world.

The Glass Ceiling

When women with the same qualifications and education as men cannot rise to the same level, as do males, this is called the **glass ceiling**. Essentially, the glass ceiling is gender discrimination based on stereotypical characteristics of women (e.g., women are better at taking care of kids than running a company). It's something along the lines of the "good ol' boy" network. The glass ceiling refers to the fact that women can climb their way up the corporate ladder, accumulate experience, but when they get to the top, they are stopped by the glass ceiling—they see above them, they have the experience to be where they can see, but they just can't get there. The argument could be made that this is one reason why we have not had a female president. The stereotype is that a female president would fall apart emotionally in an emergency and the country needs a man to act firmly and decisively. The glass escalator is the opposite of the glass ceiling. It refers to how men in female-dominated careers, such as teaching and nursing, often rise higher and faster than women in male-dominated fields.

The Equal Rights Amendment was authored by Alice Paul head of the National Women's Party in 1923. It contained three sections:

- Section 1. Equality of rights under the law shall not be denied or abridged by the United States or by any state on account of sex.

- Section 2. The Congress shall have the power to enforce, by appropriate legislation, the provisions of this article.

- Section 3. This amendment shall take effect two years after the date of ratification.

In order to be amended to the U.S. Constitution, two-thirds of U.S. states had to ratify the proposed amendment. Without this amendment, there exists nothing in the U.S. Constitution or Bill of Rights that guarantees the same rights for women as they do for men. There was opposition to the Equal Rights Amendment by those who either failed to see the need or downright opposed the idea of women being equal to men.

Even though the proposed amendment still exists as a legal document waiting for ratification, there have been no moves by the House or Senate to try again for ratification. It failed to be ratified, and when results were analyzed, as expected younger males were in favor of the amendment and older more traditional males were opposed to it. What was surprising was that while younger women favored the amendment, a significant proportion of older women opposed it. If Marx were alive, he would say of these latter women that they had developed a second-class consciousness and accepted an ideology that was contrary to their best interest.

In 1992 a televangelist, named Pat Robertson campaigned against the amendment. On January 8, 1992, Robertson said the following on his show The 700 Club, "I know this is painful for the ladies to hear, but if you get married, you have accepted the headship of a man, your husband. Christ is the head of the household and the husband is the head of the wife, and that's the way it is, period." Further, as he traveled around the country speaking out against the amendment he is quoted as having written in a fund-raising letter in 1992 the following: "The feminist agenda is not about equal rights for women. It is a socialist, anti-family political movement that encourages women to leave their husbands, kill their children, practice witchcraft, destroy capitalism, and become lesbians" (New York Times, August 26, 1992). The Equal Rights Amendment, which would have amended the U.S. Constitution to state that women are guaranteed the same rights as men, was not passed. It still hasn't been passed.

Discrimination in the Home

The division of household tasks refers to the chores around the house that men and women do. Generally, household tasks are highly genderized. For instance, males typically perform the outside chores, and women the inside chores. Women are more likely to be doing the vacuuming, ironing, dusting, laundry, childcare, and cooking – though more men today are assuming more responsibility for cooking.

The "second shift" refers to women coming home after working full-time in paid labor only to have to start their 'second shift' by assuming household responsibilities (e.g., cooking, cleaning, childcare, etc.). According to the Bureau of Labor Statistics (2014), 83 percent of women and 65 percent of men spent time doing household tasks, the average number of hours spent doing household tasks was 2.6 for women and 2.1 for men, and on any given day 20 percent of men and 69 percent of women spent time doing housework. From 2003 to 2014 men increased their share of cooking and dishwashing from 35 to 43 percent. The bottom line is that women still do a disproportionate amount of housework when compared to men.

Structural Functionalism and Gender Inequality

Functionalism sees gender inequality as a useful mechanism for the division of labor and assigning rewards. Instrumental tasks are those tasks associated with physical effort and seen as primarily male. Expressive tasks are those tasks associated with emotions and emotional support and are seen as primarily female. The functionalist perspective suggests that gender inequality is:

- functional for society because it fulfills a need. Motherhood is essential to society. They provide physical care and nurturing for future generations. By staying home and raising the children they allow men to participate in the paid labor force.

- masculine characteristics are more valued by society. Women and men perform tasks for which they are biologically best suited and women are better suited for the provision of expressive tasks.

- provides a large adaptive pool of labor which is paid. Because women tend to be found disproportionately in unskilled and low-wage jobs, they are the first to be laid off during recessions and the last to be rehired during economic recovery. They are perceived as having everything to contribute as homemakers and child care workers, but have little value to the paid labor force.

The Conflict Perspective and Gender Inequality

The conflict perspective sees gender inequality as the result of a social stratification system that gives men more power than women. Society sees women as subordinate to men, that women collectively have a false consciousness in that they accept a system that works contrary to their best interests, and that since men have the power they shape social norms to fit their needs and keep women as a subordinate group.

In 2015, there were 20 women serving in the U.S. Senate (19.3%), 104 women serving in Congress (19.4%), so in total there are 124 women serving in the House or Senate out of 619. Marx would offer these figures as support for his theory that those who hold the power are men, and that those men project their view of America in the way they vote on issues, which will always favor them. Interestingly enough, the women serving in the House or Senate are three times more likely to be Democrat than Republican.

Conclusion

The process of gender socialization is incredibly long-reaching. You can see it in many aspects of our daily life. It's all around us at work or school, on television, billboards, television commercials, and magazines. Literally you see reminders of how we are supposed to act and dress because of our gender all around us. Historically, when people step out of these very stereotypical and rigid gender roles they are met with sanctions. Sometimes those sanctions may get you merely kidded, or laughed at, or even attacked. Unfortunately, people have been killed for violating the gender role assigned to them at birth by their sex.

While there is certainly a dark side to gender socialization, one of the things you should have picked up from this chapter is that there is really no such thing as just two genders. No one fits in completely to the norms associated with the gender roles assigned to him or her by society. Each and every action or thought that is not part of those rigid norms removes you from that rigid standard. Facebook is wrong by recognizing 56 genders because in point of fact, there are probably hundreds of different genders.

Things are changing to where society seems less concerned about these rigid gender roles. Evidence for this can be found in of all places, toy stores. Though most online toy stores still divide toys into two categories, "Boys' toy" and "Girls' toys," and the largest volume of toys are still gender specific, there is a movement towards making toys less gender specific. Notice this last image is in Danish. Do you think the manufacturer would run this same ad here in the U.S.?

Terms, Concepts and Names to Know:

- Sex

- Gender

- Sexism

- Margaret Mead

- Matriarchy

- Patriarchy

- Family and Medical Leave Act

- Gender roles

- Glass escalator

- Glass ceiling

- Malala Yousafzai

- Mosuo

- Parity

- Draconian

- Hermaphrodites

Be Able to Discuss:

- How gender is socially constructed

- How the conflict perspective views gender inequality

- How structural functionalism views gender inequality

- Gender inequality in the workplace

- The division of household tasks

- The Equal Rights Amendment

- Evidence the U.S. is still a patriarchy

- Gender socialization

- What is meant by the "second shift"

References

Bureau of Labor Statistics. American Time Use Survey Summary. (2015, June 24). Retrieved April 10, 2016, from http://www.bls.gov/news.release/atus.nr0.htm

Conner, C. (2013, January 24). 19 Tips For Closing A Deal On The Golf Course. Forbes. Retrieved April 10, 2016, from http://www.forbes.com/sites/cherylsnappconner/2013/01/24/19-tips-for-closing-a-deal-on-the-golf-course/#358552b4205a

Crawford, M. (2012, September). Engineering Still Needs More Women. American Society of Mechanical Engineers. Retrieved April 10, 2016, from https://www.asme.org/career-education/articles/undergraduate-students/engineering-still-needs-more-women

Davis, S. (2003). Sex Stereotypes in Commercials Targeted Toward Children: A Content Analysis. Sociological Spectrum, 23, 407-424. Retrieved April 11, 2016.

Dewey, C. (2013, October 27). 7 ridiculous restrictions on women's rights around the world. The Washington Post. Retrieved from https://www.washingtonpost.com/news/worldviews/wp/2013/10/27/7-ridiculous-restrictions-on-womens-rights-around-the-world/

Goldman, R. (2014, February 13). Here's a List of 58 Gender Options for Facebook Users. Retrieved April 9, 2016, from http://abcnews.go.com/blogs/headlines/2014/02/heres-a-list-of-58-gender-options-for-facebook-users/

Grant, J., Mottet, L., Tanis, J., & Min, D. (2010, October). National Transgender Discrimination Survey Report on health and health care. Retrieved April 9, 2016, from http://www.thetaskforce.org/static_html/downloads/resources_and_tools/ntds_report_on_health.pdf

Kaneshiro, N. (2015, April 21). Ambiguous genitalia. Retrieved from https://www.nlm.nih.gov/medlineplus/ency/article/003269.htmAmbiguous genitalia

Lambda Legal: Know Your Rights. (2015). Retrieved April 9, 2016, from http://www.lambdalegal.org/know-your-rights/transgender/restroom-faq

Lopez, M., & Gozanlez-Barrera, A. (2014, March 6). Women's college enrollment gains leave men behind. Pew Research Center. Retrieved from http://www.pewresearch.org/fact-tank/2014/03/06/womens-college-enrollment-gains-leave-men-behind/

O'Donnell, J. (2006, March 22). Should business execs meet at strip clubs? USA Today. Retrieved April 10, 2016, from http://usatoday30.usatoday.com/money/companies/management/2006-03-22-strip-clubs-usat_x.htm

Robertson Letter Attacks Feminists. (1992, August 26). The New York Times. Retrieved April 11, 2016, from http://www.nytimes.com/1992/08/26/us/robertson-letter-attacks-feminists.html

Chapter 18: Aging

Aging Today

In October 2011, 100-year-old Fauna Singh finished the Toronto Waterfront Marathon, a 26.2 mile run. He did not win the race, but he finished it. Singh, who is a British citizen born in India, crossed the finish line in just over eight hours and 11 minutes, and he wasn't the last to finish the race. In February 2014, 102-year-old Frenchman Robert Marchand finished a 2.5 km bike race. In October 2015, 100-year-old, American Lou Hollander finished the Ironman World Championship, a 100 mile race. Hollander is a physicist and spends three hours a day exercising and has done so most of his life. Finally, Diana Nyad is an American journalist and long-distance swimmer. In 1975, she swam around Manhattan, a 28 mile swim, and in 1979, she swam from North Bimini in the Bahamas to Juno Beach, Florida a distance of 102 miles. And in 2013, at the age of 64, Diana Nyad swam from Cuba to Florida a distance of 110 miles.

For most Americans the age of 65 represents the age at which someone enters "old age." But there are different ways of measuring age. Here in the United States we use a number and that number is more often than not 65. But why do we use the age of 65 as the point at which someone becomes "old?" In the late 1800's, Bismarck in Germany, wanted to increase his popularity by creating a social welfare system. He wanted extend benefits to older Germans who reached old age without family or money. After meeting with his actuarial specialists, Bismarck chose the age of 65 at which point older Germans would be eligible to draw a pension from the German government. His actuarial people suggested he set the age at which Germans could draw their pension at 65 years because they knew very few Germans would reach that age. The age of 65 in the late 1800's equates to 105 today. When Franklin Delano Roosevelt created the Social Security system in 1935, he chose the age of 65 years as the point at which Americans could draw their pension from the U.S. government. The age of 65 was in Bismarck's time and in President Roosevelt's time virtually arbitrary. But in the 1930's when Social Security was created, the average age at death was much younger than it is today. No one then could have predicted that 75 years later people would be living routinely 15 to 20 years after reaching the age of 65.

Americans tend to think of age as a number, but in some parts of the world age has more to do with what someone is capable of physically doing than it has to do with a number representing years of life. For some cultures, functional age is what defines a person and not chronological age. As someone once wrote, there are only two certain things in life, taxes and death. We will all die sooner or later of one disease or another. It is therefore important to study how we age so we understand what is normal aging and what is not.

Dimensions of Aging

In 2010, 13 percent of the total population, 40 million people, were age 65 and over in the United States. The number of seniors 65 years and older will increase from 35 million in 2010 to an estimated 72 million in 2030, or 20 percent of the U.S. population (2010 Aging Population Report, 2010). The first thing that we needed to do is to look at the dimensions of aging. Aging is a very individualistic and unique process. No two people experience aging in the same way. The first dimension is chronological age, or the number of years we have lived since birth. Today average longevity in the U.S. is 78.8 years (Centers for Disease Control, 2015).

The second dimension of aging is biological aging. This refers to the physical changes that we experience related to our physical functions. There are normal declines that are experienced with aging, but not everyone experiences aging in the same way. We will come back to this subject later in this module.

The next dimension is psychological aging. Psychological aging has to do with the way that we age mentally and how our personality may or may not change with age. One myth that exists about the elderly is that they become more rigid and more set in their ways as they age. But the truth is research has not found significant changes in personality as people age. However their personality was at earlier stages in their life is the best predictor of what it will be like in later life.

Finally, there is social aging, the fourth dimension of aging. This has to do with people adhering to social norms as they age and go through various life stages. However, as the Baby Boomers are entering later life, these cultural expectations are changing as they relate to the elderly. Historically, society was less understanding of social age violations. For instance, in 2014, Eleanor Cunningham of Howes Cave, New York celebrated her 100th birthday by going skydiving. This was the third time she had went skydiving after having taken up the sport at the age of 90 years (New York Dailey News, 2014). In 2011, a German woman named Rajo Devi Lohan became the oldest person in recorded history to ever give birth to a child at the age of 70 years. On the other hand, and as unbelievable as it may seem, in 1933 Victoria Medina of Peru gave birth to a child at the age of 5 years (Mikkelson, 2015; UPI, 1939). Finally, at the tender age of 103, George Kirby of London married his 91-year-old sweetheart, Doreen Luckie (right). They broke the world record for oldest newlyweds.

Social aging has to do with timing. For instance we expect people to get married in their 20's or maybe 30's but not in their 90's or older. We expect young men full of testosterone in their 20's or 30's to risk jumping from a plane at 13,000 feet, but we don't expect that of a 100-year-old woman. Society expects women to give birth in the late teenage years to 20's, maybe even into her 30's, but not in their 70's. In the Western world, these violations of social norms are no longer looked down on, in fact we smile, and maybe hope that we're still able to do those things when we reach that age. But in many other countries of the world these activities would be considered violations of social norms and maybe sanctioned. Aging in other societies may be a very different experience than what it is here or in the Western world in general.

Finishing up with the idea of social norm violations, would it surprise you to know that the rate of STDs among seniors is skyrocketing? According to the Centers for Disease Control (2015), between 2007 and 2011, the rate of chlamydia infections increased by 31 percent and the rate of syphilis among the aged increased by 52 percent. How do we feel about that? Is that a violation of a normative standard? Don't we automatically think that sex between people ends when they hit 65 years? "Ah, honey, tomorrow I turn 65, so we'd better spend today in bed having lots and lots of sex, ok?" Yes, that is funny, but in reality sex doesn't stop at the age of 65 nor even in later life in general, again because aging is a very unique experience.

The New York Times reported that sex in retirement communities is becoming more common. Why? According to the New York Times, there are four reasons:

- assisted living facilities and retirement communities "are becoming like college campuses" by cramming a lot of people together into a relatively small environment,

- seniors are living longer today,

- seniors may think they are immune from STDs because that's something only discussed when speaking about young people, and

- the invention of drugs that make sex more possible in later life. In a study done by Reese et al. (2010), 40 percent of college age people use condoms in 40 percent of their sexual encounters, while seniors only use them in 6 percent of sexual encounters.

Theoretical Views on Aging

One of the first theories to look at aging was called disengagement theory by Cumming and Henry (1961). The theory advocated that in order to make room for younger generations, older people needed to give way by retiring and disengaging from society while at a time in their life that was associated with physical and mental decline. Additionally, much lower salaries would be paid when hiring younger workers to replace older retirees who earned higher wages that are typically paid to long-time employees. In this way disengagement theory argued this was functional for society.

Disengagement Theory

A major flaw with **disengagement theory** was the assumption that older people were in fact in a state of mental and physical decline. Today, people remain active routinely into their 70's and 80's. Again, aging is a very individual process. Income also affects the activities older people engage in. In our culture older retirees with adequate funds in retirement can pursue many activities, whereas people who are barely scraping by in later life may not have those same opportunities. The major flaw with disengagement theory is, as I say, that it puts forth the notion that mental and physical decline in later life is a normal part of the aging process, but research says that is not the case. In fact, forcing seniors to retire has a negative impact on their health and well-being both physically and mentally.

Activity Theory

The next theory that attempts to explain aging is **activity theory**. This theory advocates that people in later life are actually benefited from remaining engaged and active in later life. The theory suggests that disengagement is actually harmful to successful aging. By remaining engaged seniors can protect their self-esteem, self-efficacy and psychological well-being. A criticism of activity theory suggests that while remaining active may be beneficial for some, it might be dysfunctional for others. For those elderly who are physically capable of continuing their same activities, results are typically positive and seniors are able to maintain their psychological well being. On the other hand, for those elderly who are not physically capable of carrying on as they have been, the effects on their psychological well being could be damaging should they try to remain active and engaged when they are not physically able to do so.

Conflict Perspective

Finally there is the **conflict perspective**, which sees the negative aspects of aging associated with prejudice and discrimination leveled by younger generations. The perspective argues that younger generations award the highest social status to people in their 50's, then in their 20's to 40's, and the least amount of status to people under the age of 20 and older than the mid to late 60's. In general, the conflict perspective argues that the value of seniors is lessened because of the stereotypes associated with aging and therefore seniors are seen as no longer able to contribute to the labor force as they have at earlier points in their lives. Also, because of their higher salaries and the increased cost of health benefits provided by employers to seniors, drive the cost of employing seniors in comparison to lower costs associated with employing younger workers. A criticism of the conflict perspective is that it associates ageism with modern society. But in point of truth the elderly begin to lose status in the past several hundred years with industrialization. **Modernization theory** suggests that prior to industrialization, fathers passed their land and property down to their oldest son, and in return, the adult son would allow his father to be head of the family and awarded status accordingly. However, industrialization, which was occurring in the cities, drew young men from the land to the factories, which then reduced the status of the elderly father because inheritance became less valuable.

Life Expectancy and Age Dependency

According to the Centers for Disease Control, the average longevity in the U.S. is 78.8 years from birth, which is 81.2 years for females and 76.4 years for males. The U.S. ranks 43rd in average longevity globally (See figure 1, pg 262). The country with the highest longevity is Monaco at 89.5 years and Japan in 2nd place at 84.7 years.

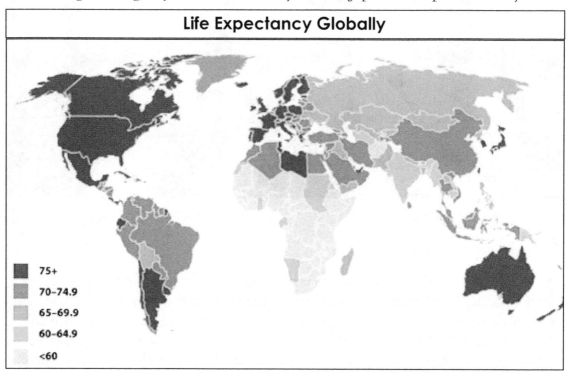

Life Expectancy Globally

75+
70–74.9
65–69.9
60–64.9
<60

As people in virtually all societies of the world are living longer, the elderly are usually thought of in one of two ways: either they are more valued by their culture or are seen as burdens. Here in the U.S., this is referred to as the "graying of America."

As the population ages, it shifts the burden of care, both physical and financial, to younger generations. The cost of medical care and subsidized housing for the poor elderly is expensive and the costs will continue to increase as the population ages. The **dependency ratio** is the proportion of those people younger than 15 or older than 64 to the working-age population (i.e., 15-64 years). In the U.S., the dependency ratio is 50 percent (Age Dependency Ratio, 2016). In other words, the working half of the U.S. population, those 15 – 64 years of age, support the non-working half, those 15 years and younger and those 65 and older.

Biological Changes and Aging

As we age, there are certain biological changes that occur for the majority of people. Those changes include the graying of our hair, and hairlines recede, we gain weight in the way of fat which replaces muscle mass, there is bone and muscle loss, lung capacity decreases, our cardiovascular system and renal systems decline, we lose brain cells, and there are vision changes as well. While learning and memory can decline, the old adage seems especially true here: use it, or lose it.

Other changes include a greater likelihood of having high blood pressure, coronary artery disease, diabetes, arthritis, and osteoporosis (primarily in women). Unfortunately, we do get shorter as we age.

However, while the picture I have painted seems bleak, it is important to remind you of something I mentioned earlier: the aging experience is unique and different for everyone. The way one-person experiences later life is not necessarily the way another person will experience it. Remember our 100-year-old athletes? I may be younger in years, but in truth they could run rings around me at half their age. Generally, while the above physical and health issues have a greater chance of affecting you in later life, for many, they do not.

Living with Zest and Zeal

I'm reminded of the old beer commercial where the narrator says, "Go with the gusto!" As I've just stated, aging is unique to everyone, but there are things that seniors can do to enhance their quality of life. Physically, seniors need to remain active. A sedentary lifestyle isn't good for anyone, but that may be especially true in later life. Exercise helps pump blood and reduces the strain on your heart. Generally, everyone should get some kind of cardio exercise at minimum three times a week and sustain that elevated heart rate for at least 30 minutes. While swimming is the best overall exercise, brisk walking is also an excellent exercise. For seniors who are unable to participate in cardio activities, any activity is better than none. A healthy diet is also important. As we age, our body is less able to process food as it did when we were younger, therefore a healthy diet is essential to maintaining good physical (and mental) health. While our genes may set the stage for many aspects of our physical self, a lack of exercise and good nutrition can reduce the potential of having "good" genes.

While physical health is important, so is mental health. Seniors need to stay engaged with their social world. Maintaining ties with others is a good way of having a good social support network. Social support networks are important throughout the life course, but may be even more important in later life. Research has found time and time again the importance of maintaining regular ties with friends and family members as beneficial (Binstock & George, 2006).

Religion and Aging

Many people believe that people become more religious as they age, but the research doesn't support that. However, for those who are religious, and especially if they are able to attend church, there are a great many social and psychological benefits.

Cohen and Koenig (2003) found that religion can play an important role in successful aging. In a study done by Ayele et al. (2015), researchers reported that life satisfaction was associated with religiosity (e.g., praying, reading religious literature, listening to or watching religious broadcasts). Religious beliefs were also used as a coping mechanism for a majority of the sample when faced with health or illness issues. This helps to reduce stress, which is research has found to be very harmful to the body. Also, when seniors attend church, they remain engaged with society, and this is crucial for their overall well-being. Additionally, friends and fellow parishioners serve as important members of a senior's social support network. Social support networks can provide a variety of assistance to seniors. In addition to physical help, support networks can provide information about services available for seniors, or can serve as bridges between the elderly and those who might either provide services or know of someone or something that might be able to respond to their needs.

Senior Living Situations

The goal of many social service agencies is to provide information and help sufficient enough to allow seniors to remain in their homes as long as possible. Controlling for physical abilities, research has shown that independence is associated with improved mental health when compared to those institutionalized elderly.

When seniors are unable to live in their own homes independently, there are a number of options for senior housing. Retirement communities are a popular option for those seniors who want independence, but may want to live in an age-segregated community. Some seniors have a preference for living in age-segregated communities whereas others prefer to live in age-integrated communities—the latter, which is known as aging in place. It depends on the personality of the individual senior. Sometimes seniors move to retirement communities because they want to escape the harsh winters of Northern states. However, one significant disadvantage of retirement communities is that they can be expensive. According to Genworth.com, the average cost of a one-bedroom, independent living or retirement community in the U.S. in 2012 was $2,750 a month. That puts it out of reach for many senior Americans.

Another option for seniors who can't remain in their homes, primarily because they need assistance with daily needs, is the assisted living facility. Assisted living facilities are made up of a number of one or two-bedroom apartments in a private setting. Usually at least one meal per day is provided as part of the senior's rent which is served

in a communal dining hall, but seniors can cook for themselves if they prefer. Further, physical and medical assistance can be provided on a limited basis to those seniors who only need minor assistance. Usually, assisted living facilities offer a great number of activities for seniors. The advantages of assisted living include autonomy for those who don't need physical assistance, within a community of other seniors, with a variety of activities. The disadvantage is some slight loss of freedom (i.e., rules), and like retirement communities, cost. Another option for seniors is continuous care retirement communities. Essentially, seniors "buy" their apartment within the assisted living wing of the facility. In the assisted living wing, life is similar to that of the assisted living facility. The difference is that as the level of care for the senior changes, the senior is transferred to another part of the facility where more intensive care can be provided. The idea is that when seniors "buy" their apartments in these continuous care facilities they are buying care until the end of life. Once a resident is moved out of his or her apartment, the unit is resold. The advantage is that once a senior moves into the facility, they never have to move again. The disadvantage is that these communities can be very expensive.

Finally, for seniors who are unable to care for themselves, need continuous care, and independent living is not possible, there are nursing homes. For seniors who need an intensive amount of care, assisted living facilities are not an option, and they must be moved to a nursing home. It is assumed that once someone enters a nursing home they will remain there until the end of their life, which is why they have such a negative image in American society. There are over 16,000 nursing homes in the U.S. today, and approximately 4 percent of seniors live in nursing homes (2010 Aging Population Report, 2010). Approximately 80 percent of nursing home residents need help with activities of daily living (ADLs), which include help with bathing, dressing, using the bathroom, and eating. Because women always outnumber men, women make up the majority of seniors in nursing homes. Of those elderly who enter a nursing home, the average length of stay for those who are able to leave the nursing home is 272 days; for those who never leave the nursing home, the average length of stay, typically until death, is 892 days (Benz, 2012).

Terms, Concepts and Names to Know:

- Actuarial science

- Dependency ratio

- Chronological age

- Functional age

- Psychological age

- Social age

- Self-efficacy

Be Able to Discuss:

- Disengagement theory

- Activity theory

- Conflict perspective on senior status

- Modernization theory

References

Ayele, H., Mulligan, T., Gheorghiu, S., & Reyes-Ortiz, C. (2015). Religious Activity Improves Life Satisfaction for Some Physicians and Older Patients. American Journal of the American Geriatrics Society, 47(4), 453-455.

Binstock & George, (2006) Binstock, R. H., & George, L. K. (Eds.). (2006). Handbook of aging and the social sciences (6th ed.). Boston: Academic Press. (see Note 6.23 "Applying Social Research").

Cohen, A., & Koenig, H. (2003). Religion, Religiosity and Spirituality in the Biophysical Model of Health and Ageing. Ageing International, 28(3), 215-241.

Federal Interagency Forum on Aging-Related Statistics. (2016, December 31). 2010 Aging Population Report. Retrieved April 12, 2016, from http://www.agingstats.gov/agingstats-dotnet/Main_Site/Data/2012_Documents/Highlights.aspx
General Social Survey. (2010). Retrieved from http://sda.berkeley.edu/cgi-bin/hsda?harcsda+gss10.

Mikkelson, D. (2015, February 7). Youngest Mother. Retrieved April 12, 2016, from http://www.snopes.com/pregnant/youngestmother.asp

100-year-old New York woman sky dives for birthday celebration. (2014, November 9). New York Daily News. Retrieved April 12, 2016, from http://www.nydailynews.com/life-style/100-year-old-woman-skydives-birthday-article-1.2004847

Population Reference Bureau. (2011). The world at 7 billion: World population data sheet: Life expectancy. Retrieved from http://www.prb.org/publications/datasheets/2011/world-population-data-sheet/world-map.aspx#/map/lifeexp

Reese, M., Herbernick, D., Fortenberry, J., Dodge, B., Sanders, S., & Schick, V. (2010). National Survey of Sexual Health and Behavior. Retrieved April 12, 2016, from http://www.nationalsexstudy.indiana.edu

The World Bank. (2016). Age dependency ratio. Retrieved April 12, 2016, from http://data.worldbank.org/indicator/SP.POP.DPND

Unknown. (2016). 2015 Cost of Care. Retrieved April 12, 2016, from https://www.genworth.com

Chapter 19: Mental Health and Illness

What is the Sociology of Mental Health?

Sociologists have a different perspective about mental health than does psychology or biology. Sociology asks the question: are mental health problems the result of the social environment or biology? Sociologists would argue that some or many psychological problems are the result of the social environment and not necessarily hormones or other chemical deficiencies. In other words, something in the social environment may contribute to a clinical diagnosis of mental illness. Further, a society may not recognize a particular pattern of thoughts and behaviors as a mental illness while other societies recognize them as such. For instance, somewhere between .05 and .5 percent of Americans have been diagnosed with gender dysphoria—an illness recognized by the American Psychological Association. However, many countries around the world do not recognize an illness called gender dysphoria.

Historically, all behavior that was abnormal earned the individual the label of deviant, and woe to you if you were labeled as a deviant during the middle ages. People with mental illnesses would be associated with witchcraft and the Devil. Very often witches, perhaps suffering from some type of mental illness, had a very good chance of being burned at the stake. Without science to explain abnormal behavior, any kind of deviance was perceived as an indication of the supernatural.

Mental Health During the Middle Ages

Prior to the 1600's, those suffering from what we now know to be a mental illness were often labeled as witches or agents of Satan. Historically mental health problems were thought to be the result of demonic or spirit possession. In earlier times, without knowledge of medical science, these were the explanations for such deviant and odd behavior. Consequently, these beliefs led to fear, discrimination, and even death. The penalty for being a witch was most often death after being tortured to confess their acquaintance with the Devil.

In the 1600's the title of "insane" led to their being "put away" in some sort of facility. Michel Foucault, a French philosopher, reported that in 1656 the Hopital-General opened in Paris to house all those judged insane or abnormal in their thinking or behavior. Foucault goes on to state this was the first time in history where the mentally ill, or the "mad" as they were called, were separated from the general population for the protection of society (Foucault, 1965). Those with what we would call today a mental illness, were housed with the deviant and abnormal—many of whom were criminals. In the eighteenth and nineteenth centuries efforts were made to separate the insane from the criminals. Eventually this led to some of the severe cases of madness being institutionalized but others being released back into society—though society didn't really accept either group back into the fold.

One of the first mental illnesses recognized by society was depression. Edgar Allen Poe wrote about his "melancholia" (an earlier name for depression). Kay Jamison researched Poe's life and found characteristics that today might earn Poe the diagnosis of manic-depressive. Jamison wrote, "fellow students at the University of Virginia, where Poe studied, described him as a volatile personality and an "impulsive, chaotic" gambler," while another student wrote of Poe, "[we] considered him cracked." Apparently, Poe's mood varied by season of the year, something Jamison reports is characteristic of manic-depression. Also, his drunkenness fit with the diagnosis as Jamison reported that sixty-one percent of manic depressives abuse alcohol or drugs (Jamison, 1993).

The Social Construction of Mental Illness

The definition of mental illness can change over time and by culture because it is socially constructed. An illness only exists when society agrees to its existence. For instance, approximately ten percent of the American population is clinically depressed (Center for Behavioral Health Statistics and Quality, 2015). Here in the U.S. there are very specific criteria that have to be met in order to be diagnosed with major depression. If you don't meet those criteria, someone might just be considered sad. In some countries where mental illness is not well-defined, someone may be considered sad or just moody, but if they were here in the U.S. they might meet the criteria for major depression.

In 1892, the short story "The Yellow Wallpaper" by Charlotte Gilman Perkins was published. The story centers around a woman whose husband believes she is suffering from what he calls a "temporary nervous depression" with a tendency towards hysteria—something thought to be common among women in the 1800's. Her treatment included exercise, fresh air, and abstinence from working. However, the treatment, and subsequent isolation, end up driving the woman into madness. Perkins' story mimicked her own experiences with depression. Like the character in the short story, Perkins' doctor had prescribed a rest cure which required that she live a "domestic life" with little mental stimulation. This was congruent with the male attitude towards women at the time—that they were weak and frail and prone to episodes of hysteria. Perkins committed suicide in 1935. Perkins along with the character in her book show just how mental illness is socially constructed—for men in the late 1800's women suffered from temporary bouts of hysteria and depression, but were not regarded as having a more serious and long-term illness as depression is now regarded.

Perkins' life and short story both support Ehrenberg's (2010) belief that what used to be considered instances of sadness have evolved into a diagnosis of depression. Some would argue that the line between normal sadness and depression has been blurred by moving to a diagnostic model of depression that attempts to simplify the condition so that a diagnosis is more easily reached.

Statistics on Mental Illness

Perhaps as many as half of all adult Americans experience some mental health condition in their lives and more than half of those experience moderate to severe symptoms. As much as twenty percent of Americans experience a mental health condition each year (National Association of Mental Illness, n.d.). Mental illness is responsible for as much as forty percent of disability cases in the US. Despite this, only about between twenty and sixty percent of people with mental illness seek treatment (Doebbeling, 2016; Corrigan, 2014).

Anxiety disorders are the most commonly experienced mental illness in the U.S., affecting perhaps as many as 40 million American adults (National Institutes of Mental Health, n.d.), but only about one-third of those with anxiety disorders seek treatment. Three to five times as many people with an anxiety disorder

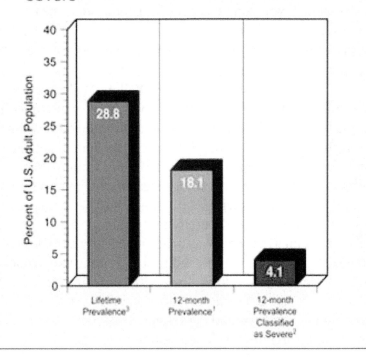

Percent of U.S. population experiencing a mental health issue,
(National Association of Mental illness)

- **12-month Prevalence: 18.1% of U.S. adult population**[1]
- **Severe: 22.8% of these cases (e.g., 4.1% of U.S. adult population) are classified as "severe"**[2]

go to a doctor than the general public and they are also six times more likely to be hospitalized for mental health treatment.

According to the Anxiety and Depression Association of America (2016), below are the most common types of mental illness in the US along with incident rates:

- **Generalized anxiety disorder** affects 6.8 million adults, or 3.1% of the U.S. population. Women are twice as likely to be affected as men.

- **Panic disorder** affects 6 million adults, or 2.7% of the population. Women are twice as likely to be affected as men. Very high comorbidity rate with major depression.

- **Social anxiety disorder**. 15 million, 6.8%. Equally common among men and women, typically beginning around age 13. According to a 2007 ADAA survey, 36% of people with social anxiety disorder report experiencing symptoms for 10 or more years before seeking help.

- **Phobias**. 19 million, 8.7%. Women are twice as likely to be affected as men. Typically begins in childhood; the median age of onset is 7. Obsessive-compulsive disorder (OCD) and posttraumatic stress disorder (PTSD) are closely related to anxiety disorders, which some may experience at the same time, along with depression.

- **Obsessive-compulsive disorder**. 2.2 million, 1.0%. Equally common among men and women. The median age of onset is 19, with 25 percent of cases occurring by age 14. One-third of affected adults first experienced symptoms in childhood.

- **Posttraumatic stress disorder**. 7.7 million, 3.5%. Women are more likely to be affected than men. Rape is the most likely trigger of PTSD: 65% of men and 45.9% of women who are raped will develop the disorder. Childhood sexual abuse is a strong predictor of lifetime likelihood for developing PTSD.

- **Major depressive disorder**. The leading cause of disability in the U.S. for ages 15 to 44.3. Affects more than 15 million American adults, or about 6.7 percent of the U.S. population age 18 and older in a given year. While major depressive disorder can develop at any age, the median age at onset is 32.5. More prevalent in women than in men.

- **Persistent depressive disorder**. A form of depression that usually continues for at least two years. Affects approximately 1.5 percent of the U.S. population age 18 and older in a given year. (about 3.3 million American adults). The median age of onset is 31.1

Mental health: How Do We Define It?

The American Psychological Association, in its Diagnostic and Statistical Manual V (APA, 2013) defines mental illness as disorders characterized by "dysregulation of mood, thought, and/or behavior. Mood disorders are among the most pervasive of all mental disorders and include major depression, in which the individual commonly reports feeling, for a time period of two weeks or more, sad or blue, uninterested in things previously of interest, psychomotor retardation or agitation, and increased or decreased appetite since the depressive episode ensued."

Specific disorders include the following as outlined by the Centers for Disease Control (August 11, 2016):

Depression

Depression is characterized by persistent sadness and sometimes irritability (particularly in children) and is one of the leading causes of disease or injury worldwide for both men and women. Depression can cause suffering for depressed individuals and can also have negative effects on their families and the communities in which they live.

Risk factors:

- Is associated with an increased risk for mortality from suicide as well as other causes, such as heart disease

- Is associated with lower workplace productivity and more absenteeism, which result in lower income and higher unemployment.

- Is associated with higher risk for other conditions and behaviors, including: Other mental disorders (anxiety disorders, substance use disorders, eating disorders)

Symptoms:

- Feelings of sadness, hopelessness, depressed mood

- Loss of interest or pleasure in activities that used to be enjoyable

- Change in weight or appetite (either increase or decrease)

- Change in activity: psychomotor agitation (being more active than usual) or psychomotor retardation (being less active than usual)

- Insomnia (difficulty sleeping) or sleeping too much

- Feeling tired or not having any energy

- Feelings of guilt or worthlessness

- Difficulties concentrating and paying attention

- Thoughts of death or suicide.

Statistics:

- More than 1 out of 20 Americans 12 years of age and older reported current depression (moderate or severe depressive symptoms in the past 2 weeks) in 2009-2012.

Anxiety

Anxiety disorders are characterized by excessive and unrealistic worry about everyday tasks or events, or may be specific to certain objects or rituals, for instance, spiders, snakes, tall buildings. Social phobias are anxiety-producing fear of social interaction, especially of large groups consisting of strangers. In obsessive-compulsive disorder (OCD), individual's experience a fixated obsession, which can be a thought, feeling, or idea, that is recurrent and will not go away. When coupled with a compulsion, for example a recurrent behavior, that is defined as obsessive-compulsive disorder or OCD. Treatment for anxiety disorders can involve treatment with appropriate medications, but are also helped by a process of desensitization—a process whereby the individual is exposed to the anxiety producing object or thought. Additionally, anxiety disorders can also be treated by "response prevention –not permitting the compulsive behavior, to help the individual learn that it is not needed" (Sadock & Sadock, 2007).

Psychotic Disorders

Psychotic disorders are characterized by "dysregulation of thought processes." For instance, schizophrenia includes symptoms of delusions, such as feeling they are someone else, or feeling superior to others like a god, and hallucinations, which includes seeing or hearing things that are not real. "Schizoaffective disorder is a disorder in which, as its name implies, individuals have features of both schizophrenia and mood disorders" (Sadock & Sadock, 2007). It is customary to treat psychotic disorders with antidepressant medications and therapeutic interventions (Andreason & Black, 2006).

Bipolar Disorder

Bipolar disorder, also casually referred to as manic-depression, is a mood disorder where patients experience extreme fluctuations in mood—from severe depression to episodes of mania or euphoria (Campbell, 2009). "Mania is characterized by clearly elevated, unrestrained, or irritable mood which may manifest in an exaggerated assessment of self-importance or grandiosity, sleeplessness, racing thoughts, pressured speech, and the tendency to engage in activities which appear pleasurable, but have a high potential for adverse consequences" (Andreasen & Black, 2006). Like depression, medication is the first line of treatment but is most effective when combined with psychotherapy.

How Does Society Respond to Mental Illness?

Unfortunately, stigmas about mental illness in general abound among Americans. Research has found that a majority of adults in the US have negative attitudes about mental illness and the mentally ill (Crisp et al., 2000; Bryne, 2001). For example, Moses (2010) found that stigma directed at adolescents with mental health problems was just as likely to come from family members, friends, and teachers as it was from strangers. Forty-six percent of these adolescents described experiencing stigmatization "by family members in the form of unwarranted assumptions (e.g. the sufferer was being manipulative), distrust, avoidance, pity and gossip, 62% experienced stigma from peers which often led to friendship losses and social rejection" (Connolly, Geller, Marton & Kutcher (1992), and 35% reported stigma perpetrated by teachers and school staff, who expressed fear, dislike, avoidance, and under-estimation of abilities. Mental health stigma is even widespread in the medical profession, at least in part because it is given a low priority during the training of physicians and GPs (Wallace, 2010).

In a survey of over 1700 adults in the UK, Crisp et al. (200) found that:

- the most commonly held belief was that people with mental health problems were dangerous – especially those with schizophrenia, alcoholism and drug dependence,

- people believed that some mental health problems such as eating disorders and substance abuse were self inflicted, and

- respondents believed that people with mental health problems were generally hard to talk to. People tended to hold these negative beliefs regardless of their age, regardless of what knowledge they had of mental health problems, and regardless of whether they knew someone who had a mental health problem. More recent studies of attitudes to individuals with a diagnosis of schizophrenia or major depression convey similar findings. In both cases, a significant proportion of members of the public considered that people with mental health problems such as depression or schizophrenia were unpredictable, dangerous and they would be less likely to employ someone with a mental health problem (Wang & Lai, 2008; Reavley & Jorm, 2011).

Research has found that the public associate drug addiction, prostitution, and crime with mental illness (Albrecht et al., 1982; Skinner, et al., 1995). Sadly, some research has found that people not only withhold pity and help from the mentally ill, but display anger and hostility largely because they feel the mental illness is within the control of the mentally ill person (Socall &Holtgraves, 1992; Weiner et al., 1988).

So how does the public react to the mentally ill? Generally, research has found four ways in which the public reacts to the mentally ill:

1. they withhold help,

2. they avoid them,

3. they believe that treatment should be forced on the mentally ill so they can become "normal" again, and

4. perhaps as much as 40 percent of Americans feel that the mentally ill should be locked away somewhere away from the general public (Weiner et al., 1988; Piliavin et al., 1969; Schwartz et al., 2001).

One of the worst ways in which the public treat the mentally ill is by avoiding them altogether. In a study done on 1444 US adults, researchers found that more than half of respondents were unwilling to spend an evening or socializing with the mentally ill. Further, they did not want to live next to work with, or have a family member marry a mentally ill person (Piliavin et al., 1969). Tragically, some research suggests that even health care workers hold some of the aforementioned attitudes toward the mentally ill (Link, 1987; Phelan et al., 2000; Roman & Floyd, 1981). However, it is incredibly reckless and counterproductive for health care workers to hold such negative attitudes towards the mentally ill given their roles in treatment of these same people. Perhaps ironically, re-search has found fewer stigmas directed at the mentally ill in Asian and African countries than in the Western world and are virtually non-existent in Islamic societies (Fabrega, 1991).

What Leads to Stigmatizing the Mentally Ill?

Now that we've established that the general public stigmatizes the mentally ill, we need to ask why that is the case. As has already been established, the vast majority of Americans believe that people suffering from some form of men-tal illness (e.g., depression, schizophrenia, alcohol dependence, and drug dependence) should be avoided at the least, but many Americans believe those suffering from men-tal illness are a danger to not only to themselves but also to society (Pescosolido et al., 1996). These views are grounded in history. Throughout recorded time those who were "different"with mental health problems were not only avoided but often victimized. Historically, and even today, the public believes that the mentally ill are a danger to society, but these beliefs are not backed up by fact (e.g. Swanson, Holzer, Ganju & Jono, 1990).

The media has no small part to play in this process of stigmatizing the mentally ill. Research has identified three ways in which the mentally ill are perceived by Americans. First, the mentally ill are portrayed as "homicidal maniacs" who thrive on the murder of innocent others. Second, the media often portray the mentally ill as naïve and childlike—as people who are incapable of caring for themselves. Three, often times the media seem to imply that the mentally ill are victims of their own weak character—in other words, their condition is their fault (Gabbard & Gabbard, 1992; Hyler & Gabbard, 1991; Mayer & Barry, 1992).

Conclusions

The research is very clear: the mentally ill are no more a danger to society than any other group, yet they are treated as lepers—people to be avoided or locked away. Mental illness is common in the US with perhaps as many as half of all Americans experiencing some form of mental illness in their lifetime, and 10-20 percent experiencing depression annually. People who suffer from mental illness are usually able to hold down jobs, contribute to society, raise a family, while keeping their illness hidden. In fact, with medications and psychotherapy, mental illness is largely controlled, though it should be remembered that the mentally ill are more likely to commit suicide largely because they do not seek out help and support because of the societal stigma placed on the mentally ill.

When writing about his father's mental illness, 18-year-old Theo Bennett (2015) stated: "If we don't recognize mental illnesses as physical health issues, then we will never get people the treatment that they need. One of the few certainties that I have learned from living with a father with bipolar disorder is that mental health is just as important as physical health. In fact, mental health is physical health; the two are inseparable. It baffles me that many people continue to make a distinction between the two." Albrecht, G., Walker, V., & Levy, J. (1982). Social distance from the stigmatized: a test of two theories. Social Science Medicine, 1982, 16, 1319–1327.

Terms, Concepts and Names to Know:

- Charlotte Gilman Perkins

- Gender dyspohoria

- General anxiety disorder

- Panic disorder

- Social anxiety disorder

- Phobias

- Obsessive compulsive disorder

- Post-traumatic stress disorder

- Major depressive disorder

- Persistent depressive disorder

- Depression

- Anxiety

- Psychotic disorders

- Bipolar disorder

Be Able to Discuss:

- Attitudes and beliefs towards mental illness

- Mental illness down through history

- The social construction of mental illness

- American Psychological Association's definition of mental illness

- Stigmatization of the mentally ill

References

Albrecht, G., Walker, V., & Levy, J. (1982). Social distance from the stigmatized: a test of two theories. Social Science Medicine, 1982, 16, 1319–1327.

Andreasen, N., & Black, D. (2006). Introductory Textbook of Psychiatry. (4th ed.). Arlington, VA: American Psychiatric Publishing, Inc.

Anxiety and Depression Association of America. (2016). Facts and statistics. Retrieved August 8, 2016, from https://www.adaa.org/about-adaa/press-room/facts-statistics

Bennett, T. (2015). Changing The Way Society Understands Mental Health. National Association of Mental Illness. Retrieved August 13, 2016 from http://www.nami.org/Blogs/NAMI-Blog/April-2015/Changing-The-Way-Society-Understands-Mental-Health#

Bernice A. Pescosolido Jack K. Martin Bruce G. (1996). Public Report on the MacArthur Mental Health Module, 1996 General Social Survey. Retrieved August 13, 2016 from http://www.indiana.edu/-icmhsr/docs/Americans'%20Views%20of%20Mental%20Health.pdf

Birch, D. (1993, April 28). Poe's latest analyst calls him manic-depressive Researcher links illness, inspiration. Retrieved August 17, 2016, from http://articles.baltimoresun.com/1993-04-28/news/1993118157_1_david-poe-edgar-allan-poe-poe-life

Bryne, P. (2001). Psychiatric stigma. The British Journal of Psychiatry, March 2001, 178(3).

Center for Behavioral Health Statistics and Quality. (2015). Behavioral health trends in the United States: Results from the 2014 National Survey on Drug Use and Health (HHS Publication No. SMA 15-4927, NSDUH Series H-50).

Centers for Disease Control (August 11, 2016). Mental Illness. Retrieved 11 August 2016 from https://www.cdc.gov/mentalhealth/basics/mental-illness.htm

Connolly J, Geller S, Marton P, Kutcher S. (1992). Peer responses to social interaction with depressed adolescents. Journal of Clinical Child Psychology, 21:365–370.

Crisp, A., Gelder, M., Rix, S., Meltzer, H., & Rowlands, O. (2000). The British Journal of Psychiatry, 177(1), 4-7.

Corrigan, P., Druss, N., & Perlick, D. (2014). The impact of mental illness stigma on seeking and participating in mental health care. Psychological Science in the Public Interest, 15 (2), 37-70.

Doebbeling, C. (2016). Mental Illness in Society. Retrieved August 8, 2016, from http://www.merckmanuals.com/home/mental-health-disorders/overview-of-mental-healthcare/mental-illness-in-society

Fabrega, H. (1991). Psychiatric stigma in non-Western societies. Comprehensive Psychiatry, 1991, 32, 534–551.

Gabbard, G. & Gabbard K. (1992). Cinematic stereotypes contributing to the stigmatization of psychiatrists. In: Fink PJ, editor; Tasman A, editor. Stigma and mental illness. Washington: American Psychiatric Press, 1992, 113–126.

Hyler, S., Gabbard, G. & Schneider, I. (1991). Homicidal maniacs and narcissistic parasites. Stigmatization of mentally ill persons in the movies. Hospital Community Psychiatry, 1991, 42,1044–1048.

Jamison, K. (1993, October 7). Touched with Fire: Manic-Depressive Illness and the Artistic Temperament. The New England Journal of Medicine, 329, 1133-1134.

Link, B. (1987). Understanding labeling effects in the area of mental disorders: an assessment of the effects of expectations of rejection. American Sociological Review, 52, 96–112.

National Institutes of Mental Health. (n.d.). Any anxiety disorder among adults. http://www.nimh.nih.gov/health/statistics/prevalence/any-anxiety-disorder-among-adults.shtml

Link, B. (1987). Understanding labeling effects in the area of mental disorders: an assessment of the effects of expectations of rejection. American Sociological Review, 52, 96–112.

National Association of Mental Illness. (n.d.). Mental health conditions. Retrieved from http://www.nami.org/Learn-More/Mental-Health-Conditions August 16, 2016.

Mayer, A., & Barry, D. (1992). Working with the media to destigmatize mental illness. Hospital Community Psychiatry. 1992, 43, 77–78.

Moses, T. (2010). Being treated differently: stigma experiences with family, peers, and school staff among adolescents with mental health disorders. Social Science Medicine, April, 70(7), 985-93.

National Association of Mental Illness. (n.d.). Mental health conditions. Retrieved from http://www.nami.org/Learn-More/Mental-Health-Conditions August 16, 2016.

Oppenheimer, C., & Hankin, B. (2011). Relationship Quality and Depressive Symptoms

Among Adolescents: A Short-Term Multi-Wave Investigation of Longitudinal, Reciprocal Associations, Journal of Clinical Child Adolescent Psychology, 40(3), 486–493.

Phelan, J., Stueve, A. (2000). Public conceptions of mental illness in 1950 and 1996: what is mental illness and is it to be feared? Journal of Health Social Behavior, 41,188–207.

Piliavin, A., Rodin J., & Piliavin, J. (1969). Good Samaritanism: an underground phenomenon? Journal of Personality and Social Psychology, 13, 289–299.

Roman, P., & Floyd, H. (1981). Social acceptance of psychiatric illness and psychiatric treatment. Social Psychiatry, 1981, 16, 16–21.

Sadock, B., & Sadock, V. (2007). Kaplan & Sadock's Synopsis of Psychiatry: Behavioral Sciences/Clinical Psychiatry (10th ed.). Philadelphia, PA, Lippincott, Williams & Wilkins.

Skinner, L., Berry, K., & Griffith, S. (1995). Generalizability and specificity of the stigma associated with the mental illness label: a reconsideration twenty-five years later. Journal of Community Psychology, 1995, 23:3–17.

Socall, D. & Holtgraves, T. (1992). Attitudes toward the mentally ill: the effects of label and beliefs. Sociology Quarterly, 1992, 33, 435–445.

Swanson, J, Holzer, C., Ganju, V., & Jono, R. (1990). Violence and psychiatric disorder in the community: evidence from the Epidemiologic Catchment Area surveys. Hospital Community Psychiatry, July, 41(7), 761-70.

Swartz, M., Swason, J., & Hiday, V. (2001). A randomized controlled trial of outpatient commitment in North Carolina. Psychiatriatic Service, 52, 325–329.

The Indiana Consortium of Mental Health Services Research, Indiana University. (1996). Americans' Views of Mental Health and Illness at Century's End: Continuity and Change. Retrieved August 8, 2016, from http://www.indiana.edu/~icmhsr/docs/Americans'%20Views%20of%20Mental%20Health.pdf

Weiner,B., Perry, R., & Magnusson, J. (1988). An attributional analysis of reactions to stigmas. Journal of Personality Social Psychology, 55, 738–748.

Chapter 20: Sociology of Work

The Historical Evolution of Work

For most of human existence, humans gained their livelihood by gathering and hunting, human survival depended on some combination of:

- gathering plants, fruits, insects, grubs, and reptiles,

- hunting large and small animals, and scavenging animal carcasses. These tasks often required the development and use of tools. The ability to communicate was also essential to the development of human life and work.

Today there are only a few hunting and gathering societies. The !Kung San of the Kalahari Desert provide a good contemporary example of gathering and hunting societies. The !Kung incorporate 85 types of plants and nuts from the local ecology into their diet for the majority of their food calories. They use poisoned arrows to hunt wild game animals and they literally out run them (i.e, the animals tire of running before they do).

The !Kung live in the Kalahari Desert in Namibia, Botswana and in Angola. They speak the !Kung language, which is marked by the extensive use of a clicking sound.

The !Kung are organized by a gender-based division of labor: men hunt and women gather. The !Kung have a great deal of leisure time and devote little time to meeting subsistence needs. On average the !Kung only spend an average of 12-19 hours per person per week gathering and hunting. Because they spend relatively little time hunting and gathering, they are able to enjoy leisure activities like socializing, dancing, and participating in religious ceremonies.

They live a nomadic lifestyle due to periodic depletion of local resources. The !Kung actually plan child birth according to how long it will take before they need to move to another location. The child should be old enough so that it can make the trip walking without the mother having to carry it. The !Kung share resources with one another and are very communal. Unlike some hunting and gathering societies, the !Kung provide care to those elderly members of their society who are unable to do so themselves because of health or disability issues.

In recent years African governments have tried to get the !Kung to settle in specific areas and switch their lifestyle to one of raising crops rather than the nomadic hunting and gathering. Slowly but surely the !Kung are adapting to this new change in their way of life and they seem very able to farm in land previously thought unfarmable.

The Agricultural Revolution

pproximately 12,000 to 10,000 years ago, farming began to change the nomadic patterns of earlier societies like hunting and gathering societies. This was a gradual shift over several hundred years and it was largely motivated by increased populations and changes in the environment. People began to settle in specific areas and stayed there; hunting and gathering for survival became a method of survival in the past. As the shift from hunting and gathering societies progressed, man became better at inventing technology that made farming more efficient.

Farming techniques including horticulture (cultivation of plants using tools to turn the soil), "slash and burn" techniques (chopping down and burning trees to open land to crop cultivation and which is still practiced in many parts of the world), and the ability to irrigate crops resulted in even greater population growth. While faming resulted in a more dependable food supply, it was also much more labor intensive.

Agricultural societies maintained strict gender roles for societal members, with men doing the more physically demanding tasks and women doing less physically demanding tasks while also being responsible for cooking and childcare. Generally, men cleared and plowed the land while women were responsible for planting crops.

As farming became even more efficient, it also became less labor intensive, which freed laborers for other purposes. As towns and cities developed, there were more people who, because they were not needed to help farm, began to develop other skills and talents. People become more skilled at specific crafts and it was at this time that the arts and philosophy began to emerge as occupations. Unfortunately, with the advent of cities, some cities had more resources than others and often this led to war. Consequently, technology also began to change weapons that were needed for defense and warfare. The oral tradition began to be replaced with written records of a people as new forms of writing came into existence. As societies became larger, they also became more enmeshed in bureaucracy.

Pre-Industrial Societies

As agricultural technology and efficiency increased, surplus increased. The result was occupations began to spring up in these newly burgeoning cities. Perhaps as much as 5 percent of the population of these societies worked in craft occupations like weavers, brewers, potters, blacksmiths, and woodworkers. These kind of craft occupations were called artisans. To be an artisan you had to have skill, talent, and often strength. When power was necessary for the artisan to practice his craft, power was either supplied by humans or water, and sometimes in Northern Europe by wind.

Usually, these crafts were familial in that family members worked the business. Apprenticeships, where someone outside of the family is trained in the skills of the craft, were not uncommon. Work tasks were primarily assigned on a person's status. Members of society with ascribed status, status that is passed down and not earned, generally held more prestigious occupations. On the other hand people with lower status did more menial work including agricultural.

Historically, time was not thought of as we think of it today. In the middle ages, time was a matter of when you could work—in other words, between sunrise and sunset. There were no clocks.

Traditional Societies

In traditional societies, which were pre-industrial, work was assigned based on gender and status based. Family ties were important and the family functioned as a work and economic unit. The family functioned well as the work unit because there was a hierarchical command structure already in place with the family patriarch at the top. Also, family members could trust each other to perform their assigned tasks. The motivation to perform a job well was natural since it was in the best interest of the family.

Slavery

Slavery, which is discussed more thoroughly in the module on social stratification, was a widely used source of labor, though it was very inefficient. Generally, societies had laws that reinforced the boundaries between slaves and citizens. Being a slave could mean living a relatively comfortable life if you were lucky enough to be a house slave, in which case you were treated almost like one of the family, or worker slave, in which case you could lead a miserable life. Slavery was completely inefficient as an economic model because it was almost always oppressive, provided only punishment and no rewards or incentives, their was no loyalty to the slave owner, and no motivation to see the slave owner profit from their work (except to do just enough work to stay alive).

Unlike the type of racial slavery practiced here in the U.S. prior to the end of the American Civil War, being a slave wasn't necessarily a lifetime of bondage. It was common for slaves to be able to buy their freedom depending on the slave owner. In ancient Rome, some slaves were considered as family members and lived with the family in their homes (Wallace-Hadrill, 1996). Manumission was the practice of a Roman slave owner freeing his slaves. Apparently, it is common for slave owners to free their slaves in recognition of their dedication over some period of time. While some slave owners freed their slaves outright, some were allowed to buy their freedom. This was an important motivator to slaves to be hard-working and loyal to their masters. Once freed, former slaves who had been formally (i.e., performed by a magistrate) freed were eligible to become Roman citizens.

In the U.S. when slavery was still practiced, occasionally a slave might be freed after the slave owner's death if it was stipulated in his will, but it was rare. This was the case with Sally Hemmings. She was a slave that was owned, and apparently loved, by Thomas Jefferson. She accompanied him to Paris where he served as the U.S. Minister to France. He is reported to have had at least one child with Hemmings. In his will, Hemmings was freed upon his death.

Sally Hemmings

Time and Work

For most of recorded history, you had breakfast and went to work before the sun came up, and you finished your work when the sun went down. There were a number of things that came together to make the notion of "time" something meaningful. Up until then, the "time" was very loose in its meaning. Someone might be told to do something by "mid-day," or by "sunset," but not that they need to have something done by a specific time. Time, as measured by hours and minutes, and as we know it today, simply didn't exist up until the 1700's. Even then it was restricted to the nobility because of the expense of buying and maintaining a clock.

The shift in the meaning of "time" can be traced back to the beginning of the Protestant Reformation. Calvinism, a Protestant sect, advocated that God would bless, or had already blessed, those who worked hard and spent little. In other words, the value of work became not only more important, but tied to God and the Heaven that awaits all those that please Him. Time became something more valuable because squandering it was displeasing to God.

Protestantism became closely allied with the advent of capitalism. The printing press, which had been invented in the 1500's, also had a part to play in a change the way people viewed the concept of time. Protestantism believed that each man should be able to read and interpret the word of God. Unlike Catholicism, which believed that the Bible should only be read and interpreted by the church, Protestantism believed that every man should be able to posses a copy of the Bible. As Protestantism spread throughout Europe, those who could afford to buy a Bible, largely made economically possible by the invention the printing press, had to learn to read. This set the stage for industrialization. The value of hard work was esteemed, Protestant values began to be intertwined with the rise of capitalism, which represented a totally new type of economic system, hard work was believed to please God, men were beginning to read in larger numbers, and the use of water to generate power necessary in the early stages of industrialization all came together. The stage was set for a complete reinvention of the concept of "time." These things were all necessary to form the foundation for industrialization.

Guilds

People who possessed certain trade skills that were valued by the society in which they lived, often belonged to a guild. Guilds dominated the way work was organized in medieval Europe until the 1700's. There were guilds for weavers, blacksmiths, metalsmiths, shoemakers, stonemasons, and other crafts. The guilds limited those who could join and thus kept out competition and preserved their way of life. Aside being very restrictive in terms of who could join, they were self-regulating (i.e., the policed themselves). Actions of individual members were scrutinized for irregularities or

personal misconduct; guilds tried to maintain an image of the modern professional.

The first step to enter a guild was to perform an apprenticeship. Apprenticeships were hard to get and highly sought after, but the guilds had complete control over who became an apprentice and eventually a member of the guild. An apprenticeship was that period in which someone with no or limited experience began to learn the trade or craft. Apprentices learned the skills of the craft and began to be socialized into the norms and values of the particular guild. For the most part, you had to apprentice for a craft before you were able to learn the craft, other ways of learning the craft simply weren't available.

Generally, there was a formal arrangement entered into between the parents of the apprentice and the master craftsman under which they would learn the trade. The apprentice agreed to work for the master craftsman a certain period of time, while learning the trade, in exchange for his room and board. Apprenticeships were so sought after by parents that they would often pay a master craftsman to let their son apprentice for him. Upon completion of the apprenticeship, the former apprentice became a journeyman. The journeyman worked under the master craftsman until such time as the master craftsman either died or handed over his business to the journeyman who would be the next master craftsman.

Guilds were highly successful, maybe too much so. They flourished for centuries as successful social and economic institutions, but their power and prestige eventually eroded as political entities began to oppose them. The guilds, which had always practiced free trade but only by controlling the number of men allowed into a guild, came up against capitalism, which had at its heart the idea of completely unfettered competition and free trade. Little by little laws were passed outlawing the guilds first in France in the late 1700's and finally by Germany in 1869. New and alternative methods of production, coupled with the rise of capitalism, completely undermined the guilds and led to their demise. Eventually, the industrial revolution transformed their skills into tasks that could be completed by machines.

The Industrial Revolution

In the mid to late 1700's, new forms of power were transforming industry into businesses that could produce far more than before. Water power in the beginning provided power to machinery, but it was the invention of the steam engine that forever changed the course of history.

Inventor James Watt is credited for patenting the first commercial steam engine in 1781, but the engine itself had been invented centuries earlier. The industrial revolution was born in Great Britain and from there spread out to other corners of the world. The steam engine was allowed for production on a scale never before seen. Whereas prior to the industrial revolution the production of goods was more or less limited to family homes, which made sense since it the business was family-owned and ran. But with steam power came factories. Production increased dramatically. Steam power was distributed via belts, usually made of leather, to machinery throughout the factor. Whereas water wheels might have generated enough power to allow a saw to cut wood, steam power easily quadrupled that power.

The shift to large-scale production meant the building of factories and hiring workers. Large numbers of workers now worked in one place, something called a factory. Work was no longer something that was kept in the family, in fact, the factories produced the modern bureaucracy, which is far from being family-like. As factories grew larger and larger, and required more and more workers, a division of labor sprang up replacing the old familial hierarchy. Class divisions of workers emerged with the owners on top, supervisors below them, and the wage workers at the bottom. Marx would later refer to these workers as the proletarians, a term which referred the workers lacking ownership of the means of production and therefore had no personal interest in the product itself. This increased social stratification among the people. The workers received a small amount of money in exchange for their labor, but the factory owners, the ones who owned the means of production, grew wealthy off of their labor.

A distinct and separate working class had sprung up as a result of **industrialization**. It was at this point that there began to be resistance to the new technologies that were displacing workers and tradesmen. In the early 1800's workers began to fight back. By forming a class consciousness, as Marx would later write, the workers began to see themselves as all part of a mistreated group. More and more workers were being hurt or killed on the job, and in those days, there were no benefits to disabled workers or financial benefits to survivors of husbands and fathers killed on the jobsite. Factories were dirty, noisy, and dangerous places to work. Workers grew angry. Their wages were just barely enough for them and their families to live on, and additionally they had to tolerate miserable working conditions. A response to these conditions was Luddism. **Luddism** was a movement in which workers openly opposed the spread of technology that displaced workers. They often went so far as to destroy the machinery. Eventually this did result in the formation of unions in the mid to late 1800's, but unions were often met with violence as factory owners fought back. Riots broke out throughout the industrializing north, and many workers were killed, and while conditions eventually get better for workers, many died along the way.

Capitalism and Market Economies

With industrialization came huge class divisions. The upper class who owned the means of production, the land, the railroads, the banks, and the mines, and then the workers, most of whom worked for subsistence wages. Historically, land had always been the primary source of wealth, and wealth was therefore transferred down from father to son in the form of the land, but that changed under capitalism. Factories replaced land as the primary source of wealth.

Adam Smith (1723 – 1790), a Scottish philosopher, is considered the father of the modern free market economy. In 1776, he wrote "The Wealth of Nations." In the book he laid out his belief that a free-market economy would be guided by reason and self-interest, which in turn would lead to competition, and would lead to overall economic prosperity. Smith called this the "invisible hand." Supply and demand would lead the marketplace in a prosperous direction for all. Smith also believed that breaking work down into smaller tasks would lead to greater productivity. In turn, he believed this greater productivity would result in lower prices for consumers and an overall increase in the standard of living for the society.

The following is from Adam Smith's "The Wealth of Nations":

> To take an example, therefore, from a very trifling manufacture; but one in which the division of labour has been very often taken notice of, the trade of the pin-maker; a workman not educated to this business (which the division of labour has rendered a distinct trade), nor acquainted with the use of the machinery employed in it (to the invention of which the same division of labour has probably given occasion), could scarce, perhaps, with his utmost industry, make one pin in a day, and certainly could not make twenty. But in the way in which this business is now carried on, not only the whole work is a peculiar trade, but it is divided into a number of branches, of which the greater part are likewise peculiar trades. One man draws out the wire, another straights it, a third cuts it, a fourth points it, a fifth grinds it at the top for receiving the head; to make the head requires two or three distinct operations; to put it on, is a peculiar business, to whiten the pins is another; it is even a trade by itself to put them into the paper; and the important business of making a pin is, in this manner, divided into about eighteen distinct operations, which, in some manufactories, are all performed by distinct hands, though in others the same man will sometimes perform two or three of them.
>
> I have seen a small manufactory of this kind where ten men only were employed, and where some of them consequently performed two or three distinct operations. But though they were very poor, and therefore but indifferently accommodated with the necessary machinery, they could, when they exerted themselves, make

among them about twelve pounds of pins in a day. There are in a pound upwards of four thousand pins of a middling size. Those ten persons, therefore, could make among them upwards of forty-eight thousand pins in a day. Each person, therefore, making a tenth part of forty-eight thousand pins, might be considered as making four thousand eight hundred pins in a day. But if they had all wrought separately and independently, and without any of them having been educated to this peculiar business, they certainly could not each of them have made twenty, perhaps not one pin in a day; that is, certainly, not the two hundred and fortieth, perhaps not the four thousand eight hundredth part of what they are at present capable of performing, in consequence of a proper division and combination of their different operations.

Note that Smith estimates somewhere between a 240 and 4800 fold increase in productivity by dividing the labor in this pin factory. That was no small feat. But, in 1776 when the Wealth of Nations was published, no one appreciated the idea of a mass market...who would want to manufacture so many pins? In other words, tradesman manufactured goods for the local community and not for exportation throughout the country. That was unheard of.

Karl Marx considered capitalism an exploitive system in which factory and business owners would extract their profits off the labor of the workers. Marx believed that the wages paid these workers was too little for the profit their labor was generating for the factory owners. Countering Marx's argument was that even though the system was unevenly divided (i.e., classist), the result of this process benefited everyone and raised the standard of living for the workers. Essentially, it is the same theory as trickle-down economics.

In his book Wealth of Nations, Adam Smith was able to show how a small pin manufacturing company could go from manufacturing 240 pins in a day to 4800 in a day. But as I pointed out above, no one thought it was a good idea to produce that many pens because there was no appreciation for mass-market.

Scientific Management

Frederick Winslow Taylor decided to put Adam Smith's work to the test. He believed that he could increase productivity and reduce problems between the workers and management by making work more efficient. He did a series of time and motion studies. Taylor believed that if he could make the task fit the worker than the workers output would increase, and because he'd be less overworked, there would be less dissatisfaction with management. So by adjusting the task to fit the worker he was able to show how he could increase productivity. In one study he able to increase the productivity of coal shoveler simply by making the shovel fit the body build of the worker. However, with more complex tasks he failed and worse there was resistance to scientific management practices.

So, while Smith and Taylor were both able to demonstrate how work could be made more efficient and increase productivity, there was still no appreciation for a mass-market.

Henry Ford and a Mass Market

Adam Smith's, "Wealth of Nations", and Frederick Winslow Taylor's scientific management, set the stage for the last piece of the puzzle to bring it all together. Henry Ford invented the assembly line. Ford believed the production operations could be performed more efficiently when workers stayed in one place and the automobiles, in various stages of manufacturing, moved past them. As the automobiles moved past them on the assembly line, workers would perform their individual tasks. Some might put on the wheels, others might be responsible for setting the body of the car on the frame, some might be responsible for installing the seats, and so on. By the time the finished automobile rolled off the assembly line hundreds of workers had played a part in building them. Following the ideas of Smith and Taylor, and breaking the operation down into smaller tasks, Ford was able to dramatically increase production output.

Henry Ford

The American assembly line became the standard that all other countries aspired to in their manufacturing processes. Even Adolf Hitler was said to have admired Ford's idea.

But even though Ford had made production more effective with his assembly line, why would he want to manufacture thousands of automobiles? That was far more than the Detroit market could accommodate. It was here that Ford again showed his genius. Ford understood that in order to have a market for the thousands of automobiles he turned out every year, he had to expand his market. He decided to ship his automobiles all over the country. Based in part on the "putting-out" system used in the 1600-1700's, Ford had to create market demand for his automobiles throughout the country. While goods were sometimes shipped to far off places, they were generally small-scale. Ford's concept of a mass market was anything but small-scale.

When Henry Ford built his first plant in Detroit and he hired workers he soon realized that the assembly line was always good as the dependability of his workers. When workers would fail to show up for work it's severely disrupted the production line. Ford man offered workers a wage of five dollars per day to work in his factory. This was an unheard-of amount in those days. Workers flocked to Ford. Absenteeism fell dramatically. There was no short supply of workers. However, other employers in the Detroit area hated Ford for what he had done. By offering workers five dollars a day they had lost workers to Ford and the only way they could retain their workers was to match Ford's wage of five dollars per day. They referred to this wage as Ford's "welfare wage."

While Ford was able to retain his workers by paying them five dollars a day, workers became dissatisfied with the assembly line work. The work was incredibly taxing, they worked long hours, and factories were often hot unpleasant places to work. So while Ford had guaranteed the production of his automobiles by paying workers five dollars a day, he had inadvertently increased their dissatisfaction with their work. Worker dissatisfaction is significantly associated with loss of productivity and in some cases even sabotage.

Bureaucracies

As industrialization spread, systems of management began to become routinized. A formal hierarchy of workers began to take shape with the owners at the top, management in the middle, and workers at the bottom. This was the early form of a bureaucracy. The larger the industry became, the more complex the system of management became. But for every new layer of management created between the workers and the owners, the more dissatisfied workers became. Production often slowed. It was at about this time that Marx was producing some of his most critical and influential work.

Bureaucracies are administrative systems of organization. Their existence goes back to pre-industrial societies. Bureaucratic organizations had been around since Roman times in the West and Chinese in the East. They were necessary for landlords as they collected taxes from their peasant renters, enforcing laws and policies, and maintaining control over the people. They also helped in the keeping of written records by organizing tasks and establishing a hierarchical structure in the process.

Max Weber began to characterize the functions and hierarchical form of the modern bureaucracy. He portrayed bureaucracies as very efficient systems and held them up as an ideal type. Weber outlined a number of features of a bureaucracy that distinguished it from other types of organizational systems. Those characteristics are:

- A bureaucracy maintains written records, and all policies and rules are committed to paper. The organization functions according to those written rules and regulations without exception.

- There is a clear division of labor. A formal hierarchical structure is clearly mapped out. This hierarchy is based on layers of management. At the top are the owners or representatives of the owner (i.e., what we call CEOs today). Below them are layers and layers of management, with the level above holding authority over the lower levels or ranks. At the bottom are the workers. The formal depiction of a bureaucratic hierarchy is that of a pyramid; power and authority flow downwards.

- At each level of the bureaucracy tasks are clearly laid out and written down. Workers were specialized in their specific tasks.

- Bureaucracies are impersonal in nature. The workers of a bureaucracy must be able to work together in the pursuit of the organizations tasks. Personal issues (e.g., prejudice, gossip, and other aspects of a person's personality that are not compatible with the worker being able to do his or her job effectively) are left at the door as the worker begins their job.

- Promotions within bureaucracies are based on merit and expertise.

- The ideal bureaucracy is rational. It is there to use information effectively and efficiently in the pursuit of its goals.

Weber believed that if bureaucracies could function according to those formal principles and structure of the organization, they would be completely efficient, an ideal type. Of course, no bureaucracy lives up to the ideal type. While companies maintain written records, there exists in all bureaucratic organizations shortcuts, policies are all not rigidly enforced, and sometimes records are rewritten when scrutinized by outsiders. While there is a clear formal organizational structure in a bureaucracy, there is also an informal structure as well. This is where people have connections with others in the structure the nature of which is not approved by the organization. Another example of the informal structure is the lowly secretary. While secretaries are at the bottom of the hierarchy, informally they have much greater knowledge and power than the formal depiction of the hierarchical structure of the organization. Workers are expected to leave who they are at the door; the only thing the bureaucratic organization wants is their labor as far as the completion of the tasks assigned to them. Again, this is an ideal. Workers can't help bring their personal lives to work with them. Usually organizations overlook this unless it disrupts the harmony of the organization and ultimately productivity. Bureaucracies are supposed to be goal-oriented and that's what makes them rational, but bureaucracies can be sidetracked, goals can be changed, and inefficiency can disrupt the function of the bureaucracy.

Finally, workers are supposed to be promoted based on their skills, but this is not always the case. One major violation of this component of bureaucracies is nepotism (i.e., the hiring of relatives who lack necessary experience or skills to do the job efficiently). The Peter Principle, a term coined by Laurence Peter, refers to the fact that often workers are promoted to the level of their inefficiency. In other words, if a worker is performing task X efficiently, he or she may be rewarded with a promotion that involves performing task Y, but one doesn't necessarily have anything to do with the other. The worker could have been fantastic at performing task X, but hopelessly inefficient at performing task Y.

The Japanese company has long been the model for efficiency and productivity. Organizations around the world have tried to emulate the Japanese company in order to increase productivity. Overall, those attempts almost always ended in failure. Non-Japanese bureaucratic organizations failed to see the relevance of culture on the Japanese company.

To understand the Japanese company, you have to go back to industrialization in Japan. Like in most industrializing nations, industry is built in the cities as it is assumed that will be the most efficient location. The same pattern occurred in Japan and factories were built in the cities. Unfortunately, there the supply of labor in the cities was meager because most people, including women, already had jobs that many chose not to leave. Factory owners were forced to recruit workers from the countryside and bring them into the city, but the problem was that males were needed in the country for agricultural purposes. The only labor source left available for factory owners were young women. In order to bring these young women into the city with them to work in their factories, factory owners had to promise they would more or less serve as their surrogate family in the city. The company would be responsible for their food, shelter, clothing, and safety— even chaperoning young women to social gatherings where males would be present. This is the heart of the Japanese company—it became like a family to its workers.

The efficiency and effectiveness of the Japanese company is largely the result of this family-like atmosphere. While fewer Japanese companies are able to guarantee lifetime employment, which used to be the norm. Japanese workers are cross-trained, like American workers in larger companies, but whereas in American companies cross training is almost always horizontal, in the Japanese company cross-training can also be vertical (i.e., to fill in for their direct superior). Workers are able to fill in for co-workers and superiors if necessary, which is incredibly efficient for the organization. Whereas in Western organizations decision-making flows down from the top, in Japanese organizations decision-making is bottom-up. The practice invests workers into the company (i.e., their family). They have a stake in the success of their company as they do in decisions related to their real families. It is not uncommon for workers to socialize with superiors after work and this serves to strengthen the family like connections or bonds but also allows workers to make suggestions for improvement. These suggestions are seriously investigated because their workers are so committed to the company. American companies tried this feature in the way of installing "suggestion boxes." Not only was the practice a failure it actually backfired when workers realized that management was just using the suggestions boxes to bolster morale.

It may seem strange to Americans, it is considered protocol for a Japanese worker to go to his or her superior and ask their permission to marry. Yes, I know. I can't see too many American workers doing that. But the practice is characteristic of the family-like environment of the Japanese organization. Finally, because the company is like family to a worker, a worker's identify may be tied to the organization. It is not uncommon for a Japanese worker to introduce him or herself by giving their name and the company they work for even if the introduction has nothing to do with business (Ouchi, 1981).

When returning to our discussion of bureaucracies, it should be noted that they are not the most effective form of management in all work situations. For instance, in software and Internet companies, companies that require a great deal of innovation, bureaucratic rule is counter-productive. Instead a laissez-faire type of management style is necessary—one that let's workers have a great deal of autonomy as they "think outside of the box."

McDonaldization of Society

George Ritzer, a sociologist, coined the term the "" to refer to the process by which society is being ran like your local neighborhood McDonalds. In other words, all tasks are routinized and rationalized—in other words, efficiency is the name of the game and standardization is the way to accomplish that. There are very few things in our life that aren't routinized. For instance, if you want to go to the bank, you get in your car, drive on a road to the bank, pull up to the drive-up window, put your deposit in the little pop-out tray or the vacuum tube canister, a voice says hello, asks if that's all you need, you say "yes," your deposit slip comes back to you, you take it out of the tray or canister, drive on a road home, get out of your car, and come inside your house. Now, the next week you have to deposit your check. Guess what? The routine will be identical, week, after week, after week. It's all routine and standardized. Life is no longer unique or special, it is simply routine.

As society has become McDonaldized, so has our work. We do the same things virtually every day. The same rituals. The same outcomes. The old expression when someone asks you what's new fits well here, "Same 'ol, same 'ol." Ritzer says there are four features of McDonaldization as it relates to society, but they apply to the modern workplace as well (i.e., the modern bureaucracy):

1. efficiency is the name of the game,

2. calculability (more concerned about the quantity, cost, and time),

3. predictability (you can predict what a hamburger will taste like in Moscow by eating one at your local McDonalds—it's the same everywhere), and

4. control (control means predictability and efficiency). From start to finish, everything is rationalized.

In the workplace, as maybe in other areas of our life, you become dissatisfied with your job. Because most of us work in bureaucracies, if you're not satisfied with your work, you are likely not producing at a rate or quality that your superiors want. You are scolded, or maybe even threatened. Because you can't afford to lose your job, you try to work harder, but the harder you work, the more dissatisfied you become. In the end, you may have a job, but you might hate it, or as Marx or Weber might argue, you are alienated from your work.

Theoretical Views on Work

The conflict perspective views work as an economic system (i.e., capitalism) that exploits and oppresses workers. In this view, the "have's," those who own the means of production (e.g., wealth, land, equipment) function to maintain the status quo that benefits them at the expense of the "have-nots" (i.e., the workers). In addition to exploiting workers for their labor, the conflict perspective sees capitalism as a system that separates workers from the product of their labor, in other words, alienates them from their work. Historically, in agricultural societies workers were able to reap the benefits of their work directly, which tied them to their work. Capitalism, Marx argued, serves to reduce that source of self-satisfaction and reduces the bond workers have to their work. As an example, when a car rolls off an assembly line, hundreds if not thousands of workers have helped produce that car, so no one individual worker can feel a sense of pride and self-worth in the production of that car. Further, Marx believed that capitalist organizations treated workers like "mere commodities" that could be "hired and fired at will" (Barkan, 2012).

Structural functionalism sees the ultimate goal of the economy as providing goods and services. Society is only made possible by the existence of an economy that involves the production of goods and services. The primary economy in most of the world today is that of capitalism. Structural functionalists say that workers benefit from capitalism by earning wages, which are then used for their support and survival. In the process of working for necessary wages, we gain some sense of self-worth and self-fulfillment from that work. Work, to a large degree, shapes our identity. Another latent function of work is that workers make friends by interacting with co-workers. These co-workers, and especially the co-workers that become friends, help build a social support network that contributes to the health and welfare of the worker.

Symbolic interaction unlike the conflict perspective and structural functionalism, looks at work from the individual or micro level. Chiefly, symbolic interactionism focuses on how we define ourselves, our job, and our problems from the social interactions that occur within the workplace. Each worker has to negotiate their own role within the organization and find their own "meaning" of work.

Unemployment and Outsourcing

Unemployment occurs when someone is not employed, but who wants to be employed in the workplace. People who don't work voluntarily cannot be considered as unemployed. Most unemployed people are involuntarily unemployed in that they are laid off or fired, but are actively seeking employment elsewhere. In our capitalist society, most people have to work for wages that are then used to pay for goods and services they require for survival. In the US, as of December 2015 the unemployment rate was 5 percent, which is down by half since late 2009 when it was at about 10 percent (Bureau of Labor Statistics, 2016).

Underemployed workers are those who are working in jobs that do not make full use of the experience and education the worker possesses. For instance, an aerospace engineer working at McDonalds because his or her unemployment insurance has ran out and they have to put bread on the table for their family. In March 2016, the U.S. underemployment rate was at 14.5 percent (Ryan, 2016).

There are widespread consequences of unemployment or underemployment. When a person loses their job, and cannot immediately find another, they are forced into having to live off of unemployment insurance benefits. However, unemployment benefits are always substantially less than the worker's earnings before being laid off or fired. (Note: many people believe that workers are not eligible for unemployment benefits if they are fired, but that is untrue). In most states, unemployment benefits only last up to 26 weeks (i.e., six months), though several states extend those benefits slightly (Stone, 2014). Most people try to live according to their means, but for many people that's not the case. Approximately 5 percent of Americans are one paycheck away from poverty, or what is referred to as the "near poor" (Morello, 2014). Generally, those with more education are least vulnerable to being in near poverty and those with the least education to be the most vulnerable (Hokayem & Heggeness, 2014). Americans are 40% poorer today than they were in 2007 according the Pew Research Center (2012). When a worker loses his or her job, and especially if they are near poor or lack significant savings, the domino effect occurs. Without their former income, they may be unable to make payments on their home and are foreclosed on. As a result of these troubles, the laid off or fired worker's credit rating plunges. Eventually, the laid off or fired worker has to file bankruptcy. The laid off or fired worker tries to find a job, but many companies will look at his or her credit rating and make a hiring decision in part based on that rating. If the laid off or fired worker finds a job utilizing his or her skills and education, they can start to rebuild their credit and their life, but it will take years to recover. But if the laid off or fired worker cannot find a job that utilizes his or her skills and education, and has to take a job that doesn't value those skills or education, he or she is underemployed and their financial situation is only slightly better off than it was when they were unemployed. Depending on the industry, he or she might never be able to find a job that values their skill and education enough so that they are brought back to the earnings and lifestyle he or she had before they were laid off or fired.

Outsourcing is when a company contracts out some parts of its operation. When those parts are contracted abroad, it is called offshore outsourcing. From an organizations point of view, outsourcing results in reduced costs and therefore greater profits. From a worker's point of view, it may lead to unemployment if the worker's job is outsourced. From a societal point of view, offshore outsourcing transfers jobs out of the country and therefore there is a loss of American jobs. With the loss of jobs in the U.S., there is a loss in tax revenue and reduced money spent on purchases. From a global perspective, offshore outsourcing has led to a reduction in global inequalities as it has brought jobs to workers in third-world countries.

Terms, Concepts and Names to Know:

- !Kung San

- Horticulture

- Craft occupations

- Sally Hemmings

- James Watt

- Luddism

- Adam Smith

- Wealth of Nations

- Capitalism

- Henry Ford

- Putting-out system

- Bureaucracy

- Ideal type

- Laurence Peter

- George Ritzer

- Unemployment

- Underemployment

Be Able to Discuss:

- The three theoretical perspectives on work

- Gender based division of labor

- Concept of time before and after the industrial revolution

- Traditional societies

- The efficiency of slavery

- The effect of the cotton gin on slavery in the American South

- Guilds

- Water as a power supply

- Scientific management

- Mass market

- Peter Principle

- The Japanese company

- McDonaldization of society

References

Adam Smith, An Inquiry Into the Nature and Causes of the Wealth of Nations, Vol. I ed. R. H. Campbell and A. S. Skinner, vol. II of the Glasgow Edition of the Works and Correspondence of Adam Smith (Indianapolis: Liberty Fund, 1981). Chapter: [I.i] CHAPTER I: Of the Division of Labor.

Barkan, S. (2012). A Primer on Social Problems: Sociological Perspectives on Work and the Economy. CreativeCommons. doi:http://2012books.lardbucket.org/books/a-primer-on-social-problems/s15-02-sociological-perspectives-on-w.html

Bureau of Labor Statistics. (2016, April 15). Labor Force Statistics from the Current Population Survey. Retrieved April 15, 2016, from http://data.bls.gov/timeseries/LNS14000000

Georgia Public Broadcasting. (2006). The Roman Empire: Slaves and Freemen. Retrieved April 12, 2016, from http://www.pbs.org/empires/romans/empire/slaves_freemen.html

Hodson, Randy, & Sullivan, T. (2008). The Social Organization of Work. Belmont, CA: Wadsworth.

Hokayem, C., & Heggeness, M. (2014, May). Living in Near Poverty in the United States: 1966–2012. US Census Bureau. Retrieved April 12, 2016, from http://www.census.gov/prod/2014pubs/p60-248.pdf

Morello, C. (2014, May 1). Five percent of Americans hover just above poverty. The Washington Post. Retrieved April 12, 2016, from https://www.washingtonpost.com/local/five-percent-of-americans-hover-just-above-poverty/2014/05/01/1d8fe754-d16a-11e3-a6b1-45c4dffb85a6_story.html

Pew Research Center. (2012, August 22). The Lost Decade of the Middle Class Fewer, Poorer, Gloomier. Retrieved April 12, 2016, from http://www.pewsocialtrends.org/2012/08/22/the-lost-decade-of-the-middle-class/

Ryan, B. (2016, March 31). U.S. Gallup Good Jobs Rate 44.4% in March 2016. Retrieved April 12, 2016, from http://www.gallup.com/poll/190370/gallup-good-jobs-rate-march-2016.aspx

Stone, C. (2014, January 14). Where Things Stand for the Unemployed. Retrieved April 12, 2016, from http://www.cbpp.org/blog/where-things-stand-for-the-unemployed

Wallace-Hadrill, A. (1996). Houses and Society in Pompeii and Herculaneum. Princeton, NJ: Princeton University Press.

Made in the USA
Columbia, SC
10 July 2018